ELEMENTS OF

GOVERNMENT

ELEMENTS OF GOVERNMENT

An Introduction to Political Science

Thomas R. Adam · New York University

Random House · New York

First Printing

 Published in New York by Random House, Inc., and simultaneously in Toronto, Canada, by Random House of Canada, Limited.

Library of Congress Catalog Card Number: 60–6197

Manufactured in the United States of America by The Haddon Craftsmen, Inc.

Acknowledgments

Any formulation of the elements essential to the study of government amounts to the author's views of the collective scholarship, past and present, relating to this field. Unavoidably a condensation of this nature may strip the researches and theories of learned and experienced men of their living flesh, reducing them to bare bones arranged in patterns of the author's choosing. Responsibility for using other men's scholarship in this cavalier fashion lies directly on the writer. Accordingly, it is more than a formal gesture to emphasize that this book constitutes a personal arrangement of material largely collected and systematized by contemporary scholars in the area of government. The existence of abundant and stimulating resources of this kind provides incentive for such a book as this—the hope of communicating some part of the excitement of ideas and the wealth of information must serve as an excuse for the liberties taken.

A member of a university is part of a *universitas* of scholars and students. To my students, past and present, are due acknowledgments for their unremitting efforts to train me in the principles and practices of simple communication and elementary relevance. To my immediate colleagues I must acknowledge that I no longer recognize where I have borrowed, and adopted as my own, ideas and original information generously contributed in the interchanges of a heartening fellowship.

Without involving him in responsibility for textual contents, particular acknowledgment for providing stimulating patterns of approach and criteria for judgment are due to my colleague in several seminars that birthed this book—Professor Arnold J. Zurcher.

Services contributed by Miss Marilyn Sermul, academic secretary and research student, are gratefully acknowledged.

Contents

ONE • FORMS AND STRUCTURES OF GOVERNMENT 1

1. The Nature of Political Science 3
2. Patterns of the Modern State 11
3. The Structure of Constitutions 35
4. The Nature of Political Office 52
5. Systems of Representation 80
6. Instrumentalities of Representation 108
7. The Legal Order 130
8. Instrumentalities of Force 155
9. The Pattern of Administration 178
10. Parties, Pressure Groups, and Public Opinion 203
11. Political Attitudes 227
12. Devolutionary Forms—Regional and Local 248

TWO • THE BUSINESS OF GOVERNMENT 271

13. The Nature of an Internal Order—Civil Rights 273
14. Government and the Economic Order 295
15. Government and Welfare 319
16. Political Aspects of Agriculture and Labor 339

THREE • INTERNATIONAL RELATIONS 361

17. Nature of an International Order 363
18. Organs and Methods of International Relations 380
19. Universal and Regional Organizations 402
20. Relations with Underdeveloped Peoples 425

Bibliography 443
Index 459

Illustrations

DIAGRAMS AND CHARTS

Sample Proportional Representation ballot 96
(courtesy of the National Municipal League)
Sample primary election ballot 102
Diagram of the United States Court System 134
Labor Participation in OPA 185
The Tax Dollar—Where It Comes From, Where It Goes 302
The Federal Reserve System—Organization chart 305
The United Nations System 404

HALFTONE ILLUSTRATIONS

between pages 150 *and* 151

CONSTITUTIONS: The shrine of the American Constitution; King John signing the Magna Carta

POLITICAL OFFICE: The badge of authority in ancient Greece; the election of a ninth century tribal king; a constitutional monarch at work (King Frederik IX of Denmark); President Eisenhower at a press conference

SYSTEMS OF REPRESENTATION: A Swiss town meeting; voters in London; a Moscow polling station; canvassing votes in Kenya; a U.S. voting machine

The Anglo-Saxon Witan; The Parliament of Elizabeth I; a U.S. Senatorial investigating committee

THE LEGAL ORDER: The Twelve Tables of the Law in ancient Rome; the British Court of Criminal Justice—the Old Bailey; the U.S. Supreme Court of 1888

between pages 310 *and* 311

ADMINISTRATIVE STRUCTURES: an Egyptian office-holder; the structure of the government of Paris in 1500; civil service reform

PARTIES AND PRESSURE GROUPS: a classical Greek orator; a labor orator in Union Square; celebrating a Parliamentary election in Trafalgar Square; a whistle-stop campaign speech; a demonstration at a national nominating convention

GOVERNMENT AND THE ECONOMIC ORDER: tax collecting in ancient Egypt; housewives protest new taxes on corn in Delft, Holland

THE INTERNATIONAL ORDER: the General Assembly of the United Nations; a vote in the Security Council; the International Court of Justice in action; a UN-conducted plebiscite in Togoland

ONE

FORMS AND STRUCTURES OF GOVERNMENT

Chapter I

The Nature of Political Science

The collective reason is shaped by the wisdom and experience of other ages, expressed in things established. There can be limited change because, though society is a divine creation, it has evils which must be experienced and, if possible, abolished.

ARCHBISHOP RICHARD HOOKER:
Laws of Ecclesiastical Polity (1593)

The study of politics is an inquiry into matters of serious concern. Individual patterns of living are enmeshed in political processes. The state is something more than an inescapable background to all forms of social action; it influences our ideals, our economic prospects, and even our intimate social relationships. There can be little question of the desirability of understanding the structure of control contained in the apparatus of government. However, it does remain open to question what kind of knowledge, and how much, ordinary citizens who do not practice politics as an avocation or engage in public service can acquire. Can information on the art and practice of politics be transmitted as an ordered body of learning, lucid enough to be understood without special training and sufficiently practical in character to be applicable to everyday affairs?

The area of "politics" lacks the definiteness and precision that allow chemistry, medicine, or even music, to be studied as a strict discipline. Originally, politics embraced all aspects of community life. Aristotle regarded the Hellenic *polis* as "an integrated system of social ethics, which realizes to the full the capacity of its members, and therefore claims their full allegiance."[1] This is obviously too comprehensive an idea to be reduced to clear description and tested rules of practice. Today, political institutions are narrowed to a single factor in the totality of community living. While this facilitates description and study it opens the door to unrealities. Practical affairs do not lend themselves to being boxed in academic categories.

To formulate rules of political organization and behavior sufficiently exact to afford accurate predictions of future events lies beyond the capacity of existing tools for political analysis. In this respect, political science differs in nature as well as in degree of exactitude from the experimental sciences. However, the term "science" may be properly applied to social studies in the sense of "a higher form of knowledge," somewhat as the seven ancient studies were called "Liberal Arts" (grammar, rhetoric, logic, arithmetic, music, geometry, astronomy). The reward of political studies is attainment of a form of practical wisdom such as may be based on insight into the pattern even of a force that cannot be predicted in its particular manifestations. A boxer, for example, while he does not expect to foresee every move of his opponent through previous study is reasonably certain that neglect of the theory and practice of the manly art would render his stay in the ring brief and unpleasant. An individual who drifts without curiosity or conscious direction among the currents and eddies of organized society becomes tempting prey to better informed entities with superior mastery over their social environment.

Practice and Theory of Politics

Politics in action, the manipulation of events to achieve some immediate end in the field of government, calls into play a variety of factors. Obviously desirable is practical experience of the workings of the particular organizations involved. Then there are gifts of personality that may ease the task of leadership. Systematic theory may not be essential to the solution of any specific problem, but if single operations cannot be related so as to form a general pattern government will lack coherent policy. Just as the elements of biology and chemistry underlie the practical art of medicine, so political theory may be held to be essential preparation to the business of ruling or being ruled.

Even when political science is narrowed by leaving out the practitioner's art, it still stretches over an uncomfortably wide range of knowledge. A dividing line may be drawn between political theory and political philosophy, though both are required to constitute the body of political science. Theory is systematic, using tools from the disciplines of law, logic, history, psychology, and sometimes the natural sciences to analyze forms and functions associated with governmental activities. Primarily it is a study of methods and means, with considerable emphasis on their institutional character. A tendency exists to treat human values as irrelevant to the strict purpose of analysis. Sometimes this may be carried to the length of attempting, pseudoscientifically, to isolate the political institution as a thing-in-itself devoid of human attributes.

In search of the exactitudes of the experimental sciences, political scientists may be tempted to strip mankind of its exasperating variables, reducing the scope of their inquiry to man as a "political animal," a creature of measurable responses, tailor-made for scientific investigation—if only he could be shown to exist. In the same way that economics has outgrown the concept of "economic man," so modern political theory prefers to admit that it is merely a partial inquiry into human affairs. Its findings are an incomplete account of the human situation until they are correlated with those of biology, religion, and other physical and social sciences. For example, a leading concern of present-day theory is the analysis of political power. Considerable ingenuity has been shown in uncovering and isolating factors related to the dominance of men over one another within the framework of political institutions. On this basis, the conclusion might be offered that modern communities cannot escape subordination to organized force. Such a political "fact" might be rendered absurd by some discovery in technology that placed an easily contrived weapon, some equivalent to the "equalizer" of frontier history, in the hands of everyone.

The systematic study of political affairs is too important to human welfare to be sacrificed to grandiose dreams of a master theory. Careful inquiries into actualities in the political field can be, and are being, carried out by political scientists who accept a limited place for their theories. Their object is to relate one form of activity to another to form a pattern. In terms of that pattern questions can be raised to be answered by the private judgment of men of action, whether rulers or citizens. Though it is not the business of political theory to reach decisions concerning particular events, if it failed to contribute essential factors the final say of the man of action would be based on insufficient information. The student of political theory has many tools at hand to further his inquiries. Selecting the correct tool for a specific purpose, and changing it for another when circumstances warrant, constitutes an important part of the skill of the trained investigator. A golfer would be seriously handicapped if he could not bring himself to relinquish a putter for any other club in his bag. A student would be hopelessly bunkered if he sought to solve all problems of government by forcing them into the frame of "who-gets-what?"

Major lines of inquiry include the juridical approach, in terms of comparative public law; administrative theory; the process of decision-making; opinion formation; theories of group organization; and the mechanics of dominance, a tool shared with the psychologists. Whether used singly or in combination these methods seek to discover how things are done. Why men choose one form of political association as against another is a question that lies within the province of political philosophy, as distinguished from theory.

Without the introduction of values, some choice made of ends or aims, discussion of methods becomes a mere declaration of personal tastes. It is not practicable to argue concerning the efficiency of any method until prior agreement has been reached concerning what objective the method in question is expected to achieve. Every member of a political community adopts either a political philosophy or a political attitude. An attitude may be described as a point of view that can be felt and perhaps communicated but not explained—at least not in logical terms. Walter Lippmann, for example, expresses a clear-cut political philosophy, while the "cop hater" operates on the level of an attitude. To what extent then may political philosophy be learned as a discipline to replace responses born of emotion, personal idiosyncrasies, and isolated experiences?

One answer is that our social heritage comes to us in part through tradition, in part by means of training our reasoning powers, and only in part through accidents of personality. Tradition works on two levels: the first is an unavoidable patterning imposed by the cultural environment of early childhood and later social ties; the second is the wider perspective of human achievement contained in the written views of previous generations. Continuity in the development of organized society has been aided by the body of knowledge known as the history of political thought. Taken together these two levels of tradition provide a framework in which each generation may devise dominant forms of political philosophy without breaking the link with past experience.

Use of reasoning power to determine proper ends for political association appears obviously desirable. Yet few groups can be held to rely wholly on their logical faculties in determining objectives of government. The English, for instance, while a reasonable people still use mystical terms such as "the honor of the Throne" to describe some of the ends sought by the governmental process. Likewise Americans would be reluctant to dismiss "devotion to the Flag" as outside the purposes of political association.

In earlier times, philosophers tended to assume that political association must have one and only one true end and aim. The search for this master purpose through centuries of political philosophy has been almost equivalent to the quest by ancient alchemists for a philosopher's stone. As alchemy's dream of one all-embracing formula led eventually to multifarious but partial discoveries, the foundations of modern chemistry, so political philosophers have retreated from the dogmatic idealism of Plato's *Republic* or Augustine's *City of God* to admission of a hierarchy of ends that may vary in time and change with social necessities. In the corresponding field of religion it has not yet proved possible to win acceptance of clear-cut objectives which might serve to bind all mankind in one universal Church. Perhaps it is even more unlikely that agreement can be reached on a single end for all forms of political association. Basic survival may prove the sole objective mankind holds in common in the foreseeable future. Humanity may have to huddle together in a frozen mass of terror until the madness of self-destruction is past.

The experience and wisdom of the past present certain major ends capable of being ordered and arranged to serve as the basis for a personal political philosophy. Formation of such a philosophy requires the application of a point of view that reflects the dominant ethical and social traits to the actualities of the environment. Ready-made political philosophies seldom fit individual outlooks. However, several major purposes for political association have proved themselves acceptable in varying degrees over many centuries. For example, the aim of *social union,* the fostering of co-operation between individuals and groups to form a perfect community, may be considered deep rooted in human nature. Archbishop Hooker, a sixteenth-century forerunner of modern ideas, declared: "Authority in Church and State is justified by the need to establish unity." In the Preamble to the American Constitution priority is given to this purpose: "We the people of the United States, in order to form a more perfect union. . . ." Devotion to the nation, the self-sacrifice of patriotism, is proof enough that the idea has meaning at deep emotional and moral levels. Totalitarian fanaticism shows the reverse side of a blind passion for unity at all costs. Also anarchy could be mentioned.

Again, among Western peoples the safeguarding of the individual in certain ideal relationships with his fellows has remained a stubbornly defended end of government. Though *freedom* is a vague idea undefinable even to skilled legal minds, it constitutes an aim millions of men throughout history have defended with their lives. The establishment of *justice,* the second purpose mentioned in the American Constitution, has been little clarified since Plato declared it the true objective of political association. Nevertheless, where men lose interest in trying to put this concept into practice such nightmares as Hitler's Germany are a sure result.

On a lower level, though still based on belief in individualism, *security,* the opportunity for personal life reasonably free from physical and economic hazards, frequently has been raised as a dominant purpose of political organization. Thomas Hobbes, a seventeenth-century political philosopher, was so convinced that the life of the individual outside the political order was "solitary, poor, and nasty, brutish, short," that he argued in favor of almost complete submission to the authority of the state, the Leviathan that shelters, at the price of dominating, a cowering mankind. This philosophy, based on a failure of nerve, proves tempting to peoples distracted beyond endurance by social disorders.

Realistic forms of political philosophy are associated generally with the idea of the state as power. The object of government, then, is to enable some particular group or type to dominate their fellows. Marx leaned toward this viewpoint in his interpretation of the political state as primarily an instrument to subject the proletariat to the economic tyranny of a ruling class. Though this approach does provide some insight into the affairs of many political bodies, it is incomplete because the lust for power is not a thing-in-itself but the consequence of an outlook capable of being examined in the light of wider philosophic patterns. Plato, in his *Republic,* puts into the mouth of Thrasymachus, a contemporary philosopher, the frank statement: "I proclaim that Justice is nothing else than the interest of the stronger." This perverse opinion remains based on the conviction that the end of the state is justice. As has been previously pointed out, politics cannot be divorced from man's total nature; if that nature is lacking in moral or religious standards, political ends will be correspondingly amoral.

While learning places the resources of past wisdom at the call of the individual, it does not provide any absolute truth to override the need for practical judgment. The gathering of information, particularly on a comparative basis, concerning how political societies operate, the analysis of institutional forms, and, above all, understanding of systems of power, provide a framework that makes sound judgment possible. Until this preliminary work has been done, personal opinions as to the true end of the political state should be treated cautiously as tentative hypotheses. Though the study of politics is normally approached with basic preconceptions, the disciplined mind will look forward to a process through which vague opinions may be transmuted into reasoned convictions.

Note

[1] Barker, Ernest (tr. and ed.), Aristotle, *The Politics of Aristotle,* New York: Oxford, 1948, p. xlvii.

Supplementary Readings

Barker, Ernest, *Reflections on Government,* New York: Oxford, 1958.

Catlin, George E. G., *Science and Method of Politics,* New York: Knopf, 1927.

Easton, David, *The Political System,* New York: Knopf, 1953.

Gettell, Raymond G., *Political Science,* Boston: Ginn and Co., revised edition, 1949.

Hocking, William Ernest, *Man and the State,* New Haven: Yale, 1926.

Laski, Harold J., *The State in Theory and Practice,* New York: Viking, 1935.

Lasswell, Harold D., *Politics: Who Gets What, When, How,* New York: Meridian Books, 1958.

———, and Kaplan, Abraham, *Power and Society,* New Haven: Yale, 1950.

MacIver, R. M., *The Web of Government,* New York: Macmillan, 1947.

Macridis, Roy C., *The Study of Comparative Government,* New York: Doubleday, 1955.

Merriam, Charles E., *Systematic Politics,* Chicago: University of Chicago Press, 1945.

Weldon, Thomas D., *States and Morals; A Study in Political Conflicts,* New York: McGraw-Hill, 1947.

———, *The Vocabulary of Politics,* Baltimore: Penguin, 1952.

Chapter 2

Patterns of the Modern State

Political science lacks a vocabulary of technical terms. It is endowed, perhaps too richly, with sonorous expressions that have become focal points of emotional, intellectual, and ethical beliefs. Definition of concepts in the manner of the natural sciences is, however, not practical. The most that can be achieved is a level of precision sufficient to allow communication about institutions and events that are matters of common experience. The use of any particular word in relation to politics has to be kept fluid, subject to change reflecting advances in other branches of knowledge or even to shifts in the outlook of each generation. For example, the concept of colony no longer possesses the meaning it had to nineteenth-century Englishmen, much less to its originators, the ancient Greeks. Willingness to admit new factors into the interpretation of this idea is closely related to ability to adapt to changing circumstances. In modern England or France "empire mindedness" is recognized as more than semantic obstinacy; it constitutes grave defiance of the trend of the times.

Characteristics of the Modern State

An agreed-upon description of the state, the basic institution of political association, would be a valuable meeting place of minds. Before there could be such agreement on a world-wide basis, however, communism would have to be reconciled with capitalism, religion to atheism, and innumerable other conflicts in human tastes and aspirations resolved. Verbal explanation of the meaning of the state involves a declaration of values, relative in some degree to circumstances of time and place.

In order to provide a summary of leading characteristics a description of the modern state may be borrowed from the writings of Sir Ernest Barker:

> A modern State is generally a territorial nation, organized as a legal association by its own action in creating a constitution (such action being in some cases, as in Great Britain, a process along a line of time rather than an act at a point of time) and permanently acting as such an association, under that constitution, for the purpose of maintaining a scheme of legal rules defining and securing the duties of its members.[1]

An examination of the major constituents of this description may illustrate the latitude permissible in constructing a personal understanding of the nature of the state.*

PHYSICAL FACTORS The word "territorial" embraces the new study of political geography. Is social union wholly a matter of choice and human will, or may it not be conditioned by accidents of terrain? Certainly in the past men have clustered where they were drawn by physical factors, in fertile valleys such as the Nile and the Indus, along natural lines of communication—most notably the Mediterranean littoral.

> The important fact for the political geographer is that the activities of the people in a State are conditioned by the relationships which exist between the physical or geographical *milieu* and its human inhabitants. It follows, therefore, that the State does not consist of the territory alone, nor of the people who live in that territory, but is a much more complex organization in which the territory, the people and their interrelationships are indissolubly welded to form an entity which possesses an individuality, a character, which marks it off from other States.[2]

Certainly the state is no mere resultant of physical factors; we lack sufficient knowledge to generalize concerning effects of climate on political organization, or to characterize states in terms of the

* A specifically American definition is given by Chief Justice Chase in the case of *Texas v. White:* "A state, in the ordinary sense of the Constitution, is a political community of free citizens, occupying a territory of defined boundaries, and organized under a government sanctioned and limited by a written constitution and established by the consent of the governed."

fertility of their soils, ease of communication, or any other factor in environmental location. Nevertheless, physical attributes of the land, its size, suitability to human needs, accessibility to other areas, could not be omitted from a meaningful description of any existing political state. To borrow a phrase from economic geography, political association may be considered subject to "space-conditioned particularity."

States can be described as large or small, rich or poor, strong or weak. Generally such characteristics refer in large part to the territorial element. Iceland and Switzerland are both small states, but through the factor of location the former is poor and the latter rich. Strength of course depends on human qualities and organizational skills as well as upon geographical fortune. Nevertheless the difference in rate of growth in power, economic and military, between the United States and Australia in the last hundred years can be attributed in part at least to physical causes.

THE IDEA OF THE NATION The common use of the term *nation–state* suggests that nationalism is the dominant and primary characteristic of statehood. From an historical point of view this is incorrect. Western peoples for the greater part of their history considered themselves members of Christian states, bordered and sometimes threatened by pagan or Islamic states. While nowadays nationalism has become a psychological and emotional focus for social union it is only one of several bonds that provide the conviction of "belongingness." A will toward unity is the underlying force, of which modern nationalism is merely one manifestation. The various factors held necessary to constitute a nation may be regarded as the means customarily used to promote unity. Nations themselves are born of an effort of will, sometimes immediate, as was the case in the American Revolution, or, more frequently, through many generations of growing clearness of purpose. It is by no means an inevitable process; while the drive toward oneness may overcome serious ethnic, cultural, and language divisions, as in the nascent states of Malaya and Nigeria, similarity and contiguity do not necessarily evoke the spark of nationhood. The separation of Canada from the United States provides a familiar example.

Among the factors that contribute to the making of a nation–state are (1) contiguity of peoples, (2) common language, (3) ethnic identity, (4) common cultural and historical experience, (5) religious uniformity or religious toleration, (6) a continued will to unite for the sake of greater strength in overcoming external foes and for the development of material and cultural resources at home. This last is the one element that cannot be dispensed with; numerous examples may be found of well-established nation–states that lack one or more of the other major factors.

Nowadays the need for greater union finds few workable alternatives to nationalism. Religion, loyalty to kings or emperors, membership in regional aristocracies or elites, no longer suffice to support the superstructure of present-day government. The uniqueness of the national bond has led perhaps to overgreat emotional emphasis. It is difficult to explain why men should place devotion to the nation in the front rank of personal virtues. However, a strong feeling that without patriotism we might perish leads to acceptance of loyalty to the nation as a matter of faith.

In seeking an objective understanding of political association it is legitimate to subject nationalism to critical analysis. On the other hand it should be remembered that the drive for greater union amounts to a race against modern trends toward physical and spiritual catastrophe. If, in the historical and psychological circumstances of our times, nationalism happens to be the clearest path toward effective unity, it may be evaluated as a means toward a greater end rather than as an end in itself.

THE FRAMEWORK OF LAW Professor Barker's definition of the state assigns to it "the purpose of maintaining a scheme of legal rules defining and securing the duties of its members." This may appear self-evident to English-speaking people, as all political states that carry the inheritance of Magna Charta are fashioned in terms of law, particularly the customary type known as *common law*. The necessity of "a scheme of legal rules," however, may be overstressed in the fast-changing world of today. New states such as Pakistan and Nigeria lack a previous bond of accepted law. Accordingly they may center their nascent unity on some traditional elite: in Pakistan the army and leaders of Islam; in Nigeria an educated minority and traditional chieftains. Perhaps the Soviet states, Russia, China, and their satellites, should be described as founded on ideologies with their legal frameworks subsidiary to

Party dogma. Identification of the state with law may be the distinguishing mark of a Western tradition of statehood rather than a universal characteristic.

Nevertheless, the most successful and enduring political associations in human experience have been states constituted under, through, and by law. Ever since Rome imposed the *Pax Romana* through the limits of the then known world, world leadership has been held by peoples who championed law. This may be ascribed to something deeper than organizing ability. Supremacy of law is based on belief in human rights, which in turn are assertions of the sanctity of individual personality. The state as the guardian of human individuality may be a Western concept; as inheritors of the idea, however, we are entitled to an opinion, grounded in history as well as morality, that it will prove the only lasting type of political association.

The English political philosopher T. H. Green fits individual rights, law, and the state into an ordered pattern in the following passage:

> Now for the member of a state to say that his rights are derived from his social relations, and to say that they are derived from his position as a member of a state, are the same thing. The state is for him the complex of those social relations out of which rights arise, so far as these rights have come to be regulated and harmonised according to a general law, which is recognised by a certain multitude of persons, and which there is sufficient power to secure against violation from without and within.[3]

By its own internal nature, law constitutes a force applied equally throughout the community and furthering a natural social cohesion. It may be described as a distinct pattern of human relationships. Tradition, together with the common thought configurations of the day, have to be externalized in a matrix of generally accepted rules before political consciousness can arise. For these reasons law may be considered the basis of all political order, the foundation of the state. In the words of Euripides

> . . . for the bond of all men's states
> Is this, when they with honor hold by law.[4]

PLACE OF THE CONSTITUTION A state without a constitution resembles an animal lacking a skeleton. Though this is a practicable life form, as jellyfish and their kin have long indicated, the limitations are obvious. A political aphorism might be coined: No constitution, no continuity. Habits of human association assume institutional forms when a high degree of social organization is reached. Society is considered generally to stem from the institution of the family, increasing in extent and complexity with the addition of a superstructure of wider institutional patterns. Likewise the political state, with beginnings in tribal and clan loyalties, developed in the manner of a crystal through the aggregation of institutional facets around a basic pattern. By identifying the character of a state with the internal logic of its institutional structure, that is, its constitution, it becomes possible to use the experience of the past to solve the immediate problems of the present. Men are more at ease when the difficulties they encounter are not all strange or new but may be faced by well-ordered, habitual responses.

The American Constitution provided a great landmark in the association of the idea of a state with a constitution. This was not so much because of its content, outstanding though that was at the time of writing and still is, as on account of the bold innovation of a written constitution. A self-conscious declaration of the institutional pattern that would create and limit the nature of a particular state was an almost unheard-of experiment in the eighteenth century. Its historical success has made it the rule rather than the exception among modern states. However, a division deep enough to affect political character remains between states that have self-consciously framed their constitutions and those that have acquired them through long habit and tradition. In the former, reason, logic, and enunciated ideals limit institutional forms; in the latter, custom and habit prevail. Before the birth of the American Constitution and its many imitators, Edmund Burke was able to write:

> The states of the Christian world have grown up to their present magnitude in a great length of time and by a great variety of accidents. They have been improved to what we see them with greater or less degrees of felicity and skill. Not one of them has been formed upon a regular plan or with any unity of design. As their Constitutions are

not systematical, they have not been directed to any *peculiar* end, eminently distinguished, and superseding every other. The objects which they embrace are of the greatest possible variety, and have become in a manner infinite. In all these old countries, the state has been made to the people and not the people to the state.[5]

Too great reliance on a planned constitution may endanger the growth of natural social union, which the state itself is designed to serve. Thus the Russian people have been marshaled into endless toil under a constitution that replaced their old political forms with the dogmas of alien philosophers. The present Soviet state is a gigantic gamble that a people may remain united when uprooted from their past and committed to a future that exists only in the minds of dedicated fanatics. Communist China presents an even more extreme example. These terrifying experiments may succeed, in so far as former traditions had led this great segment of the world's peoples into futile misery. Nevertheless the ruthless use of dogmatic constitutions to force helpless populations into untried social experiments spells something very different from the Western state as the agent of voluntary social union. In its place, Burke's *systematical* or ideological state uses the accumulated capital of social unity to purchase a gambler's chance on a dogmatic dream of a "new life."

Throughout the modern world, emerging nation–states in Asia, Africa, and elsewhere are hesitating between new and old uses of a constitution. The fate of almost two thirds of the world's population is in balance on this question. Though in Western lands we have learned how to make our constitutions, written or traditional, serve the purpose of social union under the forms of the state, our missionary efforts elsewhere are lamentably inadequate. As the president of Pakistan pointed out when turning his country over to military rule, illiterate and hungry masses cannot be expected to understand the finer points of constitutional democracy. It may prove necessary to back our belief in the Western form of statehood with determined efforts to create the material conditions that would permit the greater part of the world's peoples to enjoy its advantages.

THE ROLE OF GOVERNMENT Before the factors of territory, people, and law can be combined to form a state, a catalyst variously known as "organization" or "government" must be introduced. Government is not one of several characteristics of a political state, it is the state in operation. If institutions of government are ignored, the state remains on the level of a philosophical idea. For it to assume the condition of reality in terms of events and happenings awaits the manifestation of governmental forms. Though government is the life force of politics it should not be confined to the bounds of statehood. Every form of human association is likely to be given institutional form through the dynamics of government. Even the basic grouping of the family in former times was structured by government; the Roman principle of *patria potestas,* through which the father held life and death powers over his offspring, made government the organizing factor in home life. Religion in Western lands has invented governmental forms in the established churches that are certainly not inferior to those adopted by political communities. Economic organization in modern times is largely dependent on techniques of government. Thus the key institution of business, the corporation, was created specifically for "the better governance of commerce." To reduce the idea of government to physical force wielded on political terms is to misunderstand the self-operating character of a major part of human association. Patterns of control of men by their fellows are to be found in every type of human activity. Physical force is only one—and a very crude—example of the instruments employed in establishing such control. Influence stemming from admiration, awe, affection, and perhaps most of all enlightened self-interest, permits the formation of operational groups in terms of hierarchies of authority and obedience. The talent of mankind for cooperation enables individuals with special skills or abilities to exercise functional authority over their fellows without the employment of force. Even in the limited field of political association, government possesses many tools besides those of physical terror.

THE DOCTRINE OF SOVEREIGNTY The state in action, then, may be viewed as one of the manifestations of the government of men. Though it is only one kind of human government, sharing many of its instruments with economic, religious, and even educational associations, the pattern it presents is sufficiently distinct to be examined as a separate entity.

Sometimes political government is held to be superior to all other ways of governing men because it contains a mysterious essence called *sovereignty*. As a sovereign body, it is held, the government of a state may claim final authority over all aspects of the behavior of its people. Common experience refutes any such claim; it is not necessary to go back to the Christian martyrs to recall incidents where individuals, groups, and whole communities have maintained beliefs and attitudes in rightful defiance of political authority. Interference and persecution amount to power only where they are effective in achieving their intended ends. In matters of economics as well as those of belief it is questionable if human behavior is subject to control by the arbitrary fiat of any sovereign body. It is well to remember the fable of the emperor's clothes reduced from magnificence to nudity by the independent vision of a single child. Assertion of the doctrine of sovereignty is generally the mark of an ideological or systematical government, where the aim of cooperative living is subordinated to the master plan of dogmatists.

Among peoples whose respect for individualism permits the concept of limited government, sovereignty is not regarded as essential to political rule. It retains a rightful place as a theoretical explanation of relationships existing within domestic and international systems of law. As such, it is best left to the understanding of specialists in jurisprudence. In the United States, for example, there are sovereign States bound in indissoluble union in a sovereign Republic. Britain and many European lands revere living sovereigns. Nowadays these are marks of respect, not factual descriptions of totalitarian power.

One distinctive feature of political government is its prevalence throughout most of the branches of human activity. It may not represent the final word in any particular activity—it certainly does not in religion or education and does so most doubtfully in economics—but it is needed everywhere to link the diverse interests of men into proper relationship with one another. The origin of the word *government* is from the Latin *gubernare,* which in turn derived from a Greek term for the director of a ship. This remains an excellent analogy: the task of political government is to coordinate the behavior of groups and individuals through whose particular skills and energies the actual business of life is being conducted. Political government cannot tell people how to be virtuous or even efficient along practical lines; it is limited to guiding them in relating their personal abilities to those of other members of the community. To repeat, it is an instrument of social union or cooperation, and not the source of human perfection.

Types of Government

Classification of forms of government is not a scientific pursuit. Whereas a biologist such as Haeckel could devote nearly 3,000 pages to the classification of radiolaria, a minor form of marine life, political scientists have achieved slight methodological advance beyond Aristotle's comparative study of 148 constitutions of his contemporary city–states. One reason for the lack of objective standards in the classification of governmental systems is that value judgments confront the investigator at the very start of the inquiry. It is possible to observe radiolaria with detached interest and to arrange the observed variations in forms into some logical system. To attempt, however, to examine the passions, interests, and behavior of one's fellow men as one would a marine animal is to misunderstand the capacity of the intellect. Aristotle and all his successors started with value judgments, systematizing their observations to conform to a priori assumptions. As value judgments vary from age to age and even according to location, any formulation of types of government must be treated as a matter of convenience.

HISTORICAL CLASSIFICATION For some purposes an historical classification is helpful. Western civilization has experienced certain dominant forms that may be assumed to be closely related to its social structure. The organization of government around a single personality is one of the oldest and most persistent forms. Sacred chiefs or war leaders, revered in tribal times, transformed themselves into kings as their followers settled into established territories. One-man rule became institutionalized under the name of *monarchy*. However, many variant patterns of this theme are interspersed through the tapestry of history. The *tyrant*, constantly recurring in Greek city–states, the *dictator*, frequently required to redress the political balance in the republic of Rome, have never disappeared from the annals of politics. Organized submission to the arbitrary will of an individual is an historical fact that may not be ignored in the evolution of government. Though the phase of monarchical government seems spent, at least in the West, one-man rule certainly has not been abandoned. Dictators and near-dictators hold a substantial part of the world's peoples in thrall today. In Western Europe, Spain and Portugal have accepted over two decades of dictatorship; the Near East is dominated by Nasser of Egypt; and Caribbean, Central American and Latin American republics are constantly threatened with the return of strong-man rule. A significant trend toward the institutionalizing of arbitrary authority has appeared among the recently independent nations of Asia. Pakistan, Burma, Thailand, have placed themselves under military dictatorships; the future of representative government in Indonesia is obscure. In tropical Africa emergent national governments are finely balanced between personal rule and representative forms. Neither previous history nor current events provide a safe basis for prognosticating the approaching end of one-man rule as a major system of government.

Another system described by Aristotle as the rule of the few and somewhat later by Nikita Khrushchev as collective leadership, has contended with one-man rule for two thousand years or more. To use modern terminology, it might be described as the dominance of a single, well-organized *interest group* over other community groupings. Perhaps the most obvious examples are the hereditary aristocracies that alternated in power with absolute monarchies in European history to the time of the French Revolution and beyond. An aristocracy of birth, however, does not exhaust the historical varieties of this form. Merchant groups ruled many prosperous European states. Republics, such as Holland before the rise of the House of Orange, Venice and the states of the Hanseatic League, organized their governments on the principle that the men who knew what was good for business knew what was good for the people. Even the American Republic in its early days restricted participation in government in favor of the more stable business element.[6]

Karl Marx built on the historical fact that political government could mean control of the community by and for a particular interest group, a theory that is plaguing the world today. According to Marx, government is an instrument of the class struggle; systems of government have progressed along predetermined lines from slavery to feudalism to capitalism, with no alternative but to advance from those to communism. The motivating force is described in the first sentence of the *Communist Manifesto* of 1848: "The history of all hitherto existing societies is the history of class struggles." All varieties of government outside the Communist states are thus declared by Marxists to be instruments of the bourgeois class, the profiteer of capitalism. This sweeping generalization has confused popular thinking well beyond the limits of practicing Marxists. Capitalist societies and Communist states are looked upon as specific types of government, whereas in fact their forms of government are separate and distinct from economic or social ideologies. Thus the parent state of Marxism–Leninism, Soviet Russia, is unashamedly a government by the few. The Party hierarchy has been declared in the Russian constitution "the vanguard of the working people in their struggle to build communist society and is the leading core of all organizations of the working people, both public and state."[7] This provision has been implemented to give the Communist Party virtual control of the nomination of candidates for election under Article 141: "The right to nominate candidates is secured to public organizations and societies of the working people: Communist Party organizations, trade unions, cooperatives, youth organizations and cultural societies." The fiction of a transition stage called the *dictatorship of the proletariat* reconciles this form of government with ideals of universal equality.

Terms commonly associated with government by the few, *aristocracy, oligarchy, plutocracy,* indicate value judgments rather than differences in methods. A favorable view of the minority group in power earns them the title of aristocracy; distaste for their composition or objectives places them in the category of oligarchy or plutocracy. The existence of this form of government in the past and its likely continuance in the future is hardly subject to question. Generalizations, however, that all political government is government by the few and that all other forms of rule are cunning pretenses have never advanced beyond the level of cynical speculation.

Just as men in the past submitted at times to the rule of absolute monarchs, so at others they also dispensed with ruling groups or classes, as when they attempted direct self-government in ancient Athens. Government by the few merges into government by the many through the device of representation, which replaces the fixed ruling group with officeholders chosen and maintained in power through the process of election.

Representation may be regarded as a modern fashion in government, though its uses were well known in classical times. For example the balance of power in Republican Rome was held between the aristocratic *senate* and the commonalty, partly through the institution of the *tribunes* chosen directly by the popular assembly and empowered, in the words of the historian Sallust, to act as "the guardians of all the rights of the plebs." It is customary to equate historical forms of representative government with Aristotle's classification of government by the many or Rousseau's idea of the supremacy of the general will. These theories, however, may be considered irrelevant to the actual steps which led to the development of representative institutions in Western lands. A device designed to allow interest groups to speak with single voices did not carry with it any implication of majority rule. In medieval England, for example, it was the Estates of the Realm—the baronage, the clergy and the commons—that were represented as separate bodies in the joint task of advising the monarch. It was not the people as a numerical mass but the community as a balanced social organization that constituted the early parliaments of England. Representative government may be characterized historically as government by discussion, because debate proved the general means for persuading the spokesmen of diverse interest groups to adopt common measures for the whole state.

Nowadays the scope of discussion has widened beyond the halls of legislative assemblies to include large sections of the general community. This has been made possible through the development of communication techniques, newspapers, periodicals, radio, television, and all other physical arts and crafts of propaganda. Modern forms of representative government might be described as control by persuasion rather than rule through discussion. In any case, the distinguishing feature of representative institutions is that they provide a means whereby the interest groups of the community can arrange themselves in constantly changing patterns of social dominance. It is not the essence of representation in general to grant to a numerical majority the final authority in controlling public affairs. Under certain social conditions majority rule may reflect the power balance of interest groups in a particular society at a given time, but it is questionable whether this is a common or widespread condition. Ordinary observation of everyday life indicates that the social structure is too complex to be resolved into a single-minded majority and dissenting minority. The American Constitution, for example, was conceived by its authors as a bulwark against the dangers of majority rule. With perhaps more clarity than is common today Madison associated majority rule with conditions of "pure democracy" where citizens were able to participate individually and directly in public matters in town-meeting gatherings. He distinguished this species of government from the one proposed.

A republic, by which I mean a government in which the scheme of representation takes place, opens a different prospect, and promises the cure for which we are seeking. Let us examine the points in which it varies from pure democracy, and we shall comprehend both the nature of the cure and the efficacy which it must derive from the Union.

The two great points of difference between a democracy and a republic are: first, the delegation of the government, in the latter, to a small number of citizens elected by the rest; secondly, the greater number of citizens, and greater sphere of country, over which the latter may be extended.

The effect of the first difference is, on the one hand, to refine and enlarge the public views, by passing them through the medium of a chosen body of citizens, whose wisdom may best discern the true interest of their country, and whose patriotism and love of justice will be least likely to sacrifice it to temporary or partial considerations. Under such a regulation, it may well happen that the public voice, pronounced by the representatives of the people, will be more consonant to the public good than if pronounced by the people themselves, convened for the purpose. On the other hand the effect may be inverted. Men of factious tempers, of local prejudices, or of sinister designs, may by intrigue, by corruption, or by any other means, first obtain the suffrages, and then betray the interests of the people. The question resulting is, whether small or extensive republics are more favorable to the election of proper guardians of the public weal; and it is clearly decided in favor of the latter by two obvious considerations.[8]

The modern use of the term *democratic government,* therefore, is ambiguous. The historian Carl Becker offers an excellent description from the historical point of view:

A democratic government has always meant one in which the citizens, or a sufficient number of them to represent more or less effectively the common will, freely act from time to time, and according to established forms, to appoint or recall the magistrates and to enact or revoke the laws by which the community is governed. This I take to be the meaning which history has impressed upon the term democracy as a form of government.[9]

It may be noted that here democracy is defined as a method of representing the common will and not merely expressing majority opinion. If the *demos,* the people, in democracy, is defined in statistical terms as a majority of the adult population, reliable means for discovering their will on all questions of government have not advanced beyond those employed by ancient Athens, where they were vitiated in our eyes by the institution of slavery, which turned a minority into an artificial totality. A more subtle concept equates the *demos* with the community as an organized group where various elements are evaluated in terms of their usefulness rather than by counting heads. This leads into a metaphysics of society that opens the way for assumptions such as those held by the Soviets, that democracy consists of integrating all the particularities and singularities of human life into a common order dictated by an unchallengeably "scientific" dogma. It is healthy to shudder away from any attempt to force into even theoretical conformity with such sinister imaginings types of government that exist to promote cooperation among people who are respected as individuals.

Modern representative government is a device that serves to reflect a dynamic pattern of social organization. Failure to understand this clearly may lead to unspeakable tyranny in the name of democracy. An inherent factor that separates representative institutions from the wider ideal of democracy is acceptance of the limitation of political power. Social organization as a thing-in-itself is maintained by a representative type of government; it does not claim the overmastering function of redesigning all human relationships through political means. Confusing political democracy with the total will of the community opens the way to the excesses of tyranny.

In brief, it is inexact to refer to democratic government as a specific type or form of rule. Where a community has achieved a high degree of social union, expressed in terms of equal participation in activities and general agreement on standards, governmental forms will reflect this common consent. In the present imperfect condition of mankind, representative government provides a satisfactory degree of compromise. Theoretically, however, a true democratic society should be defined as one wherein political government has become unnecessary. Karl Marx was logical when he postulated the withering away of the state as inevitable in a society where completely equal opportunity existed for all to satisfy their needs. His followers claim the title of democratic government for a form of rule which their own theory marks as transitional tyranny.

Viewed historically, the predominance of representative forms coincides with increase in the rate of social change. Technology, of course, is a major factor in compelling men to alter their patterns of relationship. Roads, railways, mass production, and electronics have transformed more social power structures than have all the devices of political organization. Ability to mesh the gears of governmental power with a constantly changing balance of new and old interest groups is the chief attribute of the representative system.

Perhaps the modern emphasis on this form of political organization may be related to a discovery by mankind, no longer separated by physical barriers, of the necessity and wisdom of compromise as the guide to survival. This idea of political compromise has been summarized by the English philosopher John Morley:

> Those who have thought most carefully and disinterestedly about the matter, are agreed that in advanced societies the expedient course is that no portion of the community should insist on imposing its own will upon any other portion, except in matters vitally connected with the maintenance of the social union. The question where this vital con-

nection begins is open to much discussion. . . . It is expedient in certain affairs that the will of the majority should be absolutely binding, while in affairs of a different order it should count for nothing, or as nearly nothing as the sociable dependence of a man on his fellows will permit.[10]

ANALYTICAL CLASSIFICATION Types of government may be classified according to their structures as instrumentalities of power, as well as in terms of the sources of their authority. This is not a very rewarding avenue for preliminary study as it tends to resolve into detailed descriptions of existing governments throughout the world, with categories determined by the arbitrary views of the investigator. There are, however, certain broad patterns that require examination under this heading. An outstanding example in modern times is a classification of governments based on the degree of association sought between organized regions included in the territory of the state.

FEDERAL GOVERNMENT For all practical purposes modern federal government may be said to have been inaugurated by the Constitution of the United States. The device has spread rapidly in the last century. A roll call of federal or quasi-federal states taken today would include such diverse political communities as the Union of Socialist Soviet Republics, West Germany, Nigeria, Australia, India, Canada, the French Community, Switzerland, and, of course, the United States itself. The link connecting these widely different systems of political authority is the attempt to preserve a measure of political autonomy within a single state for territorial regions that acknowledge the authority of a central government. As Professor Wheare describes the need:

It would seem that federal government is appropriate for a group of states or communities if, at one and the same time, they desire to be united under a single independent general government for some purposes and to be organized under independent regional governments for others. Or to put it shortly, they must desire to be united but not unitary.[11]

At the heart of any federal system lies the question of the division of powers or functions between central and regional authorities. Recognition of the need for such a division creates a federal structure. It is of lesser consequence whether the problem is solved by enumerating the powers granted the central government and leaving residual powers to the regions or states (in the fashion of the American Constitution), or by making the central authority the holder of residual power (a solution favored in Canada). The important point is that a balance of interests between regions and nation should be sought through a political constitution.

Federalism, then, is the instrument of peoples who have not grown into a single community through long habit. It is not required in the tight little island of the United Kingdom, though even there rumblings from the proud Scots and Welsh communities periodically challenge unitary assumptions. Unitary states such as Britain, the Netherlands, Belgium, Spain, and Italy, are constantly under pressure to enlarge themselves by creating empires, commonwealths or communities. The headlong rush toward closer association, sparked by the breakdown of distance and the interlocking of economic and cultural systems, has transformed federal government into a conservative method of political union. It remains a device tested and proved by history, while more recent forms such as the French Union (now the French Community) and the United Arab Republic are in an experimental stage.

SEPARATION OF POWERS The aspect of federal government that distinguishes it most clearly from unitary forms is its built-in character of self-limitation. Each delegation of governmental power is restricted to a definite sphere or specific functions; the extent to which the general and regional governments may exercise authority is expressed in constitutional terms. The doctrine of the separation of powers in the American Constitution is described by Justice Van Devanter as follows: "The Constitution establishes three great coordinate departments of the national government—the legislative, the executive and the judicial—and distributes among them the powers confided to that government by the people."[12] Constitutions of federal states, then, have as a primary function responsibility for limiting and defining the powers of government bodies. This establishes a pattern that affects relationships between political institutions on all levels. Thus the separation of powers between executive, legislative, and judicial organs is more commonly to be found in federal than in unitary systems. This separation also aids in the task of creating a watchdog for the constitution. Where power is divided among several political institutions, each claiming exclusive powers within definite bounds, it is obviously necessary to have an arbiter to settle disputes by giving authoritative interpretations of the constitution.

JUDICIAL REVIEW. The guardian of governmental limitations required by federal systems may take various forms. When federal government was first combined with a written constitution in the United States, it was assumed that the judiciary would determine the proper bounds of state and general governments through legal interpretation of the Constitution. In 1803, Chief Justice Marshall asserted the claim of the Supreme Court to the power of judicial review in the case of *Marbury v. Madison:*

> It is, emphatically, the province and duty of the judicial department, to say what the law is. Those who apply the rule to particular cases, must of necessity expound and interpret that rule. If two laws conflict with each other, the courts must decide on the operation of each. So, if a law be in opposition to the Constitution; if both the law and the Constitution apply to a particular case, so that the court must either decide that case, conformable to the law, disregarding the Constitution; or conformable to the Constitution disregarding the law; the court must determine which of these conflicting rules governs the case; this is of the very essence of judicial duty. . . . In some cases, then, the Constitution must be looked into by the judges. And if they can open it at all, what part of it are they forbidden to read or obey? . . . From these and many other selections which might be made, it is apparent, that the framers of the Constitution contemplated that instrument as a rule for the government of courts, as well as that of the legislature. Why otherwise does it direct the judges to take an oath to support it?

Since *Marbury v. Madison* the Supreme Court in the United States has managed to maintain its position as the ultimate arbiter of the limitations on national and state governments, subject only to such amendments as the people of the United States may choose to decree. One hundred and fifteen years after *Marbury v. Madison,* Mr. Justice Holmes was able to say: "This court has no more important function than that which devolves upon it the obligation to preserve inviolate the constitutional limitations upon the exercise of authority, federal and state, to the end that each may continue to discharge, harmoniously with the other, the duties entrusted to it by the Constitution."[13]

SUPREME LAW The essence of any federal system is that its constitution must constitute a supreme or paramount law of the land, superior to statutory enactments by the general or state legislatures. This may be achieved by granting a national supreme court power to invalidate legislative acts contradictory to the supreme law of the constitution. Canada and Australia are federal states that have followed the United States practice. However, not all federal systems entrust the interpretation of their supreme law to a strictly judicial body. Switzerland denies to its highest court the right to invalidate any law of the general legislature, though it may abrogate cantonal law on constitutional grounds. Supremacy of the Swiss constitution is maintained by submitting to a referendum of the whole electorate, on the demand of 30,000 citizens or 8 cantons, any law of the general legislature.

A different method has been adopted in the 1949 Constitution of the Federal Republic of Germany. Though a Federal Constitutional Court was established with full powers to interpret the Basic Law, the Court itself may be considered to have only a quasi-judicial character. The Constitution states that the Court shall consist of federal judges and other members, who may not be members of the legislature or be government officials. Half the members of the Federal Constitutional Court are elected by the lower house of the parliament (the *Bundestag*) and half by the upper house (the *Bundesrat*). It approximates then an elective constitutional council as well as a court of law.

A recent addition to federal systems, the French Community,[14] has gone further in vesting interpretation of the Constitution in conciliar rather than judicial hands. France's Constitutional Council consists of nine members, three appointed by the President, three by the President of the National Assembly, and three by the President of the Senate. They hold office for a nonrenewable period of ten years. Before any law that touches on the Constitution is promulgated it must be submitted to the Constitutional Council. A text declared unconstitutional may not be promulgated as law.

Although Article 13 of the Constitution of the U.S.S.R. declares that "the Union of Soviet Socialist Republics is a federal state, formed on the basis of a voluntary union of equal Soviet Socialist Republics," the device it uses to enforce constitutional federalism casts doubt on whether there is a true federal relationship. Neither an independent judiciary nor a constitutional council is granted powers to challenge unconstitutional acts of the general government. The Presidium of the Supreme Soviet, a standing committee of the national legislature that exercises most of the legislature's powers when the legislature is not in session, annuls decisions of national and regional governments if they do not conform to the Constitution. In effect this means that division of powers between general and regional governments lies at the mercy of whatever interpretation the men temporarily in control of the national government may consider expedient. Regional autonomy on a clearly defined basis is replaced by unenforceable promises that every Union Republic may secede from the Union at will and may conduct direct relations with foreign powers.[15]

COMMONWEALTHS AND COMMUNITIES A need to increase the degree of association between peoples without curtailing independent development of regional areas has led to experiments in forms of union less exacting than federal ties. A notable and successful example is furnished by the Commonwealth of Nations, formerly the British Commonwealth. The Imperial Conference of 1926 described membership in the following terms: "They are autonomous communities within the British Empire, equal in status, in no way subordinate one to another in any aspect of their domestic or external affairs, but united by a common allegiance to the Crown and freely associated as Members of the British Commonwealth of Nations." Even the tie of common allegiance to the Crown has now disappeared with the admission of the Republic of India as a full member. What holds the Commonwealth together is an historical experience in the development of law and representative institutions together with common interests and a will to cooperate on issues of fundamental importance. This may seem to be insufficient to merit classification as a form of government. Under cover of the vague phrase "free cooperation," however, a comprehensive and complex system for consultation and exchange of information has grown up which places governments within the Commonwealth in unique relationship to one another.

Though this is a purely conciliar system with no power to make decisions, it may yet claim governmental character. It should be recalled that British Parliaments and Ministers of State were once in the same situation, empowered only to offer advice to the sovereign. A glance at some of the centrally organized associations developed to promote Commonwealth relations illustrates the extent of mutual cohesion. The Commonwealth Parliamentary Association, with fifty branches in legislatures throughout the Commonwealth, boasts a General Council, frequent Conferences, and several Journals; the Commonwealth Economic Committee, with members nominated by their respective governments, serves as a research and investigatory body into many phases of economic activity; the Commonwealth Scientific Conference and Standing Committee is a clearing house for scientific, industrial, agricultural, and medical research in Commonwealth countries. The titles alone of some of the other bodies indicate the degree of practical interlocking: Commonwealth Shipping Committee, Commonwealth Agricultural Bureau, Commonwealth Air Transport Council, Commonwealth Telecommunications Board, Standing Committee on Commonwealth Forestry, Association of Universities of the British Commonwealth, English-Speaking Union of the Commonwealth.

The United States has started to experiment with the commonwealth system by creating the Commonwealth of Puerto Rico, an associated rather than integrated territory with a higher degree of autonomy than that of a State of the Union. It is possible that there may develop, among governments of peoples that are linked by historical and interest ties, voluntary cooperation along the lines of freely constituted commonwealths. As a safety valve against evils of national exclusiveness the commonwealth plan offers association on a continuous basis without the commitment of political union.

The Constitution of France's Fifth Republic diagrams a variant form of government standing somewhere between federal union and the voluntary cooperation of a commonwealth system. Title XII, "The Community of Free Peoples," states that "the Federation, and the States which express the will to join it, may, in order to associate and develop their civilizations, form a Community of Free Peoples." How this is going to be done is not spelled out in detailed fashion. However, France has led Western peoples in the grant of full citizenship to nearly all the inhabitants of her overseas possessions. Cultural identification has advanced in French West Africa and Equatorial Africa, in Caribbean and Pacific lands, in a manner lacking in corresponding British or American territories.

In its beginning, federalism aimed at creating a national union between peoples with strong claims to independent existence. Now the problem is taking the shape of associating nation groups for their better advancement in a common civilization. *Commonwealths* and *communities* may provide the blueprints for governmental forms that offer approximate solutions to this need.

Notes

[1] Barker, Ernest, *Reflections on Government,* New York: Oxford, 1958, p. xiv.

[2] Moodie, A. E., *Geography Behind Politics,* New York: Rinehart, 1948, p. 19.

[3] Green, T. H., *Lectures on the Principles of Political Obligation,* London: Longmans, 1942, p. 146.

[4] Way, A. S. (ed.), Euripides, *The Suppliants,* Loeb Classical Library, London: Heinemann, pp. 312-313.

[5] Hoffman, Ross J. S., and Levack, Paul (eds.), *Burke's Politics,* New York: Knopf, 1949, p. 470.

[6] The homogeneity of the economic and social interests of the members of the Constitutional Convention has been analyzed in striking fashion in Beard, Charles A., *An Economic Interpretation of the Constitution of the United States,* New York: Macmillan, 1935. Beard's viewpoint perhaps overstresses economic interests as against convictions of public responsibility that were at least equally powerful motivating forces in the character and attitudes of gentlemen of that period.

[7] Constitution of the Union of Soviet Socialist Republics, Article 126.

[8] *The Federalist,* Modern Library, New York: Random House, 1937, No. 10, p. 59.

[9] Becker, Carl L., *Modern Democracy,* New Haven: Yale, 1941, p. 7.

[10] Morley, John, Viscount, *On Compromise,* The Thinkers Library, London: Watts, 1956, p. 60.

[11] Wheare, Kenneth C., *Federal Government,* New York: Oxford, third edition, 1953, p. 36.

[12] *Evans v. Gore,* 253 U.S. 245 (1920).

[13] *Hammer v. Dagenhart,* 247 U.S. 251 (1918).

[14] "A Federation shall be created between the Republic and the peoples of the Overseas Territories, who, by deliberation in their Territorial Assemblies, may express the will to do so." Article 67, Constitution of the Republic of France, 1958.

[15] Constitution of the U.S.S.R., Articles 17 and 18(a).

Supplementary Readings

Arendt, Hannah, *The Origins of Totalitarianism,* New York: Harcourt, Brace, 1954.

Becker, Carl L., *Modern Democracy,* New Haven: Yale, 1941.

Beer, Samuel H., and others, *Patterns of Government: The Major Political Systems of Europe,* New York: Random House, 1958.

Cassirer, Ernst, *The Myth of the State,* New York: Doubleday, 1955.

de Toqueville, Alexis, *Democracy in America,* Vintage Books, New York: Knopf, 1954.

Finer, Herman, *Theory and Practice of Modern Government,* New York: Holt, revised edition, 1949.

Friedrich, Carl J., and Brzezinski, Z. K., *Totalitarian Dictatorship and Autocracy,* Cambridge: Harvard, 1956.

Gierke, Otto Friedrich von, translated by Maitland, Frederic William, *Political Theories of the Middle Ages,* Boston: Beacon Press, 1958.

Green, T. H., *Lectures on the Principles of Political Obligation,* London: Longmans, second edition, 1942.

Lindsay, A. D., *The Modern Democratic State,* New York: Oxford, 1947.

Marriott, J. A. R., *The Mechanism of the Modern State,* London: Oxford, 1927.

Sait, Edward McC., *Political Institutions: A Preface,* New York: Appleton, 1938.

Spahr, Margaret (ed.), *Readings in Recent Political Philosophy,* New York: Macmillan, 1935.

Chapter 3

The Structure of Constitutions

Political systems are literally systems of institutional interrelationships. The pattern created by the connections of the various institutions of rule to one another and to the general functioning of society form what is called a *political constitution*. In the words of Aristotle, "A constitution may be defined as an organization of offices in a state, by which the method of their distribution is fixed, the sovereign authority is determined, and the nature of the end to be pursued by the association and all its members is prescribed."[1] Clearly, then, every state functions under some form of constitution, even though it is only one suitable to a gang of brigands. Value judgments concerning types of constitutions are unavoidable at the start of an inquiry into methods of classification. Some writers prefer to keep the term *constitutionalism* distinct from the general concept of a constitution.[2] Constitutionalism may then be reserved for a particular pattern of the organization of government, generally one favorable to the rule of law and popular consent as the basis of political authority. There is some practical value in making a distinction of this kind. The study of political constitutions as reflections of human folly and malice, as well as of mankind's aspirations, is a dreary task. It seems justifiable to make some axiomatic judgments concerning desirable standards for political government and to dismiss the deviant types, the Caligulas and the Hitlers, to a semantic limbo of nonconstitutional tyranny. At least this has the merit of confining studies to the governmental forms with which we feel directly concerned.

Structure of Constitutions

Constitutions normally systematize patterns of government in terms of three major categories. In the first place, the source of political authority in the state may be described in a manner that indicates limitations on governmental power as well as reasons for obedience. Secondly, the principal organs of government are established and their functions and interrelations determined. In the third place, objectives of government may be declared in terms of the treatment of individual citizens, both as regards legal rights and economic betterment.

SOURCES OF POLITICAL AUTHORITY An outstanding development of the last few decades has been the almost universal acceptance of "We, the People," as the final authority decreeing the organization of the state. An example of this type of declaration may be drawn from Article 1 of the Italian Constitution of 1947. "Italy is a democratic Republic founded on labor. Sovereignty belongs to the people who exercise it within the forms and limits of the Constitution." This concept has now been adopted throughout non-Western lands. The 1946 Constitution of Japan states: "The Emperor shall be the symbol of the state and of the unity of the people, deriving his position from the will of the people with whom resides sovereign power."

General acceptance of the state as the Instrument of the People does not ensure what we would consider popular control of government in very wide areas of the modern world. It is, however, an important development in the outlook of mankind as a whole towards the idea of the state. Americans, in particular, have reason to take pride in the world-wide success of a concept on which they established their Republic. Our enemies as well as our friends flatter us through seeking to surpass us in the development of our own principles.

A working analysis of any specific governmental pattern is not greatly advanced by accepting at face value rhetorical declarations that all power belongs to the people. Before any state may be regarded as a service institution of its people, the popular will must be given institutional forms through which it can express itself on basic questions of organization and power. The examination of these forms is a practical method of evaluating the worth of different constitutions.

Thus, under the Constitution of the United States, "We, the People," are organized as a general electorate voting in our several States according to the qualifications required for electors of the most numerous branch of the State legislature. This electorate possesses decisive power in the choice of the principal officeholder of the Republic, the President. Also it selects one House of Congress, the House of Representatives, through universal suffrage, limited to a minor degree by State-imposed restrictions. Barriers to the organization of the community as a single people remain in the method of electing Senators and in the imperfections of the electoral system itself. Similarly, the British people control the composition of their Parliament, and through Parliament the Government and Constitution, by their organization as an electorate in constituencies under conditions of universal suffrage. In contrast, the Union of Soviet Socialist Republics provides, in Article 3 of its Constitution, that "all power in the U.S.S.R. belongs to the working people of town and country as represented by the Soviets of Working People's Deputies." Organization of an electorate with free choice is then crippled by the provision that candidates may be nominated only by public organizations and societies of the working people, controlled in law and in fact by the Communist Party. The 1954 Constitution of Communist China contains similar safeguards against the people's finding organizational forms of expression outside the Communist apparatus. Article 1 of the Constitution of the Chinese People's Republic defines Communist China as "a people's democratic state led by the working class and based on an alliance of workers and peasants." This again permits all organization of the electorate to remain within the grip of the Communist hierarchy. France's Fifth Republic determines the source of all governmental authority in unequivocal terms.

National sovereignty belongs to the people, which shall exercise this sovereignty through its representatives and by means of referendums. No section of the people, nor any individual, may attribute to themselves or himself the exercise thereof. Suffrage may be direct or indirect under the conditions stipulated by the Constitution. It shall always be universal, equal, and secret.[3]

West Germany also has explicit provisions concerning the manner in which the general body of citizens constitutes the final source of political authority.

All state authority emanates from the people. Every citizen has the right and the duty to take part in the formation of the political life of his *Gemeinde* [community], *Kreis* [county], *Land* [state] and of the German Democratic Republic. The right of co-determination takes the form of: voting in popular initiatives and referendums; exercising the right to vote and standing for election; entering upon public offices in general administration and in the administration of justice.[4]

THE AMENDING POWER The *people* as an organized community may not be considered to act as the source of state power unless practical means are provided for the alteration or amendment of their Constitution according to popular will. A useful test of the sincerity of governmental organization to its declared principles lies in an examination of the amending process.

At this point the concept of a people has to be distinguished from a formless mass of individuals living in a certain area. In modern times the nation acts as a matrix to mold a conglomeration of individuals into the form of a people. The basic characteristics then, of nationhood, common traditions and a will towards social unity, must be integrated into the idea of popular will. This may be done by adding an extension in time to other physical characteristics of a people. Thus a people as a *nation* may be considered to be organized around the traditions and principles of previous generations. Though the guardianship of such traditions, themselves a principal bond of social unity, permits great latitude for each generation to adapt old customs to new circumstances, it also entails an obligation to pass on the inheritance to future generations. Limitations may be expected upon the power of temporary majorities to overthrow fundamental law by immediate action. The test of these safeguards lies in whether they permit popular will to formulate itself with due deliberation or whether they are means to place constitutional revision in the hands of a self-perpetuating power group.

Thus the Constitution of the United States divides the amending power into two distinct processes: the proposal of amendments and their subsequent ratification. "The Congress, whenever two thirds of both Houses shall deem it necessary, shall propose Amendments to this Constitution, or, on the Application of the Legislatures of two thirds of the several States, shall call a Convention for proposing Amendments. . . ."[5] Congressional proposal of amendments, particularly with the proviso of a two-thirds majority of both Houses, sets up a requirement that a substantial majority of the electorate should be in favor of such a proposal, perhaps over a considerable period of time. It does not constitute, however, an enduring obstacle to the popular will. If Congressional obstinacy barred a proposed change from popular consideration over any period of time, the second alternative (of application by the legislatures of two thirds of the States for the holding of a Constitutional Convention) could serve as an avenue for the expression of organized public opinion. Though there has never been an application by two thirds of the State legislatures for the holding of a Convention to amend the Constitution, the existence of this power ensures that Congress will not attempt for an unreasonable period to defy widespread demands for a change.

The process of ratification provides substantial though indirect means for the expression of a popular mandate. In the words of the Supreme Court:

> The Fifth Article is a grant of authority by the people to Congress. The determination of the method of ratification is the exercise of a national power specifically granted by the Constitution; that power is conferred upon Congress, and is limited to two methods, by action of the legislatures of three fourths of the States, or conventions in a like number of States. . . . The framers of the Constitution might have adopted a different method. Ratification might have been left to a vote of the people, or to some authority of government rather than that selected.[6]

Thus the concept of "We, the People," as the ultimate authority in American government is implemented in practice under safeguards. The American people may not act as an amorphous mass to alter the fundamental law of the nation. They are organized as voting bodies in their several States. This introduces a geographic factor which may offset determination of change by a simple majority. Further, the question at issue is not put directly to a popular vote: if Congress decrees ratification by State legislatures, the voting community may have no opportunity for immediate intervention; even the more popular method of ratification by specially elected State conventions is subject to conditions imposed on the choice of such conventions by individual State legislatures. Despite these precautions against direct action by a numerical majority, the electoral system of the United States is so balanced that the steady will of a continuing majority normally will prevail over a reasonable period of time. Eighteen years elapsed between the passage of the Eighteenth Amendment decreeing prohibition and its repeal by the Twenty-first Amendment. During the last decade of enforcement it is questionable whether prohibition was supported by a majority of the voting population. However, an ambitious social experiment, "noble in purpose," in President Hoover's words, was entitled under the American system to prove itself in a period of grace uninterrupted by the changing winds of majority opinion. Another factor in the concept of a supreme people extending in time as well as in numbers is the added sense of responsibility given to the making of decisions. If it is realized that an amendment, once made, may take twenty years to repudiate, the people are more likely to bring the highest quality of judgment to the process.

Historically speaking, the British Constitution attributes all political authority to the Crown. Accordingly, the British people are a community organized as subjects of the Crown. However, during centuries of political evolution the Crown itself has become a symbol of national unity rather than a center of power. The monarchy represents "sovereignty subject to law," which may be interpreted as government in accordance with constitutional principles. Parliament is the guardian of the complex of historic laws, starting with the Constitutions of Clarendon of 1164 and running through Magna Carta, the Bill of Rights, the Reform Act of 1832, to the Parliament Act of 1911 and the Statute of Westminster of 1931. In legal theory at least constitutional change may be brought about by an Act of Parliament. The people, then, control their Constitution through the indirect means of electing members to the House of Commons. Significant changes in the constitutional structure nowadays entail expression of the popular will through a general election. As Parliament may be dissolved at any time and a new House of Commons elected within three weeks, a Government in power lacks valid excuse for altering the fundamental law of the land without first seeking the approval of the organized electorate.

It may be said that popular control of constitutional principles is of more recent origin in Britain than in the United States. The British community lacked institutional means through which they might express majority opinion until Parliament became an approximately representative body under the Reform Act of 1832. Implementation of the concept of the people as the source of authority in the state was carried out during the nineteenth century through the creation of an electorate, honestly representative and endowed with the means to establish or overthrow Governments within a comparatively brief period of time. A step in this process may be illustrated by an extract from a speech made by the enlightened Conservative Prime Minister, Benjamin Disraeli, on the subject of the Reform Act of 1867:

> The working classes will now probably have a more extensive sympathy with our political institutions, which, if they are in a healthy state, ought to enlist popular feeling because they should be embodiments of the popular requirements of the country. It appeared to us that if this great change were made in the constitutional body there would be a better chance of arriving at the more patriotic and national feelings of the country than by admitting only a favored section, who, in consideration of the manner in which they were treated, and the spirit in which they were addressed, together with the peculiar qualities which were ascribed to them, would regard themselves as marked out, as it were, from the rest of their brethren and the country, and as raised up to be critics rather than supporters of the Constitution.[7]

Parenthetically, it might be added, Disraeli dramatized the need for a popular base for government in Britain through a political novel which described the English people as divided into two nations, the Rich and the Poor. His solution—the application of political authority stemming from an enlarged suffrage to redress the economic balance—may be contrasted with Marx's and Engels's belief in the inevitability of class war. The stable welfare state of modern

Britain provides substantial evidence that Disraeli was a shrewder judge of political evolution than Karl Marx.

Use of the popular initiative and referendum for proposing and ratifying amendments to a Constitution indicates that the people are accepted as the final source of authority for the structure of a state. The Swiss Confederation uses this device to grant final power to the Swiss nation over cantonal representation. There is, however, a qualification to preserve the federal character of the organization of the Swiss state. "The revised federal Constitution, or the revised part thereof, shall enter into force when it has been accepted by the majority of the Swiss citizens taking part in the vote thereon *and by a majority of the states*."[8] The Constitution of the Italian Republic places the power of proposing changes in the basic law in the hands of a bicameral Parliament. Parliament must vote for such proposals on two separate occasions with at least three months intervening between votes. If, on the second vote, the proposal is passed by a majority of two thirds of each chamber, it becomes law. Otherwise the proposal is submitted to a popular referendum on the demand of one fifth of the membership of either chamber, or by 500,000 electors. Australia and Japan both require that constitutional alterations should be decided by popular referendum. In the case of Australia the people must approve as voters in their several states, as well as in their capacity as a national electorate. "If in a majority of the States a majority of the electors voting approve the proposed law, and if a majority of all the electors also approve the proposed law"[9] then and only then may the Constitution stand amended. This extreme insistence on popular control on both the federal and national level has resulted in a "rigid" type of Constitution that tends to hamper social development in a rapidly growing territory.

The Constitution of the Fifth Republic of France introduces a novel element into the concept of the people as the source of state authority. The actual power of the people to alter the structure of their government is limited in two particulars which may be regarded as overriding national ideas. "No amendment procedure may be undertaken or followed when the integrity of the territory is in jeopardy. The republican form of government shall not be subject to amendment." A *mystique* of the nation as a historical force overcomes the claim of any single generation to cede its territory or change its basic form. In our modern age this may be considered a gallant flaunting of the romantic tradition.

The Soviet Constitution deals with any claim of the Russian people to alter their structure of government in a brief sentence. "The Constitution of the U.S.S.R. may be amended only by decision of the Supreme Soviet of the U.S.S.R. adopted by a majority of not less than two thirds of the votes in each of its Chambers."[10] As the fundamental law of Russia is otherwise rigged to prevent the Russian electorate's exercising any free choice in the selection of the Supreme Soviet, this provision disposes of any awkward attempt by a persistent majority of the community to alter the structure of a "people's democracy." Failure to trust the people with any practical means to control their political destinies disposes of the rhetorical claim in Article 1 of the Constitution that "the Union of Soviet Socialist Republics is a socialist state of workers and peasants."

The origin of constitutions, then, may not be taken as the principal clue to the final source of authority in their respective states. Bold declarations concerning the "sovereign" character of the people or any other body should be tested against the practical powers accorded an organized community to determine its own fundamental law. Communities exist only in terms of organization, and such organization may take many forms, from that of the traditional nation to the ideological groupings newly encountering modern technology. The provision of organization patterns permitting participation by the people as a whole is the final test of constitutional validity.

STRUCTURES OF GOVERNMENT The second great function of a constitution is to determine the relationships that should exist among major organs of government. A constitution may be likened to a blueprint of the machinery of state. It should be added that it is the type of blueprint that would seriously threaten the sanity of trained engineers or architects. Generally, constitutions create rigid patterns of relationships which are either based on historical conditions no longer relevant or reflect social theories untested in practice. In both cases the dynamic element in the practical affairs of men is neglected. As Thomas Carlyle wrote in exasperation of the paper constitutions that France produced between the Revolution and the rise of Napoleon, "they will not march."

This criticism may be leveled anew against many of the constitutions adopted by peoples recently elevated to the rank of statehood. One reason for this common weakness is that written constitutions are laws, constructed by lawyers generally for the convenience of other lawyers. While it is possible to agree with Gilbert's operatic Lord Chancellor that

> The Law is the true embodiment
> Of everything that's excellent

it has limitations as a means of designing dynamic relationships. Few business enterprises could hope to survive and flourish in the changing marts of commerce if bound at origin by rigid rules concerning the relationships of one type of activity to another. If Production was ruled immutable master of Sales, and Research and Advertising were frozen in positions occupied at the founding of the business, the adaptability of the corporation to actual conditions of operation might be severely handicapped. Political circumstances are as subject to change as economic conditions; it is unrealistic to assume that the major organs of government activity can have their interrelationship determined by a master plan in the form of a legal constitution.

Countries whose constitutions have not been reduced to written form avoid some of the difficulties inherent in a "rigid" governmental structure. Thus Great Britain, with an "elastic" constitution based on conventions and customs as well as laws, has been able to maintain greater discretion in the arrangement of governmental powers than is exemplified in the political structure of the United States. Exercise of the type and degree of political authority needed to meet a given situation is a comparatively simple process under the British system. Thus if some emergency arose that might readily be solved by government's temporarily assuming functions of private enterprise (say the publication of newssheets and the operation of transport), the elastic structure of British government permits immediate action. A situation of this character occurred in the 1920s, when the national trade-union movement proclaimed a general strike against the Government. Winston Churchill enjoyed a pleasant interlude as Government editor and publisher of the London *Times*. The Cabinet have only to decide that this is the proper course to obtain the necessary laws from Parliament with a minimum of discussion. The whole apparatus of the administrative services in all the government departments, including those of the armed services, could be engaged in a disciplined approach to the problem under the direction of the Prime Minister or of a small committee of the Cabinet. The courts of law could not challenge the actions of the Government on constitutional grounds. Speed and efficiency of action to meet the crisis might find its only check in the unwillingness of local government bodies to cooperate. At this point, the conventional procedure of the constitutional system dictates that the national government negotiate with local authorities concerning matters customarily within the local field of action. On the whole, however, a situation of this nature might result in almost total governmental power being concentrated temporarily in a few executive offices. Constitutional principles would be in no way injured, and the normal balance between governmental activities would be restored at the close of the emergency.

Rigid constitutions, on the other hand, attempt to impose a lasting framework of structural interrelationships. In practice, important changes are taking place constantly in the balance of power and responsibility among the great organs of government. However, since such alterations might seem to challenge the constitution, they may not be openly acknowledged. A form of political fiction appears that pretends things are as they always were, when they are patently different. This has the effect of confusing the general public and hindering the determination of responsibility in specific fields of political action.

For example, the Constitution of the United States declares: "All Bills for raising Revenue shall originate in the House of Representatives; but the Senate may propose or concur with Amendments as on other Bills."[11] When this clause was written, it embodied the tradition of the British Parliament that only the popularly elected House could be entrusted with the power to impose taxation. If strictly carried out this provision would bar the Senate from initiating measures requiring major tax assessments. In practice, the Senate has turned the clause into a mere formula:

the act of initiation has been reduced to little more than the power to provide a revenue bill with a title. The Senate interprets its Constitutional authority to amend as license to rewrite completely any revenue bill originating in the House. Although changes in the character of the Senate and in its method of election have given some reason for this assumption of power, the community acting in the capacity of general electorate is deprived of effective control over the tax structure. Direct responsibility for taxing no longer lies with the popularly elected body—the Senate as a whole is not subject to election at any one period. Lines of responsibility between the people and the government have become blurred in this as in many other matters where the Constitution hinders adaptations in the balance of power among the major organs of government.

Perhaps the Fourth Republic of France was the most notable example in recent times of a state paralyzed in action by its own constitution. In drawing up a constitution for the Fifth Republic a bold effort was made to prevent this danger inherent in rigid constitutions. The presidential office received extraordinary powers intended to make it the arbiter in times of necessity between the exigencies of the national situation and a rigid allocation of governmental powers. Thus, in describing the function of the President the Constitution states: "He shall ensure, by his arbitration, the regular functioning of the governmental authorities, as well as the continuance of the State."[12] In a later Article he is given extraordinary powers to carry out such arbitration.

> When the institutions of the Republic, the independence of the nation, the integrity of its territory or the fulfillment of its international commitments are threatened in a grave and immediate manner and when the regular functioning of the constitutional governmental authorities is interrupted, the President of the Republic shall take the measures commanded by these circumstances, after official consultation with the Premier, the Presidents of the Assemblies, and the Constitutional Council.[13]

It is too early to judge how well this solution will work in practice. Granting emergency authority of this character to the head of the state approaches the Roman concept of appointing a dictator for a limited period. Constitutions that depend, in the last resort, on the judgment and integrity of a single man are questionable guarantors of the traditions and liberties of a people. Perhaps it is wiser to recognize the incapacity of any constitution to predetermine the patterns of relationship among organs of government that wield dynamic instruments of power. The function of a constitution is to make general grants of authority over the community and to limit the exercise of power by any individual, office, or body. It is another and probably fruitless task to parcel out the public power in neat packages for the use of predesigned offices.

THE STATE AND THE INDIVIDUAL Political government is or should be concerned above all with the welfare of the individual. A theory of great influence in the development of American and British institutions was based on the concept that the individual and the state were bound together by a mutual compact. This explanation of political ties, somewhat inaccurately termed the *contract theory,* is associated with the writings of John Locke. Locke's own view of an original compact is not that of an historic event but rather the general agreement that men demonstrate to belong to a particular society and to accept the bonds of social union. The effect of this theory among English-speaking peoples has been, on the whole, good. It has stripped the state of the semimagical life-of-its-own, inherited from days when institutions, like natural forces, had attributed to them the personalities of gods or demons. Still, government viewed as a resultant of the need of individuals for mutual protection and advancement does not readily assume a stable form acceptable to everyone. The analogy of a legal contract whereby the state pledges itself in perpetuity to grant certain rights and privileges to the individual and his descendants in return for obedience and loyalty has proved tempting, particularly in the United States. It is, however, a weak foundation for actual rights enforceable at law. These may not be considered to have a true contractual base, as the parties that made the original compact are not the same as the parties seeking enforcement. The law of contract requires that there should be a true meeting of minds of existing persons before mere agreement, a *nudum pactum,* becomes a repository of rights enforceable by the public power. Personal rights, as distinguished from rights against things, die with the person who originally acquired them.

BILLS OF RIGHTS Ever since the American people insisted on the addition of the first ten amendments to their Constitution, written Constitutions throughout the world have included solemn engagements between the state and the individual. For example, Article 25 of the 1946 Constitution of Japan states that "all people shall have the right to maintain the minimum standards of wholesome and cultured living." The Soviet Constitution guarantees, by law, freedom of speech, of assembly, and of the press, and generously adds freedom of street processions and demonstrations. It also makes a solemn constitutional declaration that "citizens of the U.S.S.R. have the right to rest and leisure."[14] Almost all written constitutions have outdone their American exemplar in the extent and specificity of the rights guaranteed to individuals. As declarations of intention, the numerous Bills of Rights embodied in modern constitutions may be said to have an elevating influence. A more cynical viewpoint might find them analogous to New Year's resolutions, lavishly made but seldom observed.

In judging the true nature of any constitution, promises made in respect to individual rights may be regarded as polite rhetoric until the means for the enforcement of these rights by the individual are clearly spelled out. Thus the American Constitution still leads a great part of the world in specific freedoms accorded individuals through the clear remedies available if any Constitutional right is denied. It is worth noting that our major liberties are protected by a direct prohibition aimed at the branch of government possessing power to disturb them. "Congress shall make no law respecting an establishment of religion, or prohibiting the free exercise thereof; or abridging the freedom of speech, or of the press; or the right of the people peaceably to assemble, and to petition the Government for a redress of grievances."[15] In support of this prohibition lies an ordered structure: an independent Supreme Court with power to declare such laws invalid and an independent Executive bound to refrain from the enforcement of invalid laws. The compact between the individual and government in the United States may be considered a working arrangement based on the total organization of the state and not upon the appended rhetoric of a paper constitution.

The United States and Great Britain share a like constitutional safeguard that protects the individual against the arbitrary will of officialdom. In the United States Constitution, Amendments 5 and 14 forbid the federal and State governments respectively "to deprive any person of life, liberty, or property, without due process of law." The whole structure of traditional law as interpreted by an independent judiciary is thus brought into force as an arbiter between the individual and governmental power. Great Britain has cherished this principle for many centuries under the name of the "rule of law," and has elevated it to the position of the structural key of her conventional Constitution. It is the absence of a basic apparatus of this order that makes a mockery of individual rights paraded in the constitutional declarations of totalitarian states.

A trend toward reliance on an independent judiciary as an effective guarantor of the rights of the individual against government is shown by almost all modern constitutions based on Western standards. This acceptance of judicial arbitration extends from postwar Japan to the recent creation of an independent Ghana. Even France appears to have moved away from her long-held tradition that complaints against the government by a citizen may not be heard in ordinary courts of law but only before tribunals administering administrative justice. The Constitution of the Fifth Republic declares that "the President of the Republic shall be the guarantor of the independence of the judicial authority," and, in another place, "no one may be arbitrarily detained. The judicial authority, guardian of individual liberty, shall ensure respect for this principle under the conditions stipulated by law."

The Place of Constitutions

Written constitutions are best regarded as declarations of intention. In stable political societies these declarations are implemented by structures of established law and custom known to the community and consequently dangerous for government authorities to flout. There is, however, no magic in a constitution to render it automatically self-enforcing. Even countries blessed with an independent judiciary and a tradition of law observance may have their fundamental law overturned by the force or fraud of those possessed of actual power. The final bulwark of any constitutional structure is the willingness and ability of the community to enforce obedience to basic standards on their officeholders by extralegal as well as legal means. Perhaps this point has never been more clearly and sensibly expressed than in Jefferson's words in the Declaration of Independence.

Prudence, indeed, will dictate that Governments long established should not be changed for light and transient causes; and accordingly all experience hath shewn, that mankind are more disposed to suffer, while evils are sufferable, than to right themselves by abolishing the forms to which they are accustomed. But when a long train of abuses and usurpations, pursuing invariably the same Object evinces a design to reduce them under absolute Despotism, it is their right, it is their duty, to throw off such Government, and to provide new Guards for their future security.

Notes

[1] Barker, Ernest (tr. and ed.), Aristotle, *The Politics of Aristotle,* New York: Oxford, 1948, Book IV, Chapter 1, p. 156.

[2] A defense of modern constitutionalism may be found in Hermens, F. A., *The Representative Republic,* Notre Dame: University of Notre Dame Press, 1958. The origins of the doctrine are traced by Professor McIlwain, *Constitutionalism, Ancient and Modern,* Great Seal Books, Ithaca: Cornell University Press, revised edition, 1958.

[3] Constitution of the Republic of France promulgated October 4, 1958, Article 3.

[4] Constitution of the German Democratic Republic promulgated October 7, 1949, Article 3.

[5] Constitution of the United States, Article V.

[6] *Hawke v. Smith,* 253 U.S. 221 (1920).

[7] Disraeli, Benjamin, "Franchise and Reform. 1867," *British Historical Speeches and Orations,* Everymans Library, New York: Dutton, 1937, p. 289.

[8] Constitution of the Swiss Confederation, Article 123. Author's italics.

[9] Commonwealth of Australia Constitution Act 1900, Section 128.

[10] Constitution of the U.S.S.R., Article 146.

[11] Constitution of the United States, Article I, Section 7, Subsection 1.

[12] Constitution of the Republic of France, 1958, Title XI, Article 5.

[13] *Ibid.,* Article 16.

[14] Constitution of the U.S.S.R., Article 119.

[15] Constitution of the United States, Amendment 1.

Supplementary Readings

Amery, L. S., *Thoughts on the Constitution,* New York: Oxford, second edition, 1953.

Bagehot, Walter, *The English Constitution,* New York: Appleton, 1914.

Brown, George W. (ed.), *Canada,* Berkeley: University of California Press, 1950.

Campion, Sir Gilbert, et al., *British Government since 1918,* London: G. Allen, 1951.

Einaudi, Mario, "The Constitution of the Italian Republic," *The American Political Science Review,* 1948, **42,** No. 3, 661-676.

The Federalist, Modern Library, New York: Random House, 1937.

Friedrich, Carl J., *Constitutional Government and Democracy,* Boston: Ginn and Co., revised edition, 1950.

———, *Constitutional Reason of State, the Survival of the Constitutional Order,* Providence: Brown University Press, 1957.

Hoffmann, Stanley H., and Wahl, Nicholas, "*The French Constitution of* 1958," *The American Political Science Review,* 1959, **53,** No. 2, 332-357.

McIlwain, Charles Howard, *Constitutionalism, Ancient and Modern,* Great Seal Books, Ithaca: Cornell University Press, 1958.

Pritchett, Charles H., *The American Constitution,* New York: McGraw-Hill, 1959.

Spiro, Herbert J., *Government by Constitution,* New York: Random House, 1959.

Swisher, Carl B., *American Constitutional Development,* Boston: Houghton Mifflin, second edition, 1954.

Thomson, David, *Democracy in France: The Third and Fourth Republic,* New York: Oxford, 1954.

Wheare, Kenneth C., *Modern Constitutions,* New York: Oxford, 1951.

Wormuth, Francis D., *The Origins of Modern Constitutionalism,* New York: Harper, 1949.

Zurcher, Arnold J. (ed.), *Constitutions and Constitutional Trends since World War II,* New York: New York University Press, 1951.

Chapter 4

The Nature of Political Office

Political authority is one of the several ways in which men command their fellows. Obedience on the part of the individual or the group stems from a variety of conditions. Religion binds men together under a hierarchy of values generally embodied in an institutional framework; family life requires the subordination of the young to the mature; the educational process is based on the acceptance of discipline; and, above all, economic processes in an advanced society necessitate a complicated pattern of functional authority. To draw distinctions between one type of authority and another is always a delicate operation. A factory foreman's orders, for example, are followed perhaps as much from acceptance of his superior competence and from understanding of the need for coordination of activities as from any direct fear of penalties for disobedience. Are not the instructions of a policeman clearing a traffic jam obeyed on much the same grounds, or must it be assumed that they are effective only through the threat of physical force—that it is the gun and not the man that is being obeyed?

An oversimplification of political power in terms of force throws little light on the complexity of the modern state. The habit of cooperation is rooted in both man's instinctual and reasoning nature; physical force itself is a manifestation, sometimes a very perverse one, of this basic characteristic. All the means through which men influence or compel one another into obedience in ordinary life may be found in the institutions of the political state. It is better, then, to seek to distinguish political power not as a special or unique type of authority but as general authority directed towards a particular objective. This objective is perhaps best expressed by the Latin words from which the term "republic" are derived: *res publica,* the affairs of the people as a political community. There are many modern variations, such as "the general interest" or the "common good," but these carry value connotations beyond the factual comprehensiveness of the original phrase "affairs of the people."

Political authority is, then, the power used to advance the affairs of the people. This power has been embodied or institutionalized since earliest times in a particular form, that of political office. The nature of political office carries with it the true distinguishing features of state authority, which in fact might be described as that authority exercised by the holders of public office. The idea of public office has become confused in modern thinking and one way to unravel its meaning is to trace the origins of the concept. The word "office" is derived from two Latin words, *opus,* which may be translated as work, and *facere,* to do. Service, duty, and function are primary meanings.

The nature of public office in Republican Rome provides a good starting place for the examination of Western ideas. The Roman magistracy, the sum of all governing offices in the Republic, was the central element in the constitutional structure. The great offices of state, the consuls, the praetors, and at times the overriding dictator, held decision-making authority that was not dependent on legislative grants or even the ordinary law of the land. This basic power, known as *potestas,* constituted the governing instrument of the community, and it was a very elastic and authoritative form of rule. However, the principle of checking the dictates of one office through a right of veto, termed *intercessio,* exercised by equal or superior offices, maintained a satisfactory balance of power, particularly as the principal offices, those of consul and praetor, were held by two men at the same time. A further check lay in the annual election by the common people of ten tribunes of the plebs, who had absolute power to veto any act of any of the magistrates. Though these tribunes had no governing authority of their own, their persons were inviolate against either arrest or physical force on the part of the magistrates.

Public power being thus concentrated in the hands of a few

responsible men, the major question of government centered in the selection of officeholders. The Romans had two criteria for the right to hold office. One was very similar to our own: election by the free citizenry organized in their traditional clans or *gentes*. The other requirement was worth, or, as Cicero terms it, *dignitas*. This restricted candidates to specially designated classes, the patrician class for senators, or the businessman's class of *equites* or knights for other offices. Though these classes were basically hereditary, movement between them was practicable and fairly common. Cicero himself was promoted to senatorial rank, and the great general Marius, seven times elected consul, was of humble origin. Two censors, elected every five years, acted as a supreme court of public morals, determining whether the members of the honored classes were behaving in a manner worthy of their rank. If considered unworthy by the censors they were demoted. In the social circumstances of ancient Rome this system ensured that public office should be held by educated men with some background and previous training.

Three principles established by the Roman theory of office holding remain important today. The first is that the affairs of the people as a political community are settled by the decision-making authority of specific officeholders; this is sometimes described as "responsible government," as the citizenry can pin responsibility for any public act or policy on a definite individual. The second is that public power is delegated to officeholders through some process of election by the general community. The third principle, more controversial in modern times, is that public office should be awarded only to those who have proved their worth in some formally designated manner.

Insistence on personal character and public repute as prerequisite to office holding is perhaps indicative of a conservative attitude. The English poet and philosopher Samuel Taylor Coleridge gives clear expression to this point of view.

There is no qualification for government but virtue and wisdom, actual or presumptive. Wherever they are actually found, they have, in whatever state, condition, profession or trade, the passport of heaven to human place and honour. . . . Nothing is a due and adequate representation of a state that does not represent its ability as well as its property. . . . Woe to the country which would madly and impiously reject the service of the talents and virtues, civil, military or religious, that are given to grace and to serve it; and would condemn to obscurity everything formed to diffuse lustre and glory around a state. Woe to that country, too, that, passing to the opposite extreme, considers a low education, a mean contracted view of things, a sordid mercenary occupation, as a preferable title to command. Everything ought to be open; but not indifferently to every man. No rotation; no appointment by lot; no mode of election operating in a spirit of sortition or rotation can be generally good in a government conversant in extensive objects. . . . I do not hesitate to say that the road to eminence and power, from obscure condition, ought not to be made too easy, nor a thing too much of course. If rare merit be the rarest of all rare things, it ought to pass through some sort of probation. The temple of honour ought to be seated on an eminence. If it be opened through virtue, let it be remembered too that virtue is never tried but by some difficulty and some struggle.[1]

Perhaps the greatest difficulty in modern times is to distinguish a major public office, the repository of the decision-making power of government, from the mass of representatives and the army of government servants. Here the distinction made by the Romans between the *magistratus,* holder of an office, and the skilled technical staff, the *apparitores,* needed to carry out the work, can be of use. Our multitudinous bureaucracy joins in and is part of the decision-making process of government, but it does so as organized and ordered under the various offices of state. The true character and nature of these offices accordingly determines the form of government. This is particularly true of the United States, where an overshadowing office, that of the Presidency, encompasses, juridically at least, all executive power belonging to the general government. The personal authority of the temporary officeholder has become obviously less important than in Roman times; it is the conduct of the office itself that now counts. This to some extent has become a matter of administrative organization and planning, tempered by the claims of competing offices and representative bodies.

In the United States members of the House of Representatives or of the Senate are not considered in the eyes of the law to be holders of public office. This is probably a wise distinction, as the political power of representatives is different in character from the traditional duty of the officeholder, who has the clear-cut responsibility of *acting* in the daily conduct of public business. Public office, then, is the operational core of governmental organization. The manner in which offices relate the political holder to the ranks of the supporting bureaucracy, the ordering of the great offices themselves in a hierarchy of authority, existing relationships between the offices of state and the representative bodies possessing the powers of the purse and of lawmaking, these are the true determinants of any particular form of government.

The Concept of an Executive

In the terminology of political science, government commonly is divided into three parts: executive, legislative, and judicial. The American Constitution devotes an article to each of these major powers. Despite the hallowed use of the term "executive," in both the legal and operational description of the governmental organization of a state, it is difficult to provide an agreed-upon definition of the term that will fit the practical working of any government system. Article II, Section 1, of the Constitution of the United States declares that: "The executive Power shall be vested in a President of the United States of America." Further on in this section a Presidential oath of office is spelled out: "I do solemnly swear (or affirm) that I will faithfully execute the Office of President of the United States. . . ." In Section 3 of the same Article it is laid down that "he [the President] shall take Care that the Laws be faithfully executed." It is hardly surprising that debate still rages as to the true meaning of executive authority under the Constitution. If the "executive power" granted to the President constituted a transfer of the authority previously vested in the British throne, then a vague but mighty reservoir of authority —that of the royal prerogative, the power of almost unlimited action in an emergency—would lie at the hand of the President. This would make almost meaningless the generally accepted principles of a separation of powers and checks and balances. However, the idea has proved tempting to some Constitutional interpreters, and at least one President, Theodore Roosevelt, was a convinced advocate of the "inherent" powers of the Presidency.

If the term "executive" relates to the President's oath faithfully to execute his office, the character of that office is the dominant factor. Sections 2 and 3 of Article II succinctly describe the duties of the President, ranging from command of the armed forces to the granting of pardons, and including the sending of messages and the recommendation of measures to Congress. This constitutes the description of an office that deals on the highest level with the affairs of the people in domestic and foreign matters. It is hard to twist these vital but scattered duties into a specialized type of political power.

A third possibility, sometimes put forward by ardent advocates of Congress, is that the executive power is wholly contained in the provision that the President "shall take care that the laws be faithfully executed." This would limit the office of President to carrying out the instructions of Congress in the capacity of an administrator. How this could be reconciled with the Constitutional obligations of his office to negotiate with foreign countries, protect the nation as commander in chief, and appoint all the major officers of government is difficult to see. The confusion seems to arise from the assumption that all the various methods that a President may invoke to carry out the multifarious duties of his office must somehow be fitted into a single pattern of executive authority. A clearer picture of the actualities of American government may be obtained by viewing the authority of the President as related to his duties and checked by the claims of other centers of power with equally clearly defined duties. It is the office and not the nature of the power that separates the President from Congress or the judiciary.

In the general government of the United States the office of the President overshadows all others. Under a federal system, however, the general government shares power with the state governments. State offices, particularly those of the fifty governors, control a considerable part of the governing apparatus. As in ancient Rome, though on a much larger and more complicated scale, a multiplicity of offices possess decision-making power; each and every officeholder including the President has his authority checked by the Constitutional claims of other offices. Instead of the simple, military-style chain of command, political power rests on an elaborate pattern of coordination between interlocking centers of authority.

The Office of President

Though in every country great offices of state are tailored to a particular constitutional design, it is practical to group them under general categories. Where the office of president is a center of effective authority it is customary to speak of a *presidential system of government.* The United States may claim to have originated this form as well as to be its outstanding example at the present time. In essence, this type of government is based on a unification of responsibility for the major acts of decision-making needed to conduct the daily affairs of government. It may be contrasted with the *parliament system,* where the leaders of the representative assembly share responsibility for government business under the watchful eyes of the elected representatives.

Cf. + contrast

In modern America the office of President has become the repository of vast obligations of vital importance to the daily running of the country. A few decades ago, in the Presidency of Franklin D. Roosevelt, it was still possible for one man with the aid of highly skilled personal assistants (nicknamed the "brain trust"), to execute the office on the level of decision-making on all major questions. A mushroom growth of government activities spurred by the necessities of hot and cold wars has magnified the duties of this key office beyond the decision-making capacities of even the most gifted of statesmen. Accordingly, it is common now to refer to the *institutionalization* of the President's office. In plain language, the officeholder has been forced to rely in large measure on decisions reached by his ostensible subordinates. Unaltered, however, is the key principle that the President is personally responsible to other branches of government and to the community at large for the conduct of his office, whoever may have made the particular decision in question. It may be truly said that a modern President executes his office in the sense of selecting trustworthy decision makers, coordinating responsibilities and providing in broad lines a general policy for them to follow.

PRESIDENTIAL FUNCTIONS The duties of an American President may be summarized roughly under the following headings.

(1) *Policy Direction.* Initiation of domestic, foreign, security, and budget policies is for the most part the care of the President's office. Though the President initiates rather than finalizes through his Constitutional authority to send messages and recommendations to Congress, his power in this respect is continually increasing. This is largely because modern government has become so far-reaching and complex that important policies can be framed only in the light of a mass of specialized and sometimes exceedingly secret information. The office of the President alone has access to the bulk of relevant material. Another factor in the rise of the policy-making power of the presidential office is the interconnection that has developed between the major phases of domestic, budgetary, security, and foreign policy in the course of the last two decades. Congress lacks the Constitutional authority, the continuity, and, it may be added, the organization, to encompass all these problems in a single policy.

(2) *Administrative Coordination.* The vast administrative network of the general government is under supervision by the office of the President. Efficiency, economy of operation, and the maintenance of proper interrelationships constitute a presidential responsibility. Congress has shown a growing tendency to delegate to the President a considerable measure of its powers to alter the internal structure of departments and commissions. A series of Reorganization Acts now permits the rearrangement of departmental structure to a considerable extent at the discretion of the President's office.

(3) *Relations with Foreign Powers.* An accepted interpretation of the Constitutional provisions that the President has power, with the advice and consent of the Senate, to make treaties and that he shall receive foreign ambassadors and public ministers, places the principal responsibility for the conduct of foreign relations in the office of the President. Nowadays, this authority stretches over a great diplomatic apparatus abroad, a highly developed intelligence service, and a recent outgrowth of technical and economic aid. It is true that Congress, particularly the Senate, has a share in major policy determinations. However, since the rejection of the Treaty of Versailles by a Senate hostile to President Wilson, the

role of Congress has been regarded as largely negative—a veto power held in reserve against unpopular foreign adventures.

(4) *Control of the Armed Forces.* Protection of the country against foreign foes and internal insurrection is a Constitutional duty of the office of President as commander in chief. For considerable periods in American history this has been a latent authority requiring slight exercise by the current officeholder. Present generations of Americans live in less fortunate circumstances. A shadow of external violence or even internal subversion penetrates almost all phases of daily living. It no longer suffices for the President's office to act as a coordinating and directional center for the organization of the various branches of the armed services. Problems involving the financial solvency of the nation, control of economic production, stock-piling of raw materials, compulsory direction of manpower into the armed services, have to be determined by the President's office in terms of defense necessities. The important Constitutional principle of civil control over the military apparatus depends on the proper execution of the office of President. Bold assertions of authority have to be made at times, as when President Truman removed General Douglas MacArthur from command during the Korean War.

(5) *Check on the Legislative Process.* The American Constitution continued in part the British principle that the law of the nation is made by the king in Parliament. The President's office was made part of the legislative process, the stamp of presidential approval being required in ordinary circumstances to convert a Congressional bill into a statute of the United States, enforceable as law. Whereas in the British system the approval of the Crown had become largely symbolic by the eighteenth century, the veto power of the American President remains an active function of that great office. The power is not that of veto in any absolute sense but rather a right to refer back any measure for serious reconsideration. If a two-thirds majority of both Houses of Congress subsequently repass the bill it becomes law without a presidential signature. The nature of the obligation resting on the office of President is to examine all Congressional measures from the point of view of the principal office elected by the people at large. Congress, through its method of election by geographical constituencies and

States of unequal numerical and economic strength, can fall under the dominance of special interests. The office of President stands as censor of legislative enactments that are clearly not directed to the national interest.

(6) *Symbolic Personification of the Nation.* In the office of the President the nation receives a form of living embodiment. Living symbols are perhaps anachronisms; nevertheless, even a modern community finds value in having its existence as a nation evidenced by a human personality bearing high office. In his capacity as Chief of State the President occupies an office that may present itself to the whole community in time of need as standing above partisan struggles and beyond the selfish interests of particular groups. In this respect the office of President may be used as a sounding board to echo truly national opinion.

(7) *Guardian of Justice.* Law does not provide an automaton process for the rule of society. Enforcement and interpretation of law depend upon the quality of organization provided and the character of the men who operate it from day to day. A body of laws can operate only as part, though an important part, of a wider concept of justice. The time-honored but by no means obsolete obligation of a political ruler remains the dispensation of justice. In the office of the President a fount of justice still springs. The great enforcement agencies under control of his office apply the general rules of law in discretionary terms corresponding to the presidential concepts of justice. Again the Constitution places in his hands the pardoning power designed to alleviate the abstractions of law with human ideas of justice. It is the President who selects replacements to the bench from the august justices of the Supreme Court to the level of the Federal District Court. The words of the seventeenth-century Lord Halifax might well apply to the office of President of the United States:

> . . . and if it be true that the wisest Men generally make the laws, it is as true that the strongest do often Interpret them: and as Rivers belong as much to the Channel where they run, as to the Spring from whence they first rise, so the Laws depend as much upon the Pipes thro' which they are to pass, as upon the Fountain from whence they flow.[2]

INSTRUMENTALITIES OF THE PRESIDENT'S OFFICE As has been pointed out previously, the last two decades have seen a growing institutionalization of the office of President. A landmark in this process was the Reorganization Act of 1939, which created a framework of specific agencies and bureaus to serve as an infra-structure to the presidential office. Nowadays the President carries out his functions by presiding over a network of agencies that comprise his office.

(1) *Bureau of the Budget.* A director of the Bureau of the Budget with a skilled professional staff coordinates, in the name of the President, the policy decisions of the major departments and agencies. As its name implies, it derives its direct authority from control over the preparation of the Budget for the President's consideration. In the process of working with each department to determine estimates, the Bureau has developed supervisory powers over the policies of departments and independent agencies, at least in so far as the expenditure of public funds is concerned. A large and undetermined area of decision-making associated with the office of President is carried out within the Bureau.

(2) *White House Staff and Cabinet Secretariat.* An official staff organization above the level of personal assistants and secretaries now surrounds the person of the President. Six posts have been created to carry out liaison and coordinating duties with Congress, the civil service, the independent agencies, the press, and other bodies with which the President's office has to deal. In addition, Cabinet business has been regularized from informal gatherings of the President and major department heads into a more effective instrument of continuous consultation through the creation of a Cabinet secretariat, capable of recording proceedings, maintaining the continuity of agenda, and following through decisions.

(3) *The National Security Council.* The day-to-day safeguarding of the nation's security has become an overwhelming burden on the President's office. This responsibility, though it remains in the hands of the President himself, has been in some measure alleviated by the National Security Act of 1947. A Council composed of the Secretary of State, the Secretary of Defense, the Secretary of the Treasury, and the Chief of the Joint Chiefs of Staff meets weekly under the chairmanship of the President (in his absence

the Vice-President may preside). Other important officials, such as the head of the Central Intelligence Agency, may be coöpted from time to time. This continuing body, with its own special staff together with the staff resources at the disposal of its separate members, provides a collective judgment in support of the President's office.

It is interesting to note a revival of counseling by the great officers of state as an essential element of modern government. Under the Tudor monarchs, the English Crown developed into an office capable of meeting severe governmental strains through the perfection of a conciliar system. An essential feature is the participation in the operation of the highest office of the principal agents of government acting as advisers and not as holders of power in their own right. The President in his proper person still retains the authority to make the final decision though the difficult process of judging the situation has been largely collectivized. A somewhat similar concept is to be found in the Constitution in relation to the conduct of foreign affairs. "He [the President] shall have Power, by and with the Advice and Consent of the Senate, to make Treaties. . . ." In its original form the Senate comprised only twenty-six members, appointed by the State legislatures on the basis of their wisdom and experience in national affairs. It was hoped that such a body might serve as a true advisory council to the office of the President, perhaps along lines similar to those practiced by the Privy Council in Britain. Party divisions wrecked confidential relationships between the President and Senate before the end of Washington's first term. Since that time emphasis on the doctrine of a separation of powers has deprived the Presidency of constitutional means to gather round his office as loyal advisers the principal political figures in the nation. Indeed, to accomplish such an end it might be necessary to abolish party politics. There is, however, recognition that so great an office as that of President should be constituted to reflect the highest judgment of collective power holders subjecting their views to the final decision of a chief of state.

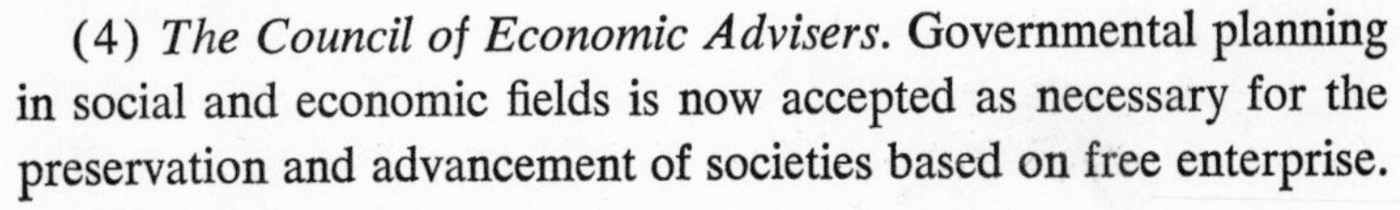

(4) *The Council of Economic Advisers.* Governmental planning in social and economic fields is now accepted as necessary for the preservation and advancement of societies based on free enterprise.

Though the type and extent of governmental supervision differs radically among Communist, socialist, and free-enterprise economies, the use of political means to safeguard the economic welfare of the community is common to all modern states. Accordingly, the office of President of the United States has had to reach out beyond execution of the laws, negotiation with foreign powers, and preservation of national security into a field of economic prognostication and social planning. Political and administrative instrumentalities devised in the eighteenth and nineteenth centuries proved inadequate to meet modern needs of this character. What is required is an institutional means of linking together the authority and craft of political policy makers and administrators with the wisdom and practical experience of those concerned with the operation of the economy. The solution, admittedly an imperfect one, adopted by the Employment Act of 1946 was the creation of a Council of Economic Advisers to serve the office of the President. A principal function of this Council is the preparation of the Economic Report the President is required by law to submit annually to Congress to guide it in the preparation of a legislative policy to safeguard and advance the national economy. Other ancillary duties of advising concerning the integration and direction of the economic policies of the great departments and agencies flow from the constant study by the Council. It is proper to regard this Council as part of the presidential office because it is headed by three men who are personal appointees of the President. In selecting three representatives of established economic and business attitudes the President commits his office to a recognizable economic point of view. Though he retains personal authority for decision-making, the manner in which problems are presented to him, and the alternatives for action suggested, are the business of his Economic Advisers. In this institution there might appear to be the risk of overreliance on the professional or academic economist as judge of economic developments and policies. Though the economist, today, may claim an important place in the organization of the nation's productive, distributive, and financial machinery, he does not rank as a fully representative leader of our economic structure. The President's office has not been equipped as yet to provide complete linkage between the holders of economic power and the trustees of political authority.

THE APPOINTING AND REMOVAL POWERS Selection and control of the principal decision makers in the daily conduct of the national business constitutes the great continuing responsibility of the office of President of the United States. Besides the heads of departments, independent commissions and agencies, there are approximately one thousand officeholders of non-Civil Service status attached to the office of the President.[3] Chief Justice Taft, with his own experience of the Presidency in mind, gave great weight to the importance of the removal power in his opinion in the case of *Myers v. United States.*[4]

> The view of Mr. Madison and his associates was that not only did the grant of executive power to the President in the first section of Article II carry with it the power of removal, but the express recognition of the power of appointment in the second section enforced this view on the well-approved principle of constitutional and statutory construction that the power of removal of executive officers was incident to the power of appointment. . . . The reason for this principle is that those in charge of and responsible for administering functions of government, who select their executive subordinates, need in meeting their responsibility to have the power to remove those whom they appoint. . . .
>
> Made responsible under the Constitution for the effective enforcement of the law, the President needs as an indispensable aid to meet it the disciplinary influence upon those who act under him of a reserve power of removal. . . . The degree of guidance in the discharge of their duties that the President may exercise over executive officers varies with the character of their service as prescribed in the law under which they act. The highest and most important duties which his subordinates perform are those in which they act for him. In such cases they are exercising not their own but his discretion. . . . In this field his cabinet officers must do his will. He must place in each member of his official family, and his chief executive subordinates, implicit faith. The moment that he loses confidence in the intelligence, ability, judgment, or loyalty of any one of them, he must have the power to remove him without delay.

A breach in the authority and comprehensive responsibility of the President's office has been made by the creation of regulatory commissions, of which the Interstate Commerce Commission and the Federal Trade Commission are examples, through Congressional statutes giving these bodies positions of great independence. In the case of *Humphrey's Executor* [*Rathbun*] *v. United States,*[5] the Supreme Court held that the President lacked discretionary power to remove the principal officeholders of such bodies.

The debates in both houses demonstrate that the prevailing view was that the [Federal Trade] Commission was not to be subject to anybody in the government but . . . only to the people of the United States; free from political domination or control or the probability or possibility of such a thing; to be separate and apart from any existing department of the government—not subject to the orders of the President. . . .

We think it plain under the Constitution that illimitable power of removal is not possessed by the President in respect of officers of the character of those just named. The authority of Congress, in creating *quasi* legislative or *quasi* judicial agencies, to require them to act in discharge of their duties independently of executive control cannot well be doubted; and that authority includes, as an appropriate incident, power to fix the period during which they shall continue, and to forbid their removal except for cause in the meantime. . . .

The power of removal here claimed for the President falls within this principle, since its coercive influence threatens the independence of a commission, which is not only wholly disconnected from the executive department, but which, as already fully appears, was created by Congress as a means of carrying into operation legislative and judicial powers, and as an agency of the legislative and judicial departments.

The logic of this decision seems to diminish the office of President of the United States to that of only one among several offices charged with discretionary decision-making authority in the daily conduct of the nation's affairs.

State constitutions place the office of governor in varying degrees in an analogous position. Several State offices, that of Attorney General is a common example, are exempt from the supervising authority of the governor. However, an important difference between national and State constitutions on this point is that, in the case of the States, independent offices are generally subject to popular election. They may be regarded as direct delegations of power from the electorate. The United States Constitution provides for popular election to only two great offices, those of President and Vice-President. It is difficult to reconcile the ambiguous position of officeholders in the independent regulatory commissions with the main principles guiding the American system of national government. An unresolved question remains: to whom are these officials responsible for the conduct of their office, if they are answerable to neither President nor people?

THE PRESIDENT AS PARTY LEADER Whether the role of party leader of one of the two great national parties is an integral part of the office of President of the United States is, perhaps, open to question. There is, of course, nothing in the Constitution that requires or designates the President to fulfill such a function. It may even be argued that the assumption of a strictly partisan character interferes with the duty of the President to serve as chief of state. On the other hand, the operation of the presidential office has long required a measure of control over one of the major political parties. In any case, in the American party system the title of party leader carries with it ambiguous claims to effective authority. A skilled politician, such as former President Truman, may blend party leadership with the Constitutional power of the Presidency in a manner that greatly enhances the authority of that office. Other Presidents may prefer to avoid partisan characterization, once elected, in order to increase their standing as symbol of national unity.

Among all the great offices of state existing in the modern world the American Presidency may claim to rank high in comprehensiveness of authority, constitutional stability, and openness to popular choice. In the words of Pascal, "the greatness of the establishment" provides an unsurpassed challenge to the personal greatness of the holder of the office.

The Office of Minister

Governmental organization in the nation–states of Western Europe generally takes the form of a *ministerial system,* which may also be described as a *parliamentary system* or alternatively as a *cabinet* form of government. Great Britain provides an outstanding example, but the system is employed with minor variations in the Scandinavian democracies, Italy, West Germany, Belgium, Holland, and, in a more equivocal manner, in the new Fifth Republic of France. With the outstanding exception of the Soviet bloc, the majority of modern states throughout Asia, Africa, and Latin America have based their governmental forms either on the American presidential concept or on some type of ministerial system.

To some extent the office of minister of state is a product of the historical evolution of European political institutions. As the term implies, a minister was originally a servant, agent, and adviser ministering to the needs of a sovereign prince. All state power, at least in theory, resided in the person of the prince, who held the sole governing office. As the medieval monarch was gradually transformed into a symbolic chief of state, the reality of governing power devolved upon the offices of the great ministers of state. Open claims to an authority inherent in the office itself raised a constitutional question by what right (in the fine old phrase of English law: *quo warranto*) a minister exercised command over his fellow citizens.

In England this question was settled by an historical compromise. Parliament's claim as a representative assembly to embody the sovereignty of the people provided a basis for the exercise of power by a minister acting as an agent of Parliament. In addition, the minister drew authority from the great reservoir of public power remaining in the Crown, though no longer exercised by the monarch personally. This reserve power is known as *the prerogative;* in modern times it may be roughly described as authority to do anything necessary for the security or welfare of the community which has not been preempted by Parliament or forbidden by parliamentary law or the conventional constitution. In present-day concepts, prerogative power stems from the organization of the community as an historical nation, in contrast to the temporary majorities of a voting electorate. The Crown as symbol of the nation remains the juridical center of such power.

An example of prerogative power is the capacity of a minister to make rules binding on the community with the force of law through Ministerial Orders. These codes, known generically as Statutory Instruments, now require the inspection of Parliament.

In some cases Parliament has the right to annul them by the archaic method of a "prayer" addressed to the Crown. Orders dealing with a limited list of sensitive matters require positive approval by Parliament. However, normal methods of parliamentary debate and amendment do not apply to these Orders, which constitute a great body of direct ministerial lawmaking, under only the very general supervision of the representative body. For example, the constitutions of most British colonies on the road to self-government rank as Statutory Instruments and not Acts of Parliament.

From the juridical point of view, ministers of state in Britain have a wider and more elastic range of authority than the American President. In part this may be attributed to the lack of any accepted doctrine of the separation of powers in the British constitution. A more pragmatic factor, perhaps, is the comprehensive system of immediate checks on the exercise of power by any single minister.

THE DOCTRINE OF MINISTERIAL RESPONSIBILITY When the monarch ceased to play an active part in the government of the state, control over his ministers, both as regards selection and the conduct of their offices, fell to a large extent into the hands of Parliament. A binding constitutional convention developed restricting the holding of ministerial office, with some minor exceptions, to members of Parliament. Tenure of office was for no fixed term but quite literally at the pleasure of a parliamentary majority. This provision makes each minister of state responsible to the dominant group in Parliament for every official act as well as for the broad policies of his office. Through the device of a "question" period in the House of Commons any member may force a minister to explain policy decisions or episodes arising in the work of his department. Should the minister fail to satisfy a substantial portion of the House with his answer a full debate may be ordered. Unless the minister wins support from a majority, the conventions of the constitution require that he resign his office. Even if the minister was not personally involved he must accept personal responsibility for the fault of his departmental officials. In a comparatively recent incident a popular minister resigned office as a consequence of the displeasure of the House over the highhanded action of certain of his officials carried out without the prior knowledge of the minister.

CABINET RESPONSIBILITY The decision-making process vital to the operation of government would run wild under a parliamentary system unless some method of establishing a hierarchy of authority and policy making was established. It is perhaps one of the great advantages of a presidential system that it substitutes the single will of one man, the President, for that of his predecessor, the monarch. A clear-cut transfer of authority of this nature was not possible in the evolution of the ministerial type of government. Instead the ministers were forced to band themselves together, at first to consolidate their power against the personal rule of the prince, and later to preserve their authority in face of their rivals in Parliament. This led to the growth of certain constitutional conventions which now serve as the binding force of Cabinet rule. First, all major policy decisions concerning the government of the country are made by the Cabinet as a collective body. A majority of the Cabinet decides the issue with each Cabinet member exercising equal voting power. Second, the proceedings of the Cabinet are secret, neither Parliament nor the electorate receiving any information as to what goes on behind the doors of the Cabinet room at 10 Downing Street. Third, once a decision has been reached every Cabinet member, without regard to how he argued or voted in private, is bound to defend that decision in public as if it were his own. Where a Cabinet minister finds that his conscience does not permit him to accept the decision of a majority of his colleagues, he is bound to resign his office. Through the strict operation of this doctrine of Cabinet responsibility for all major measures of government it is possible to present a united front to Parliament and to the people.

A further refinement is the responsibility of the whole Cabinet for the conduct of any one minister, even though the matter may never have reached the level of a Cabinet decision. There is, accordingly, no opportunity for open debate or disagreement among the political heads of the departments of state such as is customary in American political life. The British are essentially a sporting people and the team spirit of one for all and all for one is followed readily enough in public affairs. One consequence of these constitutional conventions is a degree of merging of the individual ministerial offices into a collective committee, the Cabinet. This is not to be identified with the so-called principle of collective leadership lately discovered by the Communist Party of the Soviet Union when their tyrant expired. Certainly Cabinet responsibility is an important check on the authority of individual ministers, but it is only one among several checks. The practical as opposed to the theoretical power of the Cabinet to make decisions as a collective body depends on the capacity of its members to retain their offices should the voting pattern of a majority offend a minority of powerful colleagues. Even a minority of one, if that one were the Prime Minister, would, in all probability, require the resignation of the whole ministry.

THE PLACE OF THE PRIME MINISTER In contrast to the President of the United States, the British Prime Minister does not owe his authority to the law of the constitution. In fact it is only in recent times that any legal recognition has been given to the post of Prime Minister; to single out any one of Her Majesty's ministers as possessed of unique powers threatens the useful fiction that the government of the country is carried on in the name of the sovereign by functional, and supposedly self-effacing, agents. In any case, the title of Prime Minister is now accepted at law to the extent at least that he is granted precedence at official functions immediately after the Archbishop of Canterbury. Theoretically, the public power of the Prime Minister is restricted to that of the great office of state, usually that of First Lord of the Treasury, to which he has been appointed by the Crown.

The true nature of the commanding position of a Prime Minister in a parliamentary or ministerial system of government is that of a political boss. He may coordinate or even direct the whole policy of the Government in power because it is he who selects all the other ministers and may remove them at will. This overriding authority stems from the constitutional convention that requires the monarch to make a direct and personal appointment of a principal minister when the previous ministry has resigned as a result of a defeat in Parliament or at a general election. The convention further requires that the monarch should select a political leader able to command the support of a majority of votes in

Parliament. Normally, then, an automatic selection is made of the accepted leader of the majority party in the House of Commons. There may be circumstances, however, when personal decisions are required of the reigning sovereign. Thus the resignation of Sir Anthony Eden left the majority party in the House of Commons without an acknowledged leader. The Queen had to make an immediate selection between two or more possible candidates. Presumably, though these matters are never divulged, she consulted the elder statesmen of the party before summoning Harold Macmillan to form a new Government. Even when the choice is made directly by the sovereign it is far from arbitrary; if a substantial group among the majority party should fail to agree, the position of the new Prime Minister would become untenable.

Once chosen, a Prime Minister has the right under the conventions of the constitution to nominate all other ministers for royal appointment. Thereafter he and he alone has direct access to the sovereign of Britain concerning the business of government. He is free to suggest at any time that any minister should be removed from office, and invariably his advice will be taken. If it was not he would resign and a parliamentary general election would follow in all likelihood. It can be seen that, translated into American terms, this is almost an ideal situation for a political boss. As long as the Prime Minister is able to command the support of a substantial majority of his party followers he may impose his will on the other ministers and throughout the whole of the machinery of government. A real distinction exists between presidential and parliamentary or Cabinet systems in this respect: under a presidential form a major part of the effective authority of government is derived from law and the interpretation of law; a Cabinet system, on the other hand, is based almost completely on politics, with party management the final source of practical power. As a consequence Cabinet government may be considered more flexible and perhaps more immediately attuned to the political temper of the moment than the presidential variety. A corresponding weakness, however, may reside in a tendency of parliamentary government to be influenced by the special "interests" that dominate the majority party, to the detriment of the long-term interest of the nation as a whole. The personal integrity of the Prime Minister is sometimes the only safeguard against such a development. Perhaps the administration of Stanley Baldwin may be cited as an example of the danger of overemphasis on party interests. The Conservative Party of that day feared that a rearmament program would result in the loss of the next election. Besides, the tax increase involved was distasteful to powerful business interests which underwrote party finances. Mr. Baldwin's obligation as Prime Minister to restore Britain's military might in time to avert the menace of Hitler was subordinated to his conception of his responsibility as party leader.

MINISTERIAL RESPONSIBILITY TO THE ELECTORATE The office of minister is no sinecure. The displeasure of a majority of the House of Commons or of the Prime Minister may force a minister to surrender the seals of his office at any time. Another hazard is unpopularity with the electorate. If for any reason he should become a liability to the party, the Prime Minister must take it into account. As general elections, under a parliamentary system, are not scheduled at determinate intervals but are subject to political contingencies, an administration is always sensitive to any factor that might prejudice its case if suddenly summoned before the bar of public opinion. Accordingly, ministers may be sacrificed in response to a sustained public outcry however much they are valued by their colleagues and their party in Parliament. This possibility influences a minister's conduct of his office. A department head under a presidential form of government may feel free to defy general criticism so long as he retains the confidence of the President, but a public minister, as the name implies, must win the tolerance if not the admiration of the bulk of the voting public. Once again the political character of office in a ministerial system may be stressed as compared to the stronger administrative values under a presidential regime.

Variations in the Cabinet Form of Government

The British Cabinet system has been described as an exemplar of the Cabinet form. British practices are based on the existence of a unified nation, a constitutional monarchy, and a fairly stable two-party political structure. Parliamentary government is to be found, however, in a wide range of states where one or more of these elements are lacking. The particular collegial character of the British Cabinet, with its stress on joint responsibility and secret proceedings, may be lacking in countries where coalition Governments are prevalent. West Germany and modern Italy have not experienced single-party Government since 1945. In the case of the former, a divided Cabinet has enhanced the power of the Chancellor, who is generally held responsible for all major decisions of the Government. The Italian Premier, or to use his constitutional title, President of the Council of Ministers, has had to accept a more compromising and coordinating role. Ministers not under his party leadership may insist on consideration of their views by threatening to withdraw the support of their parliamentary party from the coalition Government. The peculiarities of the political situation in any country under the Cabinet system will determine the degree of cohesion within the Cabinet and the independence of ministers in relation to the Prime Minister.

Another aspect of modern Cabinet government may be found in nations that have won independence in the last few decades. The struggle toward freedom has been carried on in general under the auspices of a single, national party; the Congress Party in India and the Convention People's Party in Ghana are outstanding examples. In both cases a two-party system has failed to develop after independence was achieved. Mr. Nehru and Mr. Nkrumah thus occupy positions of national leadership as well as party leadership. This upsets the delicate balance of checks between the authority of the Prime Minister and the role of the other Ministers and Parliament. Overwhelming concentration of political power in the hands of the Prime Minister creates a pattern of government approximating a presidential form lacking any separation of powers.

It is well to remember that both parliamentary and presidential types of rule are primarily methods of creating and maintaining offices capable of conducting the affairs of the political community but so guarded and checked in their use of personal authority that they do not endanger the freedom of the people, either as individuals or as a totality, to have the final say in directing their destiny. The measure of success achieved by any particular example of either type should be judged in terms of the balance struck between efficiency in the conduct of public business and the liberty enjoyed by the people. Adherence to abstract principles of governmental organization is of little more than academic interest.

THE FRENCH EXPERIMENT The political framework of the Fifth Republic of France is designed to encompass presidential and ministerial values within a single constitutional arrangement. The success of this experiment will depend perhaps more on the political temperament of the French people, always an uncertain factor, than on any inherent incompatibility of the two methods. According to the new Constitution, there is on the one hand a Government with its Premier and on the other hand a President. Article 21 declares that the Premier "directs the action of the Government," which in turn, by virtue of Article 20, "determines and conducts the policy of the nation." The President, for his part, appoints the Premier, and this power of selection is real and not largely nominal as in the case of the British monarch. He presides over the Council of Ministers, presumably taking an active part in the over-all direction of policy. Also, he may dissolve Parliament. As commander in chief of the armed forces he controls a major extraparliamentary force in French politics. Article 16 creates prerogative powers to be exercised personally by the President in an emergency. Separation of powers between the offices of state and the representative bodies is maintained, guaranteeing that the regime will not assume totalitarian aspects.

Though the new pattern of government in France breaks through traditional academic classifications, its provisions are not startlingly novel. In practice, presidential and parliamentary concepts of government have been borrowing heavily from each other over the course of the last fifty years. France has perhaps merely systematized with her customary logic an actual trend in the political arrangements of modern Western nations.

SOVIET CONCEPTS OF POLITICAL OFFICE Russia and the East European nations under Communist rule derived their basic state organizations from standards laid down during their previous existence as members of the Western family of peoples. Adoption of a Marxist-Leninist ideology, however, necessitated at least a theoretical break with all preceding historical tradition. An institutional framework for government had to be invented ab novo in terms of the postulates of their total revolution. As in the case of the eighteenth-century revolutionists in France, nothing very ingenious or different has been forthcoming. It may be ventured that the final outcome has amounted to little more than dressing up in mystifying jargon the accustomed offices that sustained the former autocracy. A Council of Ministers, theoretically responsible to the Supreme Soviet of the U.S.S.R., acts as the official repository of public power. The major difference between this and Western systems lies in the lack of effective legal or constitutional checks on the arbitrary authority of the ministers. Practical checks do exist, but these stem from extralegal Party control. The hierarchy of the Communist Party exercise what are quite literally life-and-death powers over ministers, individually and collectively, who serve, in fact, as mere executants of Party instructions. The governmental authority of the officeholder is separated from the political power of the Party chieftain. This arrangement works because the handful of Party leaders double as the principal ministers of state. They thus find themselves checking and controlling themselves, which in fact they do in the tradition of a feuding hillbilly settlement. Autocracy tempered with assassination is a traditional form of government among the Eastern nations. Marxism has perhaps established it on a wider base and contributed a theology to justify the blood sacrifices.

If the concept of unlimited government, or autocracy, is accepted as part both of the historical and revolutionary tradition of the Soviets their method of exercising this tyranny remains of interest. Since the death of Stalin a serious effort has been made to reconcile the naked exercise of governmental power with the theoretical principles of Marx and Lenin. The method adopted has been to identify offices of state as agencies of the collectivity. Soviet peoples are assumed to be organized in two capacities: first as a socialist community, for whom only the Communist Party and its hierarchy may speak; and secondly as a political body electing representative institutions. According to Soviet theory, then, rulers may exercise absolute authority if they can be shown to be true and disciplined agents of these collectivities. In the words of an official apologist:

The Soviet Government is a corporate body for State management. The principle of the collective discussion and solution of questions is an essential one in all the work of the Soviet Government. It enables questions to be viewed from all their aspects and correct decisions to be taken. The Council of Ministers of the U.S.S.R. is responsible for the general direction of State administration and organizes the management of the State throughout the country. It lays down the general policy to be followed, prescribes the new tasks for State management at a country-wide level and sees to their fulfillment, determines the ways and means for attaining the objectives fixed, and so forth. The U.S.S.R. Council of Ministers issues orders and decisions for all State management organs, for factories, for administrative bodies and organizations subordinate to them, for all social organizations, for the Law Courts and for all Soviet citizens. In the dispensation of justice, the courts are bound by all decisions of the U.S.S.R. Government.[6]

Control over Administration through Offices of State

In theory, political office, whether that of president or minister, places responsibility for the conduct of public affairs in the hands of determinate persons. With the size and complexity of modern administrative machinery, personal responsibility of one man or a handful of men for all the acts of government becomes a mere constitutional fiction. Has not the political officeholder become a "front man" for a powerful bureaucracy, capable of making decisions only within such limits as may be set by the effective support he may expect from his ostensible subordinates? Certainly the relationship of the politico-executive to the civil service has become in many ways as important as his relationship to the representative assemblies. The simple master–servant bond that may have existed between a Roman Consul and his *apparitores* can no longer be applied to the interdependence of political officeholder and permanent official in the modern framework of government. This situation is by no means peculiar to government but is recognized as a major reality in the large-scale organization of modern business. The pragmatic view concerning corporate management is that internal leadership is as important as external activities. In the same way, the officeholder must provide intelligent leadership to an administrative machine rather than command subordinates. On the whole, a functional relationship with a partially autonomous bureaucracy does not appear to lessen the range of responsibility of the political officeholder. Another category of leadership is added: the coordination, control, and persuasion of the administering class. The methods that have been devised to relate officeholders to the administrative machine of government will be discussed in a later chapter. It is sufficient to reiterate here that great offices of state have become increasingly institutionalized. Their holders, therefore, must serve as corporate executives in the true sense of the term.

Notes

[1] White, R. J. (ed.), *The Conservative Tradition,* London: Nicholas Kaye, 1950, pp. 64-65.

[2] Raleigh, Walter (ed.), *The Complete Works of George Savile, First Marquess of Halifax,* London: Oxford, 1912, p. 51.

[3] This figure is taken from an article by Macridis, Roy C., "The Role of the Executive in the Modern State," *International Social Science Bulletin,* 1958, **10,** No. 4.

[4] *Myers v. United States,* 272 U.S. 52 (1926).

[5] *Humphrey's Executor* [*Rathbun*] *v. United States,* 295 U.S. 602 (1935).

[6] Iojrych, A., writing on the U.S.S.R., "The Role of the Executive in the Modern State—U.S.S.R.," *International Social Science Bulletin,* 1958, **10,** No. 2, 226.

Supplementary Readings

Barnard, Chester Irving, *The Functions of the Executive,* Cambridge: Harvard, 1938.

Carter, Byrum E., *The Office of Prime Minister,* Princeton: Princeton University Press, 1956.

Corwin, Edward S. and Koenig, Louis W., *The Presidency Today,* New York: New York University Press, 1956.

Dimock, Marshall E., *The Executive in Action,* New York: Harper, 1945.

Djilas, Milovan, *The New Class,* New York: Praeger, 1957.

Freeman, J. Leiper, *The Political Process: Executive Bureau—Legislative Committee Relations,* New York: Random House, 1955.

Hazard, J. N., *The Soviet System of Government,* Chicago: University of Chicago Press, 1957.

Herring, Pendleton, *Presidential Leadership,* New York: Rinehart, 1940.

Hobbs, Edward H., *Behind the President; A Study of Executive Office Agencies,* Washington: Public Affairs Press, 1954.

Jennings, Sir Ivor, *Cabinet Government,* London: Cambridge, second edition, 1951.

Kern, Fritz, translated by Chrimes, S. B., *Kingship and Law in the Middle Ages,* Oxford: Blackwell, 1939.

Koenig, Louis, *The Invisible Presidency,* New York: Rinehart, 1960.

Lasswell, Harold D., *Power and Personality,* New York: Chapman and Grimes, 1949.

Loewenstein, Karl, *Political Power and the Governmental Process,* Chicago: University of Chicago Press, 1957.

Meynaud, J., et al., "The Role of the Executive in the Modern State," *International Social Science Bulletin,* 1958, **10,** No. 2.

Robson, William A., *The British System of Government,* New York: Longmans, third edition, 1948.

Roche, John P., and Stedman, Murray S., *The Dynamics of Democratic Government,* New York: McGraw-Hill, 1954.

Rossiter, Clinton, *The American Presidency,* New York: Harcourt, Brace, 1956.

Wirszubiski, Chaim, *'Libertas' as a Political Idea at Rome during the Late Republic and Early Principate,* London: Cambridge, 1951.

Zurcher, Arnold J., "The Presidency, Congress, and Separation of Powers: A Reappraisal," *Western Political Quarterly,* 1950, **3,** 75-92.

Chapter 5

Systems of Representation

The purpose of government has been described earlier in this book as the ordering of the public affairs of the community. This leaves unanswered the troublesome question: Who may speak for the community; by what right does any man or group of men claim to determine what are the interests of the community? In modern times Western nations have approached this problem through the elaboration of representative institutions. Universal suffrage, secret ballots, proportional representation, and many other ingenious systems have been devised to construct a general purpose for the community out of the separate wills of all the individuals constituting the body politic. Before any particular system of representation may be examined or evaluated, however, the underlying assumption as to what it is intended to represent must be disclosed. Virtually identical voting systems based on universal suffrage may be employed in political orders as widely different as those of the United States and Soviet Russia. The mechanisms of representation may be regarded as largely neutral, or, at least, as capable of application to governmental forms ranging from free governments to dogmatic tyrannies.

Representation of the Free Individual

The Western concept of the state as an instrument for the development of individual freedom requires that both the standards of freedom and practical means for their enforcement should be under continuous review by some determinate body backed by the total force of the community. Participation in the choice of such a body is essential to the personal freedom of the mature individual. By definition, a freeman is one who regards himself and is regarded by others as at his own disposal and not the mere instrument of another mind. The degree of personal freedom achieved by any individual is related invariably to the political framework in which he lives. Consequently, any representative system adopted by a freedom-loving people should ensure the greatest amount of individual participation practicable in determining political standards for the community.

The object of representative institutions, then, among free peoples is to provide a framework within which the individual may act to express his views concerning public affairs. This should not be confused with the right or power of the individual to promote his own private interests. To identify the individual's right to representation with a supposed claim to get something out of society or the state is fatal to the operation of representative systems among free peoples. Common sense tells us that a living individual can never be represented in his totality, not even by an identical twin. The concept of representation is based on a somewhat artificial division of the unity of personality into a number of clearly separated and concrete interests that may be sufficiently depersonalized to be shared with large numbers of other individuals on almost identical terms. The institution that possessed the clearest understanding of the nature and limitations of the principle of representation was, in all probability, the ancient form of the English trust. This venerable legal concept permitted some concrete interest shared by a number of people to be forwarded by directors chosen by all the parties concerned. To the outside world, such directors or trustees represented, to the extent of legal personification, the concrete interest. They acted, in reference to the management of property and the making of contracts, as if the particular interest inhered in them alone. It was the discovery that legal and social mechanisms could be devised to control trustees so that they acted fairly on behalf of their interest group that made possible the general expansion of representative organization.

It is useful to remember that representative systems control the economic and social organization of Western societies on a scale that dwarfs their political manifestations. Business corporations, trade unions, clubs, and many other building blocks of our social existence, are highly developed examples of the theory and practice of representation. They may be said to operate with greater smoothness and in many ways more effectively than corresponding political institutions because the interests involved are more concrete and certain. For example, shareholders in a commercial corporation have in common a relatively uncomplicated interest in current profits together with the growth in capital value of their corporation's holdings. Ingenious systems accordingly may be devised to permit flexible and single-minded control of corporate activities without disturbing the claim of the individual shareholder that his limited interest should be adequately represented. Obviously, the ordinary shareholder has slight claim to interfere with the details of management so long as profit returns and capital gain appear adequate in the circumstances of the times.

When we apply principles of representation that operate so well in economic and social organization to the formation of political institutions it becomes clear that the major difficulty involved is to define the major interest to be represented. Political philosophers have struggled with this problem over many centuries and their varying conclusions have provided the rationale for many types of governmental systems. English-speaking democracies may still be said to be organized around the principles enunciated by John Stuart Mill.

> It is a great discouragement to an individual, and a still greater one to a class, to be left out of the constitution; to be reduced to plead from outside the door to the arbiters of their destiny, not taken into the consultation within. The maximum of the invigorating effect of freedom upon the character is only obtained when the person acted upon either is, or is looking forward to become, a citizen as fully privileged as any other. . . .
>
> Still more salutary is the moral part of the instruction afforded by the participation of the private citizen, if even rarely in public functions. He is called upon, while so engaged, to weigh interests not his own; to be guided, in case of conflicting claims, by another rule than

his private partialities; to apply, at every turn, principles and maxims which have for their very reason of existence the general good. . . . He is made to feel himself one of the public, and whatever is their interest to be his interest. Where this school of public spirit does not exist, scarcely any sense is entertained that private persons, in no eminent social situation, owe any duties to society except to obey the laws and submit to the government. There is no unselfish sentiment of identification with the public. Every thought and feeling, either of interest or of duty, is absorbed in the individual and in the family. The man never thinks of any collective interest, of any objects to be pursued jointly with others, but only in competition with them, and in some measure at their expense. . . . Were this the universal and only possible state of things, the utmost aspirations of the lawgiver or the moralist could only stretch to making the bulk of the community a flock of sheep innocently nibbling the grass side by side.[1]

A more specifically American point of view may be quoted from that shrewd observer of our early democracy, Alexis de Tocqueville.

The lower orders in the United States understand the influence exercised by the general prosperity upon their own welfare; simple as this observation is, it is too rarely made by the people. Besides they are accustomed to regard this prosperity as the fruit of their own exertions. The citizen looks upon the fortune of the public as his own, and he labors for the good of the state not merely from a sense of pride or duty but from what I venture to term cupidity. . . .

In our times we must choose between the patriotism of all and the government of a few; for the social force and activity which the first confers are irreconcilable with the pledges of tranquillity which are given by the second.[2]

These progenitors of our present representative systems were united in the belief that representation meant that the individual had to bestir himself and pass judgment on public affairs beyond the sphere of his private claims. In plain terms, the main interest represented was patriotism, or a concern for the common good. This may sound unduly idealistic to serve as an explanation for present-day political systems. However, it remains reasonable to consider that representative systems, anywhere at any time, are successful only to the degree that this assumption approximates reality. Political representation must always be imperfect and uncertain because of the difficulty of deciding between private interest and public good. Such a question transcends the bounds of political theory or practice. The assertion of the poet–divine John Donne that "No man is an island, entire of itself" may be taken as a basic postulate of political association. The state is a product of the need for and will towards social union on the part of people in a definite area. Unless a considerable number of the individuals constituting such a state possess clear ideas concerning the values of their union, and, further, are prepared to subordinate private interests in the pursuit of these values, the life of their nation is likely to be short and calamitous.

NATURE OF THE REPRESENTATIVE In modern government the force of opinion tends to overshadow the rule of custom. Opinion implies adaptability, a restatement of principles to suit changing circumstances. At any moment of time a dominant body of opinion can be assumed to exist, affecting the direction of change. A major problem of politics is how to strain majority opinion through representative institutions so that it may provide an accurate determination of the common good. Representation, when all is said and done, is the selection and control of men. It provides no magic wand to transform the fleeting ideas of millions into an unchallengeable body of doctrine. The voting machine may not be treated as a mechanical brain. Political programs are invented by office seekers; they cannot be discovered by statistical research even when backed by the ingenuity of the modern pollster. A candidate for elective office devises a program as a vestment to adorn his naked character. They serve, as Carlyle insisted all clothes do, as symbolic expressions of character.[3]

It is character, then, a bent or habit of mind and feeling, that the voters judge beneath the guise of words and policies. There must be more to a representative than the sum total of the opinions of the majority that elects him. Personal judgment is the operative spark in any officeholder. This may not be voted into a man. Majority opinion must content itself with the selection of representatives capable of reflecting a general attitude rather than automata that repeat parrot phrases until replaced. Representative government throughout the centuries of its duration has never overcome the need for officeholders motivated by a superior interest in the common good. The problem of how to obtain these men and women is as fresh and real today as in the Athens of Pericles.

Rewards and deprivations, the incitement of individuals to excel their neighbors in the management of public affairs, is certainly the oldest and probably unequaled remedy for the defects of representative government. We still choose men, not ideas, to govern us. No substitute has been discovered for government by men with a superior interest in the common good. It remains to be seen how such an interest may be recognized, how related to majority opinion, and how maintained in the stresses of office holding. Edmund Burke defined the character of a representative in terms still valid for English-speaking peoples.

> Certainly, gentlemen, it ought to be the happiness and glory of a representative to live in the closest union, the closest correspondence, and the most unreserved communication with his constituents. Their wishes ought to have great weight with him; their opinion high respect; their business unremitted attention. It is his duty to sacrifice his repose, his pleasures, his satisfactions, to theirs: and above all, ever, and in all cases, to prefer their interest to his own. But his unbiased opinion, his mature judgment, his enlightened conscience, he ought not to sacrifice to you, to any man, or to any set of men living. These he does not derive from your pleasure; no, nor from the law and the constitution. They are a trust from Providence, for the abuse of which he is deeply answerable. Your representative owes you, not his industry alone, but his judgment; and he betrays, instead of serving you, if he sacrifices it to your opinion. . . .
>
> If government were a matter of will upon any side, yours, without question, ought to be superior. But government and legislation are matters of reason and judgment, and not of inclination; and what sort of reason is that in which the determination precedes the discussion; in which one set of men deliberate, and another decide; and where those who form the conclusion are perhaps three hundred miles distant from those who hear the arguments.[4]

POLITICAL PARTIES AS INTERMEDIARIES IN THE PROCESS OF REPRESENTATION In Western democracies, before the process of election can operate it must first be resolved into institutional forms created by political parties. These bodies are the training grounds for political leadership. They are responsible to the electorate for the character and quality of candidates for public office. The party stamp is a warranty of fitness backed by the party as a whole. The voter, accordingly, passes judgment on more than the promises and policies that emanate from the party machine. Voting loyalty is determined for a considerable portion of the electorate by the superior quality of the men holding office under the banner of the party of their choice. The burden of initial selection is, in fact, shifted from the shoulders of the individual voter to the party machine. As often as not, particularly in local affairs, a vote is cast as a token of confidence in the ability of one particular party to select the right men for office.

Representation gains in subtlety and depth from the intermediary functions of the party machine. Left to his own devices the loosely informed individual could choose only in terms of general opinions concerning virtue and desirability. Carefully gathered, professionally sifted, appraisal of the political worth of a candidate would be lacking. The ability of a party to make this appraisal is rooted in its nature as a full-time organization with the means to test candidates over years of practical service. A willingness to endure the thankless apprenticeship of party work is, in itself, evidence of an interest in the common good superior to that of the ruck of men. The quality of party organization will determine whether corruption, professionalism, or personal ambition gain too strong a foothold. It should be remembered that the machine must always defend the superiority of its products over the personalities of rival organizations before a jury of voters.

Party organization, then, provides an element essential to modern systems of representation. It is the means by which men and issues are, to some extent, stripped of the irrelevancies of vague opinion to be brought within bounds of judgment concerning a superior interest in the common good. Burke's dedicated politician, chosen for the quality of his personal conscience, merges into a party machine which stands or falls in accordance with the character of the men it trains and presents for office. The roster of worthy and unworthy candidates for public office is impossibly bulky if left to the preselection of individual voters, but there are seldom more than two or three political parties for the voter to choose from. The primary contribution of party organization to the idea of the common good is that it provides public affairs with an institutional setting of their own. Until boundary lines have been drawn between neighboring fields of commerce, religion, and culture it is hardly feasible to determine who approaches public business possessed of a superior interest in the common good.

Other Forms of Political Representation

Peoples who have not shared in the historical experiences or technological evolution of the Western nations encounter difficulties in applying Western forms of representative institutions to the ordering of their societies. The degree of social union achieved is of major importance. If nationhood cannot be taken for granted but has to be asserted against powerful conflicting claims, freedom of choice on the part of individuals is severely restricted. A voter may feel, with some justification, that the only alternative to loyal support of a single party is the destruction of the state and dismemberment of his nation. At such a stage in political development the political order is that of a community militant; individual opinions and judgments are subordinated to the need for disciplined support for the upholders of national union. Nations in Asia and Africa newly emerging from colonial dependence into national independence provide modern examples. India and Ghana remain single-party states where a vote against the party of national union indicates a willingness to risk the disruption of the state. Representative institutions flourish, but the content of representation is narrowed down to the question of the survival of a nation or system. Obviously, this form of representation should be of a transitory nature; the growth of national and political stability will either permit the voter to choose freely between two or more parties equally committed to basic national ends or the opportunities for individual choice will disappear under one or other form of oligarchic tyranny.

Soviet Representation

Communist states have adopted patterns of representative institutions based on assumptions diametrically opposed to those of

Western democracies. The key to an understanding of Communist concepts of representation lies in the first sentence of the *Communist Manifesto* of 1848. Marx wrote: "The history of all hitherto existing society is the history of class struggles." Lenin extended this idea to the proposition that the political state is nothing more than the instrument of a dominant class. Linking this with Communist dogma that labor is the source of all productive activity and human society is wholly conditioned by the means of economic production, Lenin and his successors justified the dictatorship of the proleteriat as the only logical form of state organization. The Communist Party, self-declared "vanguard" of a class, became, accordingly, the sole source of valid political opinion. Any exercise of freedom of choice outside the candidates and programs presented by the Communist Party would amount to repudiation of the national state. Within these severe limits the Soviets have encouraged representative systems, training the electorate to choose from among candidates all of whom bear the stamp of approval of the Communist hierarchy. The dilemma of the Russian voter may be likened to that of a diner in a restaurant where the menu is restricted to many delicious flavors of ice cream: if one has no taste for ice cream the only alternative is to go hungry—since there is no other restaurant to go to.

A breach in Communist logic concerning representation may be found in the organization of the Party itself. Neither initial membership nor subsequent promotion is subject to election by the community. Party programs are formulated by a closed hierarchy beyond the control of representative bodies. Dogma as handed down from Marx through Lenin to Stalin and Khrushchev, with perhaps some embarrassing interventions from Mao of China, is the official determinant of state policy. Majority opinion, then, has little part to play in the conduct of public affairs. The elaborate system of representative institutions on the surface of Soviet political life is not related to decision-making in practical matters. Instead it serves to reflect the reactions of the general community to certain qualities and practices of Communist rule concerning which the Party itself has not yet laid down a firm line. An alert oligarchy may take these reactions into account in estimating safety limits to the application of naked dogma.

Functional Representation

Another form of representation with stubborn roots in Western culture aims at participation in government by corporate bodies rather than individual persons. Historically it may be claimed that early representative institutions were designed on the assumption that the people were already organized in functional and even hereditary groupings. In medieval England and France the first parliaments were gatherings of the Estates of the Realm to consult with and advise the sovereign monarch. These concepts belong to an age lacking in both the experience and understanding of present-day individualism.

Attempts to revive corporate representation may smack somewhat of the cloistered study, as was the case with the Guild Socialist movement associated with the name of G. D. H. Cole in England.[5] Again, such forms may be employed in an effort to win mastery for some particular interest group over all others in the community. The Syndicalist movement in Europe in the early part of the twentieth century was a bid for political power on the part of the industrial worker. One of its theorists, Georges Sorel, advocated the creation of a political solidarity on the part of the workers based on the continuing "myth" of a general strike that would win them command of the machinery of government.[6]

In his radical youth Mussolini was influenced by Sorel; the later façade of a corporate state he devised for Italy took the form of a myth that cloaked the absolute supremacy of the Fascist movement. Portugal under Salazar has experimented in the forms of corporate representation to the extent of denying principles of majority rule and apportioning political representation among functional groups of the community according to the will of the dominant party. *Functional representation* assumes that the individual is concerned with public affairs solely in terms of his own functional or economic interests. At its best it denies to the individual as a social unit any direct or immediate say in affairs of state. Despite the anti-individualism inherent in this concept, tendencies exist even in advanced democracies to incorporate the electorate into interest groups and make the direction of public policy a resultant of the balance of these groupings.

Systems of Election

According to John Stuart Mill, "The meaning of representative government is, that the whole people, or some numerous portion of them, exercise, through deputies periodically elected by themselves, the ultimate controlling power, which, in every constitution, must reside somewhere."[7] In practice, then, methods of election determine the character of a system of representation. Electoral systems may be judged in the first place according to the proportion of the total people that may participate, and in the second place in terms of the means provided to exercise individual judgment through voting.

UNIVERSAL SUFFRAGE Equality of voting privileges for all adult members of a political community is now accepted as a theoretical base for popular sovereignty. However, even in countries with a long tradition of popular rule the principle is subject to substantial modifications based on social custom. Thus, as late as 1959 the model democracy of Switzerland rejected female suffrage in federal elections. In the United States the principle of the equal vote lies close to traditional social organization. Eligibility to vote in elections for the federal House of Representatives is determined, however, according to the Constitution, by the rules which each State establishes for eligibility to elect the most numerous branch of its own legislature. Some of the States have been ingenious in limiting the electoral rolls: literacy tests, common in Northern as well as Southern states, artificial registration requirements, and age qualifications varying from seventeen to twenty-one provide methods of eliminating a portion of the less determined citizenry. Perhaps the impact of compulsory military service is too recent for acceptance of its full implications on the political level. Nevertheless, the logic that holds that a youth is possessed of sufficient patriotism and intelligence to fight for his country but is not qualified to vote for public officials seems more suited to a conception of politics as a conflict of special interests than as a simple determination of the public good.

The Fourteenth Amendment to the Constitution of the United States contains a provision which, if applied, might remedy some of the backsliding in the carrying out of the principles of equal voting rights on a State and national level. Section 2 of this Amendment provides that seats in the House of Representatives shall be apportioned among the several States according to the total population of each State. However, should the voting rights of any of the male population over twenty-one be abridged for any reason other than crime or rebellion, "the basis of representation therein shall be reduced in the proportion which the number of such male citizens shall bear to the whole number of male citizens twenty-one years of age in such State." This Constitutional provision is not self-enforcing and Congress has not as yet brought itself to pass implementing legislation or resolutions.

It is fair to assume that in most Western countries the practice of politics—as opposed to the general theory of government—tends towards a restriction of the electorate. Party managers like to deal with manageable groups whose responses can be predicated with some degree of certainty. A general vote of the whole adult citizenry is difficult to handle along strict party lines. The devices usually employed take the form of discouraging rather than prohibiting the voter from the exercise of his right. Indifference on the part of substantial portions of the electorate remains the principal means through which politicians can control elections.

This whittling away of the basis of democratic action can readily be overcome if the political community asserts itself over the conveniences of the party politician. The Commonwealth of Australia, for example, introduced the simple remedy of compulsory voting. Under penalty of a substantial fine, every eligible voter must record his vote or submit a reasonable excuse for his absence from the polling booth. An obligation to vote has come to be accepted by Australians as no less binding—though more agreeable—than the obligation to pay taxes. In the 1921 election, before the adoption of the Compulsory Voting Act, less than 60 per cent of the electorate voted. In the following national election in 1925, over 91 per cent of the electorate voted. Party politicians sometimes decry compulsory voting on the grounds that it denies the individual the right to abstain, in itself an important expression of opinion in terms of "a plague on both your houses." However, the author, who has voted in several Australian elections, has found that invalidating a ballot with pointed remarks provides a satisfying method of abstention. Another value of compulsory voting is that it brings to light and generally sweeps away the network of residence and registration restrictions set to trap the feet of the unwary voter. As a matter of personal judgment, the author associates the acceptance of compulsory voting in the Commonwealth of Australia with the higher degree of social equality existing in that country in comparison with Britain, the United States, or most European lands. In Australia it is assumed that any adult of whatever degree of literacy or economic standing has the capacity and duty to express an opinion on public affairs.

DIRECT VERSUS INDIRECT VOTING Under a system of *direct voting* the voter passes a face-to-face judgment on a particular candidate or policy. Where *indirect voting* is employed, some intermediary is chosen to take part in an electoral group or college entrusted with the final choice of candidates. The purpose of this method is to allow the voter to act through some person well known to him in terms of group or regional associations and to avoid passing judgment on matters or qualifications with which he cannot be expected to be familiar. Indirect election through an electoral college is still, in theory, the method prescribed by the Constitution for the election of a President of the United States. In practice, candidates for the Electoral College are required by a binding convention to name in advance the Presidential candidate for whom they intend to vote. Accordingly, the College now mirrors, in a somewhat clumsy fashion, the choice of an approximate majority of the nation's electorate.

Though out of favor in most Western lands during the last century, indirect electoral systems are proving of considerable value among peoples in the process of achieving nationhood. In Nigeria, where thirty-five million Africans of disparate cultures and tribal ties are creating a nation out of a mere geographical area, processes of indirect election have bridged a difficult gap between reliance on the tribal community and acceptance of the wider national association. As a training ground for true representative government, indirect voting may still have an important part to play. It is noteworthy that the Constitution of the Fifth Republic of France has revived indirect election as a method of selecting the President of the Republic, who is also President of the French Community. Article 6 of the French Constitution states: "The President of the Republic shall be elected for seven years by an electoral college comprising the members of Parliament, of the General Councils, and of the Assemblies of the Overseas Territories, as well as the elected representatives of the municipal councils."

PLURALITY SYSTEMS When a people has become sufficiently homogeneous so that the vote of one citizen anywhere may be accounted equal to that of any other citizen, it is practicable to divide the electorate into single-member constituencies based on geographical areas. Ideally, each area should contain approximately the same number of voters, but this is seldom achieved under the State or local conditions that exist in the United States. For practical reasons the electoral district should be one that may be traversed by candidates in a reasonable time and the voters themselves should possess the communications common to a definite area. Rural districts are more likely than urban centers to have their inhabitants scattered over diverse areas. Accordingly, political manipulators at the level of the American State Assembly have some grounds for weighting the rural vote against that of the crowded cities. Unfortunately, once this practice is started it becomes a vested interest particularly difficult to alter in the climate of State politics.

Within a single-member constituency the candidate receiving the largest number of votes, a plurality, wins the election. This uncomplicated method is based on the assumption that the choice of the electorate will lie between two candidates, when a plurality will amount to a majority. Where a two-party system is deeply rooted in the political custom of the community this method approximates comfortably enough to the expression of majority opinion. Unfortunately, two-party government constitutes a very advanced state of social and political unity. It is based on general agreement concerning the ends of government and on tolerance of alternative methods to achieve such ends. On the national level, countries as closely knit as the United States and Britain have operated under a two-party system even in times of trouble. Even in these lands, however, political questions on the local level have given rise to the appearance of three or more effective party organizations. In other Western nations social and economic distinctions have impeded solution of political problems by means of an order that provides the voter with only two possible courses.

PROPORTIONAL REPRESENTATION AND PREFERENTIAL VOTING SYSTEMS Determination of majority opinion in political communities where a two-party system is not operative can become a very complicated business. A basic factor is whether or not circumstances permit the formation of any majority opinion upon a political matter. In general terms it all depends upon the question put to the electorate. If the choice to be made is a clear-cut yes or no on a matter of universal concern and understanding—say the continuance of compulsory military service—the bulk of an electorate spread over even a very extensive area can be expected to provide a definitive answer. Where issues are not general, however, but affect some groupings far more than others, there can be no true opinion to be expressed through voting mechanisms. A system of representation in a democratic society, therefore, should be so organized as to exercise some control over the formulation of issues submitted to the decision of the electorate. In a rough way a two-party system on a national scale is able to achieve this end. Because they must appeal to the general electorate, neither party may stand on "platforms" obviously designed for the satisfaction of particular interests. An example of this is the manner in which the British Labour party, originally based on industrial trade unions, transformed itself by choice of programs and issues into a national party with an appeal to all classes of the community.

In societies where particular group outlooks are so strong that the issues of politics cannot be presented in general terms a substitute has to be found for true majority opinion. This alternative generally takes the form of a balance of opinions. The individual elector contributes his particular outlook towards an unknown compromise, but does not pass any effective judgment on the major practical issues facing political decision. Whether or not the creation of true majority opinion is essential to the existence of representative democracy remains controversial. In many circumstances, honest methods of reaching a balance of conflicting opinions is all that can be achieved by a political apparatus even under a two-party system. The issue is one concerning which it is probably unwise to make sweeping generalizations. Government and politics operate at many levels in modern societies; the strata of public affairs in which the bulk of an electorate may possess a common interest is limited; other questions may be best settled through compromise without benefit of a dominant expression of opinion.

Once the principle is accepted of substituting for majority opinion a pattern of opinion resulting from representation of minority groups, ingenious mathematical devices have to be employed to insure that all groups scattered throughout a total electorate are given a proportionate say in the composition of representative bodies. Two of the most favored methods are the *list system* and the *Hare system.*[8]

The list plan of proportional representation requires division of the electorate into large groupings each of which elects as many as perhaps ten candidates. Political parties, generally numerous and closely identified with particular interests or attitudes, prepare lists for submission to the electorate. Each voter has one vote, which must be cast for a list and not for any particular candidate. A previously determined number of votes, say 60,000 in a national election, entitles a party to have one of the members on its list elected. Thus, in a constituency with 600,000 voters and ten seats to be filled, a minority party winning 10 per cent of the total vote would be entitled to one elected representative. Further complications are induced by a certain number of surplus votes in each constituency which fall below the total required to elect a single candidate. These may be disposed of by the addition of a national list to the constituencies' separate lists. A fractional party may thus gather enough surplus votes to return candidates on a national scale. The best example of the operation of the list system in a modern state may be found in the electoral laws of the Weimar Republic of Germany from 1919 to 1931. It is noteworthy that the present Federal Republic of West Germany has compromised between proportional representation and plurality voting. Each voter now receives two votes, one of which he employs directly to elect a candidate on a plurality basis; the other is given to a party

INSTRUCTIONS

Mark Your Choices with NUMBERS Only. (Do NOT Use X Marks.)

Put the number 1 in the square opposite the name of your first choice.

Put the number 2 opposite your second choice, the number 3 opposite your third choice, and so on. You may mark as many choices as you please.

Do not put the same number opposite more than one name.

To vote for a person whose name is not printed on this ballot, write his name on a blank line under the names of the candidates and put a number in the square opposite to show which choice you wish to give him.

If you tear or deface or wrongly mark this ballot, return it and obtain another.

OFFICIAL COUNCILMANIC BALLOT

FOR THE

GENERAL ELECTION

NOVEMBER 7, 1939

CITY OF NEW YORK,

NEW YORK COUNTY

36 ELECTION DISTRICT

18 ASSEMBLY DISTRICT

	CANDIDATES FOR THE COUNCIL	
	HENRY OFFEN	Liberal
	LANGDON W. POST	American Labor Citz. Nonpartisan
	MARION E. ROONEY	
	SOLOMON RUBIN	Settlm't Houses
	ALFRED E. SMITH, JR.	
	HOWARD H. SPELLMAN	Democratic
	ROBERT K. STRAUS	City Fusion Citz. Nonpartisan
	JOSEPH CLARK BALDWIN	Republican
	WILLIAM A. CARROLL	Democratic
	LOUIS DE SALVIO	Democratic
	PERCY FOSTER	Democratic
	EMANUEL A. MANGINELLI	Republican Citz. Nonpartisan
	PATRICK McHUGH	
	JOHN P. NUGENT	Democratic

SAMPLE PROPORTIONAL REPRESENTATION BALLOT

list for a *Land,* or state, constituency, the results being determined by a system of proportional representation.

The Hare system is a method of preferential voting based on a single transferable vote. A quota of votes for the election of a candidate is determined according to the size of the electorate and the number of seats to be filled. The voter registers a first, second, third, etc., choice over the whole list on the ballot. Those candidates receiving the required quota as first selections are immediately held elected. Any surplus of first selection votes awarded them over the quota needed for election are then transferred to the second choice expressed by the voter. Determination of the particular ballots considered surplus is made at random. This process is repeated until all the vacancies are filled. In the United States variations of the Hare method have been frequently employed in municipal elections. New York City elected Councilmen in this fashion from 1936 to 1947. On the local level of politics, questions are likely to be more immediate and specialized than on national or state levels. That it should be possible to form a true majority opinion on a matter as complicated yet important as a traffic plan for a city is difficult to conceive. The quality of city officials may well be improved by raising them above the demagogic choice of a plurality of voters. On the other hand, proportional representation may strain the principle of majority rule through an overgenerous grant of political power and influence to special interests and unpopular minorities. Certainly the repudiation of proportional representation in New York City elections was due in large part to the election of Communist Councilmen under such a system.[9]

MULTIMEMBER CONSTITUENCIES A compromise between the stark choice of the single-member constituency and the splintering effects of P.R. may be afforded by the adoption of multimember constituencies. For the greater part of their history the representative systems of England and colonial America were based upon multiple districts. Before modern transportation and communication, geographic areas, counties, towns, and cities formed integrated communities to a greater extent than today. The size and population density of natural constituencies were accepted as unalterable facts determining the number of members which might be elected to each. Britain did not create her present rigid single-member-constituency system until 1885. In the United States, elections on the State level employ multimember constituencies on a considerable scale; in 1955 an admixture of multiple-district and single-member constituencies could be found in 36 states.[10]

Perhaps the greatest difficulty confronting systems of popular representation at the present time is the dissolution of natural communities on a narrow geographic basis in favor of nation-wide economic, social, and cultural groupings. Representation is always a reflection of opinion, and opinion in turn depends for its formation on the possibilities of discussion among like-thinking people. The modern voter, as like as not, finds himself voting in a group to which he does not "belong" in terms of those essential characteristics which would help him to form a judgment concerning public affairs. National economic groupings such as trade unions, trade or professional associations, may provide the true discussion groups for the formation of one aspect of voter opinion. Other points of view may be contributed by the attitudes of cultural and social bodies transcending local geographic boundaries. In these circumstances the individual voter has to place great reliance on national political parties in effective rapport with his real opinion-forming associations. The concept of a "local" representative has become ambiguous under present-day conditions. It may be held the exception rather than the rule for a voter to choose a representative in the national government on grounds confined within the bounds of local opinion and discussion. In this respect, British electoral practices are more realistic than those of the United States in acknowledging limitations imposed by a geographic constituency on the choice of a voter. Candidates in British parliamentary elections are not required to be residents of the district where they seek election. For example, Sir Winston Churchill, English of the English, served for many years as Member of Parliament for the dourly Scots constituency of Dundee. This latitude permits the individual voter a greater choice in the type of representative he considers will reflect his concern for the national good, rather than his local feelings. The American custom of sending to Congress only residents of the locality does not stem from law or the Constitution but is nevertheless a very binding convention. It embodies, perhaps, a certain uneasiness concerning the whole idea of national representation that stems from the federal character of the American polity, the vastness of the land and the unresolved social differences of the different areas.

INITIATIVE, REFERENDUM, AND PLEBISCITE At its best, the electoral process represents the individual voter's opinion concerning any specific political issue in an indirect and uncertain fashion. The representative institution itself, be it Congress, Parliament, or Assembly, invariably stands between the electorate and a definitive judgment of issues. The institutions, not the voters, are the decision-making bodies. Accordingly, among free peoples a demand has always existed for a political apparatus that will accord the electorate an authoritative voice in the direct determination of concrete issues. When the free citizens of Athens, a minority even of the adult males of that city–state, met in their traditional Assembly, they made the laws by majority vote, judged law cases and decided military strategy and details of administration by the same method. In the opinion of their historian Thucydides, and many other competent observers, it was this practice that led them finally into disaster. On a lesser and more circumspect scale the New England Town Meeting preserved this ancient tradition. It has been generally assumed that this practice of "direct" democracy was, by its nature, limited to communities where the whole body of citizenry could meet together in one place. Modern communications have perhaps provided substitutes for mass meetings as instruments for the formation of opinion.

The Swiss Confederation has retained the practice of permitting the voter a direct say in the passing of laws and constitutional revisions. In many of the cantons ordinary laws as well as constitutional amendments are submitted to a popular referendum. A partial or total revision of the federal constitution may be brought about by popular initiative, consisting of a demand for change on the part of 50,000 voters. Before constitutional amendments come into force they must be accepted by a majority vote of the electorate as well as by the majority of the states. Many of the new European states formed after World War I made liberal use of the popular initiative and referendum. These instruments remain linked to the concept of self-determination. The United Nations has made a practice of requiring that a referendum be held when a Trust territory, such as the Cameroons in West Africa, seeks to become an independent state or link itself with some neighboring nation.

The term *referendum* is normally used to describe the submission of a constitution or law for consideration by the electorate; favorable action by a majority of voters is required to validate the constitution or law. A practice has now grown up of presenting a single issue, usually in dramatic terms, to the total electorate for their response. What is sought is an expression of opinion and the vote may not bind the government of the state in any legal manner. This is a favorite device in one-party states where the ordinary apparatus of representative government has been suppressed. These popular responses are called *plebiscites.* Though they have legitimate use in limited circumstances—say the determination by the people of a certain area whether they should belong to one state or another—the practice is open to abuse by authoritarian leaders. It is not difficult to frame a plebiscite question in such terms that a negative answer would appear to the ordinary voter as tantamount to treason to the community. Hitler was a master in the use of the plebiscite to create the impression both at home and abroad of a Germany united behind his regime.

Within the United States the initiative and referendum are employed on the level of State and local government. Amendments to State constitutions are subject to the process of referendum in practically all States, and at least twenty States have provisions by which, under certain conditions, State laws may be submitted to a referendum of the electorate.[11] A lesser number of States make use of the device of the *initiative,* whereby a constitutional change or law may be proposed by means of a petition submitted by a designated number of voters. When such a proposal is referred directly to a referendum of the electorate, it is known as a *direct* initiative; if, however, the State legislature is permitted to pass on the proposal in the first instance, the proper description is that of *indirect* initiative. On the level of municipal and county government the referendum process plays an important part, particularly in safeguarding the right of the citizenry to a direct say in the mortgaging of future tax obligations through bond issues.

On the national level, and even on the State level, the use of the initiative and referendum tends to blunt the responsibility of representative institutions. In Britain, where a unitary system of government is in force, no provisions exist for the use of the referendum process. Federal forms of government allow for local determination of political issues on a certain level and it is arguable that many such questions fall within the competence of the individual voter to decide. Again a great deal depends upon how the question is framed and whether detailed information needed for informed judgment is placed in the hands of the scattered voters. The experience of California, where the referendum has been widely used, tends to show that well-organized and well-financed publicity campaigns can exercise decisive influence on the fate of issues submitted to a popular referendum. In general, the concept of direct legislation serves as a check upon the proper working of representative institutions. Complicated questions of government have to be reduced to simple terms that may be answered by the voters' yes or no. The advantages of maintaining such a check reside, perhaps, more in a potential use of popular power than in actual efforts to direct the course of government through a questionnaire directed to the man in the street.

THE DIRECT PRIMARY The pattern of electoral processes in any country must be adapted to the social organization of the community. Many European nations, including Britain, have long-established social orders in which various elements of the community have developed natural leadership patterns of their own. In such circumstances political parties encounter little difficulty in nominating candidates who will be recognized by the electorate as typical of certain known social attitudes and policies. In a nation of the character of the United States, however, where social patterns remain fluid and subject to constant change, political leadership cannot be assimilated to an accepted mode of social control. The nomination of candidates for elective office by party hierarchies would diminish the power of choice on the part of the electorate in a degree dangerous to the proper working of representative government. Accordingly, American politics has invented and practiced the direct primary as a further development in popular representation. In essence, primary elections permit a voter to vote twice; once for the nomination of a party candidate, and

SAMPLE DEMOCRATIC PRIMARY BALLOT

BUTLER COUNTY

a. To vote for a candidate place "X" in the rectangular space at the left of the name of such candidate.
b. If you tear, soil, deface or erroneously mark this ballot return it to the precinct election officials and obtain another ballot.

For Delegate-at-Large to the National Convention
(Vote for not more than twenty four)

- W. HARPER ANNAT — First Choice for President, FRANK J. LAUSCHE; Second Choice for President, JAMES W. HUFFMAN
- EARL D. APPLEGATE — First Choice for President, FRANK J. LAUSCHE; Second Choice for President, JAMES W. HUFFMAN
- THOMAS A. BURKE — First Choice for President, FRANK J. LAUSCHE; Second Choice for President, JAMES W. HUFFMAN
- WARREN E. CARTER — First Choice for President, FRANK J. LAUSCHE; Second Choice for President, JAMES W. HUFFMAN
- ANTHONY J. CELEBREZZE — First Choice for President, FRANK J. LAUSCHE; Second Choice for President, JAMES W. HUFFMAN
- MICHAEL V. DISALLE
- EUGENE H. HANHART
- JOHN O. HOLLY
- BETTY M. HO
- JAMES W
- LAMBROS
- JOHN C
- DARRE L. McGHEE
- ROBER
- EKISON
- NELSO
- MARY HELICH
- GEORGE
- MARGUERIT MININNI
- ESTHER F. PINS
- FRAZIER REAMS
- ROY C. SCOTT — First Choice for President, FRANK J. LAUSCHE; Second Choice for President, JAMES W. HUFFMAN
- JAMES W. SHOCKNESSY — First Choice for President, FRANK J. LAUSCHE; Second Choice for President, JAMES W. HUFFMAN
- O. L. TEAGARDEN — First Choice for President, FRANK J. LAUSCHE; Second Choice for President, JAMES W. HUFFMAN
- ROBERT E. WALLACE — First Choice for President, FRANK J. LAUSCHE; Second Choice for President, JAMES W. HUFFMAN
- OLIVER H. WELF, JR. — First Choice for President, FRANK J. LAUSCHE; Second Choice for President, JAMES W. HUFFMAN

For Alternate-at-Large to the National Convention
(Vote for not more than twenty four)

- JOSEPH J. BALDINE — First Choice for President, FRANK J. LAUSCHE; Second Choice for President, JAMES W. HUFFMAN
- MARY BOYLE BURNS — First Choice for President, FRANK J. LAUSCHE; Second Choice for President, JAMES W. HUFFMAN
- LEONARD R. CERVENIK — First Choice for President, FRANK J. LAUSCHE; Second Choice for President, JAMES W. HUFFMAN
- WILLIA
- RUSSELL M. WILHELM — First Choice for President, FRANK J. LAUSCHE; Second Choice for President, JAMES W. HUFFMAN
- PEIRCE WOOD — First Choice for President, FRANK J. LAUSCHE; Second Choice for President, JAMES W. HUFFMAN

For Lieutenant Governor
(Vote for not more than one)

- HUBERT LYNCH

For Auditor of State
(Vote for not more than one)

- JOSEPH T. FERGUSON

For Treasurer of State
(Vote for not more than one)

- JOHN W. DONAHEY
- JOHN BROWN

For Attorney General
(Vote for not more than one)

- PAUL F. WARD
- STEPHEN M. YOUNG
- VITO ADAMO
- PAUL J. GEORGE
- MARION A. ROSS

For United States Senator
(Vote for not more than one)

For District Delegate to the National Convention
(Vote for not more than two)

- FRANK DOBROZSI — First Choice for President, FRANK J. LAUSCHE; Second Choice for President, JAMES W. HUFFMAN
- ALBERT A. HORSTMAN — First Choice for President, FRANK J. LAUSCHE; Second Choice for President, JAMES W. HUFFMAN

For District Alternate to the National Convention
(Vote for not more than two)

- GEORGE L. FLANAGAN, JR. — First Choice for President, FRANK J. LAUSCHE; Second Choice for President, JAMES W. HUFFMAN
- HARRY T. WILKS — First Choice for President, FRANK J. LAUSCHE; Second Choice for President, JAMES W. HUFFMAN

For Governor
(Vote for not more than one)

- ROBERT W. REIDER
- JOHN E. SWEENEY
- MICHAEL V. DI SALLE
- OSCAR L. FLECKNER
- FRANK X. KRYZAN

For Secretary of State

For Count
(Vote for

- GORDON
- WILLIAM E
- ARTHUR RE

For Prosecuting Attorney
(Vote for not

- ANDREW
- JACKSON

Clerk of

...of the Court ... Commencing January 1, 1957)
(Vote for not more than one)

- CARL V. WEYGANDT

For Judge of the Supreme Court (Full Term Commencing January 1, 1957)
(Vote for not more than one)

- MERRILL D. BROTHERS

For Judge of the Supreme Court (Full Term Commencing January 2, 1957)
(Vote for not more than one)

- EVAN P. FORD.

For Representative to Congress
(Vote for not more than one)

- R. WILLIAM PATTERSON

For Judge of the Court of Appeals (Full Term Commencing February 9, 1957)
(Vote for not more than one)

- JOSEPH BRUEGGEMAN

For Member of State Central Committee, Man
(Vote for not more than one)

- GEORGE L. FLANAGAN, JR.

For Member of State Central Committee, Woman
(Vote for not more than one)

- MARY B. BILLINGSLEA

For State Senator
(Vote for not more than one)

- EDWARD H. DELL

For Representative to General Assembly
(Vote for not more than two)

- DAVID F. DILLON
- MARVIN S. KLINE
- HARRY T. WILKS

For Judge of the Court of Common Pleas Division of Domestic Relations (Full Term Commencing January 1, 1957)
(Vote for not more than one)

- LTON H. COMBS
- THUR J. FIEHRER
- K F. WESSEL

County Commissioner
(Vote for not more than two)

- H. AUGSPURGER
- E. MANROD, JR.
- REIFF

For Prosecuting Attorney

- W. CHERNEY
- ON BOSCH

For Judge of the Court of Common Pleas
(Vote for not more than one)

- JOSEPH T. KIEP

For Sheriff
(Vote for not more than one)

- EDWARD C. LUBBERS
- EDDIE McDONALD
- GEORGE LESTER VAN LIEU
- CHARLES B. WALKE
- JOHN F. DOWD
- JOE W. GILLESPIE
- OSCAR M. JOHNSON

For County Recorder
(Vote for not more than one)

- EARL R. HOGAN

For County Treasurer
(Vote for not more than one)

- JOHN W. WENDEL

For County Engineer
(Vote for not more than one)

- JESSE H. POCHARD

For Coroner
(Vote for not more than one)

For Member of County Central Committee
(Vote for not more than one)

SAMPLE PRIMARY BALLOT, STATE OF OHIO, 1956

once for the election of a representative or officeholder. Practically all States of the Union have made primary elections part of their electoral processes in one form or another. There are two forms of primary. The *closed primary* requires the voter to register as a member of one party and to cast his nominating vote for designees of that party only. In the *open primary,* the voter need not declare his party affiliation, remaining free to nominate a candidate from any party list. California in the past has practiced the open primary with unusual vigor to the considerable confusion of party organization. A Report of the Committee on Political Parties to the American Political Science Association rendered the following judgment on the two systems:

> *The closed primary deserves preference because it is more readily compatible with the development of a responsible party system.* However imperfectly the idea may have worked out in some instances, it tends to support the concept of the party as an association of like-minded people. On the other hand, *the open primary tends to destroy the concept of membership as the basis of party organization.*[12]

In general, representative systems should be judged according to their effectiveness in granting a say in the affairs of government to the individual citizen viewed as a member of an existing social organization. Abstract principles have to be adapted in every country to the realities of a working order of society. A major limitation on all forms of representation lies in the fact that it is the business of a government to govern as well as to reflect the opinions of a citizen body. Where the social structure is such that a great deal of government is required to protect the social union, the individual voter may find his participation restricted to basic issues. Thus, when their nation is at war even the most advanced of electorates must exercise the greatest caution in diminishing the decision-making authority of the government in power. In a relaxed atmosphere of peace and national unity the opinions of citizen voters may influence the determination of a multitude of questions. However, at all times representation is a right to take part in the selection of a government that will govern. The actual ruling power remains in the hands of responsible officials and representative institutions, and not in the people at large.

Responsibility of the Voter

Though representative government is still government by a select few who hold public office and power, it requires individual citizens to accept obligations of a particular character and quality. In brief, they have to be sufficiently mature in a political and social sense to maintain a free society. History is not overencouraging as to any universal tendency of mankind toward free association. In certain areas during certain epochs free communities have prospered: the Western world over the last two hundred years provides a notable example. However, the bulk of mankind since the commencement of organized society have had slight experience of political liberty. Servility, intolerance, and fear are constant psychological patterns that result in autocratic forms of rule.

The continued operation of any representative system of government, then, rests on the social attitudes of the individuals comprising the nation. The first requirement is a personal concern in the maintenance and advancement of social union within the borders of the political state. If a substantial majority do not hold this as a true interest, representative institutions in practice will be a meaningless reflection of a conglomeration of personal greeds, whims, prejudices, and self-seeking. The voter, therefore, must be a patriot in the sense of proving willing to subordinate personal concerns to the security of the community.

In the second place, the voter must have achieved a certain degree of social tolerance to enable him to realize that personal freedom rests on a like possession of liberty by all other members of the community. Where intolerance is supreme, representative institutions cannot function. Fanatic groups cannot bear to surrender power once acquired, or even to permit free association and discussion within the ranks of the hated opposition. The ability to accept with equanimity the triumph of political views different from one's own is prerequisite to citizenship in a country governed by representative institutions. Again, it is the free opinion of the community that must be represented, not the dogmas of any particular group. In a country such as the Union of South Africa, for example, where the ruling group, of European descent, has committed itself socially and psychologically to the maintenance of minority rule at all costs, the operation of representative institutions is distorted out of recognition.

Thirdly, the citizen under representative institutions must not expect too much of his government. It is only a concept of limited government that allows for the degree of tolerance and self-discipline needed to carry on representative institutions. Where political authority is in a position to destroy a man's religion, means of livelihood, personal dignity, and family ties, few would be prepared to submit their fate to a majority vote. Again, when the function of government is restricted in favor of other social values it cannot claim to satisfy the total needs of the individual through political means. The god–king on whom all burdens and responsibilities may be thrown dwindles to the stature of a helpful but limited official. This necessitates that individuals accept a great measure of responsibility for the conduct of their own affairs. Independence is generally a mark of psychological maturity and is far from prevalent even in advanced societies.

If a sufficiency of these qualities exists among a substantial majority of the citizenry, representative institutions may operate to maintain a stable society with dynamic capacities. The relationship between the voter and his representative approximates that of principal and agent, but agent only for a limited, social, purpose, one that the voter is able to disassociate from the personal needs for which he alone is responsible. It is sometimes argued that successful operation of representative institutions requires an "informed" electorate, in the sense that the body of the electorate must possess the means and willingness to acquaint themselves with details of political policies. This assumption is hardly sustained by the experience of the peoples in Asia, Africa, or even Latin America, emerging into self-government through the development of representative institutions. In fact, it would limit the operation of representative institutions to a small sector of the Western world for the foreseeable future. Perhaps the misunderstanding arises from confusion concerning the exact role of the voter. It is his obligation to pass judgment on the character of a representative, rather than on the specific steps that representative employs to carry out his duties. Of course the voter also judges of the total results in practice of his representative's behavior, but his principal recourse when dissatisfied is to replace him with a representative of a different character. Illiterate and ignorant voters may pass as shrewd judgments in these respects as many enthusiastic amateurs of politics.

Representative institutions depend for their successful functioning, therefore, primarily on the existence of a voter body qualified to bear the responsibilities of free men. It follows that no particular arrangement of political machinery can guarantee to any community the smooth functioning of a representative system. Final responsibility lies on the level of the personal attitudes of the citizenry as individuals. They may ensure the success of almost any pattern of free government by raising their standards of social cooperation or they may render useless logically ideal institutions through lack of patriotism, tolerance, and self-reliance. Political analysis often resolves into the old truism that people get the government they deserve.

Notes

[1] Mill, John Stuart, *Representative Government,* Chicago: Regnery, 1949, pp. 64, 65, 66.

[2] de Tocqueville, Alexis, *Democracy in America,* Vintage Books, New York: Knopf, 1954, Vol. I, p. 253.

[3] Carlyle, Thomas, *Sartor Resartus; The Life and Opinions of Herr Tuefelsdröckh,* New York: Doubleday, 1937.

[4] Burke, Edmund, Speech to the Electors of Bristol.

[5] Cole, G. D. H., *Social Theory,* New York: Frederick A. Stokes Company, 1920.

[6] Sorel, Georges, translated by Hulme, T. E., and Roth, J., *Reflections on Violence,* Chicago: Free Press, 1950.

[7] Mill, John Stuart, *op. cit.*, p. 81.

[8] The name is derived from Hare, Thomas, *The Machinery of Government.*

[9] Zeller, Belle, and Bone, Hugh A., "The Repeal of P.R. in New York City—Ten Years in Retrospect," *The American Political Science Review,* 1948, **42,** No. 6, 1127-1148.

[10] Klain, Maurice, "A New Look at the Constituencies," *The American Political Science Review,* 1955, **49,** No. 4, 1105-1119.

[11] Smith, Edward C., and Zurcher, Arnold J. (eds.), *New Dictionary of American Politics,* New York: Barnes & Noble, 1955.

[12] Committee on Political Parties, "Toward a More Responsible Two-Party

System," *The American Political Science Review,* 1950, **44,** Supplement No. 3, Part 2, v-ix and 1-96.

Supplementary Readings

Brady, Alexander, *Democracy in the Dominions; a Comparative Study in Institutions,* Toronto: University of Toronto Press, second edition, 1952.

Bryce, James, *Modern Democracies,* New York: Macmillan, 1921.

Corry, J. A., *Elements of Democratic Government,* New York: Oxford, 1947, Chapter VII.

De Grazia, Alfred, Jr., *Public and Republic: Political Representation in America,* New York: Knopf, 1951.

Ford, Henry J., *Representative Government,* New York: Holt, 1924.

Hermens, Ferdinand A., *The Representative Republic,* Notre Dame: University of Notre Dame Press, 1958.

Larsen, J. A., *Representative Government in Greek and Roman History,* Berkeley: University of California Press, 1955.

Maine, Henry, *Popular Government,* London: John Murray, new edition, 1890.

Mill, John Stuart, *Considerations on Representative Government,* 1861, many editions.

Ross, J. F. S., *Elections and Electors,* London: Eyre and Son, 1955.

Chapter 6

Instrumentalities of Representation

Among free peoples, representative bodies constitute the principal intermediaries between citizens and their governments. Popular assemblies lack capacity for direct rule; they may determine general policies, and even make or unmake Governments, but the daily conduct of public affairs lies beyond their power. Their main role in the state, therefore, is to act as source of authority for the acts of officials from president or prime minister down to the level of tax collector. In democratic countries, almost every act of a Government in office must be legitimized by reference to a representative body. If they themselves do not govern, it may be safely said that no official or body of officials governs except by their will.

The Form of Representative Bodies

It has been noted previously that the individual citizen participates in public affairs not as an atomistic entity but as a person conditioned by and existing within a definite social organization. In order to create representative institutions that will mirror this situation it has frequently been found necessary to represent the individual citizen in two capacities through two separate bodies. As a numerical entity, he is represented in what is generally termed the popular house, which reflects majority choice. The social or traditional structure in which the voter finds himself is represented by a senate or upper house. This dual form of representative institution is called *bicameralism.* Primarily it originates in the historical evolution of a national society toward greater union. The second chamber provides a place for those elements in the nation–state that have not yet been swallowed up by a trend towards the homogeneity of numbers. Thus, in the United States the Constitution was adopted by the people in order to form "a more perfect Union," which was still a union, federal in character. As long as this degree and quality of union persists, the Senate of the United States, or some body equivalent in character, will be required to represent the federal attributes of the individual citizen. All modern states organized under a federal constitution possess bicameral legislatures; in the U.S.S.R., the second chamber is called the Soviet of Nationalities, in Switzerland the Council of States.

However, a geographic or traditionally regional division of the people is by no means the only basis for bicameralism. In many European countries the social structure retains clear-cut divisions which may not be ignored on the political level. Thus Great Britain, a unitary nation, still clings to its House of Lords, reflecting an established order in which certain minority elements are presumed to be invested with special virtues and authority. According to her 1958 Constitution, "France is a Republic, indivisible, secular, democratic, and social"; however, the Parliament remains bicameral, with a National Assembly chosen by the electorate as a numerical mass and a Senate elected by indirect suffrage to represent the territorial units of the Republic and Frenchmen living outside France.

In general, second chambers in federally constituted states have retained their authority, an influence often equal to that of the popularly elected lower house. In unitary countries such as Britain, upper houses have experienced a steady decline in effective power. To some extent this may be attributed to a breakdown of social distinctions resulting from the advance of social democracy in Western lands. Another factor is a gradual lessening of mistrust of popularly elected houses as responsible governing bodies. The need for a second chamber as a check on the vagaries of popular opinion was felt strongly in the eighteenth century. Madison argued in the Federal Convention that a strong senate was required to guard the people against their own "transient impressions."[1] Popular representation under conditions of universal suffrage has proved more stable and responsible as a means of government than foreseen in the days of the Founding Fathers. In consequence, the concept of a second chamber as a check on the will of the general electorate has fallen into disfavor. In Britain, by two successive Parliament Acts in 1911 and 1947 the power of the House of Lords to delay legislation passed by the House of Commons was reduced to a maximum period of one year.

Where the representative assembly is composed of a single house, it is known as a *unicameral* body. Local government is generally based on single, elected bodies, such as city, town, and county councils. On the State level, only Nebraska is governed by a unicameral legislature.

Functions of Representative Assemblies

Representative assemblies exercise three major functions. First, they are responsible for the raising and spending of public funds; secondly, they exert a degree of control over the executive and the manner in which officials carry out policies; third, they determine patterns or trends of policies through the making of laws. The manner in which these tasks are performed depends, of course, on the type of relationship established between legislatures and executive organs in each particular country. In totalitarian states the powers of representative bodies tend to be almost wholly formal. Even in Western democracies, legislatures have lost authority significantly to the executive branch and to their own internal leadership groups.

THE POWER OF THE PURSE Modern legislatures are variations of a basic pattern laid down by medieval parliaments. These historic bodies started their rise to power through control of taxation. The principle that the community taxed itself through its chosen representatives was established in England when Parliament first appeared in the thirteenth century. (The American colonists' slogan, "No taxation without representation," was no more than a claim to a traditional right of Englishmen.) As the raising and spending of public funds grew in significance in the process of government, the power and importance of legislatures increased. Today, government in all its branches is conditioned by the amount of money that can be raised by taxation and by the manner in which these funds are appropriated for specific purposes.

Control of public funds, being a supreme power, has to be exercised with considerable caution. On one hand there are the executive organs charged with the responsibility of carrying on the daily business of government; on the other, the legislature possessed of the power to grant or withhold essential supplies. Each country has met this problem in a different way, but in all cases a degree of compromise has had to be observed. In the United States, though the power of taxation and appropriation of funds on a national level belongs to Congress alone, the President initiates consideration of the budget through his Constitutional right to send Congress a budget message. In practice, determination of the financial needs of government departments and the relation of their claims one to another requires the single authority of the President's office. Nevertheless, the power of the Executive is merely that of a claimant; Congress decides how much money shall be taken from the taxpayer and for what needs and purposes it may be spent. In exercising this ultimate authority, both Houses of Congress have come to rely on the guidance of powerful leadership groups embodied in the committee organization. For example, the Ways and Means Committee and the Appropriations Committee of the House of Representatives comprise the high-ranking members of both parties. Individual members acting singly or in temporary groups have slight opportunity to tinker with the budget.

In the British system, the ancient powers of Parliament over the public purse have remained undiminished in theory. In practice, however, the Cabinet, being in possession of the executive powers of government, is able to dictate the budget as a whole and in detail. This authority inheres in Cabinet ministers as parliamentary leaders claiming the confidence of the House of Commons. If a majority of the House should reject the budget either in whole or in part, the Cabinet would be forced by a strict constitutional convention to resign and the issue would be placed before the country at an immediate general election. Though Parliament regarded as a group of representatives has delegated the greater part of its detailed responsibility to the majority leaders in the Cabinet, the House of Commons retains the final power of acceptance or rejection. A British government stakes its continued existence on the submission of a budget to Parliament. Debates on the estimates are the traditional occasions for critical scrutinies of the government's conduct in office. Though party loyalty and discipline may be relied on in general to curb misgivings on the part of individual members of the majority, the existence of what is known as a parliamentary as opposed to party spirit must always be taken into account. Even in the U.S.S.R. theoretical power to approve or disapprove of the consolidated budget and the national-economic plans rests in the Supreme Soviet. In contrast to Western democracies this constitutes a purely formal power subordinated to the rigid control of the Communist Party.

CONTROL OVER THE EXECUTIVE The claim of legislatures to supervise the executive acts of government is a somewhat ambiguous one, a comparatively recent addition to their historic pattern. It may be related to their modern role as embodiments of popular sovereignty. There are two major approaches to the rationalization of the claim: the doctrine of separation of powers, and the concept of responsible government. In the latter instance administrations are responsible for their conduct to a legislative body that possesses the power to make or unmake them.

The appearance of written constitutions in the eighteenth century stimulated a need for the formalization of relationships between legislature and executive. The United States may be regarded as the principal exponent of the desirability of separating the fields in which the three major branches of government—legislative, executive, and judicial—are entitled to function. Montesquieu's *Esprit des Lois,* an analysis of the French and English systems of government published in the first half of the eighteenth century, influenced the thinking of the Fathers of the American Constitution. The French author purported to find the tranquillity of the English state based upon an accepted separation of authority between Parliament on the one hand and the Crown and its ministers on the other. The historical experience of the American colonies reinforced Montesquieu's argument. From their inception, executive power had been wielded by royal governors, appointees of the English government, more often than not engaged in conflict with the indigenous legislature. The Constitution sought to resolve this struggle by delineating the proper spheres in which each of the great organs of government should operate. What was achieved amounted primarily to a division of responsibility rather than a fragmentation of the governing power.

In practice as well as theory the President's office retains considerable authority in the lawmaking process through the veto power and a duty to send messages to Congress. Executive discretion may be curbed by Congress in many ways; a major part of the President's powers stems from laws passed by the legislature, and all his principal officers are appointed with the consent of the Senate. In practice, separation of powers resolves itself into a separate tenure of power for each of the major branches of government. The fixed terms for the Presidency and for Congress do not coincide, nor can one branch be dismissed at the will of the other. In consequence, executive and legislative organs do not present a united front when seeking the approval of the electorate. Under a presidential system one party may win a majority in the legislature and the other party elect its candidate to the Presidency. Even when the same party controls both branches of government, unity of responsibility is apt to be tenuous. In general, a constitutional doctrine of separation of powers permits the legislature to check and supervise the authority of the executive but not to bring about its dismissal from office.

Responsible government, conversely, places the life of the executive in the hands of the legislature and at the same time generally gives the executive power to dismiss the legislature. Thus, the resolution of any conflict between the two branches will almost certainly be by an appeal to the electorate. Britain provides the most enduring example of responsible government. In the constitutional theory of that country the Government of the day is responsible to Parliament, which has, accordingly, the duty to overthrow it if it should lose the confidence of a majority of the members. Superficially, this might seem to place greater control over the executive in the hands of legislatures. Considerations of party politics, however, prevent a party majority in the legislature from overturning a Government composed of their own leaders, except in unusual circumstances. In fact, the capacity of the legislature to criticize and resist detailed policies of the executive is weakened by the knowledge that any revolt will bring about the fall of the Government and a general election. Control over executive officials and their policies in parliamentary countries normally lies at the level of party organization. Because the Government requires the continuing support of the members of its own party in parliament to survive from day to day, ministers are susceptible to the currents of intraparty opinion. This is particularly true in European lands, where the governments in power are frequently of the coalition type. In a stable two-party system such as that of Britain, the pressure is perhaps more indirect, though even the most powerful of Prime Ministers must remember that the discontent of even a few "back-bench" party members may topple him from office.

Under a parliamentary system, a major avenue for the exercise of influence by the legislature over executive policies lies in the presence of the prime minister and other ministers on the floor. Government policies and actions must be defended by the ministers themselves before their fellow members in the legislature. The "feeling of the House" customarily guides a wise Government in altering and adapting policy decisions. Party discipline may be trusted to ensure support within limited bounds; when the political sensitivity of a regime deserts it, "parliamentary" spirit is likely to overcome party loyalty.

Another form of legislative control is the "Question Hour" in the House of Commons, a parliamentary device for the interrogation of the Government in general and individual ministers in particular. Any act of an official, from a policeman to a minister, may be questioned by a private member according to the ancient procedure of the House. Parliament is very jealous of this right, which by custom lies outside the ordinary discipline of party lines. An example may be cited from an incident that occurred in 1958. A youth in a small town at the northern tip of Scotland complained to the local Procurator Fiscal, the equivalent of an American district attorney, that he had been assaulted by two policemen. His complaint being ignored by that official, he requested the Member of Parliament for the district to investigate the matter. The M.P., who belonged to the Conservative majority, addressed a Question in the House to the responsible minister, the Lord Advocate General of Scotland. The answer took the form of a brusque defense of the local officials. Unsatisfied, the M.P. persisted with further Questions till the interest of the whole House was deeply aroused. The Government found it necessary to allow a full day's debate to the subject, and the Prime Minister finally intervened with the promise of the appointment of an impartial Commission to investigate the whole event. Though an incident of this character is unlikely to result in a dramatic overthrow of a Government, it affects its prestige within its own party and throughout the country generally. As the standing of the administration is an important factor in determining when the Prime Minister will call a general election, ministers remain sensitive to Questions and Answers that may provoke unfavorable public response. By a strict British convention, the political minister is held responsible for every act of the civil servants comprising his department. Consequently, this device permits parliamentary review of the conduct of government at all levels.

LAWMAKING AND POLICY DETERMINATION The doctrine of popular sovereignty requires that the community should make its own laws through representative bodies chosen for that purpose. This theory, though logically satisfying, does not correspond accurately to the lawmaking process in Western countries. In the first place, the great body of laws under which a people live are passed on from one generation to another. In English-speaking lands they have been created by judicial wisdom, not legislative fiat, from the accepted customs of the community. The task of the legislature is to rearrange and amend these customary rules and to make additions where necessary. Even this authority had a humble start in medieval English Parliaments as a mere right to declare what were the ancient customs. The growth of the power of legislative bodies to make "new" laws and to change ancient customs at will reflects both an increasing centralization of government and a *mystique* of representation as equivalent to the popular will, current in the last two centuries. It has a sound basis in the principle that law should be founded on the consent of the community. However, it should be noted that in the past peoples have known other means of expressing consent to their laws than through representative institutions. It is not a denial of popular rule to place limitations on the lawmaking powers of representative bodies. Private property, for example, is the creation of law refining itself slowly over many centuries; may it be abolished by the fiat of a national legislature that claims to be the sole repository of the popular will? Certainly in the United States and among what we consider to be "free" peoples such action would be held destructive of the social unity which the political state is constituted to serve. The Constitution of the United States guards against such drastic actions through careful limitations placed on the lawmaking powers of both national and state legislatures. The final authority as to the scope and extent of lawmaking to be permitted remains a substantial majority of the people themselves, expressing their will through the means of Constitutional amendment.

Though legal theory in Britain gives Parliament unlimited power to pass valid laws on any subject, constitutional practice provides safeguards fully equivalent to those in force in the United States. An appeal to the electorate in the form of a general election is inevitable, for all practical purposes, whenever a British Parliament seeks to bring about serious innovations in the ordering of society through the process of lawmaking. Legislatures, then, are not independent sources of law in its fullest sense. Their function is to clothe immediate policy needs in the proper legal forms; when they seek to effect revolutionary changes they must submit their plans to a direct vote of the electorate.

The lawmaking functions of modern legislatures are also bounded by the initiative in the hands of the administration. The need for changes in and additions to the law are known most completely by officials in charge of the daily conduct of public business. Accordingly, the legislative program proposed by the current administration must inevitably receive primary consideration from the representative assembly. This requirement is sometimes obscured in American politics when a majority of Congress does not belong to the President's party affiliation. However, even in these circumstances the administration's choice of subjects in need of legislative action is difficult to avoid. Certainly the opposition party in Congress may present bills in their own form and in the name of their own leadership covering the same ground as the President's suggestions. In Britain, on the other hand, Parliament is restricted in practice to the consideration of measures proposed by the Cabinet. On rare occasions a private-Member's bill may be debated but this is generally a device whereby the Government may further a particular measure without committing itself wholeheartedly to its passage. Thus a change in the divorce laws passed the House under sponsorship of a private Member, relieving the Cabinet of direct responsibility on a politically unprofitable question.

Though both in theory and in practice legislatures are limited in their lawmaking function, it remains a key responsibility in their representation of popular sovereignty. In the final analysis, a national legislature plays the part of a jury of "good men and true" before whom the holders of power and influence must prove their case. Though the verdict may be restricted to yes or no, it cannot be circumvented. As long as officials and party leaders have to present their policies before this replica of the bar of public opinion, popular government may be said to prevail. Tyranny, in its many manifestations, has to resort to "fixing" the jury through the creation of one-party systems with a captive legislature.

The Operation of Legislative Assemblies

In theory, a sovereign representative assembly exemplifies government by discussion. This is an ancient and hallowed process for the rule of free men. Tacitus describes how the Germanic tribes of his day listened to the orations of their leaders and clashed their spears against their shields as a token of assent. It is, however, a method subject to severe limitations in regard to the number that may participate in debate. Bodies such as the Senate of the Roman Republic or the House of Commons in the eighteenth century could be swayed by the eloquence of a Cicero or Pitt to reach vital decisions on the floor of the House. Modern legislatures composed of from 400 to 600 members, on the other hand, seldom persuade members to action through free and realistic discussion of issues. Nevertheless, the principle of free discussion remains the feature that distinguishes popular, representative government from dogmatical tyranny. If realistic debate is no longer practicable in the general body of the assembly, it must be practiced elsewhere within the organization of the legislative body.

A good part of the operational structures of present-day legislatures exists to provide means for effective discussion before a final determination of the will of the representative body. Two principal methods have been developed through historical experience: formation of a pattern of leadership within the assembly, and the growth of party discipline. As an end result, congresses and parliaments in the Western world have come to represent more than the unorganized body of the electorate; they reflect an infra-structure of the power of political parties and traditional leadership concepts. In the Communist world, Supreme Soviets represent the mass of the people by courtesy and Communist Party organization in practical fact. The combination of accepted leadership and party discipline permits discussion to be canalized through a series of small workable groups, with the final decision between two or more coherent arguments left in the hands of the general body of the legislature.

LEGISLATIVE LEADERSHIP A constitutional basis for the internal leadership of legislative bodies in Western countries lies in a provision that the representative assembly possesses the sole power to organize itself. Thus the American Constitution grants power to the House of Representatives to "choose their Speaker and other officers," and further provides that "Each House may determine the Rules of its Proceedings, punish its Members for disorderly Behaviour, and, with the concurrence of two-thirds, expel a Member." In effect, this makes the legislative arm a corporate body, self-perpetuating as regards its rules and organization. A representative, then, though arriving armed with the will of the electorate, finds himself a member of a functioning body with an established hierarchy of power and strict rules of operation. The exercise of popular sovereignty becomes a collective, not individual, task, and one that has to be carried out within a corporate structure.

A position in the legislative leadership is won, generally, through competence, seniority, and ability to work within an organization. Tenure depends on capacity to produce results for the governing party that will meet with the approval of the general electorate. In many respects qualifications resemble those required for the executives of great business corporations. They are "organization" men, rather than dedicated idealists or popular heroes. An exception occurs in the case of prime ministers in a parliamentary system, where leadership of the legislature and the Government as a whole are combined in one personality. However, the normal operation of a representative body requires the professional talents of men immersed in its practices and dedicated primarily to its service. The American concept of separation of powers gives full scope to this type of leadership in Congress. Though party and legislative leadership may sometimes be held synonymous, this is neither invariably nor necessarily the case. When appealing to the general electorate, political parties may present leadership designed to attract popular favor or to organize support; when the election is over, the practiced masters of legislative manipulation may assume power over the business of government.

The two principal forms taken to organize legislative leadership are through committee rule or cabinet government. Where the separation of powers exists, legislatures are organized through committees forming an intricate hierarchy of power. Under parliamentary systems, the cabinet acts as a supreme committee for legislative leadership. Both Houses of the American Congress may be regarded as prototypes of committee organization, though the Senate, as the smaller body, allows greater opportunity for discussion and determination of issues on the floor. Under American conditions, chairmen of committees form an outer circle of Congressional leadership. An inner circle is composed of chairmen and members of the key committees, such as the Rules Committee of the House of Representatives.

THE COMMITTEE SYSTEM The basis for this system is the requirement that legislation and other important matters must first be considered in committee before being brought to the floor of the House. In the case of the House of Representatives, the Rules Committee further acts as a committee over committees, determining in general whether legislation proposed by any committee obtains right of way for consideration by the full House. For all practical purposes, true discussion of measures takes place in committee, either in open or closed hearings. Committees possess professional staffs that gather relevant information, either from government departments or from outside sources. If a measure is important, open hearings may be held giving opportunity to organized groups with an interest in the subject to state their case. The general public—through the press, lobbies, or pressure groups—may make their views felt at this point in the proceedings. The committee itself is of sufficient size, party balance, and informed knowledge to permit a high level of debate. The bulk of ill-informed or self-advertising bills submitted by ordinary members are weeded out and shelved at this stage without taking up the time of the House. Though a detailed examination would reveal many flaws in the American committee system, it serves to keep alive the spirit of informed discussion vital to any form of representative government.

A peculiar feature of the American Congress which sets it off from other Western legislatures is the *seniority* rule adopted by both parties for the selection of chairmen and members of important committees. This rule determines legislative leadership on a somewhat conservative basis, frequently checking the clear mandate of the electorate for fresh policies and personalities. It may be viewed as a hidden deterrent to popular control of the legislative process. As senior members in the House of Representatives and Senate are more likely to represent static or one-party areas than progressive districts, they are liable to form a leadership group out of touch with changing conditions in the national community. By the same token, seniority tends to preserve the tradition of Congress as an institution possessed of independent judgment, standing above the transient impressions of the electorate. To some extent the effect of the rule on leadership is mitigated by the practice of both parties of selecting majority and minority leaders for both Houses in party meetings.

CABINET LEADERSHIP Parliamentary systems of government combine executive and legislative leadership in one body, a cabinet of ministers. Nevertheless, considerable jealousy still exists between executive and legislative arms, and is kept in check only through skillful organization. No legislative body in a free country is prepared to surrender the conduct of its business wholeheartedly into the hands of the current administration, even though it be composed of leaders of the majority party. In Britain, this difficulty is met by giving official status with a salary attached to the

Leader of Her Majesty's Loyal Opposition. The Opposition then form what is known as a "shadow Cabinet" around their Leader. Parliament expects the Prime Minister to consult with his opposite number in the minority party concerning disposition of parliamentary time and the order of business. In this manner a joint leadership is created, weighted, of course, in favor of the majority party but still representative of the composition of the House as a whole.

The Cabinet retain the initiative in proposing measures to be placed before the House. A time-wasting flood of bills, such as originate from private members in the American Congress, is avoided. Parliamentary committees play a minor role, as they lack authority to prevent measures from reaching the floor of the House. They are called Standing Committees and are chosen each session by the non-partisan Speaker of the House. Their principal function is to see that proposed legislation is presented in sound technical form. As their proceedings are informal and secret, they give the Government of the day an opportunity to revise its proposals in terms of nonpartisan, technically skilled criticism. Perhaps because of this system, British legislation is generally more workable in the legal and administrative sense than is the body of laws emanating from an American Congress.

During the last few decades, a form of committee system has appeared within the Cabinet itself. Though such bodies as the Home Affairs Committee, the Economic Policy Committee, and the Defense Committee are primarily ministerial bodies, they form specialized interdepartmental groupings for the preparation and presentation of legislative and financial measures. In general, Cabinet leadership may be held more efficient than Congressional leadership in directing legislative policy. On the other hand, it entails greater danger of suppressing the true opinion of a representative body. In multiparty systems, such as those of France or Italy, the legislative dictatorship of the Cabinet is countered by frequent parliamentary revolts resulting in the overthrow of the Government, with consequent unsettling of the nation's business.

PARTY DISCIPLINE Modern legislatures no longer rank as good debating clubs. A freshman member of Congress who dreams of swaying the votes of his colleagues with the force of his rhetoric and the logic of his arguments will meet disappointment. The business of the House, nowadays, in Congress or any parliament, is to vote, not to talk. Generally speaking, voting patterns are set through committee hearings and other methods before members take their places on the floor of the Chamber. Very skillful professional maneuvering may still take place in debate, particularly in regard to the proposing of amendments. This, however, is generally an aspect of the party struggle projected on to a public stage so that one side or the other may be forced to present itself to the electorate in an unfavorable light. Though the magnificent traditions of informed debate such as took place in the American Constitutional Convention or the English Parliaments of the eighteenth and nineteenth centuries may be regretted, they are no longer practicable as an instrument of popular government. In historical fact such traditions were probably rooted in the existence of a comparatively small ruling group trusted by the electorate as a social elite. Nowadays, everyone feels entitled to discuss details of public business, and legislatures are no longer revered as repositories of political wisdom.

Party discipline is not a means for stifling debate, at least among free peoples. On the contrary, it throws discussion of vital policies open to the whole community. The outlines of legislative action have to be threshed out on the constituency level and are not confined within the walls of a legislative chamber. All the media of public communication—press, periodicals, radio and television commentators—play their part in a continuing discussion influencing the votes of legislators. Responsibility on the party level makes nation-wide debate possible; unless the individual legislator is prepared to stand up and be counted along party lines, effective popular control of lawmaking is seriously diminished. Representative assemblies remain an important part of the discussion process, serving as the final adjudicators of public arguments that would lack meaning if they were not brought to a final determination in legislative action.

The degree of party discipline required to implement general discussion by positive action varies among the different systems of government. Thus, in presidential systems, such as that of the United States, Congress is not responsible for the fate of the administration or even for the initiation of legislative or financial policy. Consequently, party members in Congress possess considerable freedom to take independent action individually or in groups outside the party line. They are unlikely to have to answer to the electorate for the overthrow of the government or a paralysis in policy making. Parliamentary regimes, on the other hand, are based on the strictest form of party loyalty. The fate of an administration and the ordering of an immediate general election may turn on the defection of a few votes within the majority party. In Communist lands party discipline is the bedrock on which the state itself is founded; defying the party line is viewed as treason.

The Power to Investigate

Society is ordered through laws, and in consequence the power to make or change laws amounts to command over the social structure of a nation. Representative bodies may not act blindly or in ignorance to change the ways of the community without risking destruction of the state. The concept of legislative power implies a power to gather the needed information. In the development of the English Parliament, the American colonial legislatures, and the Congress of the United States, the existence of this investigatory authority has never been challenged, though its scope in practice remains controversial. Danger of encroachment by the legislative arm on judicial functions arises when Congress or any other representative body forces testimony from individuals or groups under threat of punishment. An important element in the rule of law is abrogated when individual citizens are forced to disclose their private affairs outside the orderly procedures of courts of law. Throughout history, abuses of the inquisitorial power are notorious, and elected representatives have no special immunity against sharing in this form of ill-doing. In modern times, lawmaking impinges on the most complicated economic and social patterns of society. Consequently, the efficiency of methods used to obtain an essential background of complete and specialized information largely determines standards of legislative policy.

One of the two major approaches to the problem may be associated with a presidential system of government, the other with traditional parliamentary systems. Where a separation of powers exists, legislatures claim exclusive rights to investigatory processes connected with lawmaking. They create special committees composed of their own members endowed with wide legal powers and ample funds to roam the country, gather information, and summon and examine witnesses. In this practice they are not hindered by rules of court procedure for the protection of individual rights, nor are the Congressional inquisitors liable to actions for damages for libel, false accusation, or any other wrong suffered by those appearing before them. A cloak of Congressional immunity covers members of a legislative investigatory committee wherever they may choose to travel within the borders of the nation. Of course, such untrammeled powers have been and always will be abused. Nevertheless, the public interest requires that a sovereign legislature should possess absolute power to probe into every aspect of community affairs relevant to its responsibilities as the maker of laws. The Supreme Court in the United States has wrestled with the problem presented by the tyrannization by investigating Committees of individual citizens on many occasions, and its answers are still indeterminate. Mr. Justice Van Devanter gave the pith of the matter in a famous judgment.

A legislative body cannot legislate wisely or effectively in the absence of information respecting the conditions which the legislation is intended to effect or change; and where the legislative body does not itself possess the requisite information—which not infrequently is true—recourse must be had to others who do possess it. Experience has taught that mere requests for such information often are unavailing, and also, that information which is volunteered is not always accurate or complete; so that some means of compulsion are essential to obtain what is needed. . . .[2]

Parliamentary forms of government, particularly those within the British Commonwealth, have evolved a different type of legislative investigation, based on the closer relations existing between the legislature and the executive. Instead of entrusting complicated surveys of economic or social matters to committees composed of members of the legislature, the Government of the day chooses expert bodies on a nonpartisan basis. These are generally known as Royal Commissions of Enquiry, and the Cabinet is responsible for their quality to Parliament. This method of handling large-scale investigations safeguards against unfair treatment of private parties or interest groups; a convention has arisen that either a learned judge or expert scholar should serve as chairman of a Royal Commission. Furthermore, once such a Royal Commission has made its report, Parliament and the electorate expect the Government to implement it by legislation or make public explanation of their rejection of the findings of their own commission. On the other hand, both the legislative chamber and the administration may find themselves by-passed through the presentation of an impartial report carrying a message directly to the general public. An example of this was the Report of the Royal Commission on the Coal Mining Industry in Great Britain. Mr. Justice Sankey, as Chairman of the Commission, gave his name to one of the most thorough surveys of a national industry ever conducted. To the acute embarrassment of the Conservative Government that had appointed the commission, the Sankey Report recommended nationalization of the coal-mining industry. At the time, this represented a radical innovation in British politics. Though the administration of the day rejected the findings, they found favor with the electorate. As a consequence subsequent Parliaments were forced to implement them, thus opening the door to the nationalization of key industries as a major trend in public policy. To some extent, the expert investigating commission, once appointed, becomes a force in the formation of legislative policy independent of Parliament or the administration. An interested and well-informed electorate is capable of reviewing its findings and putting pressure on Parliament to implement them through legislation. In this way, opportunity is provided to debate definitive matters of national policy beyond the walls of the legislative chamber.

Influence of Legislatures on the Conduct of Policy

Perhaps the most complicated aspect of the operation of legislative bodies is that which touches on their power over the daily conduct of public affairs. Separation of responsibilities between legislative and executive organs may exist without providing any clear division of powers. Thus, in the American system Congress may intervene in many of the actions of the administration through its ability to grant or deny funds for the carrying out of any specific policy. The Federal Bureau of Investigation, for example, starting in comparatively humble circumstances, rapidly won the favor of the Appropriations Committees of both Houses of Congress. Successive administrations in consequence have found it politically and administratively desirable to extend the responsibilities of the FBI into a great many fields. In contrast, more controversial bodies, such as the Atomic Energy Commission, are made subject to Congressional pressures limiting their expansion or efficiency as instruments of administration policy.

Congress also possesses a Constitutional power to reorganize executive departments, abolishing or creating bureaus in any manner it may think fit. Career advancement for senior members of the civil service is, in consequence, seriously affected by Congressional actions. In practice, this results in the building up of close liaison between bureaucrats and powerful Congressmen, particularly the chairmen and members of important committees. Bureau leaders of the sprawling administrative machinery frequently find themselves subject to double authority: the formal command of the President or department head on one hand, and the informal power of a Congressional committee on the other. The end result may be administrative actions which are a compromise between Executive policy and Congressional interference. In any case, the infiltration of legislative views into the daily control of public business is an established fact. Probably the least desirable feature of this system is the breach made in a clear chain of responsibility to the general electorate. Voters are seldom aware when selecting representatives that they are endowing them with administrative authority. The President is the only official clearly chosen for this purpose. Behind-the-scenes influence, however well used, is essentially irresponsible.

Parliamentary systems in general avoid confusion of authority by giving executive and legislative leadership to the same body of men. This does not necessarily diminish the power of the legislature as a whole over the practical conduct of public affairs;

it merely shifts the brunt of legislative intervention in policy matters from the shoulders of subordinate officials to the top leadership group. A prime minister or any other minister has to justify his own actions and those of his subordinates from day to day on the floor of the legislature. If he is insensitive to the views of powerful groups within the legislative body, his tenure of office is likely to be short. As in a presidential system, compromise between the will of the Executive and the opinions of the legislature normally determines the course of administrative policy. Perhaps parliamentary systems, particularly those in multiparty countries such as Italy or France, allow for more compromise than is compatible with efficient government. A determined presidential leader, secure in tenure of his office and capable of appealing over the heads of the legislature to the people directly, may introduce a measure of purpose and direction into government unobtainable under any other system. In general, legislative-executive relationships belong to the craft of politics as a profession or art; they are seldom under direct control by the bulk of the electorate, and they serve as a reminder that public as well as private business must be conducted in terms of rules common to all corporate structures.

Legislatures as a Channel of Communication

Opportunity for the ordinary citizen to participate in the process of government depends upon a flow of information couched in terms related to his personal affairs. Administrative organs tend to treat members of the general community as "subjects" of government, persuading or ordering them along lines of predetermined policy. Representatives, on the other hand, are inclined to consult with local communities, if for no higher reason than to ensure their own reëlection. The element of democracy in Western government owes its existence to this interdependency between national legislatures and local opinion. In practice, a considerable part of the time and energy of the members of a legislative body is devoted to this liaison work. Constituents have to be kept informed of governmental happenings, not merely in general terms but in relation to the specific problems and outlook of their communities. It is the business of the representative to understand the pattern of local affairs and to explain the effects of national policies on the particular community situation. In order to do this, a representative must act as a personal focus for the complaints and wishes of individuals or organized groups within his constituency. Though it may not be in his power to satisfy many requests, it is always his duty to communicate them to proper authorities or to explain to his constituents why their needs may not be met. In the operation of this vital function, a representative is in no way obligated to subordinate his own judgment to the demands of segments of his electorate. However, he is obligated to explain and interpret, thus providing an informed link between the individual citizen and the inner processes of government.

Government leadership is dependent, by the same token, upon the individual representative as a specialized interpreter of popular desires and reactions. The consent of the people to government policies is a meaningless abstraction until it has been broken down into the responses of innumerable neighborhoods. There can be no substitute for the elected representative as communicator of the pattern of political feeling within his electoral district. Even totalitarian systems find it useful to maintain an apparatus of representative bodies to enable rulers to obtain accurate information concerning popular attitudes. With the growth in the extent and complexity of modern government, the operation of representative assemblies as liaison bodies between ruling officialdom and the unorganized community has increased in significance. It is in this aspect of their work that the quality of the individual legislator counts most heavily. Leadership and corporate organization may predominate throughout a great part of the operations of legislative bodies. However, as an instrument of communication a representative assembly functions as a gathering of independent personalities. Recourse to a personal representative rather than an impersonal organization is a major privilege of citizens of free countries. Though political parties also supply important means of communication between government and people, they parallel and supplement, rather than replace, the indispensable representative. The quality of personality, freely chosen by the locality, and surrounded by an aura of constitutional responsibility, belongs to the legislator, brought every few years to the democratic test of election.

Notes

[1] Farrand, Max, *Records of the Federal Convention of 1787,* New Haven: Yale, 1911, Vol. I, p. 410.
[2] *McGrain v. Daugherty,* 273 U.S. 135 (1927).

Supplementary Readings

Bailey, Sydney D. (ed.), *Parliamentary Government in the Commonwealth,* London: Hansard Society, 1951.

———, *Parliamentary Government in Southern Asia; a Survey of Developments in Burma, Ceylon, India, and Pakistan 1947–1952,* New York: American Institute of Pacific Relations, 1953.

Cole, Taylor, and others, *European Political Systems,* New York: Knopf, 1953.

Galloway, George B., *Congress and Parliament; Their Organization and Operation in the U.S. and U.K.,* Washington: National Planning Association, 1955.

———, *The Legislative Process in Congress,* New York: Crowell, 1953.

Gledhill, Alan, *The Republic of India; the Development of its Laws and Constitution,* London: Stevens, 1952.

Gordon, Strathearn, *The British Parliament,* New York: Praeger, 1953.

Griffith, Ernest S., *Congress, Its Contemporary Role,* New York: New York University Press, 1951.

Hazard, J. N., *The Soviet System of Government,* Chicago: University of Chicago Press, 1957.

Ilbert, Sir Courtenay, *Parliament,* New York: Holt, 1911.

Jennings, Sir Ivor, *Cabinet Government,* London: Cambridge, second edition, 1951.

———, *Parliament,* London: Cambridge, second edition, 1951.

Lidderdale, D. W. S. *The Parliament of France,* London: Hansard Society, 1951.

Marriott, J. A. R., *Second Chambers; an Inductive Study in Political Science,* London: Oxford, new edition revised, 1927.

Walker, Harvey, *The Legislative Process,* New York: Ronald, 1948.

Young, Roland, *The American Congress,* New York: Harper, 1958.

Chapter 7

The Legal Order

On a final analysis, the association of men in a political state is made possible through the habit of obedience. This is an ingrained human disposition that has manifested itself throughout history. Among peoples lacking in political organization it has taken the form of taboo, a semireligious control over individual conduct. More advanced societies have embodied the need for standards of obedience in a legal order. In this respect it may be claimed that the state is the creature of law.

The Nature of Law

For many centuries attempts have been made to reduce the nature of law into terms of a single definition. Since Plato and Aristotle, philosophers have struggled with the relationship between law and justice, contributing greatly to our insight into human nature and behavior but never reaching conclusions that have won general acceptance. Rulers have erected long-lasting systems of government on their own dogmatic definitions. One of the most famous examples is that of the Emperor Justinian, codifier of the law of Rome: "Whatever has pleased the Prince has the force of law, since the Roman people by the *lex regia* enacted concerning his imperium, have yielded up to him all their power and authority."[1] Lawyers possess what might be described as working definitions for the particular form of law in which they are engaged. One of the best known of these identifies laws as "rules of civil conduct enforced by the state." On the whole, generalized definitions of law are unenlightening and tend to be misleading if used out of context. What is known is that human society is founded on man's leanings toward order and obedience, that order normally expresses itself through rules, and that various methods of formulating and enforcing those rules have been practiced throughout history.

When applying the concept of law to modern societies under representative systems of government, a particular definition may be borrowed from the writings of the American jurisprudent, Dean Pound. "It [the legal order] is a regime of social control—the regime of adjusting relations and ordering conduct by the systematic and orderly application of the force of a politically organized society."[2] It is noteworthy that Dean Pound limits the concept of the legal order to social control. In times past, law tended to be identified with divine guidance, thus producing a rigid and inflexible political organization. The secularization of law has been an important factor in the development of the modern nation–state. The need to keep law separate from the dictates of religion or the intricacies of private conscience was well expressed by the seventeenth-century Marquess of Halifax:

> . . . a Divine groweth less, and putteth a diminution on his own character, when he quoteth any Law but that of God Almighty, to get the better of those who contend with him. . . . So it looketh like want of health in a Church, when instead of depending upon the power of that Truth which it holdeth, and the good Examples of them that teach it, to support itself, and to suppress Errors, it should have a perpetual recourse to the secular Authority, and even upon the slightest occasions.[3]

The policeman's club is an inadequate means of asserting spiritual values.

Furthermore, regarding law as a means of social control indicates certain internal limitations to the lawmaking and law-enforcing process within a political state. It is obvious that there are areas of human experience, cultural as well as religious, where the arbitrary will of the body politic has scant right to trespass. Individuality and an all-embracing legal order are incompatible ideas. Western civilization has come to look upon law as a defender of individual liberty rather than the absolute master of conduct.

The Doctrine of Legal Rights

The American Constitution would be a crippled instrument of government if it did not include its famous Bill of Rights. The first ten Amendments are a token of the strong faith of the people that law in its supreme sense existed to enhance and not diminish their liberties. Thomas Jefferson believed that rights are both inherent and inalienable, and he was bold enough to number the pursuit of happiness among them. This is still a meaningful statement, as Western man might be distinguished from his Soviet contemporary on the ground that he is unwilling to exchange the subtleties of personal enjoyment for an authorized, official version of social happiness. When legal rights serve as operative patterns in a political order, the individual remains free to develop fully as a human being in terms of his personal capacities. As the English political philosopher T. H. Green expressed it:

> In analyzing the nature of any right we may conveniently look at it on two sides and consider it as on the one hand a claim of the individual, arising out of his rational nature, to the free exercise of some faculty; on the other as a concession of that claim by society, a power given by it to the individual of putting the claim in force.[4]

An American point of view may be taken from a judgment by Supreme Court Justice Field:

> The theory upon which our political institutions rest is, that all men have certain unalienable rights—that among these are life, liberty, and the pursuit of happiness; and that in the pursuit of happiness all avocations, all honors, all positions, are alike open to everyone, and that in the protection of these rights all are equal before the law.[5]

There is an ancient legal maxim that there can be no right without a remedy. It is the business of a legal order to provide substance to public and private rights through the creation of adequate remedies. Arbitrary systems of government such as those of Communist Russia and China do not hesitate to list in their constitutions imposing declarations concerning rights their citizens are presumed to enjoy. These rights remain for the most part theoretical, as no provisions are included for their enforcement beyond the whim of officials. On the other hand, within Western democracies a legal system or order is embodied in the constitution of the land to balance the workings of political authority upon the liberty of the individual. Government is rule under the law as well as by means of the law. To ensure this concept, interpretation of law has to be separated to a certain extent from political decision-making and administrative practices.

Independence of the Judiciary

Among English-speaking peoples the maintenance of an independent judiciary has become a favored bulwark of the rule of law. Judges play a key part in the application of law because a rule made by the legislature does not become operative until it has been translated into a judgment of a court in a specific case. Accordingly it has been suggested in recent times that law is in reality "judge-made," legislatures and other bodies playing only a formal or secondary role. A sober statement of this point of view may be found in the writings of Judge Jerome Frank: "Rules, whether stated by judges or others, whether in statutes, opinions, or textbooks by learned authors, are not the Law, but are only some among many of the sources judges go to in making the law of the cases tried before them."[6] This Realist school of law appears somewhat extreme. What Mr. Justice Cardozo called the "judicial process" is a more subtle act which stops somewhere short of permitting an individual judge or bench of judges to create law out of their personal imaginings.

In the first place, the bench as a whole is a single body organized under a hierarchical discipline. On the national level, the Supreme Court may reverse any decision of a lower federal court; further, the Supreme Court may and does reverse itself. Besides being subjected to scrutiny by his colleagues, the idiosyncrasies of any particular judge are limited by the profession to which he belongs. Bench, bar and law school form integral parts of what used to be known as the mystery of law—a pattern of thinking, or perhaps even mental conditioning, that disciplines the outlook of the initiate in a manner analogous to religious faith. The veteran jurist Justice Learned Hand has summed up the true status of the judiciary:

JUDICIAL SYSTEM OF THE UNITED STATES — PRESENT ORGANIZATION

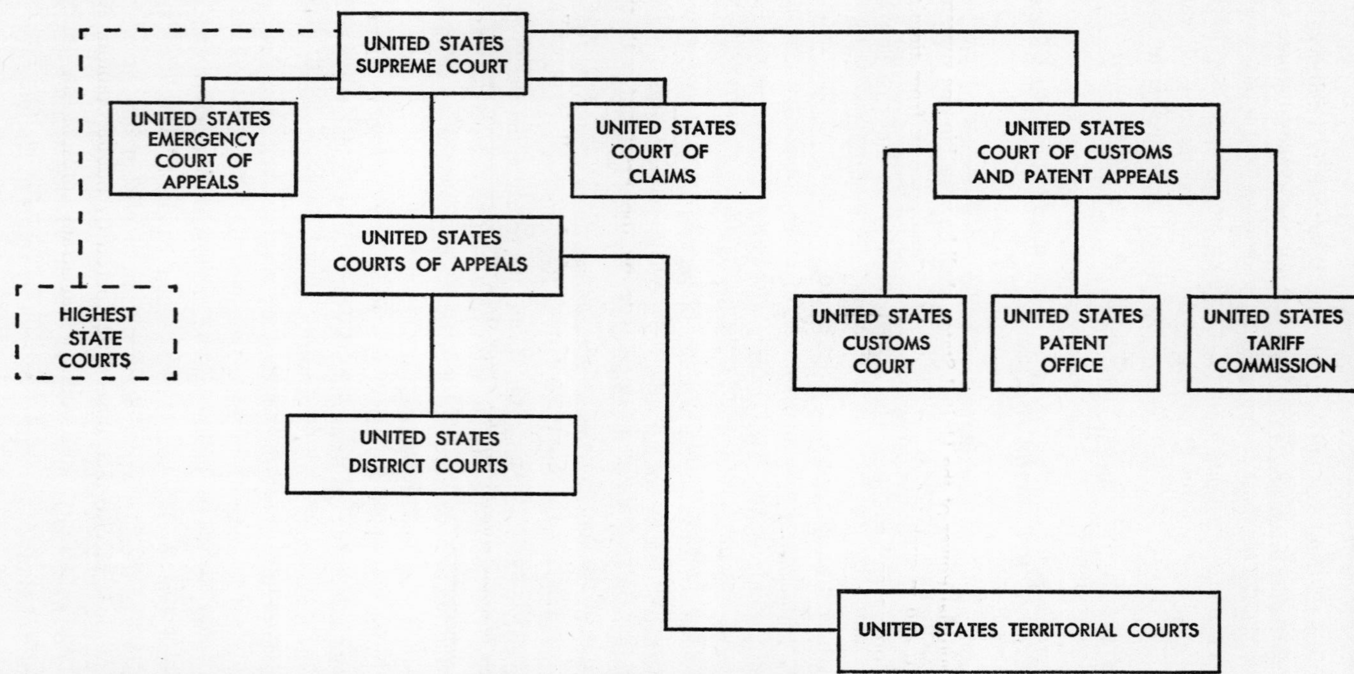

Source: Leon Schneider, *A Guide to Court Systems,* New York: Institute of Judicial Administration, 1957.

The price of their continued power must therefore be a self-denying ordinance which forbids change in what has not already become unacceptable. To compose inconsistencies, to unravel confusions, to announce unrecognized implications, to make, in Holmes' now hackneyed phrase, "interstitial" advances; these are the measure of what they may properly do, and there is not indeed much danger of their exceeding this limit; rather the contrary, for they are curiously timid about innovations.[7]

Article III, Section 1, of the Constitution of the United States declares that

The judicial Power of the United States, shall be vested in one supreme Court, and in such inferior Courts as the Congress may from time to time ordain and establish. The Judges, both of the supreme and inferior Courts, shall hold their offices during good Behaviour, and shall, at stated Times, receive for their Services a Compensation, which shall not be diminished during their Continuance in Office.

In these terse sentences a separation of powers was created between the judiciary and the other arms of the government. Of course, the independence of the judiciary is by no means absolute —all judicial appointments are made by the President with the consent of the Senate. Further, Congress retains a Constitutional right to deprive the Supreme Court of almost all its appellate powers whenever the legislature may see fit. In fact, in the heat of the feelings roused by the Civil War, Congress withdrew appellate jurisdiction from the Court when it was actually hearing a case, forcing the judges to dismiss the case for lack of jurisdiction. However, the actualities of judicial independence have won favor with the American people: even President Franklin D. Roosevelt at the height of his popularity found it advisable to withdraw an apparent threat to the autonomy of the Supreme Court.

On the local level, the judiciary is normally separated from legislative and executive control, but its independence is qualified by requirements of popular election. This is an almost peculiarly American custom, reflecting traditional distrust of the operation of law on a face-to-face basis untempered by public opinion. Accordingly, the city and county magistracy present an uneasy compromise between strict legal interpretation and the "People's

Courts" of revolutionary democracies. Historically, the system may be considered vestigial of the revolutionary origins of the nation.

In Britain, an austere independence for the judiciary is preserved through a binding convention of the unwritten Constitution. The courts of justice are presided over by the Queen's Judges who form a disciplined hierarchy at all levels. A remnant of popular justice remains in Quarter Sessions Courts, limited to dealing with petty criminal offenses. These tribunals consist of appointed Justices of the Peace, many of whom lack any formal legal training. In former times, they constituted a method of class control, the local squire-archy or men of wealth monopolizing the authority that could banish members of the lower orders to the colonies for poaching and minor infractions of the law. Today, a part-time magistrate, a practicing member of the bar called a Recorder, frequently guides a Sessions Court. The integration of the whole judicial system into the general government of the land is accomplished in England by the favorite native device of giving a man three hats to wear. In this case, the key individual is the Lord Chancellor, the presiding judge of the highest court, the House of Lords. This personage also holds, in general, the appointing power for the judiciary, a power that he exercises in practice in consultation with the other senior judges. Besides this, he is an active politician, serving in the Cabinet, presiding over the House of Lords in its political form, and subject to dismissal when the Government to which he belongs loses office. The convention that keeps this politician-minister-judge functioning smoothly in all his capacities, though peculiar to the English temperament has worked well enough over several centuries. Perhaps because judges are appointed for life and the bar from which they are drawn is a powerfully organized national body, the temptation to play politics with the courts seldom besets a Lord Chancellor.

European countries following the tradition of Roman law rather than Anglo-American precepts of common law achieve the independence of the judiciary through other means. In France, for example, a Ministry of Justice is part of the framework of government. Judges are appointed and promoted through the ministry, entering the judicial profession immediately after leaving law school, without establishing a reputation by the practice of advocacy. Their careers, then, are at the mercy of government officials, and personal independence is questionable. Their function is to interpret strictly a body of law that has been codified from the great principles of Roman law into the Code Napoléon. The principles and even details of the law are so clearly set out that neither legislators nor administrators may interfere without exposing themselves to public wrath. It is justifiable, accordingly, to consider European judges as possessed of a functional independence equivalent in practice to the personal independence of the judiciary in English-speaking lands.

Marxist-Leninist theory has slight place for law and none for an independent court system. Soviet Russia and her imitators attempted to root out the ancient tradition of law through what they called "socialist justice" applied by People's Courts. In the early days of the revolution these resembled the Committees of Public Safety that fed the tumbrils of the French Revolution. With the bureaucratization of Communism a professional court system has been revived. In outward form this now approaches that of other European countries. What remains lacking is a legal code—not a Party code—created by consent of the people and unalterable except through representative expressions of their genuine will. Until this is achieved—in other words until the Russian people have a true say in their own affairs—the elaborate system of courts is merely another instrument in the hands of the Party oligarchy.

Due Process of Law

The patterns, rituals and forms of law as an historical and rational process rank second only to the independence of the courts as safeguards of rights. A concept of law as a way of life is not easy to communicate to those who have not been subjected to the discipline of legal training. It should be recognized, however, that law represents an approach to human problems as distinctive as that of medicine or theology. Enjoyment of individual rights within organized society may take place only in terms of patterns prescribed by law. Access to law undistorted in substance or procedures is therefore vital to the preservation of personal liberty. In English-speaking countries a long battle has been fought to keep the law above politics, executive tyranny, or the prejudices of those in power. The ancient cry in England for justice according to "the law of the land" has been echoed in America through the companion phrase "due process of law." The fifth and fourteenth Amendments to the Constitution of the United States prescribe that no person shall be deprived of life, liberty, or property without due process of law. This prohibition is aimed at both the general and State governments.

The exact structure of "due process" is a changing concept that requires highly skilled legal learning to decipher in any particular instance. However, the relation of due process to the preservation of the rule of law is everybody's business. Mr. Justice Mathews has described it in terms that are valid for all English-speaking lands.

> It is not every act, legislative in form, that is law. Law is something more than mere will exerted as an act of power. It must not be a special rule for a particular person or a particular case, but, in the language of Mr. Webster, in his familiar definition, "the general law, a law which hears before it condemns, which proceeds upon inquiry, and renders judgment only after trial," so "that every citizen shall hold his life, liberty, property and immunities under the protection of the general rules which govern society," and thus excluding, as not due process of law, acts of attainder, bills of pains and penalties, acts of confiscation, acts reversing judgments and decrees, and other similar special, partial and arbitrary exertions of power under the forms of legislation. Arbitrary power, enforcing its edicts to the injury of the persons and property of its objects, is not law, whether manifested as the decree of a personal monarch or of an impersonal multitude. And the limitations imposed by our constitutional law upon the action of the governments, both State and national, are essential to the preservation of public and private rights, notwithstanding the representative character of our political institutions. The enforcement of these limitations by judicial process is the device of self-governing communities to protect the rights of individuals and minorities, as well against the power of numbers as against the violence of public agents transcending the limits of lawful authority, even when acting in the name and wielding the force of the government.[8]

JUDICIAL REVIEW The means through which due process of law is maintained against encroachment by the executive or legislative powers of government in the United States and other nations patterned on its federal system is that of judicial review. The functioning of this power in the United States and elsewhere has been discussed previously. However, it should be noted that courts seldom find it necessary to challenge the constitutionality of measures that emanate from a national legislature. Indeed, if this was a common practice a clash between the judicial and legislative powers would become unavoidable. Effective judicial review is normally operative on the level of State and local enactments, and above all serves as a scrutiny of the actions of officials, federal or State, who interfere with the liberty of a citizen under pretext of enforcing the laws. Thus, in Britain, though courts lack the power of judicial review over Acts of Parliament, they possess it in full measure over the rules promulgated by local bodies. The behavior of any British official from Minister of the Crown to policeman is also accountable to the Courts. Under the ancient writ of *quo warranto* (by what right or warrant) any official may be compelled to spell out the exact statutory or constitutional justification for his actions before a tribunal of law.

European countries that operate under codes founded on the principles of Roman law use the device of *administrative law* and *administrative courts* to protect the rights of citizens against infringement by government officials. Such courts may be regarded as disciplinary bodies employing special rules distinct from the ordinary law of the land to reconcile individual rights with governmental necessities and practices. In some respects administrative courts provide more flexible and practical remedies against governmental malpractices than do the cumbersome procedures of regular law courts. However, administrative law possesses one major weakness as compared with constitutional safeguards: The legislature of the day may alter its rules at will, thus imperiling fundamental rights of the citizenry for the sake of political expediency. A distinction should be drawn between the European concept of administrative law *(droit administratif)* and the growing use of the term "administrative law" in the United States and Britain to describe the law relating to public administration, particularly with respect to government commissions, such as the Interstate Commerce Commission, exercising quasi-legislative, quasi-judicial functions. These administrative determinations and orders approximate legal judgments in practice, but their exact position in the constitutional structure of Britain and the United States is still a matter of controversy.

Forms of Law

A major division of the legal orders to be found in the world is between those that are organized around *codes* and those that follow the principles of *common law*.

Nations that inherit a Latin tradition have shown themselves partial to modern adaptations of the Code of the Emperor Justinian, the *Corpus Juris Civilis* promulgated around A.D. 535 as a working summary of the great principles of Roman law. The new Islamic nations, Pakistan, Indonesia, and the United Arab Republic, favor codes based on the Koran and its commentaries. A distinguishing characteristic of a code is the emphasis it places on principles—philosophic, religious or moral. The duty of the judge is to apply a given principle in a logical manner to the particular case before him. Theoretically at least an answer to any legal problem may be found by diligent search of the authorized code.

English-speaking countries—Scotland excepted—lean toward the system known as the common law. This has been described as learned law, lawyers' law, or taught law. Its distinguishing feature is that it is based on a long history of the decisions of the courts, starting with the Year Books of the thirteenth century. One of the major values of common law lies in its relation to the customs of the community. Before the days of true statutory law, judges settled cases by inquiring into the customs of the community governing the particular situation. If an "ancient and good custom" was found to be applicable it formed the basis of a judgment which in turn became a precedent for other judges to follow. In technical legal language the matter had become *stare decisis.* This flavor of custom, of molding law to the habits and usages of the people, has never deserted the Anglo-American legal order. Though statutes have now usurped a great part of the field of legal relationships, laws passed by legislatures are in themselves a synthesis of customary doctrines and modern adaptations. The tradition of common law is something more than an historical accident—it stands for a stubborn belief that law stems from the practices of the community and not from ideological principles.

PUBLIC AND PRIVATE LAW Rules of law that control the internal organization of governmental institutions and the relations of officers of government to individual citizens may be conveniently described as *public law. Private law,* by contrast, concerns itself with relationships among individuals. Though convenient, the distinction is somewhat equivocal. Private relationships are seldom truly private in the sense that they lie outside the control or interest of government. All law may be said to be public in so far as it rests on the authority of the political state. However, the concept of private law emphasizes an important aspect of government: its availability to the ordinary individual as a means of furthering his personal interests. A commonplace of democracy that government exists for the benefit of the individual achieves meaningful focus in the application of private legal rights. Through the free exercise of his talents and energies an individual creates a network of relationships with his fellows. The impartial machinery of law backed by the force of government provides a means to profit from such relationships within a stable social order. An analogy may be drawn between "law power" and horsepower as instruments to increase the well-being of individuals. Their availability makes possible a great extension of the skills and force of the individual to the extent that he possesses the ability and will to make use of them. A concept of free enterprise is involved, as the competitive standard of the citizen determines his power to utilize these passive forces. In communities where government orders all major activities, the significance of private law declines. Accordingly, the extent and scope of private law in any particular country is a good measure of the role of the state as a service institution in contrast to its position as master of the people.

CIVIL AND CRIMINAL LAW The type of law that aids and assists the voluntary activities of individuals is termed *civil law* in English-speaking lands. Some confusion may arise over the use of this term, as Civil Law (capitalized) is also employed to denote forms of law based on the Roman *Corpus Juris Civilis.* In civil-law matters, government, having promulgated the rules, acts in the capacity of arbiter between the private parties. Thus when two people choose to make an agreement with each other they may take advantage of the contractual forms provided by the law of the land. In such a case the courts settle any differences between the parties according to set rules, backing up their decisions with the force of government.

Criminal law tells the individual what he may not do, and government is always an interested party. It is perhaps unfortunate that no universal definition of a crime exists; every political regime remains free to list at will forms of behavior it considers deserving of punishment. In common-law countries custom plays an important part in integrating criminal law with the general attitudes of the community. Thus, in the United States national and State governments can and do pass laws concerning the transmission or possession of obscene publications or objects. What is obscene, however, is not a matter of legislative definition or left to the fiat of some official. The courts determine the nature of obscenity according to the rules of the common law, a heritage of precedent and changing custom. Similarly, in countries that operate under codes, whether Roman, Islamic, or Marxist, a government of the day must tailor its criminal offenses to the principles that underlie their respective codes. Otherwise the pattern and machinery of law will be thrown out of gear.

Nevertheless there exists between individual liberty and political definitions of crime a borderline that free peoples require be guarded by their constitutions. Bills of Rights serve as principal instruments for this purpose. In the United States the First Amendment, as reinforced by the Fourteenth Amendment, forbids national or State government to treat as criminal offenses acts essential to the exercise of free speech or free assembly. However, law as a pattern of social control remains vulnerable on this point; legislatures have in the past imposed, and are likely to continue in the future to impose, tyrannical restrictions on private behavior through the creation of new crimes. Historically speaking, it is not so long ago that failure to attend Sabbath services at church was punishable as a crime. Many States still carry on their statute books "blue laws" that run counter to popular feeling, habits, and convenience. The final remedy lies not in law itself but in the wider field of representative government. So long as a community exercises true control over its legislative bodies, the concept of crime will approximate generally held moral and social attitudes. The surrender of such control to an ideological party or an authoritarian personality entails reversion to political infancy, with personal behavior subject to the undisputed will of the parent state.

EQUITY The common law, now shared by most English-speaking countries, had its historical origins in thirteenth-century England. Its early procedures developed in a manner too rigid to meet all social needs. As justice, above and beyond law (or rather legal procedures), was still held the province of the Crown, the king delegated to his chancellor the duty of hearing cases and righting wrongs that could not be reached by the formal processes of common law. This Court of Equity was basically a "court of conscience," the conscience of the ruler.

It is unnecessary to trace here how the rules of equity became as rigid as the rules of common law and how eventually, in both England and America, courts of equity were merged with courts of law. What remains in action today of this form of law is a type of procedure—and, one might add, a judicial license—that differs in quality from the general pattern of law. An example might be taken from the use of Injunction, a remedy in equity now open to any court of record. An *injunction* is an order by a judge addressed to someone to refrain from doing something. It might be described as a judicial anticipation of illegality that places the judgment before the trial. As a preventive measure against irreparable wrong it is a flexible and speedy instrument; it is also a dangerous one, as it may involve the court's prejudgment of a situation not yet fully disclosed by all the parties concerned under strict rules of evidence. What is of importance in relation to general government is the added flavor that rules of equity have given to the position of the judge in Anglo-American society. The social and personal consciences of judges become factors in the social struggles of the day when the judges are in a position to paralyze actions of individuals or groups by pretrial orders. Thus the rise of organized labor in the early part of the twentieth century found courts in the United States confused on how to handle startling departures from the old principles of the law of master and servant. Congress had to intervene with the Clayton Act (1914) and the Norris-La

Guardia Act (1932), which greatly restricted the use of injunctions by federal courts in labor disputes. Equity in many of its principles and remedies still serves as a humanizing influence on legal procedures; at the same time, it tempts judges to act beyond their true competence, thereby imperiling the delicate balance of judicial independence.

The Administration of Justice

The legal order assumes institutional form in a system of courts and the network of officials associated with trial procedures. A major distinction may be drawn between countries in which the legal order is highly centralized under a political ministry of justice and nations where greater judicial autonomy and local self-control prevails. The United States and most English-speaking lands fall into the latter category. In general this means that the courts order their own affairs, treating public officers, such as district attorneys and public prosecutors, as officers of the court and not as independent authorities. The link between one court and another is the chain of appeal rather than the personal subordination of a lower judge to a higher court. *Appeal* means that the findings of one court on the law of a case are subject to review and perhaps reversal by another court. For example, the Supreme Court of the United States may hear on appeal cases brought forward from the Supreme Courts of the several States when the supreme law of the land is involved. Article VI, Section 2, of the Constitution declares that

> this Constitution, and the Laws of the United States which shall be made in Pursuance thereof; and all Treaties made, or which shall be made, under the Authority of the United States, shall be the supreme Law of the Land; and the Judges in every State shall be bound thereby, any Thing in the Constitution or Laws of any State to the Contrary notwithstanding.

State court systems are not thereby subordinated to a federal court organization; all that is implied is that the existence of a supreme law of the land requires a final interpreter. It is the character of the law itself that integrates the judiciary into a national pattern. Though the existence of a federal court system superimposed over the same communities and areas as fifty autonomous State court organizations adds confusion to the American judicial scene, it serves to hinder governmental interference with the judicial process.

In Britain, though court organization is on a single national basis, the interrelationship between the superior courts is almost as complicated as in the United States. Parliament has attempted in a series of Judicature Acts to bring order into a pattern of historic confusion. In theory, there is now one High Court of Justice, with divisions that hear original civil cases, appeal cases, and criminal cases. However, at least equal criminal jurisdiction also lies with the Central Criminal Court—the famous Old Bailey. Justices of the High Court separate themselves from the parent bench in London to tour the country periodically in circuit to hear civil or criminal cases according to the division they represent. They are followed by a train of London barristers maintaining a flavor of Chaucer's *Canterbury Tales* in the conduct of English justice. Scotland preserves a separate judicature of its own, headed by the Barons of the Court of Sessions. Though the bulk of law now stems from Acts of Parliament, Scots law still applies principles of Roman law in preference to English common law. The whole congeries is held together by the functioning of the House of Lords as a supreme Court of Appeal in civil cases and in some exceptional criminal cases. As a colonial empire or Commonwealth, Britain makes law for overseas peoples. A right of appeal lies from any colonial court to the Judicial Committee of the Privy Council in London. This body in its own sphere of jurisdiction is coequal with the House of Lords.

The apparent confusion of the court systems in English-speaking lands emphasizes the independence of the single judge, even at the expense of orderly administration. There is still meaning in the expression that a judge is an officer of justice and not an officer of government. In practice, though national judiciaries operate satisfactorily in this loose manner, organization of courts on a State and local basis is open to abuse. The custom of electing judges has degenerated in many American communities to a subordination of the judicial office to party patronage. Where courts are integrated into local political machinery, lack of supervision over the conduct of inferior judges by higher judicial authority gives rise to serious dangers. An elected judge, standing alone without the support of higher members of his profession, may find it difficult to resist pressures emanating from the party and administrative machinery to which he owes his election. If appointive methods are adopted on the local level, the integrity of the courts rests too heavily on the character of lesser officeholders possessed of the nominating power. Equal access to impartial courts of law has been described previously as essential to the maintenance of a free society of individuals. Failure of the machinery for the administration of justice to achieve this end results in distortion of the basic system of legal rights. In the United States, an unresolved question exists between the need for better protection of the administration of justice on the local level and the demands of the electorate for participation in every aspect of government.

France and most other European countries have equated judges with other civil servants under centralized governmental control. However, conceptions of professional judicial autonomy have increased in Europe since 1945. The 1958 Constitution of the French Republic provides an example. Title VIII of this Constitution declares that the President of the Republic, assisted by a High Council of the Judiciary, shall be the guarantor of the independence of the judicial authority. The High Council is given power to nominate judges for France's supreme court of appeal (the Court of Cassation) and the Presidents of the Appeal Courts. It also passes on the nominations of other judges by the Minister of Justice. Above all, it acts as a disciplinary council for judges. Thus, the power of the political minister and administrative officials over the judiciary as a whole has been tempered to a considerable extent. At the same time, the hierarchy of judicial officers controlled from above in regard to professional employment and advancement remains intact.

Soviet Court systems are untroubled by any need to serve as guardians of individual liberty. This permits them to be employed as straightforward instruments of Party policies. The Constitution of the U.S.S.R. favors in principle the election of judges. Thus, the Supreme Court of the Union is elected for a five-year term by the Supreme Soviet; similarly Supreme Courts of the autonomous Republics are elected by their respective legislatures. People's Courts on the local level are elected by the voters. In a one-party state election is synonymous with party choice, however conducted. There are indications that the Communist Party is finding its open control over court operations a two-sided weapon. The general community blames any arbitrary action of an official on the Party as a whole, who are judges in their own case. A growing tendency to legalism in governmental and administrative acts, while it safeguards the Party against criticism, may in the long run place almost autonomous authority in the hands of a professional Soviet judiciary.

LAW OFFICERS OF THE GOVERNMENT Where private law flourishes among free peoples, government, though possessed of a duty to provide its citizens with access to impartial courts for the settlement of their disputes and the provision of remedies, is not entitled to intervene further. However, government is itself a major party in innumerable law suits, civil as well as criminal. A legal apparatus has to be maintained by the government apart from the courts to look after its interests as prosecutor or claimant. In English-speaking lands, these law officers lack, or should lack, any control over the operation of the courts themselves. Government has no more right than an ordinary citizen to be judge of its own case. The United States has a Department of Justice, headed by the Attorney General of the United States, to carry out the legal business of the government. Each of the several States has its own Attorney General with equivalent functions relating to State law. The most important function of this hierarchy of law officers is to prosecute crimes and other breaches of law in the name of the government. Theoretically, their standing in court during the hearing of a case is no greater than that of a private attorney; for the purposes of trial, both are accounted officers of the court. However, public-law officers have the important function in relation to the administration of justice of deciding whether or not a case involving the government should or should not be brought to trial. In the whole field of law where penalties are at issue the prosecutor, down to the level of the local district attorney, must decide whether the private citizen should be placed in jeopardy of trial. This is a very significant power and its exercise colors the character of justice being administered.

Western nations may not be said to have solved this problem in a manner that guarantees individual citizens against bureaucratic persecution through the forms of law. Ambitious, biased, or naturally tyrannical prosecutors may be found under any system. Under American conditions, where the district attorney on the local level generally is an elected official involved in partisan politics, zeal to establish a "record" of convictions may distort the practice of filing charges as well as methods used to press accusations. In Britain, the Public Prosecutor or, in his Scots guise, the Procurator Fiscal, is an appointed official subject to the temptation of bureaucratic arrogance or a professional indifference to the human problems of individuals. The long-tested remedy of English-speaking peoples against careless exercise of powers of accusation and arrest lies in the courts themselves. An independent judiciary, unimpressed by official position, may and should treat prosecutors on the level of the accused as one of the parties to a case. They are strictly accountable for their actions to the Bench, and, in theory at least, any divagation from correct lawful procedures makes them liable in a civil suit. Perhaps British courts exercise more rigid discipline over law officers than is practicable for American judges involved in elective processes that require administrative and party support.

The legal order of European countries tends to integrate the prosecutor into the judicial hierarchy itself. Examining magistrates decide whether evidence suffices to bring cases to trial, and in each stage of criminal proceedings judges act as interrogators. To Anglo-Saxon eyes this destroys the principle that the accused must be assumed innocent by the court until the weight of evidence proves him guilty. The French and general European view is that the accused, once arrested, is in practical jeopardy and will benefit more by responsible and impartial prosecution than a theoretical assumption of innocence. The disciplined hierarchy of the judiciary itself and the freedom of juries to disregard opinions from the Bench protect against too great abuses.

Under Communist justice in the U.S.S.R., prosecution of offenses against the state is highly centralized under close Party control. The office of Procurator General is established by the same chapter in the Constitution as lays down the organization of the courts. This post, to which a man is elected for a seven-year term by the Supreme Soviet of the U.S.S.R., will go only to a high-ranking member of the Party. Once elected, he appoints all the regional Procurator Generals of the so-called autonomous Republics. A flat declaration is made in the Constitution that "the organs of the Procurator's Office perform their functions independently of any local organs whatsoever, being subordinate solely to the Procurator General of the U.S.S.R."[9] A nation-wide prosecutor's office with powers at least equal to Party-controlled courts is a logical development of anti-individualistic, state-centered justice. Communist theory, as has been previously pointed out, does not accept law as a manifestation of the traditions and customs of the community limiting the power of government. Rather, it equates law with the police power of the Party, establishing a police administration in preference to an administration of justice.

THE COST OF ACCESS TO THE COURTS It is unrealistic to assume that publicly operated courts of law in Western lands provide all individuals with equal opportunities to advance their legal rights. A suit at law is an expensive business that has to be paid for out of private funds. The ordinary citizen engaged in earning a livelihood may be well advised to keep out of the courts even though he has a valuable right at stake. Though government provides facilities open to everyone, in a competitive society they are open according to the actualities of life. Poverty may be as much a bar to the assertion of technical legal claims as it is to some forms of medical attention. Though this seems regrettable in terms of abstract justice, the alternative would require assertions of state power that might prove fatal to any economy based on free enterprise. Law founded on custom and tradition may not soar too far above accepted levels of competitive self-seeking. In the field of criminal jurisdiction, however, to impose disadvantages on individuals who lack funds strikes at the nature of government itself. Where the state is a party all must be treated equally or rule will pass into the hands of privileged oligarchies. The custom of court-appointed lawyers or public defenders is employed in most Western communities to meet this situation.

Perhaps the greatest obstacle to impartial administration of justice in Western lands arises not from lack of funds but through bias on the part of law officers and the courts themselves. In the United States this bias manifests itself principally against ethnic groups, such as Negroes or Spanish-speaking Americans. In European nations class distinctions create prejudice against the economically underprivileged, sometimes scarcely concealed by the professional class from whom lawyers and judges are drawn.

Some Consequences of a Legal Order

Some basic institutions of Western society are creatures of law whose functioning depends upon the quality of the legal order and its proper administration. Perhaps the most important of these is the institution of private property—one of the most commonly used, deeply revered, and least understood terms in our language. A lawyer's definition may be given: "By 'property' is meant, as the name implies, the result of the appropriation, or making 'proper' to one's-self, of some part of the resources of the universe."[10] Confusion invariably arises from identifying the subject matter of property with property itself. In essence, property is a relationship with other people concerning "goods," which may or may not be tangible, that is, capable of material existence. For example, copyright in a musical composition is a form of property. It is the pattern of law that establishes and maintains property as a social force, not any order of nature or political declaration. This was clearly envisaged by John Locke in the seventeenth century:

> The reason why men enter into society is the preservation of their property; and the end why they choose and authorise a legislative is that there may be laws made and rules set as guards and fences to the properties of all the members of the society, to limit the power and moderate the dominion of every part and member of the society.[11]

Locke's concept concerning the relationship of property to law and government greatly influenced the Founding Fathers at the time of the writing of the Constitution. James Madison saw the

The original copy of the American Constitution has acquired a measure of the sanctity once associated with the Crown and Scepter of monarchy. Carefully preserved in a dignified setting in the National Archives building in Washington, the document symbolizes, to the stream of pilgrims to the national seat of government, the Living Constitution, under which they live and prosper. *Monkmeyer Press Photo Service*

Constitutions

The constitutional bulwarks against arbitrary tyranny have been won by the English-speaking peoples step by step over a long historical period. The determination of a united people wrested the Great Charter from the shiftless King John. The preservation of these same rights has required a like determination and unified will from each succeeding generation down to the present day. *British Information Services*

The Nature of Political Office

In classical Greece the dignity of public office was symbolized in concrete fashion (detail showing the badge of authority, from a vase painting).

A present-day constitutional mon-arch at work—King Frederik IX of Denmark in his study at the Amalienborg Palace. *Danish Information Office, New York*

Office in early times was associated with leadership in war. The tribal King was raised to power on a warrior's shield (ninth century miniature from a Greek psalter). *The Bettmann Archive*

The President of the United States communicates personally with the whole people through press conferences. *Brown Brothers*

Systems of Representation

Below left: Direct participation in law-making by the assembled citizenry is still practiced in some areas. The citizens of the Swiss canton of Appenzell, gathered for the annual open-air town meeting, raise their hands in an oath to observe the laws they have just approved. In their left hands they hold swords, symbols of citizenship admitting them to the ancient ceremony. *Wide World Photos*

Below center: Voters in a polling station at Chelsea, London. British electoral procedure is simple and unhurried, as befits a people who have long enjoyed the right to vote. *Wide World Photos*

Above right: Soviet Russia observes all the forms of elections with great seriousness, though the choice offered the voters is negligible. The election official is checking names on voters' lists at a public polling station in Moscow during elections for the Supreme Soviet. *Wide World Photos*

Center right: Africa has joined Western democracies in the use of the secret ballot. A candidate for the Kenya Legislative Assembly is canvassing votes in a proximity to the polling station that would be frowned upon under American rules. *Wide World Photos*

Lower right: The use of the voting machine in the United States assists the voter dealing with lengthy and complicated ballots. *Monkmeyer Press Photo Service*

STATE
LEGISLATIVE
COUNTY
OFFICES
DEMOCRATIC →
DEMOCRATIC →
OFFICES
REPUBLICAN →
REPUBLICAN →

Above: The Anglo-Saxon Witan, a gathering of tribal leaders and learned men, advised the King concerning the nature of law. Though they did not legislate in our sense of the word, they declared and clarified existing customary law. Alfred the Great, one of the earliest literate Kings of England, is depicted in consultation with the Witan. *The Bettmann Archive*

Above right: The Parliament of Elizabeth I functioned as a true legislative body, separate (as in present-day America) from the executive power of the Throne. The engraving depicts the Queen opening Parliament from the throne in the House of Lords, while her faithful Commons stand at the Bar of the House to hear her speech. *British Information Services*

Right: A considerable part of the practical work of the Congress of the United States is carried out in Committee sessions. Illustrated is a public hearing of the Senate Crime Investigating Committee in Kansas City. *Wide World Photos*

Written law in early days was often a jealously guarded mystery of a priestly caste. A significant step in the growth of Western law was the public display of the sacred bronze tablets containing the Twelve Tables of Law of ancient Rome. *The Bettmann Archive*

The Legal Order

Left: British Courts of Law have always relied on the dignity and authority of an independent judiciary. One of the most respected and feared of their Courts is the Court of Criminal Justice at the Old Bailey. *The Bettmann Archive*

Below: The United States Supreme Court has proved a unique balance wheel in the operation of the American Constitutional system. The Court of 1888 (illustrated here), under Chief Justice Waite (center) interpreted the power to regulate commerce as extending to inventions unknown to the Founding Fathers. In the words of the Chief Justice, "They [the commerce powers] extend from the horse with its rider to the stagecoach, from the steamboat to the railroad, and from the railroad to the telegraph." *Wide World Photos*

emerging American nation as a composite of propertied interests, and was of the opinion that "the regulation of these various and interfering interests forms the principal task of modern legislation."[12] The significance of accepting property as the creature of law lies in the resulting integration of the economic, legal and political order. Realization of the inescapable nature of this integration was perhaps denied to Western society until the rise of Communist regimes in the Soviet empires of Russia and China. In these countries and their satellites, government has broken the pattern of law, substituting ideological definitions of property that have had the effect of changing the way of life of hundreds of millions of individuals. Thus the 1936 Constitution of the U.S.S.R. abolishes the private ownership of the instruments and means of production, and distinguishes three forms of permissible property: state property (belonging to the whole people); cooperative property (property of collective farms and cooperative societies); and personal property. The last is limited to income, savings, houses, and articles of personal use and convenience. In effect this reduces the individual to a tool of the state in so far as his economic activities are concerned. The danger of this form of tyranny is by no means confined to Communist lands. Wherever property is regarded as some form of inherent right existing outside the whole pattern of law, temptation arises to interpret that right in favor of some ruling caste or statist ideology. The protection of such freedom as has been won for the economic activities of individuals in Western society rests on the acceptance of property as part of a legal tradition and order that operates as a whole. Injury to one part of the legal system reacts throughout the entire economic and social order.

Corporations and Trusts

It is hard to imagine modern America or England lacking business corporations, trade unions, charitable foundations, and even organized churches. Yet these bodies, at least in terms of their relations to the state, are products of a long and sometimes perilous tradition of law. The problem has been how to permit a group of individuals to act as one individual in their dealings with other individuals and the state. It is hardly necessary to point out the extraordinary release of energy that has resulted from permitting collective funds and a collective endeavor to continue acting as one legal person in perpetual succession. The growth of technology and communication demands such a facility, if civilization is to advance or even survive. The pressure of this need may be met in many ways, one of which is to surrender control of all collective enterprise to the political state—the Leviathan of Thomas Hobbes, the Communist Utopia of Marx and Lenin. Neither the political nor the economic order of Europe and America may claim credit for our present fortunate compromise. Legal technicians working as true artists at their craft over several hundred years have accommodated the forms of social relationships to the changing needs of the economic and cultural environment. One principal means of managing human affairs, the business corporation, has maintained our culture on a knife-edge balance between statism and individualism. In political theory, a corporate charter is a concession or franchise from the sovereign authority of the state. If this were put into strict practice by politicians, government as the responsible author of corporations would sooner or later have to administer their affairs directly, instead of merely supervising their formation and powers. Fortunately, the lawyers outwitted the politicians; in England and America another ancient doctrine, that of trusts, had found root in the law of the land, permitting collective funds and enterprise to operate as if they were one perpetual person. There was no point in state-controlled corporations if groups or fellowships could escape the necessity of enrolling under the state's banner by forming a trust. As the English legal historian F. W. Maitland expressed it:

> For the last four centuries Englishmen have been able to say, "Allow us our Trusts, and the law and theory of corporations may indeed be important, but it will not prevent us from forming and maintaining permanent groups of the most various kinds: groups that behind a screen of trustees will live happily enough, even from century to century, glorying in their unincorporatedness. . . .
>
> But, if we are to visit a land where Roman law has been "received," we must leave this great loose "trust concept" at the Custom House. . . .
>
> Then we shall understand how vitally important to a nation—

socially, politically, religiously important—its Theory of Corporations might be.[13]

Now in the United States, trusts have enlarged themselves beyond the borders of usefulness and the political order has to be brought in to redress the balance. The main point is that our culture rests on a balance between the political and legal orders, with neither gaining the mastery over the other lest the whole edifice collapse. Power, in our long established Western communities, is not merely a matter of men, organization, and money. Tradition has to be taken into account—not the tradition of vague, romantic imaginings, but a tradition of structure embodied in the complicated learning of the law, and incapable of being disentangled by anything short of the final bomb of the revolutionary anarchist.

Notes

1 Quoted from Corwin, Edward S., *The "Higher Law" Background of American Constitutional Law,* Great Seal Books, Ithaca: Cornell University Press, 1955, p. 4.

2 Pound, Roscoe, *Justice According to Law,* New Haven: Yale, 1951, p. 48.

3 Raleigh, Walter (ed.), *The Complete Works of George Savile, First Marquess of Halifax,* London: Oxford, 1912, pp. 72-73.

4 Green, T. H., *Lectures on the Principles of Political Obligation,* London: Longmans, 1942, p. 144.

5 *Cummings v. Missouri,* 18 L. Ed. 356 (1867).

6 Frank, Jerome, *Law and the Modern Mind,* New York: Coward-McCann, 1930, p. 127.

7 Hand, Learned (ed. Dilliard, Irving), *The Spirit of Liberty; Papers and Addresses,* Vintage Books, New York: Knopf, 1959, p. 121.

8 *Hurtado v. California,* 110 U.S. 516 (1884).

9 Constitution of the U.S.S.R. (1936) Chapter IX, Article 117.

10 Jenks, Edward, *The Book of English Law,* London: John Murray, fourth edition, 1928, p. 308.

11 Locke, John, Second Treatise of Civil Government, Section 222, in *Two Treatises of Government,* New York: Hafner, 1947.

12 *The Federalist,* Modern Library, New York: Random House, 1937, No. 10.

13 From the Introduction by Maitland, Frederic William, to Gierke, Otto, *Political Theories of the Middle Ages,* Boston: Beacon Press, 1958, p. xxix.

Supplementary Readings

Berman, Harold J., *Justice in Russia,* Cambridge: Harvard, 1950.

Brown, W. Jethro, *The Austinian Theory of Law,* London: John Murray, 1906.

Cardozo, Benjamin N., *The Nature of the Judicial Process,* New Haven: Yale, 1921.

Cohen, Morris R., *Law and the Social Order,* New York: Harcourt, Brace, 1933.

Corwin, Edward S., *The Higher Law Background of American Constitutional Law,* Great Seal Books, Ithaca: Cornell University Press, 1955.

Curtis, Charles P., Jr., *Lions under the Throne; a Study of the Supreme Court of the United States,* Boston: Houghton Mifflin, 1947.

Frank, Jerome, *Law and the Modern Mind,* New York: Coward-McCann, 1930.

Haines, Charles Grove, *The Revival of Natural Law Concepts,* Cambridge: Harvard, 1930.

Hanbury, Harold G., *English Courts of Law,* London: Oxford, second edition, 1953.

Jackson, Robert H., *The Supreme Court in the American System of Government,* New York: Cambridge, 1955.

Jenks, Edward, *The Book of English Law,* London: John Murray, 1928.

Jennings, Sir Ivor (ed.), *Modern Theories of Law,* London: Oxford, 1933.

Kelsen, Hans, *The Communist Theory of Law,* New York: Praeger, 1955.

McCloskey, Robert G. (ed.), *Essays in Constitutional Law,* New York: Knopf, 1957.

Maine, Sir Henry, *Ancient Law,* Everyman's Library, London: Dutton, 1917.

Pound, Roscoe, *Justice According to Law,* New Haven: Yale, 1951.

Roberts, Owen J., *The Court and the Constitution,* Cambridge: Harvard, 1951.

Robson, William A., *Civilization and the Growth of Law,* New York: Macmillan, 1935.

Rosenblum, Victor G., *Law as a Political Instrument,* New York: Random House, 1955.

Vinogradoff, Sir Paul, *Common-Sense in Law,* New York: Holt, 1914.

Chapter 8

Instrumentalities of Force

Government, even in countries where it rests on the consent of the community, implies the use of force over the individual. In fact, the generalization may be ventured that the development of the modern state has followed a pattern of the subordination of private force to public power. It is unfair to think of force and compulsion as originating in political systems. Violence and dominance are manifestations of innate characteristics that mankind shares with a considerable portion of the animal world. The political state, then, has merely canalized or institutionalized a behavior pattern that it would be beyond its power to suppress. Parenthetically, the subjugation of violence falls within the sphere of religious or cultural conditioning. Since human history first started to be recorded, some 5,000 years ago, progress in this direction, from the murderous Assyrians to the Soviet and Nazi genocides, may be considered hardly notable.

One of the least noted changes in political organization over the last hundred and and twenty-five years has been the revolution in the forms of instrumentalities through which government applied force to the individual. Among English-speaking peoples, at least, a major part of our political institutions—representative government, supremacy of law, obedience to executive power—were formulated under conditions that, in light of today's practices, might be viewed as *voluntarism;* that is, self-enforcement by the community of laws and policies without the aid of government agents was the rule rather than the exception. Physical force exercised by central authorities was occasional and sporadic, being required normally only in circumstances of a partial breakdown of community morale. Laws passed by the central government rested literally on community consent for their enforcement; it was the internal organization of the local community and not agencies of the government that exercised physical compulsion in everyday matters. Thus, in Anglo-Saxon England the *frankpledge* system prevailed throughout the land as the method of law enforcement. Under this system communities were divided into groups of ten families; a representative from each group was made responsible for law observance within his group, and, as *tithingman,* could call on the assistance of every able-bodied male who shared the joint liability for behavior within the family complex. It may be seen that, however savage-appearing and mandatory the laws emanating from a central source, they would only be enforced on the individual level in accordance with the attitudes prevailing in particular communities. This frankpledge system merged in later times into a parish constable obligation, under which the able-bodied males of any parish were appointed in turn to serve a twelve-month tour of duty as constable. Again, the force employed was that of community opinion: whatever king, Parliament, or courts of law might say, if the locality did not like the law, violators would be neither apprehended nor charged.

This easygoing relationship between the text of the law and its application lasted in England until the beginning of the nineteenth century. A true crisis in representative government or self-government occurred during the eighteenth and early nineteenth centuries —technology and communication outpaced traditional habits of public order. A choice had to be made between preservation of public orderliness and the traditional voluntarism that had served as a bulwark to public and private liberty. Some European countries took refuge in a machinery of central government superimposed by the use of organized force on the previous self-rule of local communities. In this development lay the origins of the modern police state and the institutional systems that have opened the way to the tyranny of ideological minorities over a whole people.

Britain met the difficulty in a manner that has become a model for all English-speaking lands and many other countries following the democratic tradition. The liberty of orderliness was preserved without submission to tyranny, through the creation of a new instrument of government—disciplined, decentralized, police forces. Gangsterism, both criminal and political, flourished in eighteenth-century England on a scale that would make modern American attempts appear amateur. The parish constable system had broken down in favor of hired watchmen serving the interests of property owners. The mass of the people had no protection from the cut-throats, bullies, thieves, debauchers, and a criminal class that could be manipulated to threaten the government itself. In fact it was the dangerous use of uncontrollable mobs for political purposes by the radical politician John Wilkes in the 1760s, and by the fanatical anti-Catholic George Gordon in 1780, that stirred the government to realization of the danger of the breakdown of public order. In 1829 the ministry of Sir Robert Peel obtained consent of Parliament to the establishment of a government-organized police force for the metropolis of London, and a few years later enabling Acts were passed to permit local government bodies to form similar forces. That this development averted a partial collapse in organized society may be gathered from an account by a British police historian of a Report of a Royal Commission of 1836–39 into the prevalence of crime.

The Report shows that the establishment of police forces had already effected immense improvements in public orderliness and security of person and property in some of the boroughs and in a few small country areas. The fact of the almost total absence of protection elsewhere other than the slight degree of it which was afforded by voluntary private associations for purposes of mutual help in dealing with thieves is established by a mass of detailed evidence, which was recorded by witnesses from all parts of the country, and from all classes of society. Widespread, highly organized systems of securing goods by theft and trading in them were a feature of all traffic routes; roads, railways and canals, throughout their length, along which was spread a vast network of receiving depots for stolen goods. Consignments of merchandise were left almost unguarded on their journey, from the moment of their dispatch from a warehouse to a customer, unless he made special provision for their protection. Carriers refused to be responsible for it. Rich people could afford to pay a subscription to one or another of over five hundred, so-called, Prosecution Societies, which existed in various parts of the country and they could afford also the half-crown preliminary fee for engaging the activities of a parish constable, together with the risk of the unknown expenses in which he was certain to become involved when pursuing a thief. . . . The vast mass of the people who were unable to face the cost of pursuing thieves were obliged to suffer helplessly the depredations of an army of these pests who ranged the country and preyed on its poorer citizens, in safe awareness of their helplessness and inability to retaliate.[1]

It is necessary to keep in mind the capacity of modern industrial society to dissolve into gangster-ridden disorder when evaluating the revolution in government practices brought about by the establishment of professional police bodies. Nevertheless, this new dimension in government imperils some of the principles on which government by consent is based. Substitution of professional enforcement of law and order for customary voluntarism weakens individual participation in the safeguarding of liberty. If the police idea is projected to a logical conclusion, the community may become a helpless mass, incapable of self-defense or even self-organization, manipulated by and preyed upon by disciplined mercenaries at the disposal of the regime in power. That this is no idle imagining is illustrated by the unhappy history of the Soviet states since Lenin seized power in Russia and by unsavory events in fascist and dictatorial countries in Europe and Latin America. The quality of tyranny that a police state can enforce differs substantially from that of ancient rulers who built their power on armies. Military forces are clumsy weapons with which to prescribe the daily conduct of a people; police science has reduced supervision of individuals to a fine art.

Principles of Police

Peoples that enjoy representative government have to balance the utility and even necessity of competent police forces against inherent dangers of sacrificing traditional liberties. This has been done by a careful integration of the new element of police into the constitutional structure of government. The constitutionalizing of police work may be accounted still in an experimental stage in English-speaking and many other countries. A temptation always exists to subordinate everything to order and to license police forces as irresponsible crime or antisubversion crusaders, with the consequence that the rule of law changes into arbitrary police "necessities." Britain probably still leads the world in combining police efficiency with control of arbitrary power. The principles on which her police are permitted to operate may be employed as standards on which to gauge the political validity of police organization elsewhere. The British principles may be borrowed from the writings of the historian of that institution, Charles Reith.

There are nine Principles of Police: (1) To prevent crime and disorder, as an alternative to their repression by military force and severity of legal punishment. (2) To recognize always that the power of the police to fulfill their functions and duties is dependent on public approval of their existence, actions and behaviour, and on their ability to secure and maintain public respect. (3) To recognize always that to secure and maintain the respect and approval of the public means also the securing the willing cooperation of the public in the task of securing observance of laws. (4) To recognize always that the extent to which the cooperation of the public can be secured diminishes, proportionately, the necessity of the use of physical force and compulsion for achieving police objectives. (5) To seek and to preserve public favour, not by pandering to public opinion, but by constantly demonstrating absolutely impartial service to Law, in complete independence of policy, and without regard to the justice or injustice of the substance of individual laws; by ready offering of individual service and friendship to all members of the public without regard to their wealth or social standing; by ready exercise of courtesy and friendly good-humour; and by ready offering of individual sacrifice in protecting and preserving life. (6) To use physical force only when the exercise of persuasion, advice and warning is found to be insufficient to obtain public cooperation to an extent necessary to secure observance of law or to restore order; and to use only the minimum degree of physical force which is necessary on any particular occasion for achieving a police objective. (7) to maintain at all times a relationship with the public that gives reality to the historic tradition that the police are the public and that the public are the police; the police being only members of the public who are paid to give full-time attention to duties which are incumbent on every citizen, in the interests of community welfare and existence. (8) To recognize always the need for strict adherence to police-executive functions, and to refrain from even seeming to usurp the powers of the judiciary of avenging individuals or the

State, and of authoritatively judging guilt and punishing the guilty. (9) To recognize always that the test of police efficiency is the absence of crime and disorder, and not the visible evidence of police action in dealing with them.[2]

These concepts of the preventive rather than punitive character of police work may seem idealistic, but the degree of their observance will mark the standard of individual freedom that prevails in practice in any specific community. The character and organization of the police force itself is only one of the factors involved in the maintenance of these principles. Legislatures and executive bodies are as likely to exploit police power in a tyrannical direction as the professional crime fighter. A new dimension was added to lawmaking with the great increase of enforcement power from the easygoing methods of voluntarism. Now legislators may impose measures based on prejudice, special interests, and other unpopular considerations, on the disorganized majority through perverted use of organized police forces. The ancient check of passive resistance, made effective by control of grass-roots enforcement, no longer serves to safeguard the community against the busybodies of politics. In both the United States and England the theoretical right of legislative bodies to make laws on any subject requires reexamination in terms of enforcement problems. Since representative bodies first achieved political power they have been prone to indulge their corporate prejudices by the creation of what Jeremy Bentham described as "fictional" crimes, that is, offenses against the taste of the few made analogous to injuries to the community by legislative fiat. Dancing round the Maypole, for example, was made a heinous offense by the Puritan Parliaments of the Stuart kings. When local enforcement of such laws depended on unpaid justices of the peace and a parish constable conscripted for a twelve-month term, little harm resulted from the fulminations of kill-joys at Westminster; fellow Puritans obeyed the law, and those parishes with a livelier outlook danced at will.

In present times, laws affecting personal behavior that are not integrated with community custom present grave dangers to the proper use of police power. In dealing with gambling, for example, police forces in a metropolitan community normally find themselves operating without the cooperation of the majority of citizens.

Though this is seldom the fault of the police itself, a dangerous pattern is created of a hostile police dominating the community by guile and force. The representative character of the police officer as a member of the community specially pledged to the protection of its safety is marred by forcing on him the duty of opposing the community to carry out the irresponsible will of a distant legislature. If a sufficient number of laws are passed that outrage popular custom, police forces can be separated from their community bases, made the creatures of political bodies and parties, and distorted to form a foundation for the police state.

Organization of Police Forces

The concept of the present-day police force as an extension of voluntarism in law enforcement remains valid only where community control of police bodies is real and immediate. The United States and Britain have guarded jealously the political tradition that each community employs and manages its own police organization. In the case of small and medium-sized towns and rural areas it may be said of both countries that popular control of police institutions remains a reality. Metropolitan areas and the growth of State police forces in the United States present more difficult questions of community supervision. Both nations have broken basic principles of a representative police organization by creating national "investigatory" bodies—in Britain the ubiquitous "Treasury man," in America the T-man or the FBI—based on necessities of state in place of popular observance. A limited amount of arbitrary nation-wide enforcement appears an obvious requirement of our highly integrated economic and social life. However, the contradiction in principles remains a serious threat to popular self-government until the respective areas for enforcement of specific types of laws has been clarified. Thus, national laws relating to taxation, the flow of commerce, national security, may obviously benefit by enforcement through centrally organized agencies without threatening basic principles of voluntarism. In such matters the individual is normally a member of the national rather than any local community, and his control over enforcement agencies must be correspondingly widespread. On matters of personal behavior

—drinking, gambling, prostitution, and other offenses involving customary standards of conduct—individuals may participate meaningfully in law enforcement only as members of a locality. Though the Constitution of the United States seems to favor such principles of law enforcement by a strict enumeration of the lawmaking powers of the central government, reserving to the States and people all other governmental authority, the practical evolution of the American system has dimmed the boundaries of federal or even devolutionary character of law enforcement. Thus, control of sexual morality, traditionally a matter of local community concern, has in part passed into the hands of the FBI, who have to investigate breaches of the federal Mann Act concerning the transportation of persons across State lines for immoral purposes.

State police forces represent another equivocal element in law-enforcement agencies. To some extent they may be said to represent the community on wheels. Where they are confined to patrolling highways and other areas outside organized self-governing communities, their disciplined efficiency may enhance public safety without posing any threat to the claim of the people to police themselves in their own localities. However, temptation exists, particularly in predominantly rural states such as Louisiana, to utilize a powerful State police force as a political weapon of the central State government. The imposition of tyranny through irresponsible enforcement agencies remains a danger to be guarded against constantly on the American political scene.

Despite threats from the national and State levels, locally organized and controlled police bodies still dominate the enforcement of law throughout the United States. A rapid growth in professional efficiency and uniformity of methods has not undermined local autonomy. The outstanding work of the FBI and of some State police headquarters in supplying centralized facilities for scientific crime detection has increased rather than diminished the competence of community police to operate on the local level. Generally, a city or town police force operates as a professional body under its own commissioner. Links between the commissioner and city government vary with the form of city charter in force. Principles to be observed in political control of police forces include subordination of the police commissioner or chief to the policies of elected officials, in so far as these are concerned with objectives of community law enforcement. An equally important principle is the protection of the professional, nonpartisan character of the force through placing control of internal organization and discipline firmly in the hands of a responsible commissioner or career officials.

One obvious weakness in community organization of the police power is the varying standards in professional efficiency and knowledge that result from the establishment of innumerable separately organized bodies throughout the country. There are two ways in which this fragmentation of training and methodology is being remedied: first, the FBI has established itself as a central bureau of information for criminal records and scientific detection open to all local police bodies; second, professional standards amounting almost to guild unity have begun to unite divided police units throughout the country. The role of the State government, constitutionally responsible for the maintenance of law and order throughout its whole area, remains equivocal. The growth of centralized State police bodies with general authority in a majority of States threatens the independence of locally constituted police forces. In fact some urban police systems—Boston, Kansas, St. Louis, Baltimore, are examples—are now controlled by the State government. Generally, however, lack of integration facilities, unwillingness to contribute to the costs of maintaining adequately trained and paid police officers in rural areas, failure to provide centralized information facilities and crime laboratories, has marked the political attitude of State governments toward law-enforcement problems. One important Constitutional function of State governments is to provide, through the national guard, the final military authority to meet crises in law enforcement. As the National Guard, descended from the State militia, still represents the local community in arms, its intervention remains tied to principles of popular consent.

BRITISH POLICE SYSTEMS In some respects Britain has achieved a clearer solution than the United States to the problem of safeguarding local control of law enforcement while maintaining standards of performance at uniformly high levels throughout the nation. Unitary government has some advantage over federal structures in providing connecting links between diverse local bodies. In the first place, legal theory concentrates sovereign power in one Parliament and one executive; grants of authority to communities accordingly follow a single pattern. Secondly, the tax structure is such that the central government is in a position to hold the purse strings directly for a large number of local activities. A little less than half of the expenditures of local government is met by local taxation; the remainder is contributed by the national exchequer. As might be expected, when the central government is paying the piper it is not backward at calling the tune. National standards relating to training, conditions of employment, and pay have been imposed for police officers as well as teachers and firemen. Through an inspectorate reporting to the Home Office, common standards of police organization and efficiency are maintained without destroying the effectiveness of local control. In cities and towns, the professional police command normally reports to a Watch Committee of the town council. The American practice of making a single elected official, such as a mayor, directly responsible for police administration is avoided in the United Kingdom as likely to lead to partisan influence over law enforcement.

AUTHORITARIAN POLICE SYSTEMS Dictatorial rule by individuals or minority groups would not be feasible in a modern state without the organization of a nonpopular police apparatus. Such a body must be composed by and large of mercenaries or of ideological fanatics. Reappearance of these sinister institutions during the last thirty years has constituted a grave challenge to both the theory and practice of government by consent. It is possible to visualize a dictator's hirelings tyrannizing small plantation states such as Nicaragua or the Dominican Republic along lines similar to a well-organized gang's domination of an underprivileged neighborhood. When major nations of the civilized world place themselves under such systems for varying periods it is clear that they constitute definite if repulsive forms of political government. The origin of the present-day variety may be traced back in Europe to the breakup of the feudal system. New men (*novum homines*) of every type were scrambling for the seats of traditional power and were making force their principal justification. Able and unscrupulous status seekers such as the upstart Tudor kings of England overlaid ancient forms of rule with cunning devices bought with money from a new-come exchange economy. A network of spies, *agents de police,* and informers, supported by small numbers of armed mercenaries, greatly enlarged the powers of the central government in a society where the regional political leadership, the hereditary nobility, had practically exterminated one another in an orgy of feuding. Fortunately for the tradition of government in English-speaking lands, the Tudor dynasty found it cheaper and easier to rule as popular favorites than as despots basing their power on mercenary forces in the Continental manner. In Europe proper, however, despotic centralization was required to overcome the disorientation caused by a collapsing feudal system. The long struggle of the monarchy in a country like France against the regional nobility accustomed the government to the use of mercenary troops in internal politics. As the kings consolidated their power, they discovered that to maintain order and collect taxes it was valuable to have their armed forces dispersed in small groups over the countryside. These *gens d'armée* became the basis of a national gendarmerie for the policing of a whole country under the supervision of the central administration.

Nationally organized police forces tend by their inherent structural character to be the agents of a regime rather than agents of the community. Thus, in Italy before Mussolini established his Fascisti gangs the national police, particularly in Sicily and throughout the impoverished southern part of the peninsula, were already looked upon as an alien force. Introduction of an emotional ideology helped to coat the bullying tactics of a politicial police, but the development of the fascist form of government was a logical projection, in the institutional sense, of the national police state. Similarly, Hitler inherited from Frederick the Great, Stein, and Bismarck a machinery of government already geared for tyrannical purposes provided the occasion should arise—an occasion Hitler must be credited with creating, exploiting, and using to destroy the community with fanatic thoroughness. Lenin and Stalin could hardly have reared their monolithic structure of Bolshevik oppression without the long preparation by the Romanov tsars of a central police apparatus to serve as a model of irresponsible tyranny.

Though it is questionable whether any form of police system, however centralized and efficient, can provide the sinews of government in the face of active opposition by a determined majority of the community, it is apparent that it may achieve at least passive acceptance of minority rule by a disorganized people. For this reason it may be accounted a specific type of political government —an alternative to representative institutions and popular control. In fact, the areas of the world ruled by the police state in its various guises are probably many times larger and more populous than those open to the blessings of representative government. Power in such states tends to center in a national ministry of justice or its equivalent, where lies control of the police network and its auxiliary services. Centralized police forces permit the creation of secret police groupings, which historically have shown themselves able to turn on their ostensible masters weapons of spying, blackmail, and terror that have allowed a single individual who controls the apparatus to submit his supposed colleagues to a tyranny of fear. Khrushchev in his famous denunciation of the rule of Stalin portrayed conditions of internal terrorism within the Soviet regime that appeared almost a reversion to the cruel despotisms of the sixteenth and seventeenth centuries. The subsequent revolt of party leaders against police rule that led to the execution of Beria has probably restored a more normal balance of power within the Soviet system.

In summary, police systems should not be regarded as mere instrumentalities of power wielders but as centers of political authority in their own right. Accordingly, the character of governments is to a degree dependent on the nature of their police organizations. Representative governments must not limit popular control to the making of laws and policies; unless law enforcement on the face-to-face level is brought within community control, political rule ceases to be based on the active consent of participating citizens. Governmental systems founded on passive toleration by the majority may be benevolent, economically progressive, and even necessary for the preservation of internal order, but they do not constitute representative republics. The Greek use of the word "tyranny" as a description for these forms of guided or directed rule, though it has now been given supplementary connotations of cruelty and oppression, still appears just. Where the people do not enforce their own laws themselves, as well as make them, they must accept the rule of a tyrant.

Military Power

The ultimate force behind government is generally accounted to be that of the armed services. This is a questionable assumption in highly organized, technologically advanced societies where the military machine is geared to requirements of mechanized warfare. Use of troops to quell minor civil disorders or resistance to tax levies in Western lands would create major government crises. Both in the United States and Britain employment of military forces in the task of maintaining internal order has been infrequent and generally unfortunate, at least during the last century. In the nineteenth and early twentieth century, American State governors employed the State militia, now the National Guard, to suppress labor strikes. In 1957, Governor Faubus of Arkansas sought to promote the maintenance of a segregated school system by calling out the National Guard, ostensibly to protect public order against the effects of obedience to a court ruling. This show of military might was met by the President of the United States sending a contingent of the regular armed forces of the nation to control the situation. Actualities of policing or law enforcement were hardly involved in this display of political shadow boxing, which may have served to mark the end of irresponsible use of national military equipment by State politicians.

There is one aspect of military force, however, that still remains important in the maintenance of domestic order even under representative forms of government. The military apparatus, though lacking the capacity to engage in direct law enforcement, may enforce obedience to the Constitution and to popularly elected leaders upon the police system itself. Suppression of a police coup d'état in any form is well within the power of armed forces. Thus, in Massachusetts the firm employment of the National Guard to meet an unlawful strike of the Boston police force gave Governor

Calvin Coolidge his start toward the Presidency of the United States. A similar surprise police strike in Melbourne, Australia, in 1926 provided to the author's recollection two hours in which the citizenry were free to loot stores before troops arrived to restore order. English-speaking countries in general have only an emergency use for regular armed forces in dealing with local derelictions of police duty. A further curb on the use of military force for internal law enforcement in the United States and Britain stems from the composition of their national armies. Selective or national service, to use current terminology for military conscription, has created citizen armies of different social outlook and temper from those of former professional forces. Despite rigors of military discipline, political governments in English-speaking lands would be ill-advised to rely on the armed forces to carry through by a show of force policies to which the general bulk of the community were strongly opposed. A citizen army may be utilized only for objectives acceptable to the bulk of the citizenry.

A somewhat different situation exists in countries where a centralized national police force is balanced by a highly professionalized national army. Even when the ranks of armed forces are filled by conscripts, a professional officer corps with traditions of independence may create professionalized forces separated from trends of community feeling by an exclusive military *esprit-de-corps*. Thus, France today has an army controlled to a great extent by an officer grouping traditional even in its willingness to intervene in domestic politics. The capacity of the military leaders to replace the national gendarmerie of the civil government with their ubiquitous paratroopers was dramatically illustrated during the events leading to General de Gaulle's assumption of power in 1958. In Corsica, where an airborne raid replaced the legally constituted government with a military adventurer, it is probable that public sentiment either favored the Army's entrance into domestic politics or was indifferently neutral; the regular gendarmerie in any case were as remote from the community in terms of control as the invading military. France retains her republican sentiments, and these are perhaps as strong among the military cadre as among the civilian politicians; this identification of basic outlook between professional officers and citizen conscripts keeps the armed forces of France representative of the people. Nevertheless, the Army as an institution possesses the power to substitute itself for the civil government, at least for a limited transition period. In other words, the Army could make a revolution in France and several other European countries where law enforcement has been centralized into national police forces.

Soviet Russia faces similar problems concerning the place of military power in domestic policies. Communist systems, however, have been successful to date in keeping Party organization and loyalty dominant over traits of separate professionalism in the officer corps of their armed forces. If a time comes in any Soviet state when the Party finds itself seriously factionalized, military organization will have at least equal chance with any political executive to seize governing power. Government by force is inherently unstable between civilian applications of power and military intervention. Thus, even self-willed tyrants of the character of Stalin find it necessary to retain a façade of popular rule, lest reliance on naked force give too great advantages to the military caste.

Civilian Control over the Military

The United States prides itself that, along with other English-speaking nations, its military establishment is under civilian control. This concept is based on the historic repugnance to mercenary or professional armies displayed by the British and American peoples. When the English Parliament reluctantly granted funds to the monarchy to keep what was then called a standing army, it hedged its authorization with the precaution that funds would be granted strictly on a yearly basis and should Parliament fail to pass the annual Army Act, maintenance of a standing army in time of peace would be illegal. The American Constitution followed this practice, though it extended the grant of funds to a two-year period. In principle, then, armed forces are creatures of the national legislature, their numbers, equipment, and very existence depending on the will of every session of the legislative body. This, of itself, would not suffice to curb the power of the military command under twentieth-century conditions of national insecurity. A second principle of civilian control is that the internal organization of the military should be subject to the political executive. In the United States this is accomplished by the Constitutional provision designating the President as Commander-in-Chief of the armed forces. The military chain of command then terminates in the Chief Executive, to whom the military hierarchy owe professional obedience as well as Constitutional loyalty. In Britain, similar results are achieved by making each of the branches of the armed services responsible to a political minister and collectively to the Prime Minister and Cabinet, through a ministry of defense.

The objective of civilian control is to prevent the military arm from speaking with a single voice and raising itself to a branch of government coequal with executive or legislature. It is commonly held to be a symptom of military usurpation of political power for the operation of all the armed forces to be by a general-staff system, as in the Prussian tradition of prewar Germany. Though theoretically subordinate to the political executive, the controlling group of a general staff tends to transform itself into a policy-making body, as regards both foreign policy and domestic concern. It may and frequently does appeal directly to the people over the heads of constitutional governments in the name of national security on questions of foreign and domestic policy. Thus, in Indonesia during the month of June, 1959, the Chief of Staff of the Army forbade all political activities throughout the country to avoid factional disturbances, though the president himself was overseas and a constitutional convention was in session.[3]

Though civilian supremacy still may be held to prevail in the United States and Britain, the military establishments have risen from positions of isolated subordination in policy determination to a status analogous to junior partnership. The growth of the military element as a power center in political matters is so recent in English-speaking countries and so closely tied to necessities of international survival that it has not yet been reconciled completely with constitutional theory and practices. Foreign policy and the position of the government as a major consumer of industrial goods are particularly sensitive areas in terms of military influence. In the United States, the National Security Act of 1947 sought to regularize the contributions of the military as advisers to the President ranking with the State Department and other bodies. Thus, the National Security Council was created "to advise the President with respect to the integration of domestic, foreign, and military policies relating to the national security so as to enable the military services and other departments and agencies of the Government to cooperate more effectively in matters involving the national security."[4] The military establishment is well represented on the National Security Council, through both the Secretary of Defense as a full member and the customary presence of the Chairman of the Joint Chiefs of Staff in an advisory capacity.

Outside strict Constitutional channels, leaders of the professional armed services have played a more open role in foreign policy determinations than at any previous period in American history. This has been done through direct communications with the general public, through professional associations and publications affiliated with each of the services, and through Congressional committee members. In a recent study of the influence of the military on foreign policy decisions in the United States, Professors Sapin and Snyder reached the following conclusions:

> Unfortunately, there is not much detailed case material available from which could be derived reasonably clear notions as to the nature of military influence on *policy substance:* that is, those situations and those problems in which the values of the military, their objectives, estimates of the situation, and analyses of policy alternatives, have tended to prove dominant, to be accepted more or less unquestioningly by their civilian colleagues: those in which the military have been able to block action on a particular decision or program; those in which the military have participated but not dominated the process; and those in which there have been sharp and explicit differences between the Pentagon and one or more civilian agencies, perhaps decided by the President in favor of the civilian agencies. . . .
>
> It must be remembered that the professional officers of the defense establishment are, on the whole, capable and determined men, men of strong views, accustomed to positions of command. At present they have considerable prestige in the society and substantial organizational and material resources at their disposal. They have active public-relations units and are not without their own channels and means for influencing Congressional and public opinion. Their length of experience and security of tenure in their positions are often greater than those of the civilians with whom they deal. In other words they have

certain important advantages in their relations and dealings with civilian policy-makers, members of Congress as well as State Department officials. Faced by a reluctance on the part of civilian agencies to assume certain responsibilities or an inability on their part to provide positive policy leadership, military leaders seem to be willing, if necessary, to fill the gap. Furthermore, even when faced by strong civilian leadership, there is no reason to expect them to modify their views quickly or easily. Thus, even if the exact nature of military influence on the substance of particular policies and programs can be documented in detail only in a handful of cases, the character and extent of military participation in various phases of United States foreign policy-making . . . is in itself important evidence of military influence. Indeed, the substantial and widespread nature of this participation is quite impressive evidence of the military's major role.[5]

Further testimony on this matter may be quoted from Newton D. Baker, President Wilson's Secretary of War.

The fact is that legislative determinations of military policy are more profoundly influenced by military men than they are by the executive directly, or by spontaneous legislative impulse. Nearly every member of the House and Senate committees on military affairs, and many other representatives and senators, have pet soldiers with whom they confer and whom they regard as counsellors who will steer them clear of all the vices of opinion which they attribute to the General Staff and the executive informed by the General Staff. Ambitious young majors and captains make the social acquaintance of senators and representatives and so impress them with their military knowledge, and thereafter the Secretary of War and the Chief of Staff, when they urge military legislation, find themselves facing measures and suggestions offered by members of the committees, but drawn by these ambitious and intelligent young men, which are often excellent, but more often are unconsciously influenced by bureau or arm ambition.[6]

In the thirty-five years that have elapsed since Secretary Baker expressed these opinions in a letter the situation has not changed materially except for a substantial rise in the rank and pressure tactics of the unofficial military consultants.

Another aspect of increased military influence on the direction of national affairs in the United States and other English-speaking lands lies in the constantly growing importance of weapon and military-supply purchases in the total economic structure of the country. The armed-services budget in the United States for 1959 amounted to approximately $39 billion, the greater part of which was expended in industrial purchases. This makes the United States government the greatest single customer of airplane plants, shipyards, and many other forms of heavy industry. Supply policies determined by military technicians may affect profits and employment over wide areas of the nation's economy. Accordingly, modern principles of efficient management tend to create interlocking arrangements between private industry and professional military staffs. One common practice is for high-ranking officers who have held major responsibility for supply procurement to accept, on retirement, positions in the firms supplying their former branch of service. There are many desirable aspects of such interchangeability in terms of experience and technical knowledge. On the highest level, President Eisenhower's appointment of Charles Wilson of General Motors as Secretary of Defense was a partial recognition of the value of placing a businessman thoroughly acquainted with problems of military supply in control of over-all procurement. New economic-military concentrations of power are likely to arise from this integration of the higher levels of the military profession with great financial and industrial interests. Both Congress and the executive have shown concern that "munitions lobbies" should not arise on a new scale and with increased political influence. In June, 1959, a House of Representatives subcommittee was directed to carry out an investigation of the hiring of retired military leaders by defense contractors.[7] The delicate balance of free-enterprise societies may be affected by any prolonged duration of the tensions of a cold war that removes substantial portions of the industrial economy into a realm of financial-military control only partly subject to the policies of representative government.

Structure of Military Establishments

A major change in the relationship of the military to the political establishment took place in many English-speaking lands during the second decade of the twentieth century. The introduction of compulsory military service reintegrated the theretofore isolated professional armed services with the community. Substantial elements of the population participated in the military experience under war and peace conditions. This has had the effect of removing distinctions between European conscript armies and American and British professional forces supported by a volunteer tradition. In political terms, the concept of a "nation in arms" has had repercussions both on the constitutional control of the military and on the internal leadership and organization of the services. One of the most important long-range effects has been to alter the availability of a traditional instrument that the people as an unorganized body possessed against government in any form. When the American Constitution was presented to the people its acceptance was postulated on the addition of the first ten Amendments, known collectively as the Bill of Rights, adopted in 1791. Amendment II reads: "A well regulated militia, being necessary to the security of a free State, the right of the people to keep and bear arms shall not be infringed." This clause stems from the jealously guarded right of the English people to provide the final force needed both for the maintenance of internal order and for security against external aggression from their own efforts as armed citizens. It may be traced back to the Anglo-Saxon fyrd, the assembly of the whole people in arms, that permitted the Norman kings to offset the armed might of feudal lords by summoning the national levy. The concept of popular government was based on the final reality that political leadership had to rely on the arms of the people themselves for support of its rule. Of course, armed individuals constitute a menace to public order except under primitive conditions, and the right to bear arms is limited to membership in a regularly constituted force. The State militia provided such forces, permitting the people to participate as individuals in the final application of governmental authority. In essence, this system added another limitation to the capacity of government to act outside the active or passive consent of a majority of the community. Though the elective process might become distorted in favor of some powerful minority as regards policy and lawmaking, if enforcement finally rested on volunteer members of an armed community force, practical reality would still be given to Jefferson's statement in the Declaration of Independence: "But when a long train of abuses and usurpations, pursuing invariably the same Object evinces a design to reduce them under absolute Despotism, it is their [i.e., the People's] right, it is their duty, to throw off such Government, and to provide new Guards for their future security."

NATIONAL GUARD AND THE IDEA OF A MILITIA Requirements of present-day defense have rendered it impracticable to retain locally organized and trained volunteer units as the basis of a national army. The effective "federalization" of the State militias into the central armed forces was achieved by the Army Organization Act of June 4, 1920; in 1941 the National Guard was rapidly merged into the regular armed forces. Congressional power to raise and support armies has become predominant in the military establishment of the country. This leaves questionable the continued value of the National Guard in its State organization as an instrument through which the people may participate directly in the final use of governmental force. In practice, the preservation of internal law and order through action by the National Guard has become increasingly infrequent in the last two decades.[8]

Britain has experienced a similar process, with its ancient militia being transformed into a locally recruited volunteer Territorial Army and then after World War II into a centralized national Army based on compulsory service. Popular control of armed force has not disappeared—a conscript army is still composed of representative members of the people and will fight and obey its leaders only so long as it feels the support of community consent behind it—but it has lost a great deal of its local, institutional basis. Experience of European nations such as France which have known this system for more than a hundred years illustrates the possibility of popular military leaders' winning predominance over the normal representative arms of government through the loyalty of a militarized section of the people. Militarism is not necessarily a conspiracy by a small clique of professional soldiers but may take the more dangerous form of a transformation of effective popular participation in the power of government from the ballot box to the barrack room. Popular armies are also ruling armies.

SYSTEMS OF COMMAND Another development which may have served to increase the military voice in political affairs is the merging of the separate services under unified command systems.

On the professional service level, full unification is avoided in both the United States and Britain.

In the United States, the Joint Chiefs of Staff, under a professional Chairman, superimposed on the Chiefs of the Army, Navy, and Air Force, exercise a military influence on the general government probably unequaled at any other period in the nation's history. Emergence of the military in the English-speaking democracies as a unified force exercising influence on affairs of state comparable to that of the elected branches of government is not to be regarded as a conspiracy to subvert existing constitutional forms. Unfortunately, external security has come to play so important a part in the governing process that the military man has more to contribute than in previous periods. That he is doing so in a manner consonant with the desires and consent of a majority of the community there seems slight ground to doubt. However, appearance of new needs of this character and degree call for institutional changes in basic political structures. Military leadership and the needs of military organization must henceforth be accepted as major factors in the political life of the representative democracies.

Notes

[1] Reith, Charles, *British Police and the Democratic Ideal,* London: Oxford, 1943, p. 254.

[2] Reith, *op. cit.,* pp. 3 and 4.

[3] *The New York Times,* June 4, 1959.

[4] National Security Act of 1947.

[5] Sapin, Burton M., and Snyder, Richard C., *The Role of the Military in American Foreign Policy,* Short Studies in Political Science, New York: Random House, 1954, pp. 32-33.

[6] Baker, Newton D., "On Executive Influence in Military Legislation," *The American Political Science Review,* 1956, **50,** No. 3, 700.

[7] *The New York Times,* June 4, 1959.

[8] Rich, Bennett M., and Burch, Philip H., Jr., "The Changing Role of the National Guard," *The American Political Science Review,* 1956, **50,** No. 3, 702-706.

Supplementary Readings

Ashenhust, Paul H., *Police and the People,* Springfield: Charles C Thomas, 1957.

Bush, Vannevar, *Modern Arms and Free Men,* New York: Simon and Schuster, 1949.

Ekirch, Arthur A., *The Civilian and the Military,* New York: Oxford, 1956.

Hilsman, Roger, *Strategic Intelligence and National Decisions,* Chicago: Free Press, 1956.

Holcomb, Richard L., *The Police and the Public,* Springfield: Charles C Thomas, 1957.

Huntington, S. P., *The Soldier and the State; The Theory and Politics of Civil–Military Relations,* Cambridge: Harvard, 1957.

Huzar, Elias, *The Purse and the Sword; Control of the Army by Congress Through Military Appropriations, 1933–1950,* Ithaca: Cornell University Press, 1950.

Kaufmann, William W. (ed.), *Military Policy and National Security,* Princeton: Princeton University Press, 1956.

Kohn-Bramstedt, Ernst, *Dictatorship and Political Police; the Technique of Control by Fear,* London: Routledge, 1945.

Lasswell, Harold D., *National Security and Individual Freedom,* New York: McGraw-Hill, 1950.

Reith, Charles, *British Police and the Democratic Ideal,* London: Oxford, 1943.

———, *Police Principles and the Problem of War,* London: Oxford, 1940.

Sapin, Burton M., and Snyder, Richard C., *The Role of the Military in American Foreign Policy,* New York: Random House, 1954.

Smith, Louis, *American Democracy and Military Power,* Chicago: University of Chicago Press, 1951.

Stanley, Timothy W., *American Defense and National Security,* Washington: Public Affairs Press, 1956.

Wheeler-Bennett, John W., *The Nemesis of Power; The German Army in Politics, 1918–1945,* London: Macmillan, 1953.

Wright, Quincy, *A Study of War,* Chicago: University of Chicago Press, 1942. (2 vols)

Chapter 9

The Pattern of Administration

Laws and policies, however well conceived, do little more than set a framework for the carrying out of governmental activities. The affairs of the community as a political body have to be administered or managed along lines similar to those of other corporate enterprises, economic or social. This necessitates the organization of managerial and technical talents for the conduct of public business. What is sometimes called the public service, or more narrowly the *civil service,* represents in most countries a thoroughly diversified aggregate of skills linked together by tenuous bonds sometimes reduced to mere dependence on a common paymaster. Whether the administrative services of government form a single grouping, trade, or profession appears an unreal question. Obviously, the structure of the service depends upon what is being administered: it is difficult to discover common organizational factors that link together skilled scientists in the U.S. Bureau of Standards and mail clerks in the Post Office.

Perhaps the greatest difficulty arises from the use of the term "public administration," with a hidden implication that the administration of governmental affairs is somehow different in essence from the management of any other type of corporate enterprise. A possible distinction arises from the concept that governmental business is always in the public interest, and accordingly its administration possesses a unique quality that arises from its majestic purpose. This viewpoint appears pretentious with an overtone of pious statism. To assume that a community receives all its benefits or "goods" from the political state runs counter to common sense—except, of course, where common sense has been effectively communized. In practice it might be very hard to weigh the results of a day's work of a clerk in the U.S. Treasury against those of a junior officer in a commercial bank so as to show that the government official promoted the public interest further than his business colleague. It seems sufficient to recognize that employment by the government may involve certain distinctions from other types of gainful endeavor, without creating a special category of service. The organization of corporate or cooperative management is the central problem; government merely uses the tools already established in every part of community life to administer its particular affairs.

Bureaucracy

Before examining the internal structure of the managerial process in government it is advisable to relate the organization of government personnel to community affairs in general. Continental Europe has had longer experience of bureaucracies than the United States, and has integrated them more comfortably into its social structure. Primarily, the attitude of a community at any moment toward its government servants depends on the general feeling toward the purposes of government. Thus, in England in the eighteenth century government on the administrative level was "gentleman's" business carried out by the squirearchy and aristocracy in a spirit of amateurish arrogance. Patronage, the selling of posts, absentee office holding, were accepted by the commonalty as normal to a government run by gentlemen for the benefit of the gentry. When strong concepts of popular government began to take hold in the early part of the nineteenth century, the present type of British civil service was invented to serve the new purposes of government. It may be noted that the continuity of English society preserved a leading role for the gentry in the new administration of incorruptible clerks. They were assured a monopoly of the guiding posts, but to occupy them they had to abandon their Elizabethan braggadocio, their eighteenth-century insolence of manner, and become the cautious, competent, bowler-hatted denizens of Whitehall and the Pall Mall clubs. The nature of the organization of government service, in so far as it represents effective control of social power, reacts sharply on the internal character of ruling groups in the general community structure.

Another example of the bureaucratic structure's reflecting changes in the direction of the state may be drawn from Germany (or, rather, Prussia) after its defeat by Napoleon. The police state was discredited; the work of Frederick the Great in centralizing all affairs of the community into one large national barracks run by an officer class under the strict discipline of a royal commander had collapsed before a better fighting organization—that of the Revolutionary French armies. The Prussian monarchy sought to identify itself with the rising commercial middle-class centers of power by placing reorganization of the state machinery in the hands of Minister Stein, a protagonist of modern efficiency. Stein's outlook towards the existing government service was that it had ceased to reflect the true dynamics of German society and accordingly had become ill-fitted to carry out the true purposes of government. His denunciation remains a classical attack on a bureaucracy that has lost touch with the power sources of its own community.

We are governed by *paid, book-learned, disinterested, propertyless* bureaucrats; that will suffice so long as it suffices. These four words contain the character of our and similar *spiritless* governmental machines: *paid,* therefore they strive after maintenance and increase of their numbers and salaries; *book-learned,* that is, they live in the printed, not the real world; *without interests,* since they are related to no class of the citizens of any consequence in the State, they are a class for themselves—the clerical caste; *propertyless,* that is, unaffected by any changes in property. It may rain or the sun may shine, taxes may rise or fall, ancient rights may be violated or left intact, the officials do not care. They receive their salary from the State Treasury and write, write, in quiet corners of their departments, within specially-built locked doors, continually, unnoticed, unpraised.[1]

Though written over a hundred years ago these words readily evoke contemporary approval, at least throughout the English-speaking world. In the Western world today the proportion of wage- or salary-earning personnel in government service varies from one in ten to one in five. An understandable jealousy exists between the world of employment based on profit making and the more sheltered sphere of governmental occupations. To some extent, the distinction is becoming unreal in advanced technological societies, where great corporations and trusts no longer tailor their employment policies to simple exigencies of double-entry bookkeeping. As Professor Dimock points out:

> As specialization and hierarchical organization increase in scope and as business administration becomes more and more political—that is, concerned with policy decision, group relations, and institutional influence and survival—the bureaucratic problems and executive needs of business and government become increasingly alike. The study of power and public policy becomes as important for the business corporation and the trade union as for the politically organized state. In all major governing institutions a central difficulty is how to balance the potential efficiencies of careful planning and logical organization against the equal need for individual initiative and institutional flexibility and responsiveness.[2]

Bureaucracy, then, has become a social phenomenon and may no longer be considered merely as a symptom of political malfunctioning. A good part of the complaints concerning the spread of bureaucracy stem from people who wish to have their cake and eat it too. Modern society provides greatly enhanced security to the individual at the cost of submitting to cooperative processes that restrict, sometimes harshly, his freedom of personal maneuver. It is easy to personalize the restrictions into the colorless face of the bureaucrat—a not-too-dangerous scapegoat on whom may be laid the blame for failing to take the risks out of life without diminishing its freedoms.

The United States Civil Service

Below the level of policy-making posts, government service in the United States is now largely controlled by civil-service rules. The federal government employs approximately two and one half million civilians, of whom at least 85 per cent are under some form of civil-service protection. A major concept involved is that of appointment and promotion through "merit" in place of political patronage. This involves creation of independent authorities to administer merit systems. The senior and still most authoritative of such bodies is the United States Civil Service Commission, brought into existence under the Civil Service Act of 1883. Six other independent merit systems are administered by such bodies as the Federal Bureau of Investigation, the Tennessee Valley Authority, the Atomic Energy Commission, the Public Health Service, the Veterans Administration, and the Foreign Service branch of the State Department. Management of the federal services of government remains a compromise between the political administrator and the professional civil servant. The Commission on Organization of the Executive Branch of the Government (new "Hoover Commission") pointed out:

> In the 160-odd years since a two major-party political system developed in the United States, the American people have sought to achieve a workable balance between two vital requirements in the management of their Federal civilian employees. One requirement . . . is that the officials responsible for establishing and defending Government policies and programs, the noncareer executives, should be selected by the successful party. . . . The other requirement is that there must be numerous trained, skilled and nonpartisan employees in the Federal service to provide continuity in the administration of the Government's activities.[3]

The still largely unresolved problem, then, has been how to combine neutral competence with executive leadership. Expansion of the merit systems from mere questions of appointment to those of promotion, dismissal, and the whole career management of the government employee has created a no man's land of civil service outside the worlds of both politics and commerce. In self-defense, the civil-service administrator has professionalized his craft through schools and training programs until methods and organization have become almost as much a jealously guarded specialization as instruction in elementary schools. At the same time, the business of government remains more or less a single concern related to general needs of the community. Fragmentation of the administrative process by overspecialization inhibits achievement of the purposes of government. Executive leadership requires a disciplined integration of administrative policies under a hierarchy of responsible policy makers. In the American system such policy decision makers must draw their authority either from the President or Congress. The noncareer executive, dependent on presidential appointment and leaving office with the administration, remains the principal link between an almost autonomous bureaucracy, which has increased fourfold in strength and power in thirty years, and the elected, representative aspect of government. By the Reorganization Act of 1939, the President was given power, subject to the veto of Congress, to rearrange the administrative structure of government bodies in order to bring about a greater degree of policy integration and management efficiencies. This permits such inner circles of presidential aides as those in the Budget Bureau to initiate master designs for administrative structures to implement major policy determinations. However, great areas of bureaucratic power remain divorced from direct presidential control in the independent regulatory commissions.

A possible development with the continued increase in authority over the ordinary citizen of the unreachable bureaucrat is a democratization of the administrative process. An ancient tradition exists in English-speaking countries that the private individual is responsible both at law and in fact for self-administration of laws and policies. For many centuries before police forces came into being, communities policed themselves through Watch and Ward Committees, sheriffs' posses, and the obligatory "stop thief" chase. The Anglo-Saxon fyrd, or military service contributed free with one's own rations and equipment, antedated our Selective Service. A tendency to return to citizen cooperation may be observed in the operation of one of the largest departments of the United States government, that of Agriculture. In connection with field-service administration of price and income supports under Agricultural Conservation Programs, a farmer-committee system comprising over 100,000 farmers serving on 29,000 community committees has been put into operation. Professor Frischknecht points out:

> The farmer committee system has been pronounced a great success. [Agriculture] Secretary Brannan called it "the most representative, efficient and democratic mechanism that has ever been developed for the administration of farm programs"; the national administrative agency has called it "the strong backbone of . . . operations in the

field"; and a leading scholar in agricultural administration [Charles M. Hardin] has said that "the farmer administrators of the program are members of an administrative organization which creates its *esprit de corps* out of its services to the farmers in the pursuit of justice." Farmers also have applauded the plan. If this testimony is accurate, practical decisions are taken at the State and local levels in a democratic way by groups of farmers who directly represent active and interested constituencies.[4]

Wartime necessities in both Britain and the United States brought the citizenry and the bureaucracy together in a harmonious acceptance of joint obligations. No one who experienced life in a bombed English town would underestimate the social leadership of the civilian air-raid organization, where the lines between professional civil servant and citizen volunteer had been successfully obliterated. In the United States the strict economic control of daily life established by the Emergency Price Control Act of 1942 stretched the capacity of bureaucracy to administer. The Act which set up the Office of Price Administration (OPA) authorized advisory committees representative of the industries affected to consult with the Price Administrator. Organized labor took advantage of this provision to create a parallel establishment to the official body. The interlocking of the two bureaucracies, union and governmental, is graphically illustrated in the accompanying chart. Though mergers of this character are less likely to occur under peace conditions they provide evidence that, if stretched beyond a certain point, bureaucracies are apt to revert to forms of popular participation if the representative character of government is maintained.

British Civil Service

Bureaucracy in England flourished in its earlier days under the comfortable umbrella of a ruling-class tradition. When the eighteenth-century Whig oligarchy and Tory squirearchy loosed the reins of direct administration they did not surrender the class structure of government in Britain. Though by 1870 virtually all posts in the civil service were filled by open competition, the competitive rules were carefully prescribed in favor of a special class. This

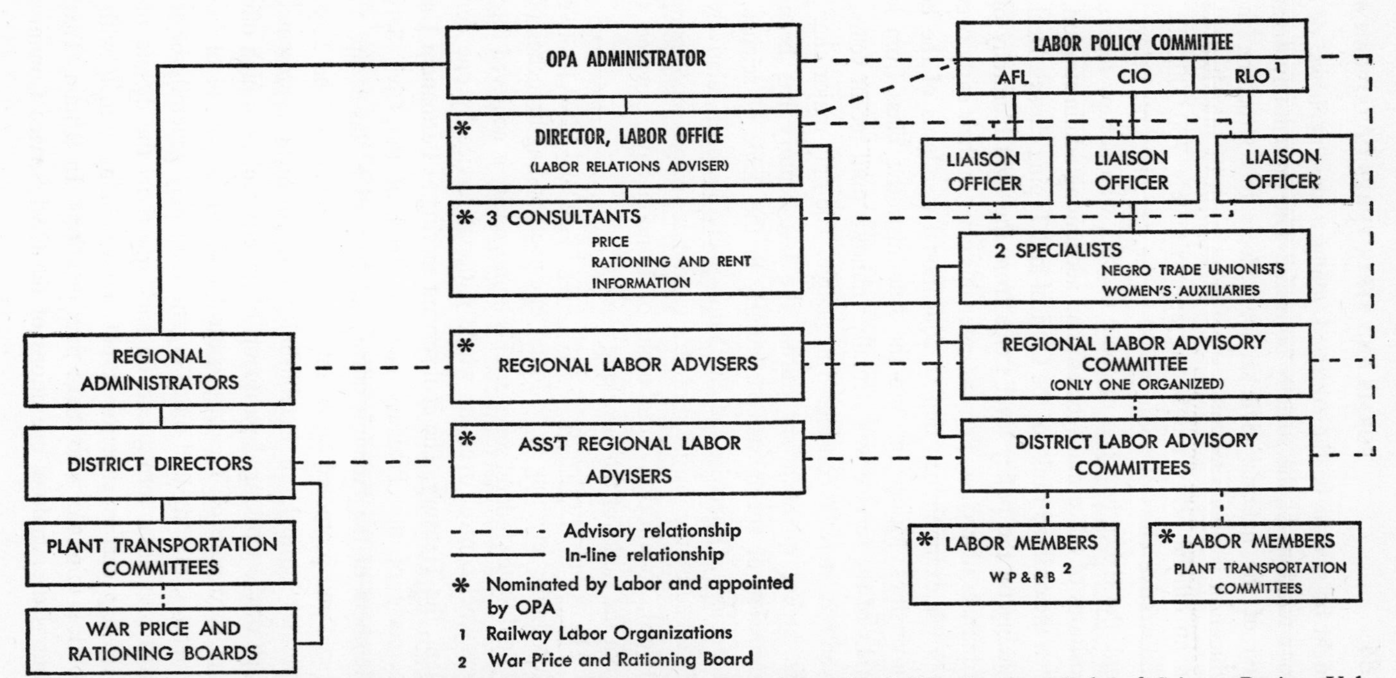

Source: John L. Afros, "Labor Participation in the Office of Price Administration," *The American Political Science Review*, Vol. 40, No. 3 (1946) p. 460.

might be said to be the educated younger sons, nephews, or even poor relations of the socially powerful. The present-day organization of the national civil service reflects this structure, though education is now accounted superior to birth or inherited wealth. In an official array numbering approximately 700,000, the Administrative class of about 4,000 is the key element; below them rank the Executive class of about 60,000, who occupy responsible positions of office management and accounting administration, and then the ordered ranks of the Clerical and Typing classes. Decision-making on the policy level stems from the tight hierarchy of the Administrative class. Persons enter this class in their early twenties through examinations tied to educational standards of the better universities. Movement into the Administrative class from lower ranks of the service was virtually unknown until recent years, and even now may be considered negligible. The only major change in the higher qualifications during the last century has been the admission of specialists, particularly in the fields of science and technology. Otherwise the club atmosphere has been relatively undisturbed by the intrusion of able candidates whose scholarships to Oxford, Cambridge, Edinburgh, or London have elevated them from the ranks of the "working classes."

The Administrative class itself may be looked upon as a career club unlike anything to be found in corresponding branches of the United States federal service. This homogeneity is achieved through personnel control over the whole national service by one department, the Treasury. The civil servant serving as Permanent Undersecretary of the Treasury acts as Head of the Civil Service. Members of the Administrative and Executive classes are transferred and promoted on an interdepartmental basis. The Treasury operates through an Establishments Department represented in each of the working departments of government by a high official. The hard core of Treasury control rests in its control of budget estimates. Staffing and office organization may generally be translated into fiscal terms, and on such questions the dictate of the Treasury carries superior if not overwhelming weight with the political ministers who make final decisions. In Britain, Treasury control overshadows operations of the Civil Service Commission, which is reduced to a rule-making body for overseeing recruitment.

A great, and to American eyes perhaps dangerous, concentration of power rests in the small Administrative class of the British Civil Service. As the members of this group are largely bound together by a common educational and cultural experience, their control of administrative methods and policies might seem to threaten the authority of the political ministry. During the first half of the twentieth century speculation arose concerning the trustworthiness of the Service in giving support to ministries whose political and social policies might differ seriously from the feelings and attitudes of the bureaucratic hierarchy. It may be said that these fears proved unfounded: socialist Labour administrations alternated with Tory administrations without shaking the disciplined functioning of a nonpartisan civil service. Perhaps the most effective check on the autonomy of the bureaucracy in Britain lies in the authority exercised by the Cabinet, and particularly by the Prime Minister, over appointments and replacements in the highest ranks. Though tenure as a whole is secure, any particular position on the level of Permanent Head of a department is subject to the will of the ministers. The Permanent Undersecretary of the Treasury, Head of the Civil Service, must accommodate himself fully to the Prime Minister's policies or accept replacement. As constitutional convention inhibits intervention by Parliament or the general public in any dispute between ministers and civil servants, the way lies open for decisive, unpublicized action by the political leader if he considers he is receiving indifferent support from the administrative apparatus.

The smooth functioning of the British Civil Service has led to attempts to imitate it elsewhere. In nations where, as in India or Ghana, the social structure still bears the impress of several centuries of a British connection, adaptations of a Senior Service system of control are still operable. Two factors appear essential: general social acceptance of homogeneous class groupings based on education, birth, or similar distinctions, and a Cabinet method of government that permits direct and unchallenged control over appointments and replacements in the higher positions of the Service. Though the second Hoover Commission recommended establishment in the United States of "a Senior Civil Service composed of politically-neutral, well-paid career administrators of exceptional skill and experience for continuing service in all departments and agencies,"[6] this recommendation has never been implemented. Under a presidential method of government, conditioned by a separation-of-powers doctrine, the appearance of an autonomous directing group within the national administrative services might add a fourth power to the existing triangle of legislative, executive, and judicial authority.

The French Bureaucracy

The government of France, from the fall of Napoleon to the Fifth Republic of de Gaulle, has been marked by a succession of ministries holding the most diverse political and social views. There is little evidence that any government has received general approval and support from the whole French community over any considerable period of time. In these circumstances, maintenance of the continuity of public affairs in France is a major achievement, for which the politicians can take only minor credit. The departments and bureaus of state as reorganized in the dynamic administration of Napoleon have possessed a life of their own sufficiently autonomous to direct the conduct of public affairs in some measure of safety through the treacherous whirlpools of unstable politics. A class structure that underlay pronouncements in favor of equality and fraternity permitted the organization of a senior service, along English lines, within the bureaucracy.

One major difference between the British and French systems, at least until recently, lay in the acute departmentalization of the French service. Under the Third Republic, each department or major bureau established the rules for the selection of its own higher personnel. This had the effect of creating distinct personnel cadres, each engaged in promoting the interests and attitudes of their departments, highly specialized in outlook and generally indifferent to the concept of an integrated administrative structure. In General de Gaulle's first government in 1945 some radical reforms were achieved towards the creation of a unified administrative structure. The senior service was brought in line with that of the

British through division into two sections, that of civil administrators and that of secretaries of administration. The civil-administrator class, corresponding to the British Administrative class, is recruited through a special academy, the Ecole Nationale d'Administration. Entrance to this school is through competitive examination held once a year; once admitted, the student is salaried during the ensuing three-year course. Though this avoids economic discrimination by permitting anyone possessed of the necessary academic talents to compete for entrance, it does not prevent a type of educational snobbery, which remains embedded in the French social structure.

Centralization of training also gives the state an opportunity to influence the moral character of its future servants. Something of the spirit of West Point or Annapolis is cherished as part of the *mystique* of French administration. One of the most useful effects of this reform has been to break down departmental careerism: in theory, at least, the products of the Administration School move freely from one bureau to another. From the point of view of political control the way is now open for a strong premier or president to discipline the bureaucracy into a single-minded devotion to the carrying out of governmental policies.

The government of France is more highly centralized than that of the United States or Britain; accordingly, the influence of the central administrative departments on regional and local affairs is a matter of greater concern. M. Pierre Laroque, a French statesman, analyzes this situation thus:

> The civil service plays a very important part in the preparation of the executive's decisions—not only by assembling information in the light of which the government can form an opinion, but also, to a great extent, by determining the measures and guiding the policy adopted by the government. It thus contributes to stability and continuity. This influence is evident chiefly in the central sphere. . . . All vital decisions are taken by the central authorities. The local representatives of the State—prefects, heads of regional and local technical services—can take decisions only when given precise instructions, and are usually mere executives. As for the decentralized local authorities, their power of initiative, though it definitely exists, is limited by shortage of funds and by the supervision of the prefects or the financial authorities.[7]

Soviet Management

Communist theoreticians describe the Soviet government as a corporate body for state management. This involves recognition of an administrative class, and lines must be drawn between political policy makers, participating masses, and obedient civil service, to achieve avowed aims of "socialist legality," "democratic centralism," socialist planning, and the leading role of the Communist Party. As usual, the Soviets manage to a considerable extent to have their cake and eat it too; that is, they continue the European tradition of a specially trained, moderately exclusive, administrative class while identifying this class with the masses by the magic of Party affiliation. It is perhaps best to permit a Soviet apologist to explain his own governmental system.

> The fact that the Party directs the State machinery in no way implies that it directly governs the country. The Party directs the organs of State management but it neither replaces nor substitutes itself for them. There is, in the U.S.S.R., a clear distinction between the functions of the Party organs and those of the State. Leadership by the Party appears from the fact that all vital questions in the life of the State are, in the U.S.S.R., decided in conformity with the Party's directives and policy. The Party's direction of the State machinery is manifested in the choice, assignment, and ideological and political training of officials, and the checking and authentication of party directives.[8]

From the non-Communist point of view this would seem to add up to a declaration that the Party bureaucracy and the administrative bureaucracy coincide, and that any points of difference are settled by the total subordination of the administrator to the Party bureaucrat.

STRUCTURES OF CENTRAL ADMINISTRATION In the majority of Western nations the structure of central administration is the resultant of historical accident. This constitutes one of the principal distinctions between the management of government affairs and that of private business. In the latter case major policy directors have a more or less free hand to plan and change administrative organization to suit immediate objectives; government leaders on the other hand are seldom free to make rapid changes in a traditional system guarded by many powerful interests. Thus, in the United States two succeeding Commissions on the Organization of the Executive Branch (first and second Hoover Commissions) have shown, in Reports issued between 1947 and 1955, that 64 executive agencies exist, all reporting in theory directly to the President, the control by the President as chief director of policy varying in practice from a direct chain of command to an almost merely formal power to make appointments to vacancies on the semi-independent commissions. Though Congress has a final Constitutional responsibility for overseeing the structure of the administrative offices, it lacks both incentive and true political power to make radical reorganization of the great network of vested interests constituting the government bureaucracy a major political objective.

Britain suffers from similar difficulties in modernizing its central administrative structure. A committee headed by a senior statesman, Lord Haldane, prepared a definitive Report in 1918.[9] This highly respected document laid down the principle that the functions of government should be organized according to the service to be rendered, not according to the clients to be served. It also declared that one of the main functions of the Cabinet was the continuous coordination and delimitation of the activities of the several departments of state. However, functional organization has made indifferent headway in Britain over the last forty years. There are too many interests involved for it to be possible to reorganize government administration as one might a department store. Bureaucracy has become a branch of government possessed of its own claim for survival and only theoretically subordinate to the unrestrained will of the executive or legislature. Professor Mackenzie of Manchester University, commenting on the present British system, points out:

> It is now certain, for better or for worse, that the Haldane Committee were correct in their tacit assumption that the departments exist in their own right as elements in the constitution. It is impossible now to return to the age which regarded them as extensions of the Minister's private office. A good Minister will control his department, he can even change it, but the department will outlive him none the less. It is a pity, however, that the Committee did not recognize at all clearly

that the Departments are staffed by human beings, and that a department or a division has as real and individual an existence as any other human community. In planning a reorganization it is fatal to forget that what you are handling is a group or groups of men and women at work. A branch or a department may be a theoretical monstrosity and yet be a "happy ship" and traditionally a "happy ship" is the only "efficient ship."[10]

Public business has grown in the last fifty years in both scope and extent to a point where it is questionable whether it can be carried out by any single administrative system. Diversity of approach and decentralization of control are becoming increasingly important objectives in the governmental systems of the Great Powers. Perhaps one of the most fruitful solutions is to attempt a separation of functional categories within government to complement a separation of powers. If government is reduced to its bare essentials, that is, maintenance of internal order, defense against foreign enemies, conduct of foreign affairs, and perhaps the modern category of social welfare, the instrumentalities required to accomplish these ends may be coordinated on the policy-making level by the responsible political leadership. Diversity and separateness among administrative agencies are not of themselves barriers to the formulation and implementation of policy by a single executive body. In fact, the political executive may have greater opportunity to further its policies through relatively unconnected agencies than might be the case if faced with a monolithic structure already committed to a rigid plan of administration. Policy control of administration on the higher level always entails authority to keep organization flexible and subordinate to immediate policy considerations. Perhaps the search for "principles" of administrative structure worthy to be observed as at least conventions of the Constitution arises through failure to reconcile some of the doctrines of the separation of powers. Executive and legislative organs both have legitimate claims to be entitled to determine the organization of the administrative machinery of government. Unfortunately, their aims are not always identical. Thus, the executive may seek to promote unity of command while the legislature may favor decentralized authority as more amenable to Congressional supervision. Constitutional or limited government has to accept compromises as the price of a proper balancing of public power. The American administrative system, in particular, serves to some extent as a check or limitation on the direct will of the President of the day. Whether or not this may be considered desirable is a question of constitutional theory and not of administrative organization.

Classification of Agencies

For the purposes of academic analysis, administrative agencies may be classified as *line, staff,* and *auxiliary* services. Though this classification facilitates examination of the subject, it does not denote the character of the agencies in reference to their effective part in the governing process.

A line agency carries out one or more of the major functions of government operating through a chain of command that links it directly with the political command structure. By and large, American departments, such as Agriculture, Commerce, and Labor, exemplify the concept of line agencies. In theory, at least, a line of command may be traced from the President through the secretary of a department by way of undersecretaries, bureau chiefs, and many intermediaries down to the field worker in face-to-face contact with the public.

An auxiliary service agency[11] is constituted to provide institutional support for other administrative agencies, generally carrying out some housekeeping function common to all, such as supply, purchase, accounting, personnel selection. An example might be cited in the United States Civil Service Commission.

A staff agency is one in which advisory and planning responsibilities predominate over operative duties. The Bureau of the Budget might fall under this heading, though in practice it also exercises many supervisory functions.

These terms may be applied to the internal structure of most governmental agencies as well as to the position of any particular agency in relation to the whole governmental structure. Thus, the British Treasury is a line agency in its operative task of collecting taxes; an auxiliary service agency in its function of personnel and supply administration for the civil service as a whole; and a major staff agency in advising the Cabinet on financial and economic policies.

Other forms of classification are apt to be based on hidden assumptions as to the purposes of government or the superiority of the impartial administrator over the partisan politician as a repository of public authority. An example of this type of classification may be taken from the British Haldane Report of 1918, a document greatly influenced by the attitudes of such Fabian socialists as Sidney and Beatrice Webb. The Haldane Committee organized government into ten main functions: Finance; National Defense; External Affairs; Research and Information; Production, Transport and Commerce; Employment; Supplies; Education; Health; Justice. It may be noted that concepts of economic control and social services play a major part in this ideal administrative structure. Also, one of the oldest and still primary functions of government, the maintenance of law and order, has ceased to interest the planners except through the organization of judicial justice. Creation of administrative machinery to bolster up some dogmatic assumption as to the nature of government runs counter to the principle that government rests on the consent of the community expressed through elected officials. It is not legitimate to confine the changing outlook of a people as to what they would like their government to do or refrain from doing through imposition of a predetermined pattern of administrative organization. At least, it is not a legitimate practice in nations that claim to maintain representative, democratic forms of rule.

Types of Administrative Agencies

In Western systems of government, the ministry or department is the prototype of administrative agency. A department is frequently described as an aggregate of bureaus, but more accurately a department is a system of bureaus linked together through the functional homogeneity of their sphere of activity and operating under a single political head. The loose federation which constitutes the normal department of state militates against despotic, hierarchical control, whether by political officials or by senior civil servants. In the United States, it permits Congressional committees to manipulate one bureau chief against another, to lessen control by the President and his appointees, and to give legislative leaders substantial influence on the conduct of daily operations. In Britain, nonofficial bodies such as the Federation of British Industries and the Trades Union Congress obtain direct say in departmental decisions through being represented on advisory councils attached to the numerous departmental subdivisions. There is nothing inherently undesirable in this introduction of a touch of the representative process into administrative activities.

An historical newcomer and almost peculiarly American addition to the administrative structure is the independent regulatory Commission. Two major factors contributed to the development of this form: first, Congress was reluctant to add to the direct power of the President over economic affairs, preferring the creation of politically neutral bodies loosely tied to the executive; second, the American electorate has resisted the "creeping socialism" implicit in the means that have found favor in Europe as necessary for economic control. Regulation of private enterprise, rather than direct governmental participation in industry, has been a leading principle of American politics over the last few decades. The Constitution vests Congress with "power to regulate commerce with foreign nations, and among the several states, and with the Indian tribes." This is a very wide power, as Chief Justice Marshall pointed out in the classic case of *Gibbons v. Ogden*.

We are now arrived at the inquiry—what is this power? It is the power to regulate; that is, to prescribe the rule by which commerce is to be governed. This power, like all others vested in Congress, is complete in itself, may be exercised to its utmost extent, and acknowledges no limitations, other than are prescribed in the Constitution. . . .

The wisdom and discretion of Congress, their identity with the people, and the influence which their constituents possess at elections, are, in this as in many other instances, as that, for example of declaring war, the sole restraints on which they have relied, to secure them from its abuse. They are the restraints on which the people must often rely solely, in all representative governments.[12]

It may be noted that this is a vital power over the national economy placed expressly in the hands of Congress and it is understandable that there should be legislative reluctance to delegate any of its authority in these matters into the unrestricted hands of the executive. The independent regulatory commission is, then, a compromise between the incapacity of Congress to undertake direct administrative responsibilities and its unwillingness to grant full authority to the political executive. An independent regulatory commission may thus be defined as an administrative body formed to apply the general rules of the legislature concerning economic and social control through the promulgation of detailed regulations, the investigation and settlement of practices, and the adjudication of relevant claims. Its independence is only partial in the United States, as the President appoints all members (though he may not remove them except for misbehavior), and Congress determines its scope of operations and even its continuance.

The organizational status of the independent regulatory commission remains a matter of considerable controversy. One point of view, strongly expressed by a 1937 President's Committee on Administrative Management, leans toward the return of these bodies to control by major departments. This would place them under direct political command of the President, so that they could no longer claim to possess quasi-legislative, quasi-judicial, authority on their own account. The first Hoover Commission on Organization of the Executive Branch of the Government (1949) rejected this drastic solution, recommending retention of the partially independent status of the commissions while suggesting minor redistribution of some executive functions. A more difficult question than that of administrative theory is involved: the underlying political problem is whether *regulation* of private enterprise (rather than direct involvement of government in the industrial process) will suffice to control economic organization under present-day conditions. The relative efficiency or inefficiency of the regulatory commissions is a minor matter by comparison with the alternative form of economic supervision contemplated—government ownership and management of key industries.

GOVERNMENT BOARDS, AUTHORITIES, AND CORPORATIONS

Where government enterprise in the economic sphere is regarded as a legitimate supplement to private endeavor, administrative structures are weighted with instrumentalities for direct management of commercial and industrial affairs. Thus, in Britain in 1956 there were approximately one million civil servants in the direct service of the central government, and over two and a half million public employees of the great nationalized industries. Government philosophy in the United States remains opposed to concepts of political management of industry, and the use of the government corporation as an administrative device has been sparing. There are two major exceptions: the Tennessee Valley Authority, a body corporate created by an Act of Congress, with control in the hands of a board of three directors appointed by the President and confirmed by the Senate; the St. Lawrence Seaway Development Corporation, created to operate jointly with the Canadian Authority a canal system between the Atlantic and the Great Lakes.

In contrast, Britain and many European countries have elevated the public corporation into a major instrumentality for the control of the national economy. It should be emphasized that this is more a choice of political philosophy than a determination of ideal means of administration. The grant of power to a public corporation (almost always monopolistic power) amounts to a judgment that private enterprise has failed to satisfy requirements of the community in that particular field of activity. This may be illustrated by some of the economic fields now occupied in Britain by public corporations. Four basic industries, coal, electricity, gas, and transport, are under public ownership and operated through government corporations. The National Coal Board has undivided responsibility for the operation of the nationalized coal mines. The production and distribution of gas is in the hands of fourteen separate Area Gas Boards (each a public corporation in its own right) loosely linked together by a Gas Council. The generation of electric power for almost the whole country—the north of Scotland has its own Hydro-Electric Board—is under the auspices of the British Electricity Authority, but distribution over the national grid is in the hands of Area Boards appointed by the Minister of Fuel and Power. Both rail and road transport are nationalized industries in Britain and their integration is achieved by the British Transport Commission, serving as holding corporation and higher management body for inferior Authorities appointed by the Minister of Transport to operate railways, bus lines, docks, and hotels.

The British Broadcasting Company (BBC) may be considered

a pioneer in a particular form of public corporation. It received a charter from the government to monopolize the field of entertainment and informational broadcasting, collecting a license fee on every radio set to meet its expenses. The Government appoints the Board of Directors and can change its personnel if it considers the corporation run inefficiently; otherwise a convention has arisen that neither the Cabinet nor Parliament is entitled to intervene in daily policies. The electorate responds quickly at any hint of political pressure against what they have come to consider *their* corporation. There are circumstances, therefore, in which the public corporation could be protected against legislative or executive interference by the public itself, acting in its capacity as the controlling electorate.

In summary, the types of agencies adopted by any government for administrative purposes are determined by the purposes for which government has received the consent of the community. However, the multiplication of autonomous or semiautonomous agencies, whether public corporations or regulatory commissions, poses unsolved problems in the conduct of representative government. More efficient management of public business may be achieved at the cost of breaking the chain of responsibility to elected bodies, legislatures, or executive groups. Particular administrative agencies, freed in large part from political supervision, may become focus points for special interests seeking to use the totality of public power to further divisive policies. National unity always requires that final supervisory power over every act of government rest clearly in the hands of popularly elected bodies or officials. The age-old problem of making the national interest superior to factional interest may find itself revived in the administrative sphere.

The Art and Practice of Administration

It has been previously observed that public administration is a branch of the general administration of corporate and cooperative bodies. Generalizations on this vast subject are properly confined to conclusions arising from many particular studies of particular cases or instances. It is questionable whether universally applicable rules may be extracted to encompass the whole structure of governmental administrative practice. There is, however, one factor that has special importance in the conduct of public business: the character of the administrator himself. Qualities that lead to success in the management of commercial enterprise or the furthering of private concerns may prove unsuitable in the advancement of governmental affairs. An administrative type, constituted to serve the outlook and structure of the particular national state in its particular stages of development, is an open or implicit objective of most governmental systems. France has perhaps the most logical answer: the special school that was remarked earlier, the Ecole Nationale d'Administration, where candidates for the senior civil service are subjected to three years' intensive training, including some forms of moral conditioning. Britain relies on the close links of her major universities to public service to produce a more flexible but still homogeneous class of upper public servants. The relatively classless society of the United States is confronted with a difficulty in finding common social bonds or standards to link its public administrators into a type grouping. To some extent this lack has been met by emphasis on professional training. A considerable number of American universities now possess graduate departments of public administration and grant degrees such as Master of Public Administration (M.P.A.) In-service training programs permit students in educational establishments opportunities to act as interns in government offices; they also provide for a continuance of formal education along specialized lines for fully employed junior officials. The objective is to build up a professional guild analogous to the guild of lawyers. Whatever the means used, the delineation of a responsible character type for senior civil servants is becoming a necessity for the successful continuance of representative forms of government. The modern state has extended its influence and control into so wide an area of economic and social life that the quality of responsible management affects every individual in the community. In brief, it may be said that government is now too serious a business to be entrusted wholly to the elected politician.

Administrative Law

A considerable amount of confusion has arisen in English-speaking countries concerning the relationship of administrative procedures as they affect the individual citizen to the guiding principle of the "rule of law," the principle that actions of the government touching on the rights of individuals must always be in accordance with law as interpreted by the courts, and never at the arbitrary will of officials. A famous interpreter of the English constitution, A. V. Dicey in his *Law of the Constitution* published in 1885, gave rise to some of the theory underlying this confusion in both Britain and the United States.[13] It was Dicey's contention that administrative justice in terms of the Continental *droit administratif* ran counter to basic principles in common-law countries. The whole conception of administrative law, particularly that portion dealing with the adjudication of claims by regulatory bodies acting in a quasi-judicial capacity, thus became a subject of political suspicion. Perhaps the most straightforward description of administrative law is as *law relating to public administration*. As such, it is just as much technical or lawyer's law as the common law itself. The difficulty arises from separating the rule-making and claim-settling powers of statutory bodies from other sources of law and treating them as a foreign element in our whole body of law. How far legislatures should go in delegating powers of rule-making and executive determination to semiautonomous, nonelective bodies, certainly involves a political question. The structure and supremacy of law itself is not, however, affected. The laws under which these regulatory bodies act are ordinary statutes of the legislature. Interpretation of such statutes is open to the courts: in the United States, judicial review extends to declaring laws invalid if not in conformity with the Constitution. Even as regards the lesser point of the right of an individual to dispute a ruling of an official before a formal court of law, care has been taken to protect individual rights at least as substantially as in other fields. In practice, it would be unrealistic to claim that a person whose rights were curtailed by some determination of the Interstate Commerce Commission was placed at a disadvantage compared with a young man subjected to the ruling of a local Draft Board, or even with an individual placed in jeopardy of trial by the overzealous action of a district attorney acting through a grand jury. In the United States, administrative adjudication is now controlled by the cautious provisions of the Administrative Procedure Act of 1946, a measure which has been widely copied on the level of the State governments.

Technicalities concerning protection of the rights of individuals against arbitrary official action are on the level of lawyer's business. The political questions that remain revolve around the desirability of delegating rule-making power out of the hands of representative legislatures and also of granting discretionary powers to officials who are neither elected nor directly controlled by a popularly chosen superior. These are weighty matters touching on the competence of representative assemblies to conduct public business in light of the growing complexity of governmental activities. The traditional method of trial and error seems the most practical approach; though the problem is real, it has not yet reached the point where it can be considered to endanger the preservation of basic individual rights.

Notes

[1] Quoted from Finer, Herman, *Theory and Practice of Modern Government,* New York: Holt, revised edition, 1949, p. 737.

[2] Dimock, Marshall E., "The Administrative Staff College: Executive Development in Government and Industry," *The American Political Science Review,* 1956, **50,** No. 1, 166-176.

[3] Commission on Organization of the Executive Branch of the Government (1953-55), *Digests and Analyses of the Nineteen Hoover Commission Reports,* New York: Citizens Committee for the Hoover Report, 1955, p. 3.

[4] Frischknecht, Reed L., "The Democratization of Administration: the Farmer Committee System," *The American Political Science Review,* 1953, **47,** No. 3, 705. [Author's brackets.]

[5] Afros, John L., "Labor Participation in the Office of Price Administration," *The American Political Science Review,* 1946, **40,** No. 3, 460.

[6] Commission on Organization of the Executive Branch of the Government (1953-55), *op. cit.,* p. 3.

[7] Laroque, Pierre, "The Role of the Executive in the Modern State—France," *International Social Science Bulletin,* 1958, **10,** No. 2, 222.

[8] Iojrych, A., "The Role of the Executive in the Modern State—U.S.S.R.," *International Social Science Bulletin,* 1958, **10,** No. 2, 229.

[9] Machinery of Government Committee. Haldane Report. Command 9230 of 1918, London: His Majesty's Stationery Office, 1918.

[10] MacKenzie, W. J. M., "The Structure of Central Administration," Institute of Public Administration, *British Government since 1918,* London: G. Allen, 1951, p. 83.

[11] This term is used in White, Leonard D., *Introduction to The Study of Public Administration,* New York: Macmillan, fourth edition, 1955, p. 31.

[12] *Gibbons v. Ogden,* 9 Wheat 1, 6. L. Ed. 23 (1824).

[13] The influence of Dicey on this question is discussed by Robson, W. A., "Administrative Law in England, 1919–1948," Institute of Public Administration, *British Government since 1918,* London: G. Allen, 1950, pp. 85-86.

Supplementary Readings

Beer, Samuel H., *Treasury Control: The Coordination of Financial and Economic Policy in Great Britain,* New York: Oxford, 1956.

Dimock, Marshall E., and others, *Public Administration,* New York: Rinehart, revised edition, 1958.

Finer, Herman, *The British Civil Service,* London: G. Allen, 1927.

Finer, Samuel Edward, *A Primer of Public Administration,* London: Muller, 1950.

Gladden, Edgar N., *The Essentials of Public Administration,* New York: De Graff, 1953.

Greaves, Harold R. G., *The Civil Service in the Changing State,* London: Harrap, 1947.

Hyneman, Charles S., *Bureaucracy in a Democracy,* New York: Harper, 1950.

Jones, Stanley W., *Public Administration in Malaya,* London: Royal Institute of International Affairs, 1953.

Robson, William A. (ed.), *The Civil Service in Britain and France,* New York: Macmillan, 1956.

Stein, Harold (ed.), *Public Administration and Policy Development: A Case Book,* New York: Harcourt, Brace, 1952.

Waldo, Dwight, *The Study of Public Administration,* New York: Random House, 1955.

White, Leonard D., *The Administrative State,* New York: 1948.

———, *Introduction to the Study of Public Administration,* New York: Macmillan, fourth edition, 1955.

Chapter 10

Parties, Pressure Groups, and Public Opinion

In order to govern a people it is first necessary to communicate with them. Patterns of communication have varied throughout history from kinship and religious organization to class structures and political parties. Though all these systems are still present in the modern world, the dominant tendency may be said to be that of *party organization*. Both dogmatical and free states rely on parties to maintain a communication link between rulers and ruled. In countries where the object of government is to further Communist or other authoritarian dogma, the party is used to transmit the commands of the ruling group to every section of the community. Free peoples use political parties principally to inform their official leadership of prevailing majority views. However, in each case a two-way channel of communication exists and it is the emphasis placed on the direction of the line of communication that determines the form of government.

Technologically advanced societies, such as that of the United States, possess a highly developed network of intercommunication. It is difficult to distinguish the role played by political parties in acquainting governing institutions with the attitudes of the community from similar practices carried out by other powerful groupings. The craft of public relations, lobbies, and pressure groups has reached a stage of development that permits almost any well-organized interest to bombard the seats of political power with its highly charged messages. Accordingly, it is sometimes suggested that political parties in democratic countries have become merely one of many alternate methods of transmitting the popular will to the institutions of government. This view bears a certain resemblance to the concept of government by *factions* discussed by Madison in *The Federalist*.

It is worth examining Madison's charges as a prelude to the understanding of the exact function of the political party in the modern, representative state.

> Among the numerous advantages promised by a well-constructed union, none deserves to be more accurately developed than its tendency to break and control the violence of faction. . . . By a faction, I understand a number of citizens, whether amounting to majority or minority of the whole, who are united and actuated by some common impulse of passion, or of interest, adverse to the rights of other citizens, or to the permanent and aggregate interests of the community. . . . It is vain to say that enlightened statesmen will be able to adjust these clashing interests, and render them all subservient to the public good. Enlightened statesmen will not always be at the helm: nor, in many cases, can such an adjustment be made at all, without taking into view indirect and remote considerations, which will rarely prevail over the immediate interest which one party may find in disregarding the rights of another, or the good of the whole.
>
> The inference to which we are brought is that the *causes* of faction cannot be removed; and that relief is only to be sought in the means of controlling its *effects*.[1]

It may be noted that Madison's factions correspond to our concepts of interest groups. They form an essential part of the organization of society and cannot be eliminated. However, in the field of government they constitute an irresponsible force because dedicated to narrow ends without regard to consequences for the community as a whole. In the history of the United States and most Western nations the danger of a clashing anarchy of interests has been overcome, at least in part, through the development of political party organization. Parties, then, form a distinct superstructure over the economic, cultural, and religious interest-group pattern. They are distinguished from all other pressure or communication groups by having as an objective the formation of a Government for all the people. This enables them to organize and serve as mouthpiece for responsible public attitudes toward the conduct of the affairs of state. An individual, for example, may be a member of some interest group that is exerting pressure on government to gain some special objective, say to reduce taxes on automobiles. In this capacity he will probably be making demands that pay slight heed to the total needs of the community, as his interest group has no responsibility in that direction. However, the same citizen may be a member of a political party that is not committed to any reduction in automobile taxation. In the second case he is making a responsible judgment in view of his concern for the type of government under which he wishes to live. His opinion as a member of a political party takes obvious precedence over the support he may express for any partial interest group. In brief, political parties serve to permit individuals to reconcile their private interests with their own concept of public necessity. The ensuing judgment must be accepted as authoritative over all other forms of personal expression.

It is, thus, fair to limit the term *political party* to a body constituted to accept responsibility wholly or in part for the total government of the community in which it is organized. The Republican and Democratic parties in the United States and most of the political groupings even in multiparty states such as France come under this category. Special-interest groups, a Prohibition party for example, that seek to advance themselves under a political cloak without any serious intention of accepting full governmental responsibilities fall under Madison's definition of *factions*. The unique place of political parties within the multifarious groupings of society remains essential to the operation of representative government. National unity among free peoples rests on the power of the individual to pass authoritative judgments in his capacity as citizen.

Functions of Political Parties

The primary function of a political party is to contest elections with a view to forming or taking part in a Government. It is worth stressing this point, as political bodies that fail over long periods to achieve governmental power forfeit the right to continue as political parties. Survival as a party depends on fulfillment of the function of active participation in governmental responsibilities. Where multiparty systems prevail, governmental authority may be shared among several parties, but each party, however small, must be prepared to accept some measure of responsibility for the total government of the community. Even when in opposition, a party is controlled by its function to provide an alternative government. It may not pursue policies so irresponsible as to unfit it to accept the burden of power. This function of being responsible to the community for an existing or potential Government overrides all others. In legal terms, it is its charter of incorporation that regulates all subsidiary action. The necessity to bid for power through the electoral process is also fundamental to a party structure. As Edmund Burke pointed out, parties serve as connectors of people with common and shared principles, and they cannot carry out this function without providing the opportunities of like-minded choice present in free elections. It is true that control over the government of a country can be won by other than electoral means. The Bolshevik party of Lenin seized power after failing to win support from the early soviets of workers' and soldiers' deputies. But a group that achieves power through such means is not functioning as a political party but as a revolutionary movement. The Communist Party later remedied the defect by arranging an electoral system that provided the forms of a contest without any of the inconvenient realities.

The second function of a political party is to nominate candidates for popular election and to provide them with the means for presenting their claims to the electorate. Politics may be properly regarded as a profession or art requiring certain standards of competence on the part of its practitioners. Though qualifications differ in kind from those customary in other forms of public service, such as law or medicine, they are no less prerequisite to the enjoyment of office. A reasonable man would no more entrust the business of government to a chance acquaintance than he would the planning of his house. Where a representative or officeholder has to be chosen by many thousands or even millions of voters, it is obvious that fitness for public service must be attested by some responsible body. Because political parties are the only organizations dedicated to the maintenance and continuity of government as a whole, they possess a superior right to winnow out candidates from the mass of enthusiastic amateurs.

The ordinary voter, then, may demand that political parties select suitable candidates for his consideration, that they discipline these candidates into support of a common policy, and that they stand responsible for the behavior of their candidates if elected to office. In rendering such services, parties enjoy considerable leeway to exercise institutional judgment. However, voters, like other consumers, judge products by results. If a party produces unattractive candidates or ones who disappoint in office, voters will withdraw their confidence and the party will lose elections. Lacking electoral victories over any period of time, the party will wither and die. Accordingly, a substantial part of any party organization is devoted to the business of candidate selection, a highly professional task requiring clear analysis of the changing views and structure of the political community. Each nation–state has developed its own system peculiar to its needs, and within large countries such as the United States methods vary from locality to locality. It may be generalized that in all cases parties charge an institutional fee for their services. This charge, levied on the free choice of the mass electorate, takes the form of including a number of candidates proposed for election more because of their value to the party as an institution than because of ability to serve the public. The "fat cat" candidate, able to contribute generously to party funds in return for nomination, has a place in most representative systems. The extent of this practice depends on the watchfulness of any particular electorate. In State elections within the United States, "organization" men may preempt the field, trusting in the casual indifference of the electorate, whereas in national elections such choices entail some risk to the party.

There are two major methods of candidate selection that determine the structure of party organization. In the United States, national parties leave the selection of representatives to local party groupings, reserving the key office of President to be contested by a candidate chosen by a party convention manipulated by the central party organization. This practice rests firmly on the convention that representatives must be residents of their Congressional district. Consequently, American parties are loose federations of State and local groupings lacking institutional centralization and relying for their cohesion on the political leadership displayed by officeholders and within representative bodies. In Britain, by contrast, where there is no residence qualification, the local party organization is under considerable pressure, financial and otherwise, to follow suggestions from the central office of the party concerning nominations. As the Prime Minister in Britain is not chosen by direct vote but through a majority of votes given to candidates of his party, the electorate in general prefer candidates pledged to strict party allegiance. The result is a highly centralized party structure possessing the power to discipline individual representatives by denying them party nomination in future elections.

The American system of local choice, though it perhaps lowers the quality of representatives in terms of political training, allows for greater participation by the ordinary voter in the affairs of local party organization. A major device to give the ordinary citizen control over internal party structure is the *primary election.* This double electoral process throws open differences of opinion within the local party structure to the final decision of the electorate, or at least that part of it sufficiently interested to register as party members. States of the Union committed to one-party control are able by this means to engage in internal political struggle on a popular basis. The function of the political party as an integral part of the constitutional machinery of elections is illustrated in the use of primaries in American politics. For some time the Supreme Court held that political parties were voluntary associations entitled to restrict membership in the manner of private clubs and that consequently the right to vote in a primary election was not protected by Constitutional guarantees. Eventually, in the case of *Smith v. Allwright,* the court reversed itself in the following terms.

Primary elections are conducted by the party under state statutory authority. . . . The United States is a constitutional democracy. Its organic law grants to all citizens a right to participate in the choice of elected officials without restriction by any state because of race. . . . The privilege of membership in a party may be, as this Court said in *Grovey v. Townsend,* no concern of a state. But when, as here, that privilege is also the essential qualification for voting in a primary to select nominees for a general election, the state makes the action of the party the action of the state.[2]

A third function of political parties is the formulation of general policies for submission to the electorate. These policies act as a connecting link between attitudes of the community and a specific governmental program. It should be observed that government policies as such remain in the hands of elected officials and representatives and are not subject to the dictation of party organization, except, of course, in Party states, whether Communist or Fascist. The duty of a political party in this respect is to outline the general direction of policy that might be expected from an administration formed from its ranks. Its formulations might be likened to the issuance of a prospectus by a commercial corporation. Though the aims and objectives listed may be considered binding only in a limited sense, they must be sufficiently clear and straightforward to permit a reasonable voter to estimate the character and basic outlook of the Government for which he is asked to cast a ballot.

Even among peoples experienced in representative systems, the nature and scope of party programs gives rise to misunderstandings and confusion. As electioneering bodies, parties are bound to dramatize to a considerable degree what they estimate to be the favorite hopes of the electorate. This is not necessarily an irresponsible process, for the wishes of the people, however difficult of attainment, deserve expression under conditions of popular government. As elected administrations, on the other hand, a party's incumbents have full responsibility for deciding in practice the degree to which campaign promises are compatible with the actual circumstances in which the country may find itself at any moment. For example, on two occasions, under Woodrow Wilson and later under Franklin D. Roosevelt, the Democratic Party campaigned on the issue of keeping the nation out of a European war. As President of the United States each of these leaders felt compelled at a later time to act in a contrary manner.

In the United States party platforms in national elections normally express basic attitudes rather than specific programs. Voters recognize that they are giving their support to individual politicians linked together by a shared point of view and by no means committed to a concrete program. This permits considerable flexibility within the party itself in the approach to political situations as they arise. As the House of Representatives has to submit itself to the electorate every two years, an alert citizenry may not be long deprived of an opportunity to punish irresponsibility or double-dealing. European countries, by contrast, tend to treat party programs as blueprints of governmental policy. Under parliamentary systems, leaders of the victorious party gain full legislative and executive control of the governing power. Consequently, they may be expected to declare themselves beforehand as to policies. In Britain, both the Conservative and Labour parties issue detailed policy statements before an election and are judged by and large by their capacity to make good on their promises if they win power. This practice inclines voters to cast their vote for specific policies with only secondary consideration for the character of the representative himself. In turn, the elected representative finds himself tied to a clear-cut party program which he may not challenge without appearing to betray his constituents. Accordingly, the level of party discipline is much higher in the British Parliament than in the American Congress. Though the British voter perhaps gains a more obedient servant than his American counterpart, he sacrifices representation based on personal judgment.

Party policies, whether made on the local or the central level, are bound at some time or other to clash with the judgment of the responsible officials in power. For the majority party to refrain from imposing its will on such occasions indicates the operation of a healthy representative system. It must be repeated that representative government is the choice of officeholders by the people at large. To substitute party ideals or party discipline for the supremacy of the elected official is to cross from the representative into the Party state. In general, political parties under Western conditions of government give substance and form to the vague generalities of public opinion. They do not, however, implement or dictate governmental policies. Again it may be said that their role is that of communicator apprising responsible officials of the limits within which they are free to formulate policy without sacrificing popular consent.

Structure of Political Parties

National political parties seek to reflect dominant patterns in the organization of the total community. To survive they must win elections, and, where voting is free and universal, victory belongs to the group that coincides best with the national balance. Party unity based on strong ideals and rigid aims may inhibit rather than promote growth. Burke's famous definition of a party as "a body of men united for promoting by their joint endeavours the national interest upon some particular principle in which they are all agreed," is too aristocratic for application to modern conditions. A small ruling class of leisured gentlemen trained in high ideals of public service might achieve unity through principle. A diverse society living on different economic and social levels must look to more practical bonds for common action. A political community is composed of groups organized around particular attitudes and narrow objectives; wider social or national union depends upon the reconciliation of these attitudes. The mass political party serves more as a substitute for principle than as the champion of a single ideal.

Accordingly, a political party should be composed of the largest possible aggregation of power groups in the community that can be persuaded to ally themselves in a quest for governmental power. Reconciliation of differences is the structural key to successful party formation. On a higher plane, it may be said that parties are formed to promote social union and not to advance ideologies. They achieve this purpose through seeking common goals in the diversity of social groupings that may be advanced by political means. As their bond of union is the prospect of sharing in governmental power, they can afford to embrace in their ranks individuals and groups with widely differing outlooks on morality, economic affairs, religion, and social customs. Tolerance rather than principle is the dynamic of party growth.

Every country must possess its own pattern of party structure to fit the particular organization of its social system. Where a considerable degree of homogeneity prevails, each party may be a loose confederation of groups almost indistinguishable from the rival party. To a certain extent this is true of the United States, where large sections of the population are content to participate in government through either major party in accordance with issues rather than prejudices or deep-rooted convictions. Elsewhere in the world, however, many nations though practicing representative government have not reached this easy level of tolerance. The newly independent nations of Asia and Africa have discovered that deeply felt social cleavages result in parties unfitted to bear true governmental responsibilities. For example, a Prime Minister of Ceylon, the late S. W. R. D. Bandaranaike, gave his opinion that the two-party system was not suited to countries where political parties were organized on the basis of race and religion as well as on political and economic considerations. In support of this conclusion he cited two lands in his area, Burma and Indonesia, where the weakening of the party system had led to the establishment of military dictatorships.[3]

Political parties, then, are the end products of a close social union. They cannot afford to center their organization on deep-rooted divisions that might give them logical coherence at the cost of destroying national solidarity. In consequence, an ideal party structure seeks to cut across economic, cultural, and religious lines by concentrating on alternative methods of achieving commonly agreed upon ends. To some degree, the party struggle is a mock battle, or, better, a form of game in which participants fight only within the rules. This leaves open a wide field for the organization of the community into contending camps for possession of the instrument of government, if government is conceived as a limited weapon for group or individual advancement. As long as men are free they will hold diverse views with some passion and heat as to how best to achieve ends that all consider desirable. Party organization sharpens, clarifies, and provides a medium of expression for, such conflicts of opinion. In Britain, for example, the Labour movement first built up a powerful trade-union organization to win a greater measure of social justice for the wage-earning class. When the balance of economic power had been redressed by the direct action of strikes and unionization, a political party was conceived that would aim at national rather than class objectives. However, in order to win governing power the Labour Party had to divorce itself from strict trade-union control and appeal to many other groups in the electorate. Its great achievement lies in the fact that it has reconciled organized labor with other economic groupings under the banner of national political policies.

A major feature in the structure of political parties under representative regimes is the division between the mass party and the elected cadre of legislators or officials. The conduct of elections, financing of party organization, and the nomination of candidates is in general carried out through the machinery of the mass party. Policy formulation, together with decision-making on the governmental level, is controlled by the elected group. Again the British Labour Party may serve as a clear-cut example. The mass party is organized around a central Executive Committee, which acts as the continuing organ of the Party Conference. Party finance, broad policy determinations, and contact with the public are handled by this Committee, on which trade unions hold 12 out of the 27 seats and constituency delegates only 7. On the other hand, the Parliamentary Labour Party, composed of Members of Parliament, does not accept instructions as to voting policies or political maneuvers from the Executive Committee. Further, the Parliamentary Labour Party as a group elects its Leader, who almost automatically becomes Prime Minister or Leader of the Opposition, depending on the course of elections. The relationship between these two centers of organization is determined from time to time by general party conferences where rival leadership groupings struggle for a vote of confidence. There are many variations in this type of party structure but the basic division between the mass party and the legislative group must be preserved in any system of responsible government. Voters elect individual men, not party labels, to conduct public affairs. Once elected, representatives may not subordinate their judgment to that of any nonelective body even though it constitutes the leadership of their mass party.

Party Hierarchies

In accordance with the normal meaning of organization, a political party is, of course, operated by a determinate group of organizers or leaders. The question arises whether "bossism" is or is not an inner structure of party organization. A well-known theory on this subject proposes the somewhat inaccurate term "the iron law of oligarchies," according to which any form of human organization tends to be operated under oligarchic control.[4] Perhaps the most general answer that can be given to this query is the Biblical admonition: "Thou shalt not muzzle the ox when he treadeth out the corn." Of course, the individuals with the energy and specialized abilities to rise to positions of authority within the party structure exercise power in terms of their own views. If their pride, sense of self-importance, and even private interests, are incidentally served, it would seem an unavoidable fee to be paid for essential services. The question is not really who is entitled to make decisions within a party organization, but rather what type of decisions organization leaders are to be free to make. Regarded from this point of view the party boss may be seen to have a position analogous to that of the executive of a commercial corporation. His freedom to act according to his own will is conditioned by his need to obtain results from an outside environment over which he possesses slight control. In other words, he is free to gamble his judgment against the circumstances, but he knows that if he loses, his job is at stake. The circumstances that challenge a party boss are the confidence of his subordinate party workers and, more importantly, that of the electorate. In local politics in the United States and many other lands, indifferent and ignorant electorates may readily be hoodwinked into permitting party bosses to exercise power unscrupulously. However, when this happens the blame may be attributed more to faulty social organization in that locality than to any inherent defect in the structure of political parties. On a national scale, bossism can operate only on a more subtle basis, concealing from the people their true interests and blinding their judgment on matters of vital concern. Communists and other upholders of authoritarian ideologies are convinced that this is what commonly takes place under representative systems of government. Believers in democracy can hardly accept this view without admitting that self-government is an illusion.

The degree of bossism tolerated within party organization, then, depends upon the social organization of the community as a whole. In a hierarchical society contented to operate on a well-defined class basis, the party organizer may be identical with the power holder in some accepted economic or cultural grouping. British political parties, for example, are perhaps more tightly controlled by an inner hierarchy than those in the United States. However, these hierarchies are in their turn representative to a considerable degree of the prevalent social order, subject to the discipline of the power groups from which they come and operating within an established field of interrelationships between class and economic substructures. The American party boss is a more conspicuous, though probably less powerful, figure, because he is generally isolated in the political field. He plays the swashbuckling role of a condottiere, a hireling to influence elections and officeholders for the benefit of more stable groups.

On the popular level, party organization resembles that of the social club, a voluntary association of people of like interests. The precinct party club in the United States and the Communist cell in Soviet lands exhibit certain similar organizational features. The major distinction lies in the fact that in the United States the party club is truly a voluntary grouping with real powers to choose its own leaders and participate in the formation of general policies. It is worth noting that in neither the U.S.S.R. nor the United States is there any compulsion to belong to a political club. Party organization is something the individual citizen may or may not employ to advance his own views concerning the government of the country. In Russia, he must pass a severe test of conformity to gain this opportunity; in the United States he need merely exercise a personal will to participate. Under both systems ordinary citizens remain aloof in large numbers, apparently content to leave party direction in the hands of enthusiasts. Where free elections are held under a two-party or multiparty system, citizens still retain their right to pass judgment on government even though they remain outside the party organization. Mass parties in a structural sense are still minority leadership groups that appeal to the voter rather than seek to integrate him into their organizational framework. In political participation, as in most forms of human activity, an individual obtains results in accordance with the energy, time, and talent he devotes to it.

Party organization is a costly matter and the question of finance ranks almost equally with the need to attract voluntary party workers. Under free enterprise systems, funds are normally obtained by rendering services to groups or individuals capable of paying for them. Parties are no exception to this rule: their finances stem from individuals and groups who feel that they will benefit by their party's accession to power. Accordingly, parties are organized around centers of wealth accumulation as well as around voting blocs. To some extent, its capacity for raising operational funds may be considered a test of the seriousness of a political party's bid for power. If a party has created an organization and a program that reflects in good part the outlook of a dominant section of the social structure, fund raising provides an additional proof of the sources and depths of its support. Conversely, if a party is bidding for power over the general community in the interests of an economic or ideological minority, its dependence on a narrow range of financial patrons will subordinate party leadership to the holders of the purse strings. Such arrangements are difficult to conceal among free peoples.

It is sometimes suggested that party organization consists of the assimilation of preexisting social groups under a leadership that promises them the advantages of political power. The type of groupings indicated are regional or geographic communities, income and occupational groups, groupings by ethnic origin, religious and educational-level associations. Obviously, political parties do cater to such forms of social organization. However, it is not necessary that, in order to satisfy organized demands, parties become mere federations of already established social formations. The hypothesis that voting blocs function in terms of specific social connections—race, religion, income level, etc.—is questionable and undependable. Citizens, as living individuals, are multidimensional creatures that confound those who would place them in single categories. For example, how could one determine the voting loyalty along bloc lines of a Catholic Negro American conducting a prosperous real-estate business in Boston? In a free country, political parties are unique organizations serving the need of individuals to express personal judgments distinct from those of their other types of social grouping.

The Operation of Political Parties

Politics as a branch of human activity is naturally subject to the corruption and ills of human flesh. The working of political parties highlights weaknesses associated with a quest for power. Within any party structure there may be found elements bent on using the machinery of government for the advancement of personal and group interests at the cost of the community. At all levels of party organization there are opportunities for the abuse of public power which are denied mainly through counteraction on the part of other factors in the body politic. An independent judiciary, for example, presiding over a legal system beyond the reach of political manipulators, serves as a major barrier against corruption of power. Perhaps more important is the sense of office, discussed in a previous chapter. The holders of authority under the constitution and laws of a land are first and foremost responsible officials and only secondarily political partisans. If this is untrue in the case of any particular state, it may be predicted that representative government will not long endure in that area. Even legislative assemblies normally regarded as party-organized operate in terms of superior obligations. Party power over the machinery of government is, accordingly, a limited power, or, more properly, an influence, that has to accommodate itself to the claims of other institutions of equal or superior standing.

In operation, then, political parties function as negotiators, connecting links between group opinion and officials, investigators and critics of official policies and actions, but seldom in the role of decision makers. Among free peoples, it is a loose and improper expression to say that a country is ruled by a party. On the other hand, party government, in the strictest sense, is a reality in dogmatic states. Under such conditions the party is held to be synonymous with the people, representing the final source of power, above law, officialdom, or constitution. Hitler, in the early days of his power, when he was undertaking acts of terrorism against his own Brown Shirts, boasted that the law of Germany was contained in his breast. In terms of the Party state he created, this was a valid premise. It follows logically that only one party can be tolerated in a dogmatic state; two or more bodies claiming to be identical with the sovereign will of the community would be intolerable.

True representative government requires that parties operate in conjunction with each other. Perhaps the clearest form is the two-party system where government is carried on in the atmosphere of a continuous debate between two recognized disputants. The important point is that each party acknowledges the rights and obligations of the other within the system, the majority party granting the minority group adequate opportunities to make its voice heard in the affairs of government and the minority accepting the final authority of a majority vote. There is scant historical evidence to support the view that political parties would exercise this restraint if freed from the bonds of a constitution and formal methods of officeholding. Both England and America have known civil wars that were essentially party wars; in the English Civil War of the seventeenth century, the victorious party beheaded the constitution in the person of the unlucky monarch. Multiparty systems are more complicated but operate on the same principle of mutual interaction in the process of government.

Where state and party are the same, as in authoritarian dictatorships, government may operate quietly and immediately, if not necessarily efficiently. Representative government under party organization, on the other hand, is a noisy, somewhat cumbersome, business, conducted amid a constant cackle of opposing voices. This is the intention of the process: a free people need not merely to be governed but to be ruled through discussion. Otherwise, the efficiencies of power are bought at the cost of voluntary association in a social union. Party politicians, if allowed to operate freely on both sides of the government fence, are gadflies that can sting any incipient tyrants into sanity or death. Of course, a price must be paid for the continual pressures, manipulations, and outcries of party men acting at all levels of national and local government: administration becomes expensive, timid, and sometimes corrupt. However, if the pressure of party politics lifts, the community loses touch with its own government. Parties are needed to reflect the attitudes of the people; where a majority of the people are irresponsible, venal, or foolish, representative government will give them the rule they deserve. In Western countries, it is fair to say that the populations of most lands have won commendable grades for sanity and public morality in the hard test of party responsibility.

In constitutional democracies, parties may be regarded as manipulative, as opposed to dictatorial, instruments of rule. They influence without commanding the actions of officeholders and legislatures. More important still, they may manipulate the expression of popular opinion. The politician, in the partisan sense of the word, is the practitioner of an art that is not to be described in didactic terms. He plays off (as a trout fisher plays his fish) the force of public power on a delicate line of balanced interests. An ideal party strategist should know the exact limits within which his advice will be taken or rejected by the executive organs, the extent to which he may prod the executive by influencing the legislature, and above all the degree to which he can arouse public opinion (or the appearance of popular concern) so as to intimidate all branches of the official government. The party game, though serious and responsible, is still a game, subject to principles now being discovered relating to the theory of games in general.[5]

One of the most controversial issues involved in the organization of parties in a modern state centers in their role in controlling public opinion. An aroused expression of public opinion on a vital topic championed by a political party provides a tempting avenue to power. To obtain such support, a party may have to focus its program sharply on one or more emotional subjects. Once committed, a temptation will arise to go further along the same route until demagoguery prevails and the party has rendered itself unfit to govern within the bonds of a constitutional democracy. The alternative practice of attempting to reflect existing opinion in as many of its facets as possible makes the party a more responsible body at the cost of reducing its dramatic appeal. The compromise most favored among stable communities is for parties to build dramatic issues out of relatively unimportant matters while playing down by tacit mutual agreement emotional questions that might prove disruptive of essential social unity. Thus, the important issue posed by conscription into the armed services in peacetime has been virtually ignored as a party topic in both England and the United States. The examples of Mussolini's Italy and Hitler's Germany still stand as warnings to Western democracy of the danger of the mass party capitalizing on emotional appeals to a vulnerable electorate.

Pressure Groups

The political state is only one among several instruments for the governance of men in modern society. Individuals, by and large, are ruled by their interests, and these interests express themselves through power-wielding institutions. In the course of his ordinary activities, a citizen may submit to the authority of the hierarchy of a business corporation that employs him, the rules of a professional or skilled grouping of which he is a member, the moral injunctions of a Church, and the instructions of many other forms of institutional bodies. Within a free society, these groupings are more or less voluntary; nevertheless, the social order they create conditions the character and type of individual expression open to members of any specific community. Political government in a representative state, then, has to provide for representation of the individual as a member of an existing social order. This is achieved in part through political parties in countries where a two-party or multiparty system prevails. However, the economic, religious, social, and cultural grouping never coincides exactly with the political organization of a community along party lines. Where a power group is underrepresented through party structure in terms of its actual social strength it will seek to redress the balance outside party politics through direct access to the seats of governmental power as a pressure group.

The uses and abuses of pressure groups may be regarded from two points of view. First, their methods of influencing government, and even their right to take part in the political process, may be challenged. This to some extent has been a traditional American attitude: suspicion of lobbies and outside groups in politics. Second, their part in government may be viewed as inevitable, and the resulting evils may be tackled at a deeper level, that of restricting their basic social power through political action. This, in general, has been the European reaction to direct intervention by business, labor, or other interests in the governmental process. In Britain, for example, the Federation of British Industries and the Trade Union Congress are recognized as forces, normally in opposition to each other, exerting direct influence on almost every level of government activity. Comparatively little interest is aroused on questions of how these bodies operate in their dealings with the machinery of the state. At the same time, the electorate treats as a major political issue the balance of economic and social power existing between such institutions.

It may be assumed that in all countries under representative government pressure groups will operate as supplements to a party system. Regulation of their activities is achieved in several ways. In the first place, since the electoral process itself may be distorted by the skillful use of large sums of money supplied by interest groups, regulation by law of election expenses is an obvious method of preventing money interests from obtaining unfair advantages over other social groupings. In a unitary state such as Britain, one general election held every few years determines governmental and party power. Reasonable and strictly enforced laws are capable of controlling the situation. The maximum permissible expenditure for each of the 630 members of the House of Commons ranges between $7,000 and $5,000, and it is calculated that the average candidate spends little more than 40 per cent of this amount.[6] In a federal state such as the United States, control of government power may be effected by elections for State office in fifty States as well as the biennial elections for Congress. With the increasing use of television and other costly media of mass communication, election expenditures present a grave danger of the social corruption of the electoral process. Well-financed interest groups operating both within and outside party alignments are given undue opportunities to sell their wares to the imperfectly informed voter. Serious efforts to keep the basic process of political discussion in the United States clear of paid "commercials" may require stern measures on the national and State levels for the further regulation of election expenses.

THE LOBBY One of the major instruments through which interest groups influence the course of government is the political *lobby*. This is in effect a professional agency employed by some pressure group to contact officials and legislators on behalf of its clients' affairs. American political history has tended to show the lobby in an unfavorable light, particularly in relation to State government. For a period in the nineteenth century, California and some other States had their legislatures virtually controlled by arrogant railway lobbyists. On the national level, suspicion of the abuse of lobbying culminated in the Federal Regulation of Lobbying Act of 1946. Under the provisions of this Act, lobbyists engaged in influencing Congressional legislation must register and submit quarterly statements concerning the source of their funds and how they were spent. Most States have followed suit with similar legislation restricting the unpublicized behavior of lobbies.

Among European nations, the lobby has been accepted generally as an inevitable part of group influence on government. In Britain, the major interest associations—Farmers Union, Federation of British Industries, Trade Union Congress, British Medical Association, British Legion, and many others—are largely integrated into legislative and executive decision-making on a consultative basis. A somewhat shadowy line exists between the officials of these great corporate bodies and the civil servants on whom political Ministers should rely, at least in theory, for guidance. Such control as does manifest itself over the lobbying process is based mainly on the jealousy of bodies such as the parliaments of Britain and France for their privileges as against semipublic organizations of almost equivalent power.

Direct influence by pressure groups on departmental officials and the civil service in general is hard to determine and difficult to control. Laws concerning bribery and corruption of government servants are normally strict in most lands. However, the great expansion of government employment has reduced the gap between the civil servant expert and his colleagues in private industry. Common training and professional interests create close bonds in many fields. Besides, the practice of alternating public and private employment has become so widespread that interest groups have opportunities to influence key government men through inducements related to their future careers. Perhaps the most useful device to control this situation is to regularize methods through which outside groups may lawfully advise government officials. This has the merit of bringing the practice into the open and of making the interest group publicly responsible for the part it plays in decision-making. Thus, in Britain the Federation of British Industries and its opposite number, the Trade Union Congress, are represented on approximately 70 and 60 government committees respectively.[7] It is not overcynical to say that government in advanced countries today has become too far-reaching and serious a business to be entrusted wholly to politicians and civil servants. The right to consultation by nongovernmental power groupings cannot be ignored. Machinery for its regulation may vary from state to state, but the principle remains that those with the most comprehensive knowledge of any situation and the clearest interest in its solution must be integrated into the governmental processes involved.

Public Opinion

The elaborate structure of political parties and interest groups is nothing more than an apparatus for the expression of opinion. Accordingly, it is very important to know whose opinion is being expressed—that of the collectivity or that of puppet masters. It has been suggested previously that within states governed by representative institutions it is difficult if not impossible to substitute over any considerable period of time private views for the voice of the people. However, this is based on the assumption that the *vox populi* really exists and is not a fiction of politics analogous to the useful fictions of law. The question whether this assumption is valid may be reduced to simple terms: Does the ordinary citizen of a modern state possess the capacity to form an opinion that is not wholly illusory concerning public affairs? A sober answer would be that it all depends upon the information given to him and the matters he is asked to consider. Obviously, governmental procedures and policies are seldom clear to the ordinary man immersed in his own concerns. Besides these, however, there are the results, the effects, of government action on daily life, and these are things a free people seldom find difficult to judge. They express themselves, with little regard to the niceties of argument, through voting and through total behavior patterns. If the absence of verbal or logical presentations is overlooked, the reality of public opinion, both on the national and on the majority level, may hardly be denied. It is only when this totality of opinion is expected to act as a public oracle that its reliability becomes tenuous. Skilled interpreters are required before public opinion may be applied to the practical conduct of government.

The main interpreters, under representative forms of government, are political parties, interest groups, and the organs of cultural communication. The first two are subject to summary punishment at the voting booth if their pronouncements run counter to basic community attitudes. The third—press, radio, television, literary and intellectual leaders—are sometimes regarded as an irresponsible force capable of bemusing the ordinary man into subordinating his political judgment to the views and prejudices projected. It is true that newspapers, books, and television personalities do not have to submit to the discipline of elections; they may fill the radio channels, the newsstands, lecture platforms, and bookstores with a clamor that drowns out the voice of the ordinary man. However, it is questionable if they can do so for very long. Though the average citizen cannot outargue them, he remains free to ignore them by the expedient of withholding his indispensable cash. As long as free enterprise and competition rules in the communication field, a monopoly of published or intellectual opinion contrary to the deeply felt attitudes of the community seems inconceivable.

Notes

[1] *The Federalist,* Modern Library, New York: Random House, 1937, No. 10.
[2] *Smith v. Allwright,* 321 U.S. 649 (1944).
[3] *The New York Times,* April 24, 1959.
[4] This theory is discussed in Michels, Robert, *Political Parties,* New York: Dover, 1949.
[5] Shubik, Martin, *Readings in Game Theory and Political Behavior,* Short Studies in Political Science, New York: Random House, 1954.
[6] Ross, J. F. S., *Parliamentary Representation,* London: Eyre and Son, second edition, 1948, p. 128.
[7] Beer, Samuel H., "Pressure Groups and Parties in Britain," *The American Political Science Review,* 1956, **50,** No. 1, 1-23.

Supplementary Readings

Albig, William, *Modern Public Opinion,* New York: McGraw-Hill, 1956.
American Political Science Association, *Toward a More Responsible Two-Party System, A Report of the Committee on Political Parties of the American Political Science Association,* New York: Rinehart, 1950.
Bailey, Sydney D. (ed.), *Political Parties and the Party System in Britain,* New York: Praeger, 1952.
Barron, Richard, *Parties and Politics in Modern France,* Washington: Public Affairs Press, 1958.
Blaisdell, Donald G., *American Democracy under Pressure,* New York: Ronald, 1957.
Brady, Alexander, *Democracy in the Dominions; a Comparative Study in Institutions,* Toronto: University of Toronto Press, second edition, 1952.
Brogan, D. W., *Politics in America,* New York: Harper, 1955.
Duverger, Maurice, translated by North, Barbara and Robert, *Political Parties: Their Organization and Activity in the Modern State,* New York: Wiley, 1954.
Key, Valdimer O., Jr., *Politics, Parties and Pressure Groups,* New York: Crowell, third edition, 1952.
Leiserson, Avery, *Parties and Politics: An Institutional and Behavioral Approach,* New York: Knopf, 1958.
Lipson, Leslie, *The Politics of Equality; New Zealand's Adventures in Democracy,* Chicago: University of Chicago Press, 1948.
McKenzie, Robert T., *British Political Parties,* New York: St. Martins, 1955.
Michels, Robert, translated by de Grazia, Alfred, *First Lectures in Political Sociology,* Minneapolis: University of Minnesota Press, 1949.
Neumann, Sigmund (ed.), *Modern Political Parties, Approaches to Comparative Policies,* Chicago: University of Chicago Press, 1955.
Overacker, Louise, *The Australian Party System,* New Haven: Yale, 1952.

Ranney, Austin, *The Doctrine of Responsible Party Government,* Urbana: University of Illinois Press, 1954.

Schriftgiesser, Karl, *Lobbyists: the Art and Business of Influencing Lawmakers,* Boston, Little, Brown, 1951.

Sorel, Georges, translated by Hulme, T. E., and Roth, J., *Reflections on Violence,* Chicago: Free Press, 1950.

Truman, David B., *The Governmental Process: Political Interests and Public Opinion,* New York: Knopf, 1951.

Chapter 11

Political Attitudes

A survey of the purposes, forms, and instrumentalities of government does not suffice to explain government in action. Before operational practices may be predicted or assessed, the general attitude of governing bodies toward the situations or times in which they find themselves must be taken into account. At any specific period in time, particular governments operate with a bias toward concrete social outlooks. Classification of such outlooks may be attempted on several levels: historical, philosophic, situational. Generalized definitions are bound to be misleading unless related to exact circumstances; nevertheless, the study of politics in operation requires the acceptance of rough categories through which general attitudes of existing governments may be described. Most of the appellations used have become part of the rough-and-tumble of political propaganda, so that dictionary meanings often become secondary to the question of who is using them about whom. Thus, a regime that styles itself conservative may be described as reactionary by its opponents and authoritarian by more detached observers. Of course, all such elements may be present in any actual governing body; the difficulty lies in determining proper standards to be applied in assessing which attitude is sufficiently predominant to decide the category.

Governmental attitudes rarely, if ever, conform to absolute philosophic or religious truths. Though they are creations of the moods and circumstances of changing society, neither religious nor ethical factors may be ruled out—these, in mixed, imperfect forms, are as much part of a current social structure as economic needs or the lust for power. Accordingly, the situation of the times rather than absolute values or principles serves as the progenitor of political attitudes. Present-day categories do not necessarily coincide with those of the recent or historic past: in days when forms of worship were all-important in Europe, governments could be classified in terms of the religious creeds they propagated and the degree of submission of the civil power to theocratic influence. Nowadays, political attitudes, at least in technologically developed lands, may be embraced by terms whose effective use commenced in the eighteenth and nineteenth centuries. Conservatism, liberalism, radicalism, anarchism, socialism, communism, fascism, provide a galaxy of isms that have been said in a somewhat exaggerated quip to have replaced the ancient creeds of religion and morality for twentieth-century man. Because these terms are so much part of the armory of political discussion, it is important to determine their practical signification as means of evaluating government institutions in action. However, value judgments lie so close to the surface in the use of any of those terms that they may not pretend to form a satisfactory basis for any truly objective system of classification. It is probably better to restrict their use to serving as a guide or indication to the character of any particular regime in comparison with contemporary bodies. From the personal point of view, one or other of these political attitudes may be favored according to the religious outlook and cultural and intellectual tastes of the individual without deference to the concept that either history, religion, or science has offered irrefutable proofs of the superiority of any one.

Of course, practical considerations will inhibit too wide a range of choice: in Communist lands, conservatism or liberalism might prove a painful selection, and if one is fortunate enough to live among a free people it would be unseemly to insult their moral standards by opting for some of the more extreme political attitudes.

Conservatism

Many political regimes which, throughout the world, pursue diverse and often contradictory policies may be recognized as linked together through possession of a conservative attitude. The essence of this outlook may be described in Edmund Burke's words as a respect for "reverent antiquity." The fact that patterns of behavior are handed down from one generation to another by processes of imitation and learning tends to equate ease and security with established custom. In the absence of strong external pressures or some internal catastrophe, only the restless and discontented favor innovations. Certainly conservatism is a deep-rooted feature in isolated tribal societies, and in all probability has been the attitude that has prevailed in human government over the longest period of historical time. In Europe, the Age of the Enlightenment, with its appeal to pure reason, the new belief in progress launched by Condorcet in Revolutionary France, the weakening of the ritual bases of tradition in thrones and churches, proved a severe threat to the authority of established custom. Even more serious were the antitraditional aspects of technology burgeoning from the industrial revolution; machines flatly challenged the ability of men to live according to the precepts and standards of their nonindustrial ancestors. This destruction of the habitual conservatism of the masses is now being repeated on a much wider scale among the seven out of ten world inhabitants who reside in underdeveloped areas.

Though the mass base for political conservatism is diminishing, powerful groups in the community may find advocacy of its principles a profitable and legitimate avenue to power. Modern conservatism need not fall into the error of ancestor worship or blind acceptance of the past for its own sake. The value of antiquity, even to such a fervent devotee as Virgil's "pious Aeneas," never lay in mere age, but in the fact that it represented the only source of established order. The upholding of a public order that maintains the continuity of national life has become the slogan of present-day conservatism. This attitude can give rise to meaningful political policies in two major directions. First, it emphasizes the function of government to place the preservation of order beyond all other calls on public force or resources; it gives precedence to security in its physical, cultural, and economic manifestations over ideological experiments, including the idea of progress. Secondly, it distinguishes order from mere repression, linking it instead with that form of social union that flows from institutional and emotional continuity. Conservative political groups may, in certain circumstances, lead in the fight to preserve popular liberty against tyranny. An example may be drawn from as far back as Magna Carta, forced on an innovating tyrant by the champions of a traditional feudal order.

As against this, conservative political forces tend to crystallize their practical objective of order into the maintenance of an outmoded and reactionary social situation through the use of public power. Concentration on order and continuity in a fast-moving social system may readily result in the disorder of institutional practices that lag behind cultural and technological developments. Of course, the established order which conservative regimes exist to defend differs in character in every country; accordingly it is not to be expected that conservative regimes or political groups in different nations will resemble one another in their methods or policies.

BRITISH CONSERVATISM Over the period of the last hundred years, the most continuously successful conservative movement in politics may be attributed to the British Tories and their successors, the modern Conservative Party. From the practical, as contrasted with the philosophic, point of view, the basis of political conservatism was laid by two nineteenth-century British Prime Ministers, Sir Robert Peel and Benjamin Disraeli. The approach of universal suffrage with the passage of the Reform Acts forced the ruling groups of Britain to seek new alignments with the unorganized masses. "Tory democracy," as conceived by the subtle spirit of Disraeli, offered improvement in the economic and social lot of the multitude through vigorous development rather than through destruction of the established order of the state and society. He accepted the fact of change and sought to integrate it into a customary pattern. "In a progressive country change is constant; and the great question is not whether you should resist change which is inevitable but whether that change should be carried out in deference to the manners, the customs, the laws, the traditions, of the people or in deference to abstract principle and arbitrary and general doctrines."[1] Of course, one of the traditions Tory democracy sought to preserve was the privileged position as regards political leadership of a particular economic and social class, the gentry. These, Disraeli declared, were the natural leaders of the people and the champions of the nation against sectionalism.

The proper leaders of the people are the gentlemen of England. If they are not the proper leaders of the people, I do not see why there should be gentlemen. . . . My honourable friends around me call themselves the country party. Why, that was the name once in England of a party who were the foremost to vindicate popular rights—who were the natural leaders of the people and the champions of everything national and popular: and you must blame yourselves alone if you have allowed the power that has been entrusted to you by the Constitution to slip from your hands, to be exercised for other interests than the general good of your country.[2]

It may be said that the party of Disraeli has governed the country at intervals until the present time with at least partial success in persuading the bulk of the electorate that "responsible paternalism" will be as bold and successful in effecting needed economic changes and social advances as theorists on the other side. Lack of theory has been perhaps both the strength and weakness of British conservatism: it has used the authority of the state to control free economic activity along lines which would be considered socialist in the United States, and, in pursuit of national unity and popular favor, it has remained true to few principles except that of belief in the natural superiority of class leadership. National unity, vigorous exercise of state authority, sanctity of property, and, more covertly, preservation of a ruling class or group, constitute the main outlines of a conservative attitude in British politics. Because this outlook does not amount to logical dogma it is able to agree with socialist attitudes as regards state control of economic activities and with Liberal attitudes in respect to liberty, particularly as they relate to the freedom of property. The pragmatic bent of all British political attitudes has proved a major factor in the successful operation of party government. Power shifts from one party to another do not entail serious changes in principles and aims of government, but indicate rather alternative approaches to generally accepted ends.

EUROPEAN CONSERVATISM The established order in most European countries in the late eighteenth and early nineteenth centuries differed considerably from that of Britain. Consequently, European conservative attitudes have developed along different lines from those prevailing in English-speaking countries in general. Though the Austrian statesman Prince Metternich had the foresight to see that the newly emancipated masses should be integrated into the existing establishment, his concept of "conservative socialism" has not generally been followed. Defense of traditionalism has taken the form in Europe for the most part of a defense of privileged institutions such as monarchies, established churches, hereditary aristocracies, and military elites. Popular support has been elicited in the recent past and may still be elicited for the outlook of "the Right" as providing order and continuity in a chaotic world.

The two institutions that have survived as a popular base for present-day European conservatism are the established church and the army. Spain liquidated her revolutionary agonies of the 1930s by basing her governmental structure on these two pillars. Portugal's regime has similar foundations. In France, the latent power of the Right is closely linked to the position of the Army in the state, and the favorite political issue of Rightist groups is the protection of the established church, particularly in educational matters. Though the devotion of European conservatism to specific institutions gives it a belligerent and sometimes even revolutionary character, the Rightist parties are not upholders of a dogmatic ideology that must be imposed on the rest of the community through the use of public force. So long as the institutions it regards as basic to the continuance of the nation–state are safeguarded, European conservatism is prepared to accept a balance of interests with other contending outlooks within a representative system of party government.

AMERICAN CONSERVATISM The established order in the United States has never crystallized into clear-cut institutions such as a ruling class, established church, and military elite. It may even be said that the conservative attitude towards politics expressed itself so completely in the accomplishment of a written Constitution that it thereafter became superfluous except in defense of basic constitutionalism. Popular opinion has come to regard the Supreme Court as the trusted guardian of fundamental tradition and continuity, thus largely removing the key issue of conservatism to a position outside the field of party politics. Of course, a conservative outlook still plays an important part in determining the character of American government, but the forces that constitute the strength of American conservatism tend to operate across party lines or outside party politics altogether. Slavery was the one institution that remained subject to bitter partisan controversy after the acceptance of the Constitution. Calhoun and the Southern wing of the Democratic party entered the political arena with an implacable conservative defense of this institution. The fact that they were prepared to carry their defense of a single institution to the lengths of civil war, which they failed to win, militated against popular acceptance of political conservatism along party lines.

The term *constitutionalism* might be substituted for political conservatism in the United States. Issues touching on the extent to which the spirit as well as the letter of the Constitution is to be observed in the hurly-burly of partisan economic and social struggle test the strength of the conservative attitude within the governing group. Historically speaking, both major parties may be considered to have shown themselves predominantly conservative on this test. What Disraeli dreamed of but never achieved—conversion of a solid core of ordinary wage earners to a politically conservative outlook—has come about naturally in the United States, perhaps through the excellence of the Constitution as a pragmatic summary of traditional values and its skillful adaptation to changing conditions.

Furtherance of the rights of property and business is sometimes associated with a conservative attitude towards politics in the United States. This can be held true in so far as the Constitution itself provides a major bulwark against the destruction of private property or free enterprise. If applied more narrowly and meaningfully, however, it does not provide a very profitable basis for the analysis of political forces. Interest groups concerned with property or business are not necessarily concerned with defense of the traditional structure as a whole. In basic questions of civil rights where fundamental traditions of society are involved, the economically privileged element is as divided as any other section of the community. There is no parallel in the United States to the politically conscious "gentry" of England, who have established themselves among the people as limited though coherent defenders of clear-cut social rights and duties.

Radicalism

The radical outlook in politics may be considered as old as the conservative, and to some extent an unavoidable corollary to the claims of tradition and stability. When an established order in politics or society begins to weigh upon the ambitions or hopes of substantial elements in the community, there will arise inevitably a demand to tear up the old order by its roots and start afresh. *Radicalism* means literally the doctrine of getting at the roots. In the development of the political institutions of the English-speaking peoples, radical thought and action have played a not inconsiderable part in determining both the pace and direction of social change. An early example of English radicalism in brutally frank terms may be taken from a reported speech of the hedgerow priest John Ball to his followers in the Peasant Rebellion of 1381.

> I counsel you therefore well to bethink yourselves, and to take good hearts unto you, that after the manner of a good husband that tilleth his ground, and riddeth out thereof such evil weeds as choke and destroy the good corn, you may destroy first the great lords of the realm, and after, the judges and lawyers, and quest mongers, and all other who have undertaken to be against the commons. For so shall you procure peace and surety to yourselves in times to come; and by dispatching out of the way the great men, there shall be an equality in liberty, and no difference in degrees of nobility; but a like dignity and equal authority in all things brought in among you.[3]

In its subsequent development the radical tradition outgrew, at least among English-speaking peoples, this naive and bloodthirsty approach to institutional change. However, emphasis on the principle of a clean break with former institutional patterns remained the essence of this approach to problems of government and society. The English Puritans, held in bondage to a hated Establishment in religion, strayed into some curious by-paths of total political and economic reform. The Levellers under the leadership of John Lilburne presented Cromwell and the Parliamentarians with the concept of government based on an Agreement of the People that was to create the fundamental law of the land through direct reference to the majority of individuals. Though this appeared shocking and even criminal to the seventeenth-century outlook of Cromwellian England, its enunciation paved the way for future democratic constitutions, particularly that of the United States.

Radicalism as a drive towards rational reform of political institutions had its great philosophic hero in Jeremy Bentham, and its active political supporters in the English Chartists. It spent its political strength in the winning of the series of Reform Acts starting with that of 1832. With the transformation of Parliament, the political power center, into a body responsive to majority opinion, English radicalism moved into channels of economic theory that favored a dominant middle-class commercial element.

Continental European radicalism centered its political philosophy in the doctrines of the Rights of Man advocated in romantic terms by Jean Jacques Rousseau. Commencing with the Jacobins of the French Revolution, political power groups employed this ideological weapon against existing governmental systems down to the culmination of the Revolution of 1848. From that time onwards in Europe, and later elsewhere, political radicalism has been outmaneuvered by its Communist opponent. The uprooting of ancient institutions and their transformation along rational lines has become too obviously an invitation to the Communist machine to seize power.

Within the United States, fundamental institutions of government have seldom been placed in serious jeopardy through the development of radical political attitudes. Opponents of slavery, in particular the radical abolitionists epitomized by William Lloyd Garrison, were willing to risk destruction of national unity in order to uproot a hated institution. Following the catharsis of the Civil War, radicalism manifested itself in movements of economic reform, the Granger movement, Greenbackism and other panaceas based on cheap money, the Populist movement, and to some degree the Progressive Party of Wisconsin. A clear distinction between American radicalism and its European counterpart is that the basic institutions of the political state were not subjected to challenge by any effective power group in the United States. The issues of American radicalism were economic reforms to be carried out within the framework of the existing political system. This variety of social and economic radicalism remains a latent and constitutionally legitimate force in both American and British society.

Liberalism

Though Liberalism has probably been the most powerful single political attitude in English-speaking and European countries during the last century, it is perhaps the most difficult point of view to define or even describe. Political liberalism is, of course, by no means identical with philosophic liberalism. In Britain, its growth has been attributed to the power of a mercantile class pursuing doctrines of laissez faire and free trade in its own interests. European critics of the liberal tradition have identified it with the supremacy of the bourgeois over both aristocracy and proletariat. Even American liberalism may be analyzed, in part, in terms of the promotion of the interests of specific groupings. With reference to liberalism in the United States, Professor Hacker has suggested that its promotion was one of the chief endeavors of the old ruling class.

> The whole rationale of the liberal democratic scheme—incorporating the ideas of individual liberty and limited government—was that it could work as long as it had only to protect a particular section of the community. It takes power to guarantee freedom. And the power of the ruling class was exercised only to carve out an area of freedom for its own members. On the one hand, it shaped the law so that property rights and freedom of expression would be sanctioned; on the other, it kept the emotions of the majority at bay.[4]

Historical factors, however, provide an incomplete explanation of the power and influence of the liberal attitude on the modern political scene. The term has a strong connotation with freedom and liberty in its political as well as dictionary meaning. This freedom is for mankind as living individuals and from the authority of the state viewed as a restraint on the development of individual personality. Thus, the liberal outlook in politics started as a defense of what we now call civil rights. One of its main products, the concept of limited government, remains a rallying point for the political organization of substantial numbers of people throughout the world. In practice, the idea of inviolable rights pertaining to the individual has been colored by the needs and habits of specific societies at particular periods of their development. Thus nineteenth- and twentieth-century liberalism in countries affected by the industrial revolution has been biased towards the safeguarding of private property rights against collective power. Because of this it has drawn to itself the support of considerable sections of the economically powerful middle classes in European and American lands. Its emphasis on religious and cultural toleration and on the dignity of the person has attracted the educated, individualistic element normally dominant among civilized peoples. From this point of view, the weakness of the movement as a governing attitude lay in its negative response to the functions of the state. Political communities cannot be controlled, organized, and sustained merely by limiting the authority of government.

In its development into a more positive type of political attitude European liberalism divided into two main lines of approach. One, a scientific or pseudoscientific form of liberal realism, may be associated with Walter Bagehot's *Physics and Politics*.[5] This book set forth the thesis that the values of highly developed individualistic societies depended upon the cherishing, politically as well as economically and socially, of an elite. Further development of this viewpoint in the writings of Mosca and Pareto has created one type of European liberal attitude that may be considered to some degree opposed to popular democracy. However, the main stream of liberal opinion in the United States, Britain, and elsewhere has achieved a positive approach to the state through serious efforts to improve the machinery by means of which democracy functions. Rule by the majority is a meaningless concept in politics if related to nothing but numbers. The superstructure of the state has to be designed according to principles related to the true end of government before majority will can operate as anything but a blind and dangerous force. It is in this effort to apply positive principles of human dignity and liberty to the working machinery of representative government that present-day liberalism has found its greatest strength. It aspires neither to be the equivalent of democracy nor to oppose it but claims the role of an essential supplement.

The stresses and strains of the twentieth century have not advanced the liberal cause in politics. External dangers, extreme social dislocations, and rapid technological changes have augmented a political need for solidarity and authoritative planning. Power groups imbued with conservative or collectivist outlooks have been better prepared to wield the authority of the state in these directions. Present terminology which places conservatives on the Right wing of social movements and collectivists on the Left assigns Liberals to the Center, a balance wheel against extreme departures in either direction.

Socialism

The collectivist point of view may be distinguished from the communal feeling that permeated the Middle Ages. The latter was based on a sense of belonging within a face-to-face group and on a measure of distrust of larger aggregations. In contrast, modern collectivism owes its origins to the uprooting of great masses of mankind from their traditional fellowships and their reorganization into the impersonal groupings of an industrial society. Consequently, mass organization for primarily economic ends has created social patterns that have reached into the political field. *Socialism* is a very wide term adopted by as antagonistic power figures as Hitler, Stalin, and the leaders of the British Labour Party. One attribute common to all is a readiness to use state authority to recast and reorder the economic system of the community. As this willingness is now shared almost equally by conservative authoritarian groups it provides a rather meaningless bond.

It is questionable whether the term socialist can be applied meaningfully to any political power group unless it is operating within the framework of a class society. Where class distinctions are recognized, the employment of political instrumentalities to win economic gains for the mass of wage earners is a clear socialist objective. The socialist motivation is almost wholly confined to the economic sphere. For this reason, manifestations of the socialist attitude in the present circumstances of the Western world are almost certain to be combined with some other powerful drive, such as *nationalism*—Hitler's National Socialism; *Communism*, in terms of dogmatic Party rule; or egalitarian reformism, as in Britain or Sweden.

Though class-conscious politics provided the original motivation for the growth of the socialist movement, this distinguishing mark began to fade when socialist parties achieved national power. Reformist parties that advocated socialist doctrines were faced with a choice of accepting established constitutional systems or transforming themselves into revolutionary dictatorships backed by a single class. The bulk of European socialists followed the lead of the German Kautsky and the British Labour Party in opting for constitutional reform. As a result of this decision, it became necessary to cross class lines and appeal to the interests of the middle class and farmers and peasants as well as the hard core of industrial workers. Present-day socialist parties outside the Communist orbit are not recognizable as instruments of a single class. They do, however, remain faithful to the basic Marxian doctrine that the order of any given society is determined by the established system for the production and distribution of wealth. Accordingly, they have made alliances of like-economic-interest groupings the basis of political power. This is only practicable when men are tied to a specific economic interest for the greater part of their lives through the division of society into social classes.

Britain, the Scandinavian countries, The Netherlands, and other European nations have found the socialist movement in politics a corrective to class injustices inherent in the traditional structure of their societies. Perhaps because of the ease with which men have moved from one economic and social grouping to another in the United States class divisions have never afforded a sufficiently powerful motivation for the growth of socialism as a force in American politics.

It is sometimes considered that the socialist attitude in politics is antagonistic to the institution of private property and the maintenance of the capitalist system. This viewpoint has ceased to be a very practical guide to political analysis. Concepts of the nature of private-property rights have altered to such an extent under the impact of national security needs and modern industrial and business practices that it is questionable whether in a country such as Britain a Conservative power group would differ greatly from its Socialist opponents in a willingness to subordinate traditional aspects of private property to wider ideas of economic management. Similarly, the capitalist system of the twentieth century has developed, particularly in Europe, through interlocking trusts into a pattern of centralized activity that provides a convenient instrument for political manipulation. If present-day socialism is accounted the enemy of capitalism it generally wears the mask of a boon companion encouraging its victim to gorge itself to death. Certainly the socialist attitude in European politics has furthered interference by the state in economic matters along lines of planning, nationalization of key industries, centralization of economic control, and acceptance by the state of responsibility for community standards of living and productivity. However, conservative groupings have shown almost equal readiness to apply the authority of the state to economic procedures; motivations and methods may differ sharply but end results frequently coincide.

Fascism

The term *fascism* is used frequently to cover a variety of political attitudes. As manifested in Mussolini's Italy and Hitler's Germany, it took the form of a collectivist doctrine distinguished from Marxian communism or socialism by an emphasis on nationalist or racist bonds of social union. In practice, however, it did not neglect economic motivations attractive to the masses, but, rather, overlaid them with a *mystique* of emotional nationalism, theretofore neglected by the Marxists. It paralleled communism in its antitraditional outlook, reviving some of the doctrines of extreme radicalism in a ruthless destruction of established institutions. The end results of fascist accession to power were similar in governmental form to the achievements of the Lenin–Stalin cult: dictatorship over state and people by a single party. Italian Fascism came into power in 1922 purporting to be a cure for national disunity and humiliation. Exploitation of national sentiments served to suppress a near anarchy of partisan disorder, and Mussolini attempted to create a popular basis for a collectivist order by organizing the

Italian community into functional syndics for economic and political purposes. This deeper revolution never went beyond the stage of a façade of paper planning, as it was basically inconsistent with the effective dictatorship of a single political party. However, Italian Fascism in its initial success of rallying a divided people around national symbols has set a pattern that is still influential in the political attitudes of some peoples emerging into nationhood. Thus, the United Arab Republic has come into being at the instigation of a politico-military dictatorship which has successfully subordinated social and economic divisions to a collectivist nationalism. In these later developments, fascist nationalism remains a powerful political attitude likely to affect forms of government in a considerable part of the world, at least during a transition period to a more stable social order.

Hitler's National Socialism was a more sinister phenomenon. The German Folk with Hitler as Leader were envisaged as something more than an historic nation. Their bond of union was to be that of a conquering horde with a mission to impose their racist fantasies on the rest of the world. Socialism then became the organization of all economic resources—labor, capital, all instruments of production and distribution—for the task of collective aggrandizement. The catastrophic consequences of this attitude when adopted by even as powerful and efficient a people as the Germans has probably stifled further development of this form of political hysteria elsewhere for a generation or so. However, traces of the Nazi outlook continue to operate on the political level, particularly in regions where social divisions on racial lines remain acute. The Afrikaner Party in South Africa has committed itself and the state it controls to a system of racial domination necessitating the application of Hitlerian methods of government for its maintenance. A clear distinction between German National Socialism and its later developments lies in the fact that racial unity now serves as the end and purpose of government in areas where the dominant race is either in a minority or perilously balanced against other ethnic divisions. Consequently, it is restricted to a problem of internal tyranny and has ceased to threaten world order as a crusading movement.

*Communism**

Compared to other major political attitudes in the modern world, communism is unique in at least two respects. First, it is doctrinal in a manner and degree that raises it almost to the level of a theological creed. This comparison is necessary in order to emphasize that communism embraces the total nature of man and does not limit itself to politics or economics as do other political viewpoints. Second, communism is only incidentally an attitude towards government within a nation–state: its logical purpose is world government. Because of these basic differences in outlook, communism is the natural enemy of every other form of political attitude, and in fact of every noncommunist government in the world. This is not so much a matter of superior malice as the consequence of a doctrinal assumption of an existing world society in which it is the duty of every communist to work for the dominance of his faith. Where German National Socialism menaced mankind as a world conqueror, communism has replaced it as world subverter.

To understand Communism as a political force it has been necessary since the time of Lenin to grasp the elements of its totalitarian ideology. It was Lenin rather than Marx or Engels who welded the economic and social philosophy of Marx to a political structure in such a manner as to effect the total subjection of the individual to the Party. It is hardly an exaggeration to say that Leninist-Stalinist Communism requires for its fulfillment the appearance of a new type of human being, a "collectivist" man who will be motivated by social dogma rather than individual feelings. This has to be achieved through the use of the political state as an instrument of total control. The basic communist dogma of dialectical materialism postulates that all truths concerning human life are interrelated and all are based on the nature of social systems which

* Here it is appropriate to point out that, throughout this book, the word *communism* has been spelled with a small *c* when it refers to the doctrine—economic, political, philosophic—that stems from Karl Marx and Friedrich Engels; with a capital *C* when it refers to the practices, policies, organizations, and (sometimes quite different) doctrines of parties that, since 1917, have called themselves *Communist*. Thus, for example, some communists proposed "free love"; (Soviet) Communists are exceedingly puritanical.

in turn may be reduced to manifestations of the class struggle. The Party alone has a true understanding of the nature of society; accordingly, all truth must be Party truth. In Lenin's own words:

> We repudiate all morality taken apart from human society and classes. We say that it is a deception, a fraud, a befogging of the minds of the workers and peasants by the landlords and capitalists. We say that our morality is entirely subordinated to the interests of the class struggle of the proletariat. Our morality is derived from the interests of the class struggle of the proletariat. . . . That is why we say that there is no such thing as morality apart from human society; it is a fraud. Morality for us is subordinated to the interests of the class struggle of the proletariat. . . .[6]

It is not difficult in Communist logic to take the next step and grant the Party, as the one source of true understanding, the guardianship of the community under a dictatorship of the proletariat. Further, a doctrine of "democratic centralization" applied to the Party itself creates a hierarchy of power wielding iron discipline.

The Communist attitude, then, resolves itself into a rigid doctrine to which the individual owes absolute submission. Consequently, whenever and wherever Communists obtain power they will forge the type of tyrannical machinery essential to the implementation of their system. Absolutist tyrannies of this nature have been endemic among political societies in the past and are not wholly unknown to non-Communist states today. The new dimension added by the Communist attitude is its spread beyond state boundaries to form a hidden government over all the believers located within other state systems. National political government finds itself challenged within its own domains by a supranational system that makes direct claims on the loyalty and obedience of its citizens. A parallel might be made with the religious movements that warred across state lines in the Europe of the sixteenth and seventeenth centuries. The consequence of this challenge to national loyalties has been, in part, a drawing together of non-Communist political attitudes in defense of a common position—the right of peoples to determine their own affairs as members of nation–states and not as part of a world proletariat.

Communism's relationship to democracy poses a difficult question. On the one hand, absolute authority over the community is claimed on behalf of a minority Party group organized on strict hierarchical lines. On the other hand, political rule is carried out with close observance of representative forms and through means of an apparatus designed to enforce mass participation in the governing process. Perhaps the Communist attitude might be described as the promotion of captive democracy. It goes beyond previous concepts of popular rule to envisage government based on the acceptance and participation of masses trained and conditioned by force and persuasion in the tenets of a single dogma. The instrumentalities employed to accomplish this mass conditioning are the socialization of all major forms of property and Party control over education and the communication of opinion in any form. Communism is, accordingly, something more than a political attitude, as its objective is total conversion of the individuals comprising the community. According to the degree in which this is achieved in practice, democratic procedures may take over in actuality under Communist governments. This concept of democracy is diametrically opposed to the traditional Western viewpoint that a democratic system of government exists in order to increase the individuality and responsibility of the individual. The Communist version is that political democracy is an instrumentality for the merging of the individual person into the dogmatic mold of a group consciousness.

Anarchism

A body of political opinion centering in concepts of anarchy exists to the left of both socialism and communism. It may be described as extreme left-wing, not in terms of its ability to disrupt the established order—which is negligible—but because of its uncompromising stand for the abolition of all forms of governmental control over human society. In essence, the anarchistic attitude conceives of mankind as inherently cooperative and hence fully capable of living together in peace and prosperity without the intervention of organized force; political government accordingly is the serpent in the garden of mankind's natural brotherhood.

In the nineteenth century, two varieties of anarchist attitude were developed: philosophic or utopian anarchism, and a violent revolutionary brand. Proudhon, in France, advocated total abolition of all political institutions and their replacement by a complicated system of voluntary barter or credit based on units of labor contribution. Though this afforded slight threat to the authority of the established governments of the day, it may be said to have provided inspiration for the development of *anarchic-syndicalism,* a more effective political movement and one still latent in European Latin countries. The organizational principle of anarchic-syndicalism is that guilds or *syndics* of workers or professionals are the true producers and upholders of the community. Because their common interests induce them to work together harmoniously, they have no need of political institutions beyond some vague meeting place where the totality of syndics can exchange views. Under European conditions, the promotion of this political attitude greatly enhanced the solidarity of the trade-union movement, though it never came within measurable distance of unseating governmental power in any particular state.

Russian anarchism advocated violent revolution as an immediate means of attaining destruction of the state. Certain of its devotees attempted this piecemeal through assassination of political figures, bringing invidious notoriety which still clings to the reputation of the cause. However, the leading proponents, Bakunin and Prince Kropotkin, conceived of revolution on a more serious scale. Bakunin contested with Marx for leadership of the First International Workingmen's Association and direction of a communist movement. Kropotkin, the theorist, argued that communism could be achieved only through anarchy. "Every society which has abolished private property will be forced to organize itself on the lines of Communistic Anarchy. Anarchy leads to Communism, and Communism to Anarchy, both alike being expressions of the predominant tendency in modern societies, the pursuit of equality."[7] Though the Russian anarchists lost the power struggle for control of the revolutionary party, enough of their point of view remains embedded in the logic of Communist dogma to cause embarrassment to present leadership. Thus "the withering away of the state" promised by Marx and Lenin as a final culmination of communism in action is a return to anarchy. In Communist lands the anarchist attitude is still considered a dangerously potent antagonist to the established order.

In Britain and to a lesser extent the United States, anarchism has taken the form of a detached, almost philosophic, critique of the basic assumptions of government. That this has hardly endangered the foundations of the state may be gathered from the bestowal of the honor of knighthood on the leader of British philosophic anarchism, the art critic Sir Herbert Read. Nevertheless, providing an organizational framework for denial of the basic postulates of government has not been without effect in English-speaking lands.

In summary, the anarchist attitude is one of unrelenting protest to any or all of the claims of governmental authority; when maintained on the level of intellectual theory it serves a purpose in confronting powers-that-be with awkward questions.

Notes

[1] Quoted from Viereck, Peter, *Conservatism: From John Adams to Churchill,* Princeton: Van Nostrand, 1956, p. 43.

[2] Quoted from White, W. J., *The Conservative Tradition,* London: A. & C. Black, 1950, p. 164.

[3] Quoted from *British Historical Speeches and Orations From the 12th to the 20th Century,* Everyman's Library, New York: Dutton, 1937, p. 4.

[4] Hacker, Andrew, "Liberal Democracy and Social Control," *The American Political Science Review,* 1957, **51,** No. 4, 1013. For a critique of this viewpoint see Cook, Samuel D., "Hacker's Liberal Democracy and Social Control: A Critique," in the same issue.

[5] *Cf.* Easton, David, "Walter Bagehot and Liberal Realism," *The American Political Science Review,* 1949, **43,** No. 1, 17-37.

[6] Quoted from Hook, Sidney, *Marx and the Marxists,* Princeton: Van Nostrand, 1955, pp. 195-196.

[7] Quoted from Spahr, Margaret (ed.), *Readings in Recent Political Philosophy,* New York: Macmillan, 1949, p. 372.

Supplementary Readings

Benda, Julien, translated by Aldington, Richard, *Treason of the Intellectuals,* New York: Morrow, 1928.

Bosanquet, Bernard, *The Philosophical Theory of the State,* London: Macmillan, fourth edition, 1951.

Chandler, Albert R. (ed.), *The Clash of Political Ideals,* New York: Appleton, revised edition, 1949.

Ebenstein, William, *Today's Isms: Communism, Fascism, Capitalism, Socialism,* Englewood Cliffs: Prentice-Hall, 1954.

Egbert, Donald D., and Persons, Stow (eds.), *Socialism and American Life,* Princeton: Princeton University Press, 1952.

Halévy, Elie, translated by Morris, Mary, *The Growth of Philosophic Radicalism,* Boston: Beacon Press, 1955.

Hartz, Louis, *The Liberal Tradition in America,* New York: Harcourt, Brace, 1955.

Hobhouse, L. T., *Liberalism,* New York: Holt, 1911.

Hook, Sidney, *Marx and the Marxists,* Princeton: Van Nostrand, 1955.

Hunt, R. N. Carew, *Marxism, Past and Present,* New York: Macmillan, 1955.

Kirk, Russell, *The Conservative Mind; From Burke to Santayana,* Chicago: Regnery, 1953.

Kropotkin, P. A., *The Conquest of Bread,* New York: Vanguard, 1926.

Lerner, Max, *America as a Civilization: Life and Thought in the United States Today,* New York: Simon and Schuster, 1957.

Mayo, Henry B., *Democracy and Marxism,* New York: Oxford, 1955.

Meyers, Marvin, *The Jacksonian Persuasion: Politics and Belief,* Stanford: Stanford University Press, 1957.

Plamenatz, John, *Mill's Utilitarianism; reprinted with a Study of the English Utilitarians,* Oxford: Blackwell, 1949.

Read, Sir Herbert, *Anarchy and Order: Essays in Politics,* London: Faber, 1954.

Sabine, George H., *Marxism,* Ithaca: Cornell University Press, 1958.

Schumpeter, Joseph A., *Capitalism, Socialism and Democracy,* New York: Harper, second edition, 1947.

Viereck, Peter, *Conservatism; From John Adams to Churchill,* Princeton: Van Nostrand, 1956.

Watkins, Frederick M., *The Political Tradition of the West: A Study in the Development of Modern Liberalism,* Cambridge: Harvard, 1948.

White, R. J. (ed.), *The Conservative Tradition,* London: Kaye, 1950.

Chapter 12

Devolutionary Forms—

Regional and Local

In a previous chapter it was suggested that an urge to engage in cooperative activities accounted for a considerable part of the willingness of men to submit to the authority of their fellows. Political obedience is, in general, voluntary rather than compelled. Accordingly, governmental institutions designed to utilize cooperative attitudes are more numerous, and, among free peoples, more powerful, than the hierarchies of force. Public services, sanitation, water supply, hospitals, recreational parks, poor relief, and other activities constitute joint enterprises in which we engage willingly through institutions cast in a governmental form.

Of course, there are objectors to one or all of these corporate enterprises, just as there are still individuals who believe in the right of private revenge as superior to the operation of law. Any civilized community has to carry out a certain amount of housekeeping in common and the legal cloak of governmental structure normally provides the most convenient framework. It is perhaps unfortunate that language denoting power and force is used to describe these public and generally local bodies engaged in performing domestic tasks for the community. Historically, at least in England and most European countries, communal activities in the field of government preceded centralized authority; integration of these scattered, voluntaristic bodies within a concept of national government under one or more supreme authorities gave rise to the political fiction that they were all emanations from a central political power. The theory that the sanitation truck sweeping the local streets operates under a grant of authority from the sovereign state or nation is perhaps constitutionally necessary but certainly is of little use in relating the community to its sanitation problems.

In the language of politics, the term *devolution* is used to describe the delegation of powers from one authority to another. Generally speaking, political devolution usually recognizes already existing situations, providing the stamp of legality on methods of social control with a long tradition of their own. Where government activities impinge increasingly on the behavior of individuals, the extent to which devolution is permitted to traditional local bodies determines the degree of citizen participation. Thus, a 1952–54 Royal Commission inquiring into Scottish demands for Home Rule made the following observation:

> When the State's interference with the individual was insignificant, it mattered little to the Scotsman whether this came from Edinburgh or London. But when so many domestic matters are no longer under control of the individual and so many enterprises require some form of official authorisation, he begins to wonder why orders and instructions should come to him from London, to question whether Whitehall has taken sufficient account of local conditions, and to criticise not government but what he regards, however erroneously, as the English government.[1]

To some extent the degree of devolution of government functions within a modern state measures the voluntary element present in the body politic. Centralized authority tends to separate itself from the community, either through the creation of power castes or through the adoption of some dogmatic ideology. Representative institutions and the electoral process provide only a partial counterbalance to the isolation of power; a substructure of community bodies responsible for the operation of public services in the localities remains essential for the participation of individuals in popular rule in the true sense of the term. The liberties of English-speaking peoples in particular have been based historically on their capacity to adapt local self-government to all forms of constitutional evolution. An ideal balance may be said to occur when the central authority plans and proclaims policies which are left to local bodies to apply under the general supervision of the national or state governments. Writing on the spirit of democracy in the young Republic in the 1830s, Alexis de Tocqueville had this to say:

> But I am of the opinion that a centralized administration is fit only to enervate the nations in which it exists, by incessantly diminishing their local spirit. . . . Granting, for an instant, that the villages and counties of the United States would be more usefully governed by a central authority which they had never seen than by functionaries taken from among them; admitting, for the sake of argument, that there would be more security in America, and the resources of society would be better employed there, if the whole administration centered in a single arm —still the *political* advantages which the Americans derive from their decentralized system would induce me to prefer it to the contrary plan. It profits but little, after all, that a vigilant authority always protects the tranquillity of my pleasures and constantly averts all dangers from my path, without my care or concern, if this same authority is the absolute master of my liberty and life that when it languishes everything languishes around it, that when it sleeps everything must sleep, and that when it dies the state itself must perish.[2]

Regional Government

Self-rule and nationalism sometimes find themselves at conflicting purposes within the same geographical area. It is an apparent paradox that strong convictions of national unity should develop institutions that interfere with practices of self-government. This occurs most often when government is regarded as one indivisible power; thus the force and strength needed to preserve the nation from internal disruption and external foes are equated with the organization used to decide building regulations, traffic plans, sewage disposal, and other local affairs. People's business and nation's business overlap but do not necessarily coincide: in general, the former is cooperative, immediate, and limited in application to particular localities, while the latter demands obedience, preserves long-range continuity, and serves interests of the community beyond neighborhood levels. A major and as yet unsolved problem of political organization is how to disentangle these two aspects of government so as to leave the cooperative neighborhood spirit free to flourish without weakening the unity of the nation in its essential tasks.

Federalism is, of course, one of the major solutions, but as it has developed in the last hundred years it leaves many difficulties unsolved. In the first place, components of a federal state are apt to be historical or cultural accidents that fail to coincide with rational economic or social groupings. Perpetuation of such arrangements may raise barriers of sentimental traditionalism against practical interests of the community for changing geographical and national structures of organization. In its extreme forms, federalism may prove so reluctant a step towards national unity that the resulting state lacks the strength either to defend itself against outside enemies or to retain its internal cohesion.

Among the new states entering the world's theater, the West African state of Nigeria provides an example of both the abuses and uses of federalism in nation building. Three historically separated groupings—the Islamic peoples of the north, Hausa and Fulani; the eastern region dominated by the Ibo; and the western territory of the Yoruba—are engaged in maneuvering for a constitutional structure that will preserve the maximum amount of regional autonomy. This has aroused many other less important tribal groupings to demand rights for themselves within an even more fractionalized nation–state. It is questionable whether the forces that preserve tribal distinctions are compatible with the building of a modern economy and the social integration needed for survival as a nation.

Switzerland, conversely, with its historic cantons and communes based more often than not on geographical as well as cultural realities, has been able to approximate true regional autonomy under federalist principles.

In the United States, regional autonomy has been in part frozen into a pattern that may be considered outmoded in respect to economic and cultural realities. States of the Union rarely represent rational subdivisions in terms of the ordinary concerns of their inhabitants; they provide a governmental and sometimes cultural heraldry that gratifies the pride of their citizenry at some cost to the efficiency of public business. One consequence of a failure to adapt regional autonomy to changing economic and social conditions has been the rise in power of the central administration. National necessities have led to broad interpretations of the federal principle of the Constitution that remove major areas of social control outside the scope of regional or State supervision. It is paradoxical that the nation responsible for introduction of federal systems of government should have expanded its area and population with the utmost vigor while it was reducing its reliance on regional self-government. Some of the blame for this state of affairs should be laid on the concept of a written Constitution which crystallized an historic grouping of the people as if it were an immutable pattern. Regionalism is merely a device to allow individuals greater opportunities to participate in the service functions of government while leaving the policy making and command of force needed for national integration to be conducted on a higher level. If regions become things-in-themselves, repositories of irrelevant loyalties and sentiments, they decline in value as practical instruments of self-government in the bread-and-butter concerns of daily life. It would be reckless to prophesy that regional combinations based on common economic interests and geographical contiguity are likely to replace traditional State governments. However, on the administrative level indications of more natural combinations have begun to appear in such bodies as the Tennessee Valley Authority, the Missouri Valley Authority, and several other lesser interstate combinations such as the Port of New York Authority.

A further instrument that may be used to promote practical regional ends is the Council of State Governments operated as a joint governmental agency by all the States for the exchange of information and service facilities. This organization serves as a central secretariat for many other associations of State officials from the Governor's Conference down to the National Association of State Purchasing Officials. It works in conjunction with an older body, the National Conference of Commissioners on Uniform State Laws. Though these bodies represent all the States, they provide a meeting place where groups of States with regional interests may plan action in common. It may be emphasized that the prevalent form of State government in the United States does not amount to true regional government, and that such indications of a development of regional administration as exist should be considered extraconstitutional.

Countries under unitary forms of government have developed what may be more practical devices for regional self-government than historic federal states. Thus, the postwar Italian Republic is divided into regions, provinces, and communes. "The Regions are constituted as autonomous bodies with their own powers and functions according to the principles fixed by the Constitution."[3] Italian *regions* are governed by elected regional councils, which select an executive committee headed by a president from their own members. They are given a wide array of matters to handle, including the supervision of rural and urban police forces distinct from the national police force. Principally, however, they are responsible for public services in the economic and social spheres. A commissioner of the central government resides in the capital of each region to exercise national administrative powers and coordinate them with regional activities. This form of linkage follows the tradition established by Napoleon when he reformed the provincial administration of France. Regional and local government is always held subordinate to the power of the central administration, not only in constitutional theory but through the active intervention of a high-ranking administrator able to call upon staff and police forces of his own.

Until recently, France has been regarded as the European model of centralized government operating down to the local level. Since Revolutionary times, the French Republic has been divided into *departments*—of which there are now about one hundred—headed by a prefect as delegate of the national government and organized to apply the laws of the central administration to local circumstances. Each department is divided into *communes,* corresponding to more traditional subdivisions of villages, towns, and districts. On the commune level, elected mayors and councils maintained a limited measure of governmental responsibility. A trend towards greater decentralization that commenced under the Fourth Republic has gathered momentum under the Fifth Republic. Article 72 of the 1958 French Constitution reads:

The territorial units of the Republic are the communes, the departments, the Overseas Territories. Other territorial units may be created by law. These units shall be free to govern themselves through elected councils and under the conditions stipulated by law. In the departments and the territories, the Delegate of the Government shall be responsible for the national interests, for administrative supervision, and for seeing that the laws are respected.

Further evidence of a deliberate policy of decentralization may be adduced from an official statement in 1959 of the balance sheet of the de Gaulle administration.

As a result of state action in the past and of the evolution of modern society, the framework and means of action of the departments and communes had little by little been reduced over the years. The recent measures are designed to enable the local communities to carry on efficiently their essential functions in the nation. These measures grant the local communities more freedom to manage their own affairs without State supervision, render local taxation more flexible, and broaden the scope of local administration.[4]

Regional arrangements in British government are complicated by problems of cultural particularism analogous to those encountered in the United States. Under provisions of the Government of Ireland Act of 1920, the people of Northern Ireland are granted a legislative body, styled Parliament, of their own, though they retain their right to elect members to the United Kingdom Parliament. Scotland is integrated into the United Kingdom Constitution through two historic events: the union of the Crowns in 1603, and a voluntary Union of Parliaments in 1707. However, a considerable degree of Scottish autonomy remains as regards both policy making and administrative practices. This is achieved on the executive level through the presence in the Cabinet of a representative of Scottish interests, the Secretary of State for Scotland. The United Kingdom Parliament may either pass separate laws for Scotland or by an "application clause" adapt ordinary laws of the land to the peculiarities of Scottish jurisprudence. In any case, lawmaking is in the hands of a legislature in which the Scottish electorate claims barely one ninth of the seats. A unique constitutional device provides some of the substance of legislative devolution while preserving a façade of undivided parliamentary authority. A Standing Committee on Scottish Bills, generally termed the Scottish

Grand Committee, composed of all seventy-one Scottish members and from ten to fifteen other members selected from the non-Scottish membership of the House of Commons with regard to the balance of parties, is given power to consider measures affecting Scotland as if it were a committee of the full House. To some extent this Scottish Grand Committee combines functions analogous to those of a powerful Congressional committee with law-making powers normally associated with a State legislature. Of course, American and British legislative practices do not coincide. First, the British Government of the day decides whether a measure is peculiar to Scotland and therefore entitled to be considered by the Scottish Grand Committee. Secondly, though this has never happened, the opposition of six members from non-Scottish constituencies could block reference of the second reading of any Bill to the Scottish Grand Committee. By and large, however, a measure of devolution of lawmaking does occur within the British legislature in favor of traditional Scottish interests.

Perhaps devolution is most marked in the field of administration. The Scottish Office, presided over by the Secretary of State for Scotland, is unique among British government departments both as regards the wide range of matters under its control and because of its dispersed location. For most practical purposes its headquarters are in Edinburgh, not London. Though this form of devolution works satisfactorily in practice, it is basically illogical and unfair to the interests of other sections of the nation. The principality of Wales, the Duchy of Cornwall, and other historic subdivisions possess like claims to special treatment; if they were all accorded similar autonomy, the administrative and political structure of the United Kingdom might begin to disintegrate.

The problem of adapting methods of regional decentralization to current needs remains acute in most English-speaking lands. The Canadian provinces have developed as cultural communities seeking, as in the case of predominantly French-speaking Quebec, to use governmental autonomy to conserve distinct ways of life. To a lesser degree, the states of the Australian Commonwealth have hindered the practical development of their continent through the preservation of historic rivalries. A very difficult question is involved concerning the use of government institutions to foster cultural distinctions that are no longer the natural resultants of enforced social and economic isolation. It may be argued—and in many quarters it is still strongly believed—that it is a duty of a system of government to preserve, at any cost in efficiency, the traditional cultural divisions of its people. As against this, attempts by government to maintain established religions that could no longer rely on their own internal strength have proved historic disasters. It is possible that cultural autonomy in fast-moving technological civilizations should fight its own battles with cultural weapons, eschewing the dangerous aid of the political state.

In the United States, the question of the devolution of governmental authority is not concerned solely with the desirability of the decentralization of power but with the larger issue of what bodies should be the recipients of such authority. The answer provided by the Constitution was in the nature of an experiment dictated by the exigencies of the times. In the words of the 1955 Commission on Intergovernmental Relations:[5]

> The American federal system began as an experiment. It was the third try for a solution on this continent to the age-old problem of striking a satisfactory balance between the needs for central strength and central regulation on the one hand and the values of local freedom of action on the other. . . . The federal system devised by the framers of the Constitution was the product of necessity rather than doctrine. . . . They were content to keep the States substantially as they knew them, but they deplored certain economic and fiscal tendencies in some States. Chiefly, they felt a very practical need for a central government of much greater strength and potentialities than the Articles [of Confederation] provided. . . .
>
> The States make their own constitutions, and the laws that govern elections, crimes, property, contracts, torts, domestic relations, and the like. Most States in their turn have tended in practice to establish a virtually federal division of powers and responsibilities between themselves, their counties, and their municipalities. This autonomy has kept under local controls most of the schools, the police, the ordinary administration of criminal and civil justice, the local taxes, and the provision of most municipal services. It has kept in local hands also the machinery of elections and with it, in the main, the control of the party system. It has enabled local option to prevail on a wide

range of domestic concerns. It has furnished local bases of power and refuge for political leaders, parties, and policies in opposition to those for the time being dominant in Washington. It has made possible a large degree of popular participation and consent.

However, the Commission goes on to point out that the historic structure of the States does not provide a final answer to problems of devolution within the American system.

The objective of decentralization cannot be attained by a readjustment of National-State relations alone. It will be fully achieved only when carried through to the lowest levels of government, where every citizen has the opportunity to participate actively and directly. The strengthening of local governments requires that activities that can be handled by these units be allocated to them, together with the financial resources necessary for their support.

The local government map of the United States discloses a maze of approximately 109,000 governmental units, many of them overlapping. This figure includes some 3,000 counties, 17,000 incorporated municipalities, 17,000 towns and townships, 60,000 independent school districts, and 12,000 special districts. It is not uncommon for the same area to be served by a municipality, a school district, a county, and one or more special districts. A considerable number of metropolitan areas embrace over 100 separate local government units. More or less hidden in this picture is a paradox that constantly plagues the States and bars an easy solution of the problem of achieving the decentralization of government—too many local governments, not enough local government.[6]

Clearly, the United States has not achieved the direct type of decentralization of national authority to the community level possible under the French or even the British system. The State stands as an historic intermediary limiting the access of the organized locality to use of the funds or powers of the central administration.

Certain types of social needs affecting local communities but felt on a nation-wide scale have brought the central administration into direct contact with local government units during the last decade. This is particularly true of the field of housing, where State aid has been inadequate or unavailable. The Housing Act of 1954, Title III, Slum Clearance and Urban Renewal, permits projects to be initiated by a local public agency that has received enabling authority from the State. After being passed upon by officials of the central government, they are executed by the local agency with financial and technical assistance from the central authorities. For all practical purposes, State government is by-passed in this process and a direct relationship established between administrative departments of the national government and local governing bodies. Whether or not these forms of direct contact will be extended, reducing the State to a formal role in many matters of social management, depends to some extent on whether there is expansion of nation-wide interests claiming government assistance and on the fiscal capacity of the States to meet these needs from their own resources. The future educational needs of the country, for example, have been proclaimed on some sides as necessitating direct federal aid to communities for better schools. An approach to the British system of a national administrative network interlocking with local self-governing bodies remains possible even within the limitations of an historic federalism.

Self-rule on the Locality Level

In principle, at least, a community enjoys local self-rule when it is free to determine the organization of its own local government. Constitutional theory in the United States gives to the State governments power to decide the forms of government that shall prevail in urban and rural areas. Home rule in the sense of liberty to frame their own charters has been granted, with considerable qualifications, to municipalities by about one third of the States. Counties or rural areas have not fared so well: only six States have seen fit to accord them similar privileges. No serious deprivation of local self-determination is involved, as the general practice permits a choice of optional charters by the local community. These optional charters are varying models of government organization drawn up by the State legislature as suitable for local communities of different sizes and characteristics. In general, the needs and wishes of local residents are adequately met by one or other of these charters. On the administrative level, supervision by State authorities is an uncertain and haphazard factor. Counties experience considerable State interference, as they are considered generally as integral subdivisions of the State's administrative system. Municipalities, particularly metropolitan centers such as New York and Chicago, are relatively free from direct interventions on the part of State officials. This contrasts with British and European patterns of central inspectorates emanating from departments, such as the British Home Office, specially organized to oversee local affairs.

GRANTS-IN-AID One of the principal devices that relate local self-governing communities to higher levels of government is known as the *grant-in-aid*. This form of aid is based on the practical attitude that, while a community should be free within reasonable bounds to undertake on its own initiative those types of governmental enterprise for which it is prepared to meet the full cost, when it is either unwilling or unable to pay for public services from local taxation, then it must accept standards of performance and supervision laid down by the contributing partner. In some cases, the local community may be free in actuality as well as theory to reject conditions imposed through a grant-in-aid by an outright rejection of the grant. There are many other circumstances, however, in which the State has imposed legal obligations on local government to fulfill certain tasks—as in the education of children and the carrying out of social-welfare plans—that are beyond the unaided fiscal capacities of independent localities. A measure of compulsion is then present to serve as agent of the higher government in return for receiving its money. Control of urban and rural governments through grants-in-aid is somewhat complicated on the American scene through the fact that a substantial number of such grants emanate originally from the national rather than a State government. The State itself, then, is acting as a partial agent, and the municipality is being guided by conditions laid down by national officials who lack any direct constitutional right of supervision. In Britain, where the national government has direct access to local governing bodies, the grant-in-aid can be used more clearly and powerfully to bring about common standards of performance from the utilization of general tax money. Britain, France, and other European countries organized as unitary states, maintain national inspectorates of high quality on both the technical and administrative level to assist as well as supervise operations of local government. The federal character of the United States inhibits the development of this form of skilled professional advice and intercommunication.

A major drawback to centralized planning for local developments is the sacrifice of local autonomy and individual participation involved in any outside control of the design of growth of a locality. In postwar Britain, planning on a national scale was adopted in order to conserve scarce resources. However, a full measure of local participation in the planning as well as execution of developments was assured by the Town and Country Planning Act of 1947. Under the provisions of this Act, county or borough councils were appointed as local Planning Authorities to work under the central ministry. If they wished they could form joint Planning Boards with two or more counties. A practice of appointing subordinate committees to represent subdivisions within the county brought planning to the level of gardening as a major hobby of the British householder.[7] In the United States, the Federal Housing Acts of 1949 and 1954 follow similar principles of inviting localities to plan their own improvements within broad lines, with the central government paying two thirds of the cost and the local government one third.

Forms of Local Government

Perhaps because of its closeness to the community, local government throughout the centuries has been wedded to a conciliar form. It should be remembered that, through a considerable part of Western history, the community, in a local specific sense, and not the individual, was regarded as the true social unit. In the fourteenth-century treatise *Defensor Pacis,* Marsilius of Padua states principles of communal government that remain valid to the present day.

> I mean by citizen any man who participates in the civil community, in the principate or the council or the jury according to his rank. . . .
>
> Now that we have defined the citizen and the more weighty multitude of citizens, let us return to our announced purpose: namely to demonstrate that the human authority of legislation belongs only to

the corporation of citizens or to its more weighty part. The primary human authority, in an absolute sense, to make or institute laws, belongs only to him from whom alone the best laws can proceed. Now this is the corporation of citizens, or its more weighty part, which represents the whole corporation, because it is not easy or possible to bring all persons to one opinion on account of the deficient nature of some, who through individual perversity or ignorance dissent from the common opinion but whose irrational protestations or contradictions ought not to impede or frustrate the common benefit. Therefore the authority to make or institute laws belongs only to the corporation of citizens, or to its more weighty part.[8]

It is a matter of convenience whether the "more weighty part" of the citizenry choose to exercise their authority through an elected council, serving as a rule-making and executive body under the chairmanship of a mayor, or prefer to elect a mayor as principal official with a council as an advisory rather than controlling body. The former is the normal pattern in Britain, while in the United States the tendency lies toward a strong mayor, city-manager, or commission form of government. One divergence from traditional patterns manifested in the United States is the development of special boards and commissions to administer particular functions of local government. Creation of school districts governed by school boards independently chosen by the electorate provides the most common example. The two principles involved in selecting forms of municipal government are community representation and control, and administrative efficiency. It is seldom possible to reconcile these two ends in an exact fashion: the strong managerial types of government stress efficiency, while conciliar forms allow for a maximum of interest representation.

Some confusion necessarily arises from the use of the term "government" to cover both the great affairs of state conducted on the national level and the type of cooperative housekeeping engaged in by local communities. The difference is more than one of scope and extent; it amounts to a distinction in kind. An individual owes obedience to and participation in the general government of his country as a major social and moral obligation. Private interests and conveniences are for the most part secondary to fulfillment of duties on which the whole security of personal rights must rest. This is far less true, if it is true at all, of local administration. Littering the streets with discarded papers, for example, is bad community manners and may quite rightly be curbed by force if necessary. It is not, however, equivalent to breaching national security or even evading payment of national taxation.

The quality of local affairs, then, is basically a compromise of legitimate interests rather than acceptance by individual citizens of a superior interest. Both the profound concern and the indifference in which local government matters are held by groups in the community may be explained by the type of interests most strongly affected. Thus, the average citizen in a large town or metropolis may look upon his city government with the skeptical outlook summed up by the slang phrase, "You can't beat City Hall." In normal life, the local administration is the purveyor of certain classes of services; the best that may be expected of it is that they provide these services without fail, efficiently, and at a minimum cost. At the same time, various groups within the community on every economic and educational level find that their personal livelihoods, social interests, or ideals are inextricably entangled with the conduct of local government. The intensity of their interest—whether it be that of the fireman struggling to maintain a family on inadequate pay or of the businessman who may stand to lose or gain great sums through the passage of certain types of zoning ordinance—gives them special status in relation to control of the machinery of government. It is sometimes suggested that the well-organized special interests that play an almost overwhelming part in the practical conduct of local administration constitute a sinister phenomenon. This point of view perhaps stems from some misunderstanding of the peculiarly voluntaristic nature of local self-government. The bulk of the community are under no social or moral obligation to engage themselves in administrative problems; basic protection of individual rights and dignity, along with group security, is provided for by participation in national affairs. The citizen may be a passive customer of local government so long as he abides by the maxim *caveat emptor* (let the buyer beware) and uses his collective power to punish if he considers himself cheated. The special groups, driven to participate by their own interests, are not necessarily selfish in the narrow sense: humanitarian bodies, groups with aesthetic interests, bodies concerned with economical use of tax funds, are as likely to prove active and effective as groups motivated by greed. If the structure of government is such that equal opportunity is granted to every type of group to make its influence felt in accordance with the degree of public support it can arouse, then individuals who wish to participate in local administration may do so freely by joining an active group or creating one of their own. The complaint that this would be too much trouble to be worth while is a measure of the individual's true concern.

If local government is regarded as primarily government through a balance of group interests, certain factors apply that are not always present in government on a higher level. The general community electorate holds a watching brief to see that no single group or combination of groups is able to distort the government apparatus in such a way as to prevent other alternative groupings from winning influence or power. This may be achieved by an electoral process carried out with strict attention to requirements of true representation. Devices such as difficult registration procedures that bar voters at election time, obscure and overlong ballots, gerrymandering electoral districts, tricky primary laws and procedures, have all been used in the past and are likely to be employed again whenever the vigilance of the community is relaxed. Cumulatively, they possess the effect of hindering the mass of the citizenry from passing judgment on the practices and performances of the administration in office. Because a proper balance of group representation is vital in local matters, the electoral method of proportional representation is most successful on this level. In France, it has proved itself a bulwark of lively community government, underpinning the sometimes shaky structure on the national level. Several American cities have experimented with this technique with results that may be considered controversial. Cincinnati, Ohio, is the largest city to have retained proportional representation over several decades.[9] Group representation is particularly important in large American cities where minority groupings such as the Negro or Spanish-speaking electorate may suffer political neglect.

The elected official on the city or county level is subject frequently to unfair disparagement. In the United States, he is apt to be caricatured as a City Hall politician, and in Britain as a dull fellow with a curious interest in sewers and water-supply systems. In part, this may be due to the fact that local government is the main provider of public services, and the citizen–customer exercises the privilege of a free man to grumble at what he is receiving and the price he has to pay. It is one of the dividends of representative government among free peoples that the supply of devoted men making voluntary efforts for slight rewards in the service of the community has never dried up. An experience in living under an authoritarian regime where only the distant bureaucrat or the Party man handles public affairs would prove illuminating to the casual citizen of democratic lands. Where citizens cease to be preferred customers and become mere objects of governmental action, maintenance of personal dignity, comfort, or convenience becomes a matter of deference to the men in office. Of course, many self-seekers and downright rogues infiltrate into elected office on the local level. Perhaps this is not always the fault of the system, but of the temper of the electorate itself. If group representation is working smoothly and powerful sections of the community are not overscrupulous as to how they gain political and administrative advantages, it may be expected that they will elect unsuitable men to office. Ever since the days of Plato men have dreamed that it is possible to have a political government that will rise superior to the weaknesses of the community it represents, but to this day it remains a heartbreaking dream. More powerful factors than political organization—the cultural and religious standards achieved by the bulk of the inhabitants of a locality—serve as the true determinants of governmental virtue. The number and quality of voluntary public servants who rise above the level of their fellows to contribute disinterested service verifies the medieval belief that communal feeling is natural to mankind. It is not necessary to postulate unusual social idealism. A citizen may extend his responsibilities from his own family and garden to embrace a neighborhood, a ward, or a whole city without shifting his viewpoint appreciably from practical and attainable graces of living. The care of local government organization among free peoples should be to safeguard this wellspring of communal fellowship from the sterile hand of administrative bureaucracy or the disease of party bigotry. It would be difficult to discriminate between types of elected officials on the local government level in the United States, Britain, and free European countries. Perhaps it would be fair to say that they all equally mirror their communities and beyond that it remains a question of cultural taste.

Local Civil Service

Efficiency in the provision of public services in local communities rests obviously on the level of expertness and integrity that prevails among professional employees. It cannot be pretended that standards that might be expected from private enterprise are common in the municipal services of any country enjoying representative institutions of government. Private corporations that handle large-scale construction, engineering, or supply problems find it profitable to organize on a national or regional basis, employing highly skilled and paid experts who can be shifted around to deal with problems that arise in many areas. Localities staff their services, even in great metropolitan areas, for discontinuous and limited tasks that make economic use of superior ability difficult to achieve.

Resulting loss in efficiency of performance should be considered a price that has to be paid to maintain control by the community over its own affairs. Elected officials cannot be responsible to the community for the operation of the public services unless they possess the power of hiring and discharging professional workers. At best, this places hiring and staffing procedures on a somewhat amateur, restricted level, and at worst opens the door to patronage, favoritism, and corruption. Though most major American cities have adopted civil-service procedures modeled on those of the national or State governments, they must by and large be accounted façades rather than strong operative checks on the patronage habits of the political element. Again, community outlook may be held responsible at least as much as organizational defects in the political machinery. A traditional American attitude that has endured for more than a hundred years is that posts in local government employment belong by right to community residents and that they may be regarded to some extent as a means of "looking after" certain worthy elements. This viewpoint hinders career opportunities for those who choose to specialize in professional aspects of public service. For example, if telephone services (closely analogous to community public services) had to be organized strictly on a local or even State-wide basis, personnel problems would certainly affect efficiency of operations and raise costs. When more and more economic activities and professional skills are unifying themselves on a national scale, the parochialism of municipal and county services increasingly burdens costs and performance.

Britain, as a unitary state, is able to avoid some of the difficulties presented by American conditions. First, there is a wide range of local officials that have their salary range, qualifications for appointment, and conditions under which they may be dismissed, determined by departments of the central government. Key appointments, such as the clerk of the county council, who is in effect the principal executive officer on the professional level, the medical officer, and even certain classes of sanitary inspectors fall within this category. This makes it possible to enforce national standards of recompense and ability over the whole network of local government bodies. Secondly, since, under these conditions, localities are unable to supply skilled personnel on the higher levels from their own resources, a practice has arisen of advertising appointments in local service on a nation-wide basis, which permits the development of professional specializations that offer a secure career to able men. A further consequence has been the rise of respected guilds among the various professions and skills, thus strengthening the position of the community civil servant against political malpractices. A tendency in this direction may be noted on the higher levels of professional appointments in American municipalities, particularly with regard to the important post of city manager. A professional organization of city managers now exists which would make it difficult for a fair-sized community to appoint an improperly trained person to such a post. However, the city-manager association is not yet strong enough to protect its members against irresponsible dismissal or abuse in office. Other positions that require high standards of professional expertness—superintendents of school systems, city engineers, medical officers—are still filled for the most part according to the unhindered judgment of local political leaders.

Relation of Local to National Government

It has been emphasized previously that the business of local government is primarily the provision of public services and not the basic ruling of the people in terms of internal order or external security. This division of functions is of fundamental importance for the protection of individual rights and the furtherance of national union. On the level of national government, individual citizens have to recognize the existence of an interest superior to their private or group interests, because the possibility of any peaceful development of interests is based on the continuance and strength of the nation–state. However, when national government descends too far into the private and particular affairs of the citizen body, intolerable strains may arise between the devotion of the individual to his personal concerns and the need for submission to a larger will. In authoritarian countries, this hazard is met by subordinating personal interests and beliefs to the force and fanaticism of Party dogma. Free peoples largely escape the dilemma by interweaving a pattern of local self-government between the citizen and the nation, at least on matters that are not essential to the existence of the state. When the question is one of services rather than obligations, it becomes legitimate to promote group interests on a particular basis. Local politics allows a limited indulgence in neighborhood and group rivalries without endangering the unity of the nation. Besides this, it keeps alive the communal sense still needed to underpin the modern experiment of naked individualism. It is questionable whether any man has strength enough to be free by himself; first there must be experience of belonging to a free community, and then pride of membership in a free nation. The particularism, inefficiency, and sometimes downright corruption, of local government is probably a small price to pay for the preservation of all these graded steps to effective liberty.

Notes

[1] Royal Commission on Scottish Affairs (1952-54) Report. Command 9212, Edinburgh: Her Majesty's Stationery Office, p. 13.

[2] de Toqueville, Alexis, *Democracy in America,* Vintage Books, New York: Knopf, 1954, Vol. I, pp. 90 and 96.

[3] Constitution of the Italian Republic, 1947, Article 115.

[4] Balance Sheet of the de Gaulle Administration, June 3, 1958–February 5, 1959. *French Affairs*—No. 84, New York: Embassy of France, Information Service, May, 1959, p. 36.

[5] The Commission on Intergovernmental Relations, A Report to the President for Transmittal to Congress, Washington: United States Government Printing Office, June, 1955, pp. 9 and 34.

[6] *Ibid.,* p. 47.

[7] For an account of British practices see Presthus, R. Vance, "British Town and Country Planning: Local Participation," *The American Political Science Review,* 1951, **45,** No. 3, 756-769.

[8] Quoted from Lewis, Ewart, *Medieval Political Ideas,* New York: Knopf, 1954, Vol. I, p. 75.

[9] See Straetz, Ralph A., *PR Politics in Cincinnati,* New York: New York University Press, 1958.

Supplementary Readings

Alderfer, Harold F., *American Local Government and Administration,* New York: Macmillan, 1956.

Anderson, William, and Weidner, Edward W., *State and Local Government in the United States,* New York: Holt, 1951.

Beloff, Max, "The 'Federal Solution' in its Application to Europe, Asia and Africa," *Political Studies,* 1953, **1,** No. 2, 114-131.

Benson, George C. S., *The New Centralization,* New York: Rinehart, 1941.

Birch, A. H., *Federalism, Finance, and Social Legislation in Canada, Australia, and the United States,* New York: Oxford, 1955.

Bowie, Robert R., and Friedrich, Carl J., *Studies in Federalism,* Boston: Little, Brown, 1954.

Chapman, Brian, *The Prefects and Provincial France,* London: Macmillan, 1953.

Clark, Jane P., *The Rise of a New Federalism,* New York: Columbia, 1938.

Commission on Intergovernmental Relations, *A Report to the President for Transmittal to Congress,* Washington: United States Government Printing Office, June, 1955.

Dawson, R. M., *The Government of Canada,* Toronto: University of Toronto Press, 1947.

Finer, Herman, *English Local Government,* London: Methuen, fourth edition revised, 1950.

Greenwood, Gordon, *The Future of Australian Federalism,* Melbourne: Melbourne University Press, 1946.

Hinden, Rita (ed.), *Local Government and the Colonies,* London: Macmillan, 1950.

Livingston, W. S., *Federalism and Constitutional Change,* New York: Oxford, 1956.

Mott, Rodney L., *Home Rule for America's Cities,* Chicago: American Municipal Association, 1949.

Robson, William A. (ed.), *Great Cities of the World; Their Government, Politics, and Planning,* New York: Macmillan, 1955.

———, *Introduction to French Local Government,* London: 1953.

Sawer, G., et al., *Federalism in Australia,* Melbourne: F. W. Cheshire, 1949.

Wheare, Kenneth C., *Federal Government,* New York: Oxford, third edition, 1953.

TWO

THE BUSINESS OF GOVERNMENT

Chapter **13**

The Nature of an Internal Order—

Civil Rights

As in the case of other human institutions, government must be judged finally according to how well it conducts its prescribed business. Application of this pragmatic standard, however, is rendered difficult by lack of general agreement as to the specific nature of the business of government. In a previous chapter it has been seen that one form of governmental order—the Communist—sets itself the task of an almost total reordering of man's nature. Obviously, if such objectives are accepted success or failure may only be determined in the dim vistas of the future. Present governmental practices would be subject to evaluation solely by the inner ranks of the hierarchical initiates. Because of the incapacity of a majority of inhabitants to judge the accomplishments of political systems with self-proclaimed ends of this character, it seems proper to dismiss them as tyrannies, that is, governments whose primary business is the retention of power in the hands of self-sufficient groupings. Analysis of the governmental process, then, in terms of objective functions of government may be limited to governments based on consent, or, in other words, the political order among free peoples.

Even among free peoples, general consensus regarding the functions of government may be reached only along very broad lines. Minimum objectives are: maintenance of internal order, promotion of general welfare, and protection against external dangers. It is useful to adopt these essential functions—essential because in their absence the consent of the community to the political system could hardly be assumed—as standards of evaluation of governmental activity. Their minimal character assures that varied and complex acts of government will be examined in terms of their relationship to basic functions of the state. However, for purposes of practical analysis these standards provide at best a point of view rather than any detailed schedule of values.

Thus, preservation of internal order appears a more down-to-earth and limited concept than advancement of human liberty. Unfortunately, if the nature of the internal order of a modern community is examined closely, the apparent simplicity and directness of the objective begins to fade. What order is to be preserved? An historic order that no longer suits changed needs, or an order that corresponds to the desires of a majority of living inhabitants? A dogmatic order of which only a minority of the community possess understanding? In line with previously discussed interpretations of representative government among free peoples, it is apparent that internal order must be imbued with the passive or active consent of the bulk of the citizenry. The extent of active consent may be judged approximately through election results, but any estimation of the degree of passive consent presents a more difficult problem. Nevertheless, it is one that institutions of government must solve in order to operate; if legislative assemblies or public officials had to await express approval from the general populace before carrying out policies or acts of government, representative government would become impossible. At the same time, failure to gauge limitations of passive consent in a free country may prove equally fatal.

Civil Rights as a Standard of Passive Consent

A pragmatic, historically proved type of internal order suitable for peoples under representative government may be based on a framework of civil rights. Observance of such rights constitutes an understanding by government of the limits within which individuals composing the political community are prepared to render their obedience. If a constitution, written or unwritten, makes definite to the citizen body the nature of its civil rights, government may generally operate freely within these limits, secure in the obedience and support of the bulk of its constituents. For, as

Aristotle points out: "To live by the rule of the constitution ought not to be regarded as slavery, but rather as salvation."[1] Certainly, the American tradition from the days of the acceptance of the Constitution onwards has tended to equate the legitimacy of government with the preservation of civil rights. In very general terms, the will of the government may impose any type of internal order on the community so long as it complies with the strictures of the basic pattern of civil rights. The art of government, then, is action within the boundaries imposed by the passive consent of the community and made known through constitutional rules or conventions determining civil rights. Decidedly, it is not the function of government to refrain from acting in order to safeguard liberties of the individual; on the contrary, it is the business of government to act and discipline the community, as chief protagonist of a cooperative effort to uphold an agreed-upon method of social existence. That aspect which liberty wears as a government-enforced pattern of mutual living is often overlooked, giving rise to the viewpoint that the state is the principal opponent, rather than the most active proponent, of individual freedom. It is true, as Mr. Justice Frankfurter points out, that "personal freedom is best maintained —so long as the remedial channels of the democratic process remain open and unobstructed—when it is ingrained in a people's habits and not enforced against popular policy by the coercion of adjudicated law."[2] Yet the protection of a people's habits against internal violence is one of the most difficult tasks confronting representative government. It cannot be accomplished by a withdrawal of governmental power from this vital field, but rather through its wise and skillful use. Thus, Mr. Justice Harlan describes in the following terms the basic political order that seems essential to personal liberty within the United States.

But the liberty secured by the Constitution of the United States to every person within its jurisdiction does not import an absolute right in each person to be, at all times and in all circumstances, wholly freed from restraint. There are manifold restraints to which every person is necessarily subject for the common good. On any other basis organized society could not exist with safety to its members. Society based on the rule that each one is a law unto himself would soon be confronted with disorder and anarchy. Real liberty for all could not exist under the operation of a principle which recognizes the right of each individual person to use his own, whether in respect of his person or his property, regardless of the injury that may be done to others.[3]

Freedom of Thought and Speech

Without means of communication between its individual components, any society, political or cultural, might be accounted stillborn. The process of discussion provides an operational framework for political systems based on the consent of the governed. Without freedom to inquire, engage in argumentation and exchange of opinions concerning all aspects of social activity, there can be no general consensus above the level of superstitious acceptance of authority. Therefore, it is the business of government among free peoples to insure conditions that make discussion possible through maintenance of a public order in which political institutions as well as private parties are restrained from repressing the flow of opinion by violence and force. Mr. Justice Brandeis gave clear expression to this point of view in relation to the American Constitution.

> Those who won our independence believed that the final end of the state was to make men free to develop their faculties, and that in its government the deliberative forces should prevail over the arbitrary. They valued liberty both as an end and as a means. They believed liberty to be the secret of happiness and courage to be the secret of liberty. They believed that freedom to think as you will and to speak as you think are means indispensable to the discovery and spread of political truth; that without free speech and assembly discussion would be futile; that with them, discussion affords ordinarily adequate protection against the dissemination of noxious doctrine; that the greatest menace to freedom is an inert people; that public discussion is a political duty; and that this should be a fundamental principle of the American government. . . . If there be time to expose through discussion the falsehood and fallacies, to avert the evil by the processes of education, the remedy to be applied is more speech, not enforced silence. Only an emergency can justify repression.[4]

These gallant words may be considered applicable outside the American sphere as well, to all forms of government based on the consent of a free people.

Considerable practical difficulties remain as to how political government should maintain the delicate balance of an order in which the climate of opinion is unmarred by forceful repression. Individual nations adopt different means in accordance with the behavior patterns of their citizens. Some fundamental factors, however, may be considered common to all civilized communities. In the first place, certain communications of ideas may constitute an integral part of a recognized offense against the community. Thus, a pamphlet entitled "1000 Easy Banks to Rob and How to Go About It" may in ordinary understanding as well as law prove a recognizable constituent of a criminal act. Public forms of expression are behavioral acts subject to the ordinary law of the land. There are several customary offenses which are peculiar to the arts of expression: obscenity, slander, and libel, among others. It is just as much the business of government to suppress these outbursts as it is its concern to safeguard the freedom of the press. It may be recalled that the rule of law is successor to and substitute for the reign of private violence. If government fails to apply the force of law to the righting of private wrongs in any widespread area, a resurgence of violence outside the law is likely to occur.

Free speech does not exist in a social vacuum; it is the product of an order protected by government. Methods of protection need not conform to the strict logic of any philosophical system; as long as they work in a given situation, government in a free society is fulfilling one of its major functions. Because many basic arrangements in American government are subject to the process of judicial review, a scholastic attitude centering in fine points of law dominates consideration of the practical question of the desirable limits of freedom of speech. Doctrines such as that of "clear and present danger" exercise a baleful fascination over the lay mind. This rule is well set out by Mr. Justice Douglas in the case of *Terminiello v. Chicago:*

> That is why freedom of speech though not absolute . . . is nevertheless protected against censorship or punishment, unless shown likely to produce a clear and present danger of a serious substantive evil that rises far above public inconvenience, annoyance, or unrest. . . . There is no room under our Constitution for a more restrictive view. For the alternative would lead to standardization of ideas either by legislatures, courts, or dominant political or community groups.[5]

However, in the same case the dissenting voice of Mr. Justice Jackson presented an opposed viewpoint.

> But if we maintain a general policy of free speaking, we must recognize that its inevitable consequence will be sporadic local outbreaks of violence; for it is the nature of men to be intolerant of attacks upon institutions, personalities and ideas for which they really care. In the long run, maintenance of free speech will be more endangered if the population can have no protection from the abuses which lead to violence. . . . The choice is not between order and liberty. It is between liberty with order and anarchy without either. There is danger that if the Court does not temper its doctrinaire logic with a little more practical wisdom, it will convert the constitutional Bill of Rights into a suicide pact.

In Britain, there is at least equal regard paid to principles of free speech as a basic constituent of individual liberty. Political methods of upholding free expression are perhaps more direct, with individual officials or Parliament itself being held responsible directly to the electorate for any apparent breach of popular conventions on this subject. The courts in general have been able to deal with situations as they arose by reducing them to the pragmatic question of whether a police officer was entitled to intervene to prevent a breach of the peace.[6]

Government responsibility for the structure of free expression through a free press, free publication, and unhindered public meetings lies at the basis of public order in representative democracies. Though there are no immutable principles as to how this order is best fulfilled, it is not too difficult for a community to recognize failures in performance and punish the administration of the day for its incapacity to fulfill a major function of government in a free country.

FREEDOM OF BELIEF In the past history of Western peoples, diversity of religious beliefs was regarded as a constant and dangerous threat to public order. Considering the fury and passion of religious convictions in former times, this was probably a far from erroneous view. Religious toleration, in those countries where it exists, is largely the creation of the system of government that has withdrawn public support from the prosecutor of belief and threatened him with the fate of the common criminal if he pursues his bigotry with private violence. There have been two major steps in ordering a community's religious passions. First, government withdrew as the protagonist of one particular creed in its internal struggle to dominate or exterminate its rivals. Second, government protects the free exercise of religious faith even when held by unpopular minorities.

In the United States, particular emphasis has been placed on the denial of state support to any organized religion. A lucid interpretation of the First Amendment in this connection has been given by Mr. Justice Black.

> The "establishment of religion" clause of the First Amendment means at least this. Neither a state nor the federal government can set up a church. Neither can pass laws which aid one religion over another. Neither can force or influence a person to go to or remain away from church against his will or force him to profess a belief or disbelief in any religion. No person can be punished for entertaining or professing religious beliefs or disbeliefs, for church attendance or non-attendance. No tax in any amount, large or small, can be levied to support any religious activities or institutions, whatever they may be called, or whatever form they may adopt to teach or practice religion. Neither a state nor the federal government can, openly or secretly, participate in the affairs of any religious organizations or groups and vice versa. In the words of Jefferson, the clause against establishment of religion by law was intended to erect "a wall of separation between church and state." . . . The First Amendment has erected a wall between church and state. That wall must be kept high and impregnable.[7]

Because of conditions pertaining to its population growth, the United States became a "melting pot" of ancient cultures. If government had not acted in terms of strict religious neutrality, latent suspicions and hatreds born of religious persecution elsewhere might have seriously threatened social and political unity.

The American political order based on strict religious neutrality is based on the American situation and is by no means applicable to the government of free peoples under other cultural conditions. Thus, in a Latin country where an overwhelming section of the community subscribe to the Catholic faith, the type of internal order government creates to meet the religious situation may differ radically from the American solution. For example, under the fundamental principles of the Italian Constitution there is included special recognition of the place of the Catholic Church. The state and the Catholic Church are, each in its own order, independent and sovereign. Their relationships are regulated by the Lateran Pacts.[8] A more equivocal status is accorded other religious groupings.

> All religious confessions are equally free before the law. Religious confessions other than the Catholic have the right to organize according to their own statutes in so far as they do not conflict with the Italian juridical order. Their relationships with the state are regulated by law on the basis of agreements with the appropriate representatives.[9]

It is questionable whether the historic Protestant minority, the Waldensians, would agree that these constitutional provisions have accorded true equality of treatment to their sect in so far as the exercise of government power and protection are concerned.

France, on the other hand, proclaims herself a secular Republic and makes no constitutional provisions for the favoring or protection of religion in any form. Britain indulges in historic confusion on the subject. An established church, the Church of England, is maintained for one section of the country—it has only missionary standing in Scotland. However, this church no longer represents the religious views of a majority of the electorate, even in England. From a purely political point of view, it is a "class" or "party" church, and is accorded no special rights in its religious operations. However, its hierarchy hold positions of great political influence as members of the House of Lords and as traditional counselors of the monarch. In payment for this preferred political position, the Church of England has to sacrifice an important part of its autonomy as a religious institution: it may not make changes in its basic ritual or creed without the consent of Parliament. In quite recent times, Parliament has refused such consent after long and heated debate in which elected politicians expounded the Faith according to their consciences and legislated the will of the Almighty.

The nature and degree of support political institutions may accord the establishments of religion, then, is largely a question of expediency related to the popular temper of the moment. Nevertheless, the question of the free exercise of religious faith may determine whether an administration is entitled to rank among free governments. If the type of internal order which a government defends interferes with basic religious practices it is difficult to assume that it enjoys even the passive consent of the community. Backward societies where a majority of one faith insist on the persecution of minority faiths may be postulated and probably still exist. However, their right to be termed a free people if they insist on majority tyranny is questionable. More common is institutional tyranny sparked by power groups and dependent on the helplessness or indifference of the majority of the people. The clearest example in present times is the Soviet campaign against religion, carried out with the instrumentalities of government. Governments based on the consent of free peoples are under a duty to create and support an internal order designed to permit the free exercise of religious practices and usages, at least as long as the bulk of the citizens are believers in one or other of the forms of organized religion.

This function of government in relation to the internal order is by no means simple to perform. At what point may the religious enthusiasm of some be curbed in favor of superior interests of the many? Mr. Justice Frankfurter elucidates this problem in terms of the American Constitution.

Centuries of strife over the erection of particular dogmas as exclusive or all-comprehending faiths led to the inclusion of a guarantee for religious freedom in the Bill of Rights. . . . So pervasive is the acceptance of this precious right that its scope is brought into question, as here, only when the conscience of individuals collides with the felt necessities of society. Certainly the affirmative pursuit of one's convictions about the ultimate mystery of the universe and man's relation to it is placed beyond the reach of law. Government may not interfere with organized or individual expression of belief or disbelief. Propagation of belief—or even of disbelief in the supernatural—is protected, whether in church or chapel, mosque or synagogue, tabernacle or meeting-house. Likewise the Constitution assures generous immunity to the individual from imposition of penalties for offending, in the course of his own religious activities, the religious views of others, be they a minority or those who are dominant in government. . . .

But the manifold character of man's relations may bring his conception of religious duty into conflict with the secular interests of his fellow-men. When does the constitutional guarantee compel exemption from doing what society thinks necessary for the promotion of some great common end, or from penalty for conduct which appears dangerous to the general good? . . . Conscientious scruples have not in the course of the long struggle for religious toleration relieved the individual from obedience to a general law not aimed at the promotion or restriction of religious beliefs. The mere possession of religious convictions which contradict the relevant concerns of a political society does not relieve the citizen from the discharge of political responsibilities.[10]

A wide range of social activities is involved in the conflict between private conscience and public duty: conscientious objection to war service, obedience to public health requirements, methods of education, among others. Legislatures and administrators on all levels have to deal with these problems through policy formation and decision-making. It is misleading to regard government as merely under a duty to refrain from interfering with the free choice of the individual. A considerable part of the planning and action of government bodies is concerned with the task of preserving an internal order balanced between the necessities of the community and the liberties of the individual. Thus, in France, as in many Catholic lands, the interlocking of the educational systems supported by the Church and the State, respectively, presents a burning political issue.

Security of the Person and Home

Where consent and not fear motivates obedience to the political order, it is the function of government to protect individuals against arbitrary harm to their persons or invasions of their privacy. Of course the greater part of government activity in this direction is of the nature of "police" work—the repression of private, unsocial deeds. However, government officials themselves possess force which may be misapplied to the hurt of individual citizens. An internal order, then, has to be constructed which will balance necessities of governmental force against the claim of the individual to reasonable security for his person. Though this is one of the most difficult of all problems of government to solve on a practical basis, failure to achieve a satisfactory compromise is disastrous to the existence of a free society. The end result of abdication to unchecked governmental power over the individual has been imaginatively portrayed in George Orwell's *1984*.

The Constitution of the United States crystallizes a hard-fought tradition of English-speaking peoples in the provisions it lays down for security of the person. Article I, Section 9, declares: "the Privilege of the Writ of Habeas Corpus shall not be suspended, unless when in Cases of Rebellion or Invasion the public Safety may require it." This famous writ, invented in England in the twelfth century and perfected by Acts of Parliament in the seventeenth century, is a proved remedy against wrongful imprisonment by officials. Shorn of legalistic detail, it provides for immediate access to a judge for determination as to whether an individual is being wrongfully detained by the authorities. It is not a prohibition on government in general as to the seizure, detention, and punishment of citizens, but rather a check by one part of the governing body, the judiciary, on the behavior of the active arm, the executive. As such, it is part of an internal order for the security of the community imposed and maintained through the structure of government itself. The whole framework of government-guaranteed personal security includes the institutions of the grand jury, trial jury, an independent judiciary to ensure fair trial, and several constitutional restrictions on the use of official force against the individual—the prohibition of physical torture or cunning fraud to obtain confessions of crime is perhaps the most notable.

The degree of security which may be afforded the individual against arbitrary official action must depend ultimately on the extent of social cohesion achieved by the community. In the fulfillment of its primary function of preserving order, government must balance dangers of violence, rebellion, and betrayal against a pattern of personal security. Thus, two recently founded nations, India and Ghana, which still preserve a framework of English constitutional law and practice, have found it necessary to permit preventive detention without trial of persons whom officials consider dangerous to the safety of the state. The lack of any absolute standard renders government responsible for the task of continuously balancing policies and actions to produce a type of internal order that will enhance individual security to the greatest extent practicable under the conditions of the times.

The Protection of Privacy

Closely linked to the need for physical security of the person is a claim to the privacy of the home. Government is concerned with the preservation of this element in the dignity of the individual because it may be considered a condition for the obedience free men are prepared to give the institutions of the state. The Fourth Amendment to the Constitution of the United States declares: "The right of the people to be secure in their persons, houses, papers, and effects, against unreasonable searches and seizures, shall not be violated. . . ." In the words of Mr. Justice Frankfurter:

> The security of one's privacy against arbitrary intrusion by the police —which is at the core of the Fourth Amendment—is basic to a free society. It is therefore implicit in the "concept of ordered liberty," and as such enforceable against the States through the Due Process clause. The knock at the door, whether by day or by night, as a prelude to a search, without authority of law but solely on the authority of the police, did not need the commentary of recent history to be condemned as inconsistent with the conception of human rights enshrined in the history and the basic constitutional documents of English-speaking peoples.[11]

The thin barrier that separates any community in the modern world from terrorism by the instrumentalities of government should be apparent to even the less diligent reader of newspapers. Insufficient credit is perhaps accorded political institutions in free countries for their generally successful struggle to avert the evils of government by fear that have beset more than half the world. Whether the barrier is one of law or convention, it is preserved only by unremitting effort and skill on the part of governmental bodies designed to rule by consent.

Equality of Opportunity

Creation through government of an internal order that will satisfy basic social and moral aspirations of the bulk of the people must always be an unfinished and imperfect business. This is particularly true when the outlook of mankind is undergoing great historic change. Thus, in the Western world the long sway of hierarchical society, where everyone had his place determined by status, came to an end only within the last three centuries. New arrangements based on equality of opportunity to profit and advance oneself through exercise of individual talents have infiltrated very slowly through the whole social organization. In 1789, the French Declaration of Human Rights declared that "all are equally eligible for all honors, places, and employments according to their different abilities without any distinction other than that created by their virtues and talents." Though it may be claimed that this principle has had revolutionary effect upon the form and functioning of the government of France, it would be unrealistic to credit political institutions with its achievement. A majority of governments in the Western world are edging toward some measure of equality of opportunity, each by its own methods according to the structure and situation of the particular society. Some skeptics are prepared to dismiss the concept itself as an illusion, or at least an ideal beyond the capacity of political institutions to implement. One drawback to this point of view is that there appears no alternative to forward action in this direction other than acceptance of the dogmatic egalitarianism of totalitarian collectivism. In simpler terms, we must choose between a free equality of opportunity and a disciplined equality of Communism.

Through the circumstances of its origin and situation, the United States has led the world in the dissemination and promotion of the doctrine of equality of opportunity. This has placed a heavy burden on her political structure to implement generally accepted but somewhat untried objectives of social organization. A candid statement on the subject may be quoted from a 1947 Presidential Committee on Civil Rights.

> Our American heritage further teaches that to be secure in the rights he wishes for himself, each man must be willing to respect the rights of other men. This is the conscious recognition of a basic moral principle: all men are created equal as well as free. Stemming from this principle is the obligation to build social institutions that will guarantee equality of opportunity to all men. Without this equality

> freedom becomes an illusion. Thus the only aristocracy that is consistent with the free way of life is an aristocracy of talent and achievement. The grounds on which our society accords respect, influence or reward to each of its citizens must be limited to the quality of his personal character and of his social contribution.
>
> This concept of equality which is so vital a part of the American heritage knows no kinship with notions of human uniformity or regimentation. We abhor the totalitarian arrogance which makes one man say that he will respect another man as his equal only if he has *my* race, *my* religion, *my* political views, *my* social position. In our land men are equal but they are free to be different. From these very differences among our people has come the great human and national strength of America.
>
> Thus, the aspirations and achievements of each member of our society are to be limited only by the skills and energies he brings to the opportunities equally offered to all Americans. We can tolerate no restrictions upon the individual which depend upon irrelevant factors such as his race, his color, his religion, or the social position to which he was born.[12]

Translating these sentiments into the texture of social life through the instrumentality of government remains an unfinished task in America, as elsewhere. The process is a continuing one. Through interpretation of the "equal protection of the laws" clause in the Fourteenth Amendment, the courts have struck down many attempts to introduce discriminatory standards into employment, housing, and education. As far back as 1867, Mr. Justice Field declared: "The theory upon which our political institutions rest is, that all men have certain inalienable rights—that among these are life, liberty, and the pursuit of happiness; and that in the pursuit of happiness all avocations, all honors, all positions, are alike open to every one, and that in the protection of these rights all are equal before the law."[13] Courts of law have perhaps pioneered attempts of government in the United States to remove the gross inequalities introduced into society by the practice of racial and religious bigotry. However, they are by no means the only agencies now committed to this task. For example, in the life career of one man, General of the Army, later President, Eisenhower a revolutionary change has been accomplished in removing barriers to equality, of opportunity for personnel of all races and creeds within the armed services. This was effected by policy decision-making on the executive level; its effects have now spread into practically all forms of personnel management on federal government level. In affairs of this sort, the administrative arm of government serves as an instigator of social change rather than as a docile executant of existing prejudices. The Dreyfus affair in late nineteenth-century France is a classic case of the involvement of government administrative practices in the forces of social change. Anti-Semitic prejudice was a distinguishing mark of the social group that dominated the administrative machinery of French government at that time. Captain Dreyfus's fate aroused disclosure, criticism, and a reordering of control centers in government, substantially reducing the authority of a prejudiced minority throughout the whole area of French society.

A struggle for equality of opportunity assumes dramatic and easily recognized forms when race or religious bigotry is involved, but more traditional barriers raised by class or economic disadvantage are apt to be overlooked. Among the older European nations this issue has now come to the forefront of the political struggle; the degree to which instrumentalities of government are to be used to provide some measure of equality of opportunity for all has become the central question of politics. Experience tends to show that government policies, while important, are still supplementary to economic and cultural forces in the achievement of this ideal. There is one field, however, the provision of free educational facilities, where the standard of equality of opportunity is almost wholly dependent upon governmental policies and action.

The Furtherance of Education

One of the most significant revolutions in Western society during the last hundred years has been the universalization of the educational process. A demand for free public education took form in the United States and England on radical political platforms; the American labor movement played an important promotional part when it was still in its socially disreputable infancy. Nowadays, provision of free educational facilities to a constantly ascending level is regarded as an unescapable responsibility of the political state. In fact, coercion of unwilling or careless parents and truant children is accepted as a needed police power. The tide in favor of state-enforced education has risen so high as to endanger other freedoms within the social order. A legal viewpoint may be cited from an opinion by Mr. Justice McReynolds in a case arising out of a law of the state of Nebraska forbidding the teaching of any language but English until after the eighth grade.

> The American people have always regarded education and acquisition of knowledge as matters of supreme importance which should be diligently promoted. The Ordinance of 1787 declares, "Religion, morality, and knowledge being necessary to good government and the happiness of mankind, schools and the means of education shall forever be encouraged." Corresponding to the right of control, it is the natural duty of the parent to give his children education suitable to their station in life; and nearly all the States, including Nebraska, enforce this obligation by compulsory laws. . . . That the State may do much, go very far, indeed, in order to improve the equality of its citizens, physically, mentally, and morally, is clear; but the individual has certain fundamental rights which must be respected.[14]

The decision of the court in this case extended the protection of the Constitution "to those who speak other languages as well as to those born with English on the tongue," thus preserving a quality of equal opportunity in learning.

Responsibility for the educational pattern of the community has placed on political institutions an added burden which has not yet been fully evaluated. As has been previously pointed out, control of education in many Catholic lands has strained relations between Church and state. In the United States, content and nature of the educational process has not yet become a matter of serious political controversy, but the costs of education conducted on a general scale are now affecting the whole field of government operations. Britain provides an interesting illustration of the interlocking of the functions of government with an educational system in determining the nature of an internal social order. Coincident with the spread of state-provided schooling, the British protected their class system through a network of private establishments perversely called "public schools." The pioneer labors of the great Dr. Arnold of Rugby created a model for the educational training of the sons of the well-to-do. In terms of its purpose the system was outstandingly successful, disciplining into a common and socially responsible mold succeeding generations of the inheritors of social power. For most practical purposes the "old school tie" was the guide to a ruling-class hierarchy. A writer on British parliamentary representation points out:

> Eton, about the most exclusive and expensive school in the country, averages well over 500 times as many Members [of Parliament] as she should have on the basis of proportion, while Harrow, not far behind, has nearly 450 times her due representation. The Harrovian has over 1,800 times and the Etonian well over 2,000 times as good a chance of entering Parliament as has the elementary-school boy—in spite of the rise of the Labour party![15]

The state school system robbed of the interested support of the economically privileged class has had to bear a weight of social snobbery and battle continuously for a sufficiency of funds. Consequently the issue between state and private education has erupted into the political arena. When returned to power, the Labour Party propose to extend governmental control over operation of the private schools so that at least they become as accessible to talented youths from lower economic groupings as they are to the sons of the well-to-do. This has already been achieved in the instance of the traditional universities, causing noticeable changes in the social origins of administrators in government and elsewhere.

Government responsibility for education may not be accounted irrelevant or overbenevolent meddling in matters that belong outside politics. Present-day conditions link educational facilities to equality of economic and social opportunity in such a fashion as to make them a major element in the determination of the character of the social order. At the cost of being repetitious, it may be emphasized that a primary function of the political state is the safeguarding and control of the internal order of the community. In so far as this is effected by the pattern of educational opportunity, government has a duty to exercise its authority. A more controversial question is raised by those who advocate that government should supervise the whole conduct of the educational process in order that it may become a tool for citizenship training or the cultivation of patriotic attitudes. Under dogmatic totalitarian governments, Communist or ultranationalist, much could be said for such a theory. Free peoples, however, consent to an internal order which is based on the independence of the individual mind and judgment and not on the supremacy of collectivist wisdom. Consequently, it is not the function of their governments to dictate the content of education; political responsibility is limited to making accessible to all groups in the community the opportunities for learning that flow from free scholarship and research.

Free Association

Individuals are related to their social environment through a network of groups: the family, unions, corporations, churches, clubs, professional organizations, political parties, and many others. Determination of the type of associations permitted, and the degree of choice open to individuals to move freely through group patterns, depends upon policies and actions of the political state. Control of group association amounts in practice to responsibility for the pattern of the social order. Even the limited government enjoyed by free peoples may not escape the exercise of this function. Two major examples may be cited from the history of Western culture: religious affiliations and membership in labor unions. The stormy history of government control over church membership is now past—unlamentedly past—history. All that remains among English-speaking peoples is a supreme law or convention of the constitution prohibiting the use of political authority in matters touching on religious association. In consequence, religious toleration has become a commonplace of life in English-speaking and most other Western lands. This desired condition, however, is the end result of painful experimentation with political practices, and its continuance rests on the ability of governments to maintain a certain kind of internal social order. An illustration of the responsibility of political institutions in this respect may be drawn from the tragic events immediately following the establishment of India and Pakistan as independent nation–states. Millions in both countries suffered death, mutilation, or forced exile in an outburst of religious hatred and intolerance. British rule had suppressed this latent violence over the centuries, but a change in the pattern of government left the community unprepared to control its own social evils. It is perhaps only in countries where processes of government have been functioning with unbroken success from time immemorial that men come to believe that peace and order in society is due to inherent virtues in the body of the citizenry. History is a more cautious teacher, indicating that the blessings of religious toleration are the fruit of exceptionally skillful and well-organized political processes.

The question of association in labor unions is more recent and as yet is not fully resolved among free peoples. Government policies in this direction belong properly to control over the economic order discussed in a subsequent chapter. However, relations of individuals to the state in terms of an internal order to which they may accord at least passive consent are closely bound up with privileges and forms of labor association. In eighteenth-century England and America, government forbade workers to associate together for bargaining purposes with their employers. Theoretically, employers were also forbidden to form trade associations among themselves to influence wages or prices. This was done to protect what government considered essential economic interests against "conspiracies in restraint of trade." Change and development in industrial society made such restrictions intolerable for skilled and unskilled workers. A crisis of consent to existing political institutions was involved for a large segment of the people. During the nineteenth and twentieth centuries government met this by political action till it evolved a pattern of free association that would permit participants in the economic struggle to retain loyalty and obedience to the political state. A landmark in the intervention of the government of the United States in this sphere was the National Labor Relations Act (Wagner Act) of 1935. Justification of this governmental action in terms of the relation of the individual to the state was expressed in trenchant terms by Chief Justice Hughes:

... the statute goes no further than to safeguard the right of employees to self-organization and to select representatives of their own choosing for collective bargaining or other mutual protection without restraint or coercion by their own employer. This is a fundamental right. Employees have as clear a right to organize and select their representatives for lawful purposes as the respondent has to organize its business and select its own officers and agents. Discrimination and coercion to prevent the free exercise of the right of employees to self-organization and representation is a proper subject for condemnation by competent legislative authority.[16]

Throughout a considerable part of the Western world, the problem has now advanced to a further stage and the protection of the individual worker against compulsory association in labor unions contrary to his personal will has become a political issue. In any case, government is committed to supervision of the rights of association in labor organizations as an inescapable function of the political state.

The Nature of the Internal Order

A viable social union is an artifact of human organization. It is the function of government to provide at least the superstructure of such an organization. In order to do this where a free people is concerned, it must build its order upon areas of common agreement. Otherwise it will lose that consent on which the obedience of the individuals constituting the community is predicated. For this reason civil rights have been treated here as natural building blocks for governmental responsibility in free countries. Of course, they may be regarded from another point of view—that of opposition of the individual person to control by state authority in any form. Though a dichotomy between the individual and the state unquestionably exists, its resolution lies properly in the realms of philosophy or ethics. The study of politics is confined to a lower level of actualities where all individuals are members of some political state and bound to it in some measure of obedience and loyalty.

The peace of the police state differs from the order maintained by the government of a free people in this particular. Individual rights are the blueprints of the latter, because this type of government could not function any other way without losing the basis of its support. Both police state and free government have this in common, however, that they must function positively and actively on a day-to-day basis to maintain the type of order to which they are dedicated. Interpersonal relationships of a character designated by the West as free provide an important part, but still only a part, of the framework of internal order. In order to win continuing obedience from the bulk of the community, government must ensure reasonable functioning of the production and distribution of material goods. The function of government to safeguard the economic order does not always coincide with its function to maintain the order of civil rights. There is nothing automatic about the operation of political institutions, and a clash of governmental functions gives rise to the passions of politics that can be settled only by the wisdom and capacity of statesmen.

Notes

[1] Barker, Ernest (tr. and ed.), Aristotle, *The Politics of Aristotle,* New York: Oxford, 1948, p. 234.

[2] *Minersville School District v. Gobitis,* 310 U.S. 586 (1940).

[3] *Jacobson v. Massachusetts,* 197 U.S. 11 (1905).

[4] *Whitney v. California,* 274 U.S. 357 (1927).

[5] *Terminiello v. Chicago,* 337 U.S. 1 (1948).

[6] Two leading British cases, *Wise v. Dunning* (1902) and *Duncan v. Jones* (1936), were settled in this fashion.

[7] *Everson v. Board of Education,* 330 U.S. 1 (1947).

[8] Constitution of the Italian Republic, 1947, Article 7.

[9] *Ibid.,* Article 8.

[10] *Minersville School District v. Gobitis,* 310 U.S. 586 (1940).

[11] *Wolf v. Colorado,* 338 U.S. 25 (1948).

[12] President's Committee on Civil Rights, *To Secure These Rights,* New York: Simon and Schuster, 1947.

[13] *Cummings v. Missouri,* 4 Wall 277, 18 L. Ed. 356 (1867).

[14] *Meyer v. Nebraska,* 262 U.S. 390 (1923).

[15] Ross, J. F. S., *Parliamentary Representation,* London: Eyre and Son, second edition, 1948, p. 109.

[16] *National Labor Relations Board v. Jones & Laughlin Steel Corp.,* 301 U.S. 1 (1937).

Supplementary Readings

Barker, Ernest (tr. and ed.), Aristotle, *The Politics of Aristotle,* New York: Oxford, 1948.

Becker, Carl L., *Freedom and Responsibility in the American Way of Life,* New York: Knopf, 1945.

Carr, Robert K., *Federal Protection of Civil Rights,* Ithaca: Cornell University Press, 1947.

Chaffee, Zechariah, Jr., *Three Human Rights in the Constitution,* Lawrence: University of Kansas Press, 1957.

Cushman, Robert, *Civil Liberties in the United States,* Ithaca: Cornell University Press, 1956.

Dumbauld, Edward, *The Bill of Rights and What It Means Today,* Norman: University of Oklahoma Press, 1957.

Holcombe, Arthur N., *Human Rights in the Modern World,* New York: New York University Press, 1948.

Konvitz, Milton R., *Fundamental Liberties of a Free People: Religion, Speech, Press, Assembly,* Ithaca: Cornell University Press, 1958.

Laslett, Peter, *Philosophy, Politics and Society,* New York: Macmillan, 1956.

Lauterpracht, Hersh, *An International Bill of the Rights of Man,* New York: Columbia, 1945.

Locke, John, (ed. Cook, Thomas I.), *Two Treatises of Government,* New York: Hafner, 1947.

Maritain, Jacques, *Man and the State,* Chicago: University of Chicago Press, 1951.

Mill, John Stuart, *On Liberty.*

Pfeffer, Leo, *Church, State and Freedom,* Boston: Beacon Press, 1953.

Tawney, R. H., *Equality,* New York: Harcourt, Brace, 1931.

Chapter **14**

Government and the Economic Order

As Keeper of the Peace, King's Peace or People's Peace, government has always been involved in current questions concerning the production and distribution of material goods. Because standards of livelihood and the hope of gain arouse strong feelings, they are likely causes of social disorder. Consequently, political institutions seek to anticipate occasions of economic strife, submerging them in a general pattern enforced by political authority. Responsibility for the economic order among free peoples does not lie fully, or perhaps even mainly, in the hands of the government. In matters of wealth production, the political state may serve in an ancillary capacity to other forces in society. Methods of participation by government in the economic process constitute some of the most controversial issues in modern politics.

The type of economic order that confronts governments of free Western nations may be described as the *market system*—essentially a system of free enterprise that entrusts the economic tasks of society to the interplay of individuals motivated by desire for personal gain. General acceptance of this system amounted to a profound social revolution brought about by the factors in social development that contributed to the dissolution of the medieval way of life and the rise of modern times. Political forms, particularly the rise of the centralized nation–state, played a significant if not decisive part in providing suitable social terrain for this experiment in human progress. Though the market system has evolved a long way from the early simplicities of Adam Smith, it remains recognizable as the social framework for economic growth in a substantial portion of the world. Of course, it is now challenged by the counterrevolution or reaction of Marxist communism that seeks to reestablish the ancient principle that all wealth flows from the exercise of political power—a viewpoint familiar to the Egypt of the Pharaohs.

In discussing the consensual order of civil rights, it was suggested that government serves as the principal protagonist of this order, with the function of declaring its nature as well as safeguarding its observance. It would be unwise to make the same assumption concerning the economic order existent among a free people in the twentieth century. Government represents only one of the factors involved and as it does not pay the piper it is not entitled to call the tune. The function of government, then, is to police rather than determine a system of production and distribution. Policing, of course, is in itself a form of intervention, making the political state responsible in part for the operational characteristics of the economic order. In particular, governmental standards are concerned with the contentment of the bulk of the people—sometimes given the ambitious name of "social justice"—and the effective economic power of the nation as a whole as weighed against that of its potential rivals. Accordingly, the single-minded advancement of any theoretical economic system—whether capitalism, socialism, or any other—may be considered an improper function for a representative government of a free country.

anti-socialist

Coordination of the workings of a partially self-operating pattern of economic activities with the expressed needs of the community is probably an ideal limit of government action. To achieve this end, political institutions must remain flexible and undogmatic in their policies though resolute to deal with total situations through exercise of governmental power. This distinguishes free nations, apparently to their disadvantage, from their Communist or totalitarian neighbors. Such weakness as exists, however, lies in the realm of defense of economic dogmas rather than in protection of standards of prosperity. Though limited government may not impose a total system of living on its citizens, it is well equipped to provide adequate force for the maintenance of existing standards or the satisfaction of reasonable needs. Methods used by governments throughout the Western world to fulfill their economic functions are the subjects of vigorous and healthy controversy. A journalistic practice of labeling the governments of free nations as capitalist or socialist is unenlightening. Only dogmatic states, Communist or Fascist, are entitled to employ the institutions of government as instruments of economic theory. Judgment of the methods employed by Western governments to intervene in economic affairs should be related to particular situations and the effectiveness of the political means used to deal with them.

Government Planning

Recognition of a government function to engage in economic planning resulted more from necessities of war than from political theory in the majority of Western countries. Planning for survival is obviously a government responsibility, and the type of total war waged in the twentieth century makes survival dependent upon a coordinated use of all economic resources. Practices grafted onto political systems under wartime conditions are difficult to eradicate, particularly if readiness for war has become a precaution essential to survival. Limits of government planning tend to be obscured in the double-talk of political controversy. Thus the British Labour Government that came into power in 1945 emphasized the ostensibly new function of planning for abundance. In practice, however, this took the form of a cautious retreat from the drastic planning of wartime. The most extreme form of planning, direction of civilian labor, was hastily dropped. Stripped of her external resources, Britain was close to national bankruptcy, and any government would have been compelled to maintain tight control over the national economy. The principal innovation of the Labour Government took the form of the nationalization of key industries, a controversial expedient which future developments have shown to be little related to a planned economy. Britain's leadership, then, tended towards a form of situational planning which has been widely followed for diverse reasons throughout the Western world.

In the United States, the framework of government planning was retained almost intact, but, as in the case of the Liberty ships, it was mothballed for emergency use. A major instance of acceptance of the principle of government responsibility for planning may be found in the Full Employment Act of 1946. In the words of this statute:

The Congress hereby declares that it is the continuing policy and responsibility of the Federal Government to use all practicable means consistent with its needs and obligations and other essential considerations of national policy, with the assistance and cooperation of industry, agriculture, labor, and State and local governments, to coordinate and utilize all its plans, functions, and resources for the purpose of creating and maintaining, in a manner calculated to foster and promote free competitive enterprise and the general welfare, conditions under which there will be afforded useful employment opportunities, including self-employment for those able, willing, and seeking to work, and to promote maximum employment, production, and purchasing power.[1]

This wordy declaration with all its saving qualifications is worthy of study as a guide to the empirical, ancillary concept of government planning in economic affairs still dominant in the United States.

A fair test of the seriousness of the intentions of government to undertake major responsibility for the over-all planning of the national economy may be made by examining the permanent instrumentalities it has created to effect that purpose. The contribution made by the Full Employment Act was the Council of Economic Advisers, a small professional body with the duty of advising the President concerning his economic reports to Congress and in other matters according to his will. Though this distinguished group has subsequently won for itself a place analogous to a general economic advisory staff it would be far-fetched to consider that it was either intended to achieve or has in practice achieved the position of a planning body over the nation's economy. Contrasted with the powerful bodies entrusted with planning in a Communist economy, it is of negligible account as a power-wielding instrumentality.

Even in Britain, planning machinery is denied a central position in the power complex of government. Neither the Cabinet nor the permanent civil service has entrusted significant authority to continuing planning bodies. On the highest policy-making levels, control of economic plans rests with the Cabinet or its ministerial committees. There is slight evidence that this task has been distinguished in any particular manner from the other functions of this supreme body that are brought into play to resolve specific situations. On the administrative level, a number of organizations exist with somewhat nebulous functions and powers. The Central Economic Planning Staff and the Central Planning Board, created in 1947, are now adjuncts of the Treasury. The Cabinet is served by the Economics Section of the Cabinet Office and by the Central Statistical Office. No more than two per cent of the higher administrative class of civil servants are engaged in this work.[2] It may be deduced that where government does not arrange its structure so as to give planning organizations a predominant share of the actualities of power, responsibility for planning the total economy is not regarded as a function of government. Promotional forms of government planning in economic matters are a natural feature of the governments of underdeveloped lands. Though India, Ghana, Egypt, and other recently independent nations attempt to concentrate national resources on what government conceives to be essential projects, this form of developmental planning should be distinguished from the planning of the total economy mandatory in Communist circles. It resembles rather the planning for survival in which free countries engage under pressure of war or equivalent threats to their existence.

In contrast, Communist states accept complete responsibility for the direction of the economic affairs of their peoples. Their dogma postulates that political institutions are resultants of economic forces, and the government by its nature is bound to dictate the economy. Accordingly, the governmental apparatus in Soviet lands is designed with this purpose in view. A Russian publicist offers a succinct description of the process.

Soviet administration does not amount simply to a system of strictly administrative measures regulating the external structures of life; it organizes the entire system of social relationships, up to and including the very basis of that system—the economy. The Soviet State assumes responsibility for administering, not merely the life of men, but the economy itself. The overwhelming majority of factories, mines, banks, transport enterprises, State farms, machine and tractor stations, etc., are supervised by State management bodies. Housing, lighting, heating, telephones, the radio, education, hospitals, the cinema, etc., all come within the competence of those bodies, which are responsible for providing for the needs of workers in all fields. . . . The more immediate tasks of Soviet State management organs include . . . the organization of the economy and of cultural education. . . .[3]

Despite the awesome magnitude of these functions, the planning machinery employed to carry them out is far from clear. According to the Constitution, the Council of Ministers, the supreme executive organ, should constitute the ultimate planning authority. Apart from the fact that this body is too large for practical decision-making, it is not the true center of political authority. The Presidium of the Communist Party, an extraconstitutional grouping, is the final master of the Soviet state. In practice, one man, as during the reign of Stalin, or shifting inner groups such as have surrounded his successors, control the blueprints that order the whole economy. Khrushchev, in 1957, decreed an important measure of decentralized administration. National Economic Councils have been set up for each of two hundred economic and administrative regions. These bodies are now responsible for the execution of production plans and for the economic results of the work of the enterprises under their supervision. Central ministries have been substantially reduced in numbers and their work restricted to more indirect planning. To some extent, this reform amounts to an admission of the failure of pure political planning to encompass all the actualities of economic interests. The regions may be said to represent the diversification of needs to be found in Soviet Russia as elsewhere. By shifting into their hands substantial control of the economy, the fiction of the solidarity of the proletariat as an economic grouping is weakened. For practical purposes, regions are being placed in competitive array against one another, with the centralized machinery of the nation–state withdrawing to the more tenable role of policeman rather than operator. Of course, so long as Russia remains a single-party state under Communist domination, the economy of the people will be subjected to a strait jacket of rigid dogma. However, the two hundred new centers of economic management will tend to produce varying interpretations of the dogma in practice, leaving room for greater adaptation to underlying realities of the processes of production and distribution.

Management of Money and Credit

That government is a money-maker in the most literal sense is obvious to anyone who has viewed a collection of ancient coins with all their oddities of shape, size and ingenious self-glorification of departed rulers. This responsibility toward the basic medium of exchange has certainly not lessened with the passing of centuries. The coining of money, a jealously guarded prerogative of political sovereignty, has widened into control of the currency and, in part, of the credit facilities of the community. Methods by which this is done or attempted vary considerably among Western states. The understanding or interpretation of these methods calls for a degree of expert knowledge not generally possessed by laymen. However, the forms and consequences of government action involve certain inescapable political issues. Since money is the means by which individuals in a modern state exchange the products of their labor and services, its dependability is of great import to the community. One of the unpleasant practices of early English monarchs, resented to the point of revolt by their subjects, was the clipping of some of the precious metal from the coinage of the realm before issuing it to the populace. A present-day citizen still feels "clipped" when his money tokens decline in purchasing value. Like his forefathers, he places the blame, probably correctly, on the government of the day. A similar situation obtains when the internal credit structure of a nation is under strain affecting the employment and business opportunities of its inhabitants. Again, government is held responsible as at least a major party to the situation.

There are three interlocking areas where government possesses responsibility of control over the financial structure of the country: fiscal policy, debt management, and the supervision of credit. Fiscal policy (public finance through taxation, borrowing, spending) is inextricably entangled with a general control of money and credit. The effects of government action in these spheres are highly technical, so that extreme simplification is misleading. It may be suffi-

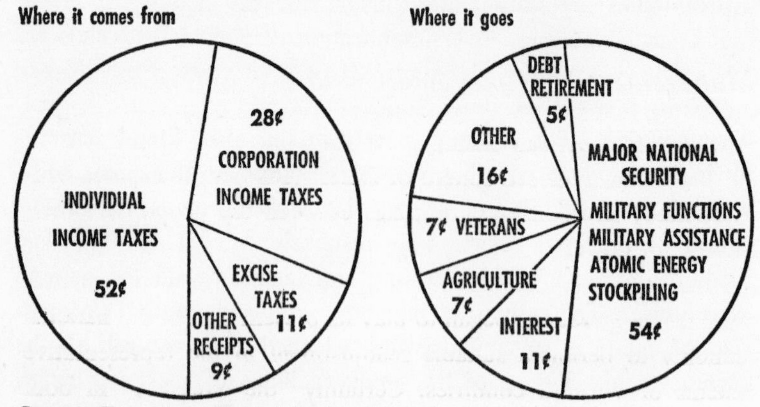

Source: Executive office of the President, Bureau of the Budget

cient to observe that the burden of taxation imposed and the rate of government spending possess obvious power to influence the character of the national economy together with the livelihood of individual citizens in their various economic groupings. In consequence, the electorate considers it a function of government to maintain the background of a general economic security through fiscal and financial policies. This requirement is complicated by a general, though understandable, ignorance on the part of the bulk of the electorate as to methods to be employed to fulfill this responsibility. For example, only a small proportion of voters in any country may be expected to understand the results of large budget deficits or surpluses on the market value of credit instruments, such as bonds. Though their personal fortunes or livelihood opportunities may be involved, they lack the technical information needed for the formulation of an effective judgment. In other words, they have lost direct control over their political institutions in this particular, being forced to rely on intermediary bodies of official or unofficial experts. With the staggering rise in government spending, taxation, and general intervention in financial affairs that has occurred during the twentieth century, this situation poses a challenge to concepts of representative government. One major function of government now rests in a shadowy borderland between arbitrary power and popular control. Electoral systems conducted on a popular basis are questionable means for the determination of vital financial policies. Oversimplification of such issues leads to demagoguery—William Jennings Bryan's electioneering slogan suggesting that the people were being crucified on a cross of gold provides an American example. At the same time, withdrawal of the issues into a closed sphere of expert judgment interposes constitutionally irresponsible groupings between the people and their exercise of power.

Perhaps insufficient time has elapsed since government control of financial operations began to play its present part in the national economy to permit a suitable readjustment in the representative systems of Western countries. Certainly "the Treasury" in both the United States and Britain has become an equivocal force which fits imperfectly into any pattern of representative control over either executive or legislative organs. Tentative developments such as the Economic and Social Council introduced into the 1958 French Constitution or the National Council of Economy and Labor created by the 1947 Italian Constitution may show the way toward some suitable adjustment. Proposed functions for the French Economic and Social Council are outlined in Article 70 of the 1958 Constitution. "The Economic and Social Council may likewise be consulted by the Government on any problem of an economic or social character of interest to the Republic or to the Community. Any plan, or any bill dealing with a plan, of an economic or social character shall be submitted to it for advice."

An illustration of the type of responsibility for the economic security of the community assumed by a present-day government through fiscal and financial powers may be drawn from a survey of the first months of the de Gaulle administration in France.

The first budgetary estimates for 1959 showed a net Treasury deficit double that of 1958. . . . Such a deficit could not possibly have been entirely financed through public bond issues. This would have led inevitably to new Governmental borrowing from the Bank of France, i.e., a new wave of inflation. Furthermore, over the last few years, the price of so many items has become tied to a particular index or to the price of a basic commodity that the inflationary trend could have rapidly worsened. Meanwhile, the world-wide tendency to an economic recession had hit France when the country was pricing herself out of her export markets. The cumulative effect of this, plus inflation at home, threatened to aggravate the already considerable deficit in current accounts. The policy of economic recovery adopted by the Government was aimed at: (1) externally, reducing the balance of payments deficit; (2) internally, fighting both recession and currency inflation. The remedies selected were: devaluation of the franc, increased investments, a balanced budget. At the same time, France made two moves to ensure her full participation in the European Common Market and increase her exchanges with the rest of the world: trade liberation and external convertibility. This was a stern policy. The methods by which it was applied might almost be described as surgical. It all forms a coherent plan, all parts of which are interconnected, based on the major tasks which France has set herself to accomplish. . . . The twofold aim of the Government was to bring the budgetary deficit down to a safer level and to create, through fiscal, monetary, and administrative reforms, conditions proper to a stable economic growth.[4]

Government activities of this character are bound to affect the private affairs of almost all citizens. The constantly rising degree of intervention by political institutions in the economic order has become a principal feature of modern systems of government.

THE CONTROL OF CREDIT Systems of credit control are more refined from the point of view of their institutional framework than the operation of general fiscal functions. This is due in part to a long standing governance of credit by nonpolitical entities comprising the banking system of a country. Governments for the most part have merely superimposed their control organs on well-established institutional arrangements. Also, total responsibility has proved beyond the capacity of political government in countries that adhere to the free-enterprise system. Accordingly, governmental intervention has been confined within a realm of customary practices that offer a traditional resistance to arbitrary political maneuvers.

The Federal Reserve System of the United States provides an example of the ancillary and service character of government control. Founded in 1913, it was given two primary functions. The first was that of a financial service institution to the federal govern-

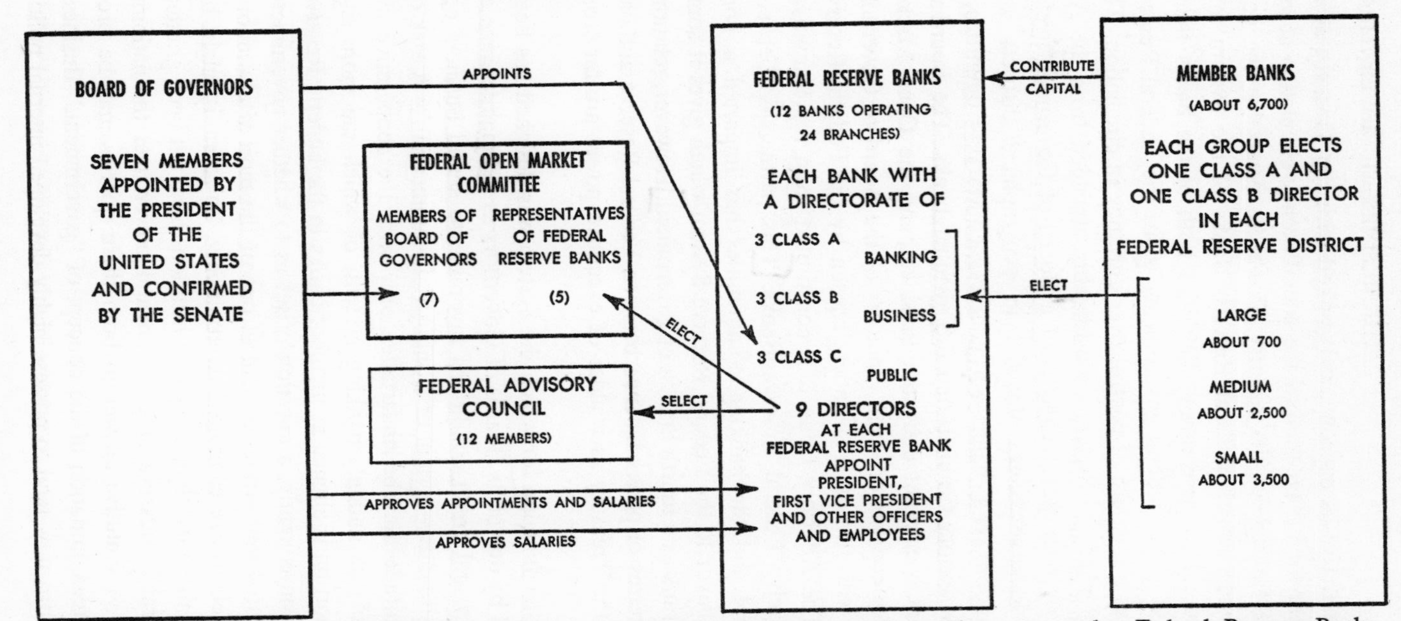

All national banks and many State banks are members of the Federal Reserve System. There are twelve Federal Reserve Banks, each serving one of the districts into which the country is divided. The policy responsibilities of the Federal Reserve are entrusted to the Board of Governors of the Federal Reserve System, the Federal Reserve Banks, and the Federal Open Market Committee. Source: Board of Governors of the Federal Reserve System, *The Federal Reserve System: Purposes and Functions* (Washington, D.C., 1954), p. 82.

ment itself. In this capacity, it is linked with the Treasury as an instrument for the creation of the actual money circulating at any one time throughout the country. Power to determine the conditions under which Federal Reserve Banks of the System may issue Federal Reserve notes—liabilities both of the banks themselves and of the federal government—gives the Federal Reserve authorities a measure of control over currency in circulation. The composition of the System (considerably amended from the Act of 1913 by later Acts) consists of a Board of Governors, twelve Federal Reserve Banks—located in geographical districts and serving as "banker's" banks—a Federal Open Market Committee, a Federal Advisory Council, and the member banks. The Board of Governors is appointed by the President and the Open Market Committee consists of seven members of the Board of Governors together with five other members chosen by the Federal Reserve Banks. The Advisory Council is constituted from representatives of the twelve Federal Reserve Banks. This partnership between the official and the banking communities has imparted a non-political flavor to the Federal Reserve System which gives it some claim to rank as a fourth branch of government. However, relationships in terms of power balance between Federal Reserve authorities and the Treasury as wielder of executive power are far from clear.

The other function for which the System was designed has been described by one of its Boards of Governors as the maintenance of "monetary and credit conditions favorable to sound business activity in all fields—agricultural, industrial, commercial."[5] A task of this magnitude may be undertaken only with the cooperative assistance of the nation's banking system, of which the more significant portion is aligned as member banks in the Federal Reserve System. Consequently, a question arises as to whether government has infiltrated into virtual control of one of the most vital sections of a free-enterprise economy. Alternatively, however, it might be asked whether private banking organizations have not been granted a considerable measure of governmental power over the national economy. A tentative answer to both these queries may be provided by reexamination of the concept of "government." Business organizations now tend to possess highly developed internal political orders of their own. In practice, they regulate considerable areas of commercial activities throughout the community. The government of commerce by business institutions is a meaningful phrase that need not carry any sinister implications. Political government may contribute its authority to existing patterns of business control without the assumption of total responsibility or arbitrary power. At the same time, recognition of the actualities of the public power exercised by business groupings may be made dependent on their acceptance of the priority of national interests as interpreted by the political state. Though this intermeshing of the political and commercial organization of the nation works well in the field of credit control, unanswered questions remain as to its general adaptation to theories and practices of popular representative government.

European countries engage in a more direct form of credit control through the institutions of central state banks. Relationships between the governors, say of the Bank of France and the political administration in power, are probably as complicated as those between the Federal Reserve Board of Governors and the Treasury. Theoretical subordination of a central bank to political authority does not alter the realities of its position as a liaison body between two almost coequal powers in the field of credit control: the banking community and the political state. A typically British compromise whereby a tight-knit banking system was presided over by the Bank of England, a private bank that had assumed governmental functions by historical accident and accretion, was ended when the Labour Government nationalized the Bank and formalized its powers over the private banking system. Now the same problem confronts Britain as troubles other countries under popular government: what is the exact limit and character of the authority wielded by the government of the day over a credit system that has been infiltrated by the political institutions of the state but is still operated by the organs of private enterprise?

Government Control of Economic Resources

Karl Marx built the towering edifice of his theory on the conviction that political power must by its very nature be the creature of economic interest. Development of governmental functions in Western nations during the past hundred years indicate that Marx and his successors underestimated the reality of a national economy —an economic structure that unites the people in all their diverse interests in a manner parallel to their political union. As the political state is the only logical guardian of the national economy it is obligated to undertake those functions essential to its maintenance and expansion. Conversely, under the principle of limited government its sphere is restricted to what touches the economy as a whole, distinct from any of the specialized interests of consumer, producer, or entrepreneur. Though particular decisions along those lines may prove complicated or controversial, the principle affords a reasonable working guide to the economic activities of the governments of free peoples.

Politics and economics are interconnected on the institutional level as they are in the lives of individuals. This does not amount to a denial of what Professor Ernest Barker calls "the just autonomy of the economic process," but indicates rather a need for a mutual division of functions within the same sphere of social activities. The line of division is determined by situational factors: technological developments, condition of natural resources, geographical location, and countless others. Thus the British may consider nationalization of coal mining essential to the safeguarding of a diminishing resource vital to their total economy, while in the United States similar government action might constitute needless interference favoring or prejudicing one partial interest in a balanced pattern of fuel supply. Conversely, in the United States, particularly in the West, water supplies underlie the whole economy of regions. Direct government action on a State and inter-State basis to construct and control water-supply systems is not regarded generally throughout these areas as a form of flowing socialism. Canada, for its part, has found that the national unity of its sparsely populated territories is bound up with the adequacy of transportation links. The government has not hesitated to treat this need as an essential natural resource, owning and operating one of the two transcontinental railroads, the Canadian National, the Trans-Canada Air Lines, the Canadian National (West Indies) Steamships Limited, and now, in partnership with the United States, the St. Lawrence Seaway.

These random examples may serve to illustrate the situational aspect of government enterprise in free lands. The only relevant theory linking them together is that where a gap exists in the structure of the total economy that is being inadequately filled by the operation of private economic power, government is obligated to act. Every particular instance may be the subject of healthy controversy, but the general responsibility of government to conserve, safeguard, and actively promote development of resources basic to the working of the economy is no longer a matter of serious political dispute.

Direct ownership and operation by government of natural or industrial resources poses certain new problems in the organization of political institutions. Britain has pioneered in the development of the public corporation as a governmental instrument for this purpose. That experience may be examined as an illustration of some of the difficulties encountered. In the first place, the profit motive is withdrawn and the stimulus of competition replaced by total or partial monopoly. The "national interest" becomes the sole standard of achievement, which at once gives rise to the question which arm of government is competent to determine the national interest and implement its determination by specific instructions. Constitutional theory in Britain would indicate that Parliament alone possesses this capacity and that its will would be carried out by the Cabinet. However, a practical need for efficient, nonpartisan management of nationalized industry has dictated a form of control through largely independent boards. Public accountability for policies adopted by the nationalized industries—in which two and one half million workers are employed—thus lies in a no man's land between the political Cabinet and the management boards. Professor Eldon L. Johnson points out that five years elapsed after the passing of the Transport Act of 1947 before a minister used the full powers given to him in that Act to issue a specific direction to the British Transport Commission, operating the national railway system, in an important matter of policy—reduction of passenger charges.[6] The direction raised a political storm in Parliament, bringing determination of what was the national interest down to partisan level. Informal pressures and influence backed by an ultimate power of appointment serve under normal circumstances to keep ministers and boards in general agreement over policies.

This, however, falls short of a single-minded control of key industries in the national interest by political bodies responsible for all details of their conduct to the general electorate.

Public ownership of industrial resources through government corporations has not achieved this end in Britain. What has been accomplished is a compromise between autonomous monopolies and political direction. The key issue of public interest remains latent: unquestionably, in any crisis government is in an effective position to impose its will, but until sharp and unmistakable needs arise the business managers conducting public corporations continue in a pattern almost indistinguishable from that of their commercial colleagues.

Government Regulation of Business and Industry

Supervision by government of business and industrial practices as a means of political control over the economy is more generally accepted in Western lands than direct participation in production and distribution processes by state bodies. The United States has developed a network of regulatory laws and agencies linking government and commerce into a closely integrated pattern of social control. Because of the predominant position of the American industrial organization in the Western community, these methods of government regulation possess great influence among technologically developed societies outside the Communist bloc.

Perhaps some of the clearest answers concerning the nature of government's right to regulate business in a free enterprise society have stemmed from interpretations of the American Constitution. For example, there is Mr. Justice Roberts's statement in the case of *Nebbia v. New York*: "The Constitution does not secure to anyone liberty to conduct his business in such a fashion as to inflict injury upon the public at large, or upon any substantial group of people."[7] A more specific delineation may be quoted from the opinions of Mr. Justice Brandeis:

> A regulation valid for one kind of business may, of course, be invalid for another; since the reasonableness of every regulation is dependent upon the relevant facts. But so far as concerns the power to regulate, there is no difference, in essence, between a business called private

Left: Prototype of the bureaucrat, from about 1300 B.C. The statuette is inscribed, "The Privy Councilor and Administrator of the Nome, mouthpiece of the King in the entire land . . . Superintendent of the Offices of the Two Lands, the Chief Royal Scribe . . . the King's Secretary, Yúny, . . . and his wife . . . daughter of the Superintendent of the Necropolis. . . ." *Courtesy of the Metropolitan Museum of Art, Rogers Fund, 1915*

Administrative Structure

Right: "The Government of Paris"—a woodcut from "Ordonnances Royales," Paris, 1500. A capsule of government organization from medieval France. The larger-than-life policy makers dominate the administrative substructure. (*Le greffe,* tax clerk; *Le receveux,* tax receiver; *Le procureux,* city attorney; *Le clerc,* city clerk). *Department of Printing and Graphic Arts, Harvard College Library*

Below: The "merit" system was introduced into the United States by the Civil Service Commission created in 1883. Illustrated is an official examination of custom house clerks and applicants for positions. *The Bettmann Archive*

Directly below: Public discussion is the beginning of party politics. An orator in classical Greece endeavors to attract an indifferent audience. *The Bettmann Archive*

Bottom: A left-wing (*Independent Workers of the World*) labor orator packs Union Square, New York City, in the era of mass rallies. *Brown Brothers*

Right: British voters jam London's Trafalgar Square to listen to the results of a Parliamentary election—celebrated somewhat in the spirit of a sporting event. *Wide World Photos*

Parties and Pressure Groups

Above: The American tradition of whistle-stop campaigning brings the candidate for the presidency face to face with the people. *Brown Brothers*

Below: Circus-parade politics permits pressure groups to blow off steam, and impress a nominating convention with their candidate's popular backing. *Wide World Photos*

Tax collectors in ancient Egypt penalized delinquent taxpayers in summary fashion. The dependence of political government on taxation has changed little in 3000 years. *The Bettmann Archive*

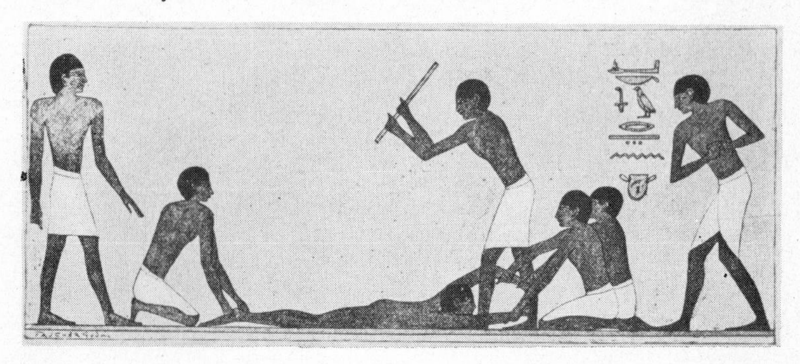

Illustrated is the tax commissioner of Delft, Holland (recumbent in foreground) being admonished by female citizens protesting new taxes on corn. Reluctance of citizens to accept tax burdens remains to this day a limitation on the scope of governmental activities. *The Bettmann Archive*

The International Order

Left: As modern in its buildings as in its aims, the General Assembly of the United Nations embodies cautious hopes for a political order that may alleviate the rule of force between independent nation-states. *United Nations*

Below: The Security Council in action. The influence possessed by Great Powers in the realities of world politics is recognized through entrusting the executive arm of the United Nations mainly to their direction. *United Nations*

The International Court of Justice (the World Court) is the principal judicial organ of the United Nations. All states, prepared in advance to accept its jurisdiction as binding, are entitled to plead their causes before this Court, at The Hague, Netherlands. The judges are distinguished jurisprudents selected from many countries. *United Nations*

In the field the United Nations has proved itself a competent and impartial body for the supervision of plebiscites. Illustrated is a plebiscite conducted in the Trust territory of British Togoland to determine the will of the people concerning the political future of their land. *United Nations*

and one called a public utility or said to be "affected with a public interest." Whatever the nature of the business, whatever the scope or character of the regulation applied, the source of the power involved is the same. And likewise the constitutional limitation upon that power. The source is the police power. The limitation is that set by the due process clause, which, as construed, requires that the regulation shall not be unreasonable, arbitrary or capricious; and that the means of regulation selected shall have a real or substantial relation to the object sought to be obtained. The notion of a distinct category of business "affected with a public interest," employing property "devoted to a public use," rests upon historical error.[8]

These common-sense interpretations of the legal authority of the state provide a broad basis for practical exercise of the regulatory functions of government. To what extent and in what direction this authority will be exercised remains, of course, a matter of political policy. Under conditions of popular rule, intervention in the economic order is likely to take many forms, not all of which contribute to a systematic pattern of control. The Voice of the People—sometimes tuned through special channels—may demand certain economic satisfactions that necessitate application of governmental power to the economic structure. Tariff laws are outstanding examples of the capacity of governments to utilize national sovereignty to shape an internal economy pleasing to powerful sections of their own people. Because in general this power appears to be used against foreign groupings, its sometimes reckless manifestations are frequently a basis for demagogic appeals. In practice, a political state's capacity to promote an internal economic situation through the erection of tariff barriers is limited more by fear of reprisals from economically powerful neighbors than from the reluctance of its own inhabitants to make economic gains through political means.

Other forms of regulation to promote special features in the national economy vary according to the situation in which each country finds itself. Thus, in postwar France rent control has been considered an important function of government in order to insure citizens housing within their means. Merchant shipping, civil aviation, and railroads have all benefited by the regulatory zeal of government in the United States, being favored with the grant of facilities or outright subsidies from public funds to promote development against external competition or in face of adverse economic conditions. These forms of promotional regulation may be regarded as political readjustment of the economic order to meet popular interests or at least demands.

Internal Policing of the Economic Order

Perhaps the greatest distinction between the political and economic order of a country lies in the fact that the economy as a whole is not organized to operate within a framework of institutional responsibility. That is, if over-all production falters or unemployment rises there is no hierarchical structure of economic bodies to assume effective responsibility before the bar of public opinion. It is because of this lack rather than on account of any particular capacities of their own that political institutions are obligated to function as policemen over the general field of economic activities. An unavoidable paradox results from free enterprise being employed as the motivating force of an economy and at the same time being subjugated to political power. This difficulty may be overcome in part if it is realized that the order of any society is as unitary as the lives of the individuals composing it. Differentiation of the economic from the political order or vice versa is a convenience of theoretical analysis and little more. In terms of actual events, only social situations exist, and they are met either singly or cooperatively by one aspect or another of the same social organization. Phrased in another way, the union of a people is the reality, both political state and economic order being mere manifestations of this central event.

One somewhat evasive way of expressing the concern of political forces in economic affairs is to designate them as guardians of "the public interest." Of course they operate (by and large) in terms of public interest, but it seems a curious implication that economic organizations do not do likewise. Perhaps the crux of the matter lies in a special claim to guardianship. If this posits a unique understanding on the part of government of the economic needs in terms of production and distribution, it appears historically unjustified. If, however, it means that the political state provides the only organization responsible to the people as a whole, it makes practical sense. Accordingly, government policing of the economy may be viewed as a reaction of the people themselves collectively to their own group and individual behavior. As such it possesses its own internal limitations: a man may rub an itching hand but he does not crush it as a hostile body.

Control of Corporate Power

Emergence of the corporate form as an instrument of economic enterprise released sufficient human energy to transform the material culture of the Western peoples. At the same time, it upset customary power balances in a manner that could not escape attention from the political state. Efficiency of organization has tended toward the development of centralized blocs of economic power. Whether or not these corporate groupings, trusts or cartels, monopolize areas of economic interest remains a controversial question. It is not their monopolistic qualities that are the principal concern of politics, but rather their centralization of social power.

Professor A. A. Berle[9] has calculated that slightly more than half of American industry is under the ownership of not more than 200 corporations. An overlapping remainder is under the control of what he calls *concentrates,* that is, situations where more than half the particular business is controlled by a few large corporations with consequent ability to dominate conditions under which smaller concerns may operate. An obvious resulting problem is how these power centers may be rendered socially responsible for their activities. Direct action by government has proved, perhaps, of less importance than other means in achieving this end. Though legislation commencing with the Sherman Anti-Trust Act of 1890 has been significant in a general control of monopolistic growth, it has barely touched the roots of the system. Concentration and centralization of business policy making is probably needed to meet existing conditions. Government is in no position (outside totalitarian systems) to substitute for commercial organization in this undertaking. Consequently, public responsibility must be infused into an existing operating pattern of nongovernmental bodies. Under conditions of popular rule, this is by no means impossible: holders of corporate power are fully aware that a change in the temper of the community could imperil their organizations in innumerable ways. Generally, it suffices for political institutions to proclaim standards of behavior that are clearly supported by the bulk of the people. Corporate organization, then, through its own internal political order will endeavor to satisfy clearly expressed public will.

Professor J. K. Galbraith[10] has suggested that the modern economy of America is controlled by an institutional balance which he terms *countervailing power* exercised between concentrates of business and labor. In so far as this true, political government possesses a latent capacity to impose its will by skillful disposition of its support to one side or the other. In general, great corporations may be likened to elephants rather than tigers: they are majestic creatures with peaceful herd instincts that render them capable of lending their unsurpassed strength to useful work. The occasional "rogue" deviate, isolated from his kind, invites destruction.

European experience of corporate power has not excited the same type of misgivings as have been manifested in the United States. In part, this may be due to the willingness of many European nations to transform concentrations of industrial control into direct governmental bodies. Britain, for example, has nationalized four key industries, and the political threat suspended over other groupings, such as the steel and chemical combines, renders them sensitive to popular favor. Another possible reason for the tolerance shown to a cartelization process throughout European industry may lie in the international functions of such groupings. Economically speaking, Europe has outgrown the restrictions of national frontiers. Though political institutions lag behind in recognition of this fact, the great cartels have provided a measure of European economic unity acceptable to the peoples themselves.

Regulation of Business Practices

What has been previously referred to as the police function of government is, in general, a responsibility for the protection of the health, safety, and morals of the community. Government must perform this task throughout all fields of human activity, because it is the only institutional organization that embraces the community as a whole. Consequently, it is concerned in the noneconomic results of business practices. Administration of Pure Food and Drug Acts may serve as a straightforward example. Whether or not the profit motive is interfered with or delicate machinery of trading disturbed, government may not tolerate the poisoning of its citizens in any manner or to any degree. Injury to individuals or groups through commercial fraud or malpractices are as much the function of government to prevent as the wrongs suffered from private violence. The scope of regulation involved is empirical, as the ingenuity of greedy men constantly creates new occasions for police action.

An unresolved controversy exists over the extension of the regulatory powers of government to adjust the national economy so as to promote one area of interest at the possible expense of others. This discussion is particularly acute in the United States, where government has been reluctant to step in directly to nationalize industrial services in the name of the public good. During the New Deal period, however, indirect methods were employed to favor certain neglected features of the economy for various social and political reasons. An example may be cited from the Rural Electrification Act of 1936, which established machinery for the provision of government loans at low rates of interest to municipalities, cooperative associations, and other bodies to enable them to engage in the supply of electricity to rural districts. An energetic Rural Electrification Administration organized in farming areas a largely cooperative electrification movement that challenged the ascendancy of private power corporations. Together with the work of the Federal Power Commission, which regulates inter-State rates on electric power, and a stimulation given to State regulation of power utilities by interchange of information and facilities from federal power agencies, these activities tended to put government in competition with private enterprise in this field. One justification put forward is that it has become a function of government to provide a "yardstick" to measure fair rates in the partly monopolistic industries called public utilities.

Wartime necessitated great expansions in this type of interest regulation. Consumer interest—when everyone could be assumed to be engaged directly or indirectly in national defense—was protected by the extreme measure of controlled prices. Once added to the armory of government power, this weapon is unlikely to be surrendered completely even under peacetime conditions. Bare hints from a current administration that it may feel compelled to request return of price controls to combat inflation exercise great influence over powerful sections of the economy. Another controversial function lately assumed by government in the United States and elsewhere is responsibility for the rate of national economic growth. In part this is a reaction from the claims and threats of Soviet countries that their directed economies will outpace Western development and render the United States and its allies militarily impotent and culturally obsolescent. The Full Employment Act of 1946 included "economic growth" among its objectives, but failed to mention methods government might employ to fulfill its responsibility in this respect. Though economic expansion previously formed part of the purpose of American life, it had not hitherto been formally attributed to government policy or action. As Professor Arthur Smithies points out: "We had always thought of it as a by-product of the pursuit of other objectives, such as the maintenance of a vigorous private enterprise economy. . . ."[11]

Theoretical limitations on the regulatory powers of government invite somewhat unreal arguments. The problem is not what government might do if it had the power, but, conversely, what government as now constituted has the actual power to accomplish. This brings the matter down to the practical organization of the governmental structure. It is clear that it does not parallel that of business or industry. Accordingly, government may assume the tasks of business only when it possesses the personnel and organizational structure to fulfill them. Even though regulatory commissions and other bodies show traits that suggest they may be on the way to becoming groupings of a business type in their capacity for management and economic planning, the great bulk of officialdom, administrative and policy-making, remains foreign to the world of economic enterprise. Any important expansion of government regulatory responsibilities may require transformation of the structure of government itself. This may prove a slow process unless hastened by the unlikely event of a violent revolution involving the physical destruction of the present entrenched power holders.

Notes

[1] *Public Law 304,* 79th Congress, Session 2. February 20, 1946, S. 380 Employment Act of 1946, Washington: United States Government Printing Office, 1946.

[2] *Cf.* Milne, R. S., "Britain's Economic Planning Machinery," *The American Political Science Review,* 1952, **46,** No. 2, 406-421.

[3] Iojrych, A., "The Role of the Executive in the Modern State—U.S.S.R.," *International Social Science Bulletin,* 1958, **10,** No. 2, 225.

[4] Balance Sheet of the de Gaulle Administration, *French Affairs*—No. 84, New York: Embassy of France, Information Service, May, 1959, pp. 7 and 8.

[5] Board of Governors of the Federal Reserve System, *The Federal Reserve System: Its Purposes and Functions,* Washington: United States Government Printing Office, first edition, 1939, p. 23.

[6] Johnson, Eldon L., "The Accountability of the British Nationalized Industries," *The American Political Science Review,* 1954, **48,** No. 2, 366-385.

[7] *Nebbia v. New York,* 291 U.S. 502 (1934).

[8] *New State Co. v. Liebmann,* 285 U.S. 263 (1932).

[9] Berle, Adolf A., Jr., *The 20th Century Capitalist Revolution,* New York: Harcourt, Brace, 1954, pp. 26 and 27.

[10] Galbraith, J. Kenneth, *American Capitalism, The Concept of Countervailing Power,* Boston: Houghton Mifflin, 1952.

[11] *The New York Times,* June 15, 1959.

Supplementary Readings

Berle, Adolf A., Jr., *The 20th Century Capitalist Revolution,* New York: Harcourt, Brace, 1954.

Burkhead, Jesse, *Government Budgeting,* New York: Wiley, 1956.

Burns, James M., and Peltason, Jack W. (eds.), *Functions and Policies of American Government,* Englewood Cliffs: Prentice-Hall, 1958.

Cole, G. D. H., *Guild Socialism Restated,* London: L. Parsons, 1920.

Dimock, Marshall E., *Business and Government,* New York: Holt, third edition, 1957.

Fainsod, Merle, and Gordon, Lincoln, *Government and the American Economy,* New York: Norton, revised edition, 1948.

Galbraith, J. Kenneth, *American Capitalism; The Concept of Countervailing Power,* Boston: Houghton Mifflin, 1952.

Groves, Harold M., *Financing Government,* New York: Holt, fourth edition, 1954.

Hunt, R. N. Carew, *The Theory and Practice of Communism,* New York: Macmillan, 1950.

Koontz, H., and Gable, R., *Public Control of Economic Enterprise,* New York: McGraw-Hill, 1956.

Robson, William A. (ed.), *Problems of Nationalized Industry,* New York: Oxford, 1952.

Schlatter, Richard, *Private Property,* New Brunswick: Rutgers University Press, 1951.

Schumpeter, Joseph A., *Capitalism, Socialism and Democracy,* New York: Harper, second edition, 1947.

Steiner, G. A., *Government's Role in Economic Life,* New York: McGraw-Hill, 1953.

Woytinsky, W. S. and E. S., *World Population and Production Trends and Outlook,* New York: Twentieth Century Fund, 1953.

Chapter 15

Government and Welfare

Controversy surrounds the question of the obligation of government to safeguard individual economic security. An unfinished debate on this topic, conducted on a level of unproved generalizations and strongly held convictions, constitutes the core of political argumentation in most modern states. As a prelude to personal involvement (almost impossible to avoid in practical life) it may be useful to examine some of the terms employed in the debate and the hidden assumptions they may conceal.

Perhaps the most widespread and generally accepted term is that of the *welfare state*. This serves as a useful summary of the extensive network of social services provided by the government of a country such as Great Britain, where the term was first generally accepted in politics. When the concept is generalized to include government responsibilities in the United States and non-European countries, particularly in underdeveloped areas, it loses much of its descriptive character in favor of a theoretical bias. In Britain, as in other European lands, social services were extended to make representative democracy workable as a political system in a class society based on economic privilege. The major question involved was political: how to retain majority support for an existing institutional framework in a community where a class system had created grave economic and social injustices. Where the European type of class organization does not prevail, the political solution of a welfare state loses much of its urgency and practicality.

American Concepts of Welfare Obligations

Present-day use of "welfare" as a political issue may involve confusion with the term "general welfare" as employed in the Constitution of the United States.[1] Thus, Senator Morse in a dissent to the Report of the Commission on Intergovernmental Relations (1955) writes:

As a constitutional liberal, I hold to the point of view that the underlying purpose of our federal system of delegated powers is to promote the general welfare of the people of the nation as a whole. . . . The ultra conservative point of view fails to give due emphasis to the general welfare clause of the Constitution. It fails to recognize that the impelling motivation of our constitutional forefathers was to form a political society of free men and women for the purpose of promoting the general welfare of all, through a system of representative government in which the people by way of checks and balances would remain the masters of governmental affairs.

The Senator raises two important issues: where the responsibility for care of the general welfare lies, as between State and central governments in a federal system, and whether "the general Welfare of the United States" is synonymous with the economic security of the individual. In reference to the latter point, it is questionable whether the Founding Fathers shared the twentieth-century viewpoint as to the obligation of political institutions to underwrite the personal security of the individual. The matter, of course, is not one of constitutional interpretation but of current necessities underlying existing political organization. Because an economic class system has not dominated American development, the maintenance of established patterns of government or national unity has not become dependent on a guarantee of certain standards of economic security to a depressed majority of the people.

A clearer approach to American doctrines concerning the social-service functions of government may be found in Professor Coker's concept of "empirical collectivism."[2] Political and social necessity serves as the guidepost to action in this doctrine. Those things are done collectively that cannot be done in any other way, and with the greatest possible economy in the use of authority, organization, and resources. Elaborate theories concerning the "rights" of individuals to economic protection through state action are disregarded. Agrarian and frontier tradition in the preindustrial phase of American society laid a solid basis for collective action through neighborly associations which was projected onto the political as well as the social sphere. With the growth of political democracy and an industrial economy, the States assumed wide responsibilities in the field of social services. By 1850, there were fifteen State universities and the principle of public, tax-supported education was widespread. Federalism has perhaps concealed the gradual growth of government intervention to strengthen the security of the individual against economic and social stresses. For financial and political reasons, the federal government was in no position to assume the burden of national social services until after the turn of the nineteenth century. The first federal grant-in-aid to the States took the form of the Morrill Act of 1862, which transferred public lands to the States willing to use the proceeds of their sale for the establishment of agricultural colleges.

By 1930, the federal government still had a minor part in the provision of social services. Grants were made to the States for the rehabilitation of disabled workers and for vocational education and agricultural extension services. The New Deal Administration of President Franklin D. Roosevelt witnessed a revolutionary acceptance of responsibility on the part of the federal government for human welfare throughout the whole country. Perhaps the enlargement of government activities had been overstressed in light of previous State and local efforts to cope with social problems. However, the massive intervention of the central government, involving the integration and bureaucratization of social services, marked a radical change in the American attitude toward social legislation. Empirical rather than theoretical reasons for government intervention still seem to have been dominant, as is illustrated by the preamble to the Federal Emergency Relief Act of 1933.

> The present economic depression has created a serious emergency, due to widespread unemployment and increasing inadequacy of State and local relief funds, resulting in the existing or threatened deprivation of a considerable number of families and individuals of the

necessities of life, and making it imperative that the Federal Government cooperate more effectively with the several States and Territories and the District of Columbia in furnishing relief to their needy and distressed people.

Ordered responsibility for a framework of social security on a national scale was assumed by the federal government under provisions of the Social Security Act of 1935. Four categories of persons whom the States had not been able to safeguard adequately —the blind, the aged, dependent children, and, above all, the unemployed—were covered by schemes under this Act. Political and economic necessities of the times, rather than any widely held views concerning proper relationships between government and the individual, guided the formulation and subsequent operation of this legislation. Twenty years later, the Commission on Intergovernmental Relations appointed by a Republican President reported:

> It has been amply demonstrated that unemployment compensation is a built-in stabilizer of the economy. By giving purchasing power to the unemployed, it helps maintain the purchasing power of the community during a recession. For example, the total amount of unemployment benefits paid out in calendar year 1953 was about $840 million; during 1954 it was over $2 billion. In calendar year 1954, benefit payments exceeded tax collections by $692 million. In the preceding year, tax collections topped benefits by $586 million. . . .
>
> The mere existence of a nation-wide unemployment compensation system is not enough. It should protect the unemployed through benefits reasonably related to wage levels, for adequate periods, and governed by reasonable eligibility and disqualification provisions.

Methods adopted by the federal government under the Social Security Act provided for cooperative action with State governments, with only one program—that of old-age insurance—administered directly by federal agencies. A federal-State system with the administrative machinery of State and local bodies operating the programs allows for flexible arrangements that can take into account the great diversity of American regional conditions.

Though general principles of social security now originate for the most part from the federal government, many obstacles remain in the way of the establishment of a centralized national policy. Because the sphere of direct social legislation does not lie within the enumerated powers granted to Congress by the Constitution, the grant of tax money has remained the principal instrument through which the federal government has induced the several States to accept a common plan. By making the grants conditional and for specified purposes, the central government is able to achieve a measure of standardization in the operation of social legislation. However, the procedure is in many ways cumbersome and wasteful. Ideally, grants should be variable according to the needs and fiscal capacities of the individual States, but the political and economic difficulties encountered have proved insurmountable up to the present. Again, conditional grants have had the effect of emphasizing the type of services supported by the central government at the expense of general assistance, for which the individual State bears the total fiscal burden. A distorted pattern of security, for which no specific administration may be clearly blamed, has been an obvious consequence. It may be claimed that an empirical solution of social problems that cannot be handled on a State or local basis is still the objective of national intervention in the field of social security. The British approach of "cradle to grave" security as a basic relationship between the individual and the State has not yet been accepted as a dominant factor in the American political situation.

British and European Attitudes

It has been suggested previously that the concept of the welfare state should be reserved for European nations, on the ground that it represented a deliberately executed structure to meet the political condition of a nation torn by class strife and injustice. Britain provides an example of the process in action. Before becoming Prime Minister, Benjamin Disraeli dramatized in his political novels the division of England into two nations—the rich and the poor. This was a political fact of major importance that might have led, as it did in many Continental lands, to political revolution accompanying the rise of democracy. Early recognition of the situation by the major political parties resulted in conscious attempts to promote national unity through government guarantee of minimum standards of economic justice. The movement culminated in the famous Beveridge Report of 1942, named after the Chairman of a Committee on Social Insurance, Sir William Beveridge. In brief, this Report integrated all previous schemes dealing with social security into a nationally operated plan so comprehensive in nature as to merit the designation of cradle-to-grave insurance. Unemployment relief, old-age pensions, family allowances, sickness benefits, workmen's compensation, funeral expenses, and national assistance grants for the needy were included in the coverage. The political circumstances of the acceptance of this Report were of importance. Dunkirk had made the British a besieged people fighting almost alone against overwhelming German might. National morale, particularly in the armed forces and among factory workers, was the sole remaining barrier against disgraceful surrender. The release of the Report at this time created a concrete social objective around which the bulk of the people could rally their future hopes. With war-inspired acumen the coalition Government conducted an unprecedented educational campaign on a nation-wide scale on the contents of the Report. Discussion guides were issued for the use of military formations, and strictly enforced orders made educational sessions on the company level as obligatory as weapon training. In the writer's personal experience, these Beveridge debates did a great deal to weld the lower ranks of the military services into a fighting force actuated by a clearly realized purpose. One effect, of course, was to commit the major political parties to full acceptance of social security as a basic obligation of the national government. Since the time of the Report, political controversy has raged over methods, timing, and costs, but never over the principles involved in cradle-to-grave insurance.

Postwar constitutions among European democracies generally recognize the obligation of the state to provide a measure of economic security for its individual citizens. Thus, Article 38 of the 1947 Italian Constitution reads:

Every citizen unable to work and deprived of the means necessary to live has the right to support and to social assistance. Laborers have the right to provisions and assured means adequate to their living requirements in case of accident, sickness, disability and old age, and involuntary unemployment. Those unable to work and the disabled have the right to education and to a beginning in a profession. Organs and institutions established or assimilated by the state provide for the fulfillment of the tasks contemplated by this article.

Similarily, the 1946 French Constitution declared in its Preamble:

The Nation shall guarantee to all, and particularly to the child, the mother, and the aged worker, protection of health, material security, rest and leisure. Any individual who, because of his or her age, his or her physical or mental condition, or because of the economic situation shall find himself or herself unable to work, shall have the right to obtain from the community the means for a decent existence.

Though these promises are not repeated in the more laconic de Gaulle Constitution of 1958, their omission may perhaps be credited to their general acceptance as an unescapable obligation of modern government.

Scandinavian countries have led the way in Europe to a form of social and economic egalitarianism based upon extensive government guarantees of individual security. Again in their case, it may be recalled that severe class divisions between a landholding aristocracy and the working masses had to be resolved to insure peaceful evolution of political institutions under conditions of democracy.

The alternative to acceptance of the welfare state in countries with a feudal background varies between proletarian revolution and class government based on military force. Spain has undergone both experiences in the last thirty years.

Types of Social Security: Old-Age Pensions

Government responsibility for provision of retirement allowances for the aged is a comparatively new development that has spread rapidly through Western countries. Once inaugurated, a tendency toward increased coverage and rising benefits becomes part of the political pattern. This may be held to be due in part to consequences of industrialism and scientific technology on living conditions. Thus, in 1939, persons sixty-five or over constituted 6.3 per cent of the population of the United States. By 1980 the percentage will have risen to 16, according to the calculations of the National Resources Committee. The effect of monetary inflation following the wars of the twentieth century has been to reduce the ability of large sections of the aged to live off savings accumulated from wage earnings from their productive periods.

Contributory insurance schemes are now preferred methods in the United States, Britain, Canada, and many other countries. The United States Social Security Act of 1935 as subsequently amended provides for a compromise between the private-insurance principle of benefits according to individual contributions and the social principle of basing benefits on actual needs. Britain commenced with noncontributory old-age pensions in 1908, but when the Beveridge Report was implemented in 1945 it included retirement pensions in the National Insurance Fund supported by contributions from employers, employees, and the government. In practice, whatever actuarial devices are adopted, taxes levied on business and wage earners must bear the major load of supporting the current generation of old-age pensioners.

Unemployment Compensation

Since the industrial revolution destroyed the type of individual economic security present in agrarian societies, political institutions in Western lands have encountered continuous pressure from the necessities of large sections of the population that are dependent for their livelihood on the vagaries of industrial employment. Representative democracy and general economic insecurity provide an explosive mixture normally fatal to established political and social orders. Abandonment of free, representative government in favor of Communist or Fascist dictatorships has proved at least a temporary answer in great areas of the modern world. Free peoples have sought to discover a workable substitute for the economic independence provided in Jefferson's day by the family farm, which he held with good reason to be a sure foundation for political democracy. Mutual insurance on a national scale, with government acting as promoter and service operator, has been the most widely accepted solution. A distinction may be drawn between such insurance schemes and government action to provide poor relief out of general tax money. Though premiums are collected from both employers and employees in the form of a compulsory tax, government thereafter acts as trustee and administrator of designated insurance funds. The parallel between private and public insurance may not be pressed too far. Direct personal interests of individual employers or employees are not necessarily served by national schemes. The insurance is an underwriting of the economy as a whole, through the correction of certain social weaknesses. In so far as every individual is dependent on the security of the whole economy, insurance premiums may be regarded as a proper hedge against risks even though no direct money benefits are ever received. From another point of view, participation in national insurance schemes may be considered one of the conditions under which business enterprises and workers are entitled to make use of the general facilities of the community.

Britain inaugurated unemployment insurance by a National Insurance Act of 1911. Most industrial nations had become fully committed to the principle before the United States turned to this solution in the depression of the thirties. The Social Security Act of 1935 faced the problem common among federal systems as to the degree of control to be exercised by national and State governments respectively. Cooperative federalism was chosen as the basis for the American system, and its operation in practice has pioneered new forms of working relations between central and State administrations. A tax-offset plan formed the heart of the financial arrangements. Ninety per cent of this federally imposed tax was allowed to employers as a credit for sums paid into State unemployment compensation funds; ten per cent of the tax was retained by the federal government to be used to make grants to State unemployment schemes. Laws passed by the States had to conform to federally imposed standards, and State unemployment compensation funds had to be paid into a trust fund administered by the federal Treasury. Considerable freedom remains with the States concerning the type of laws they adopt, extent of coverage, benefit rates, and whether contributions are paid into a single reserve fund or individual employer reserve accounts are established. This, of course, leads to great administrative complexity and considerable diversity concerning benefits and contributions. From the political point of view, certain advantages may accrue from divided responsibilities. Mass pressures on national political parties from wage earners or organized business to alter benefits or rates are cushioned through fifty State governments.

American methods of meeting government responsibility toward unemployment insurance are of importance for all federally organized states. Australia first began consideration of insurance schemes in 1910, but found the resolution of responsibilities between federal and State governments an insurmountable obstacle until 1946. In that year, a constitutional amendment was adopted giving the Commonwealth government direct power to make laws concerning unemployment compensation and similar social services. The Labour administration in power decided on a noncontributory scheme based on a portion of the income tax which came to be known as "the Social Service Contribution." In effect, this has elevated the position of central government as service institution for the individual and altered basic issues in national politics. New federations coming into being, such as Nigeria, will have to choose between the American type of decentralized cooperation and the Australian emphasis on a national level of social security.

Education

A general acceptance of state responsibility for provision of educational facilities may be traced far back into the history of Western peoples. When the learning process ceased to be a monopoly of a universal Church at the close of the Middle Ages, endowment of colleges and universities became largely a responsibility of government. In America, the New England colonies recognized public responsibility for education early in the seventeenth century. Perhaps a major reason for the solicitude of governments lay in the relationship of the power and wealth of a community to its educational standards, particularly in the field of the sciences and higher skills. With the advent of industrial technology, the need for skills produced by the educational process became apparent as a factor in the competitive struggle for prosperity between nations. The educational level of the population determined whether a nation had the capacity to make use of new technological developments, thus increasing its military power and internal prosperity. If advancement of individual interests were the sole concern of government, there would be slight reason why provision of educational facilities should take precedence over protection of health. Yet the latter is a very recent and still controversial sphere of governmental activity, while the former is a well-established tradition of government responsibility. The particular position of education may be recognized if it is assumed to be a community rather than individual interest. This traditional motivation is once more coming to the front with the threat imposed on non-Communist peoples by an efficient and strongly supported Russian educational system. It is no longer merely a question of who has the most industrial and military equipment, but also of which nation can outstrip the other in scientific, intellectual, and skilled man power.

Because of the public interest as well as private gain involved in the educational process, difficult political issues arise as a consequence of government intervention. In the first place, industrialized states normally make education compulsory for the young of both sexes up to ages varying from thirteen to seventeen. This may amount to a severe restriction on the choice of the youngsters themselves and a burden on their families, deprived of their productive labor. The denial of voluntary choice in such a matter may only be excused by the public need for a uniformly educated population. Secondly, and more importantly, control of schooling by the state renders youth in its most impressionable years liable to indoctrination along lines determined by political sources. A certain measure of indoctrination is, of course, inevitable in any organized society. Primitive peoples employ initiation rites and ceremonies to fit youth into tribal life. Advanced technological societies include in their educational curriculum "training for citizenship" in various forms and to different degrees. However, a basic issue remains between the state and the family as to the extent of control that may be exercised over the mind of the child under compulsory systems of education. The American position has been summed up by Mr. Justice McReynolds:

> The fundamental theory of liberty upon which all governments in this Union repose excludes any general power of the State to standardize its children by forcing them to accept instruction from public teachers

only. The child is not the mere creature of the State; those who nurture him and direct his destiny have the right, coupled with the high duty, to recognize and prepare him for additional obligations.[3]

Local control of educational facilities through the raising and spending of tax moneys provides safeguards against the use of schools as instruments of political or social propaganda on a wide scale. However, educational standards, as regards both material taught and teaching competence, have to be imposed from some central source. State governments possess this authority under the American Constitution, permitting a nation-wide system of competitive diversity. Though misuse of political power in the educational system is thus largely avoided, other disadvantages appear. Lacking access to federal funds, many localities and States are unable to provide facilities that would be considered barely minimal in more fortunate communities. If the standard of public education is truly a national concern, national resources may have to be pooled to permit the efficient and economical building of an adequate school system for the country as a whole. Experience with other forms of cooperative federalism indicate that this will not necessarily lead to domination of the content and form of public education by the instrumentalities of the central government. Where the federal government has intervened in education in incidental programs concerned with defense research, veteran training, or school lunches, it has discovered methods of adjusting its activities in accordance with the autonomy of the academic community or the local school board.

Political issues involved in governmental control of educational processes may be analyzed more clearly in the case of unitary states such as Britain and France. The British Ministry of Education, for example, directs the educational structure of the nation to an extent beyond anything in American experience. Though the provision of school buildings and instructional staff is a responsibility laid on local authorities, teacher qualifications, curricula, and standards of school buildings are determined by the ministry. Under the Education Act of 1944, each local education authority, of which there are approximately 146, is obligated to submit to the ministry a plan covering its educational program. Experts in the central government offices shape this plan in negotiation with local representatives.

Once agreed upon, the program is enforced by a ministerial order from the national administration and supervised by inspectors from the ministry. A concentration of educational administrators and supervisory experts in Whitehall makes ministerial policy dominant as regards technical knowledge as well as official power. As local authorities are heavily dependent upon grants from the central government to finance school operations, resistance to national policies tends to be feeble and sporadic.

Administrative regulation of public education by the national government inevitably makes educational objectives subject to debate as questions of political policy. The Labour Party has claimed in the past and still claims that insufficient expenditure on public education has accentuated class differences by giving the advantage of superior education to a minority attending what in America are called private schools. Integration of the total educational system, public and private, under some form of merit plan has been raised as a major political issue. The Labour point of view is stated by a party representative in the following terms:

> Socialists believe strongly in two different kinds of equality. In the first place, they believe in equality of opportunity. They wish to build up the kind of society in which each boy or girl will have the education best suited to bring out his natural ability and to develop his various tastes. A community which had an effective system of education would have the whole people from which to choose the best individuals to occupy all the most important posts, whether in industry, the universities, the arts or Government. . . . Obviously, absolute equality of opportunity can never be attained; some children have better parents than others, some are endowed with better physique than others. Socialists hold that it is the duty of the community to do its best so to organise its education, its health and other services as to neutralise these natural inequalities as far as possible.[4]

Nonsocialists, naturally enough, regard the neutralization of natural inequalities through state-supported education as a leveling-down process destructive of social excellence if carried out on a compulsory basis for the whole community. The issue is deeply rooted in the class division of British society, where the superiority of private-school education has become a symbol of class rule. In defense of the private-school system, which admittedly produced a ruling class throughout the nineteenth century, it is claimed that "they did not make society into different classes. That was done for them. But given classes, they instilled into those they taught a greater measure of humility and decency than any Christian aristocracy had been able to achieve before."[5]

Power to enforce educational choices on parents and children may be accounted one of the dangerous instruments in the hands of representative democracies. A social philosophy held by temporary majorities is likely to be imposed on the sensitive pattern of youthful education. In France, political efforts to secularize education and diminish the influence of Church schools has added to the turmoil of French politics for over a century.

At the same time, provision of educational facilities ranks as one of the most important services that government can render to a community. Among the new nations arising in Asia and Africa, the link between social unity, organization, and levels of education stands out in bolder relief than is the case in long-established countries. Nevertheless, the same principle applies in both instances: standards of freedom are linked to capacities for mutual communication and understanding, which in turn are products of some educational system.

Health Services

Plagues, contagions, and disease-breeding conditions have been the concern of government from earliest times. The new dimension of personal medical services for the individual is a product of modern technology. It is only in comparatively recent times that the medical profession as an organized body has been in a position to offer the ordinary individual essential services. The new gift of controlled health now constitutes a major demand on the part of the community. Whether this demand is one to be left to the individual to satisfy through his own powers or is a proper field for government action is a controversial political issue. As Britain, among industrialized nations, pioneered in this field, the policies adopted there (widely imitated elsewhere) form a useful starting point for examination of the topic.

Conditions brought about by industrialization and the rapid

growth of population on a small island served to throw light on the miserable health standards of the laboring masses. Though it is questionable whether these standards were better in preindustrial times, the crowding of the people into towns and increased demands on human skill and energy in factory employment made the health of the worker a national question. Apart from any humanitarian principles, a healthy and skillful labor force constituted the country's most important resource. Internal immigration from a healthier countryside soon ceased to revitalize urban communities, and the problem became one of conserving and improving existing resources. Reformers from the time of Lord Shaftesbury's Factory Acts to Lloyd George's National Insurance Act of 1911 could plead a solid basis of economic advantage for their proposals. The 1911 Act provided sickness benefits and medical care to all the working classes through a contributory insurance scheme to which workers, employers, and the state contributed. A network of voluntary friendly societies had previously served as insurance agents for poorly paid workers, and these were coopted into the administration of the government scheme. Initial opposition from organized medicine lessened when practitioners discovered that "insurance" patients replaced in a more profitable manner the charity cases to whom they had previously accorded free treatment under the prevailing medical ethics of the day.

It was on this established pattern of governmentally insured medical care for the working population that the more extensive National Health Service was established in 1948. The most revolutionary change was the destruction of class barriers, thus making available to all sections of the population the same type of medical care under similar conditions. This involved bringing hospitals, specialists, dentists, drugs, and appliances into the insurance network. Long experience with the previous system permitted operation of the comprehensive scheme with remarkably little friction. Costs, however, in the first year were more than double the original estimate and have been increasing, though no longer at the original precipitate pace. Investment in health coverage has added a burden to the British taxpayer that limits his freedom to indulge in other forms of national expenditure. Many industrial countries now follow the British pattern to a greater or less degree. Australia since 1946 has provided on a national level for sickness benefits, free drugs and hospital treatment, and maternity benefits.

Government implemented health-insurance plans in the United States have lagged behind those of other industrial countries perhaps because higher standards of living have robbed them of some of their urgency. Besides, it is only within recent years that voluntary medical-insurance plans have been placed in widespread operation. If the British experience is any guide, voluntary schemes provide a useful preliminary phase, accustoming the medical profession and the general public to the pattern of collective health services.

Housing

Acceptance of responsibility by the state for adequate housing for the people is a development of the second half of the twentieth century. War damage in Britain and Europe and a suspension of building activities in the United States during the war period placed governments under pressure to meet public demands in this respect. Empirical necessities rather than ideological theories prevailed in America and Britain; evidence of this may be found in the fact that the British Conservative Party outstripped its Labour rivals in the housing programs it initiated while in office. Nevertheless, once governments have committed themselves to responsibilities of this kind it is difficult to retreat from them under conditions of representative democracy. Adequate housing tends to be added to clean water supply and safe health conditions as a collective obligation for which government is the proper agent.

In the United States, Constitutional and political theory favors the State governments as principal parties in housing programs. In the words of the 1955 Commission on Intergovernmental Relations, "Responsibility for the initiation and administration of public housing, slum clearance, and urban renewal programs rests with State and local governments." However, Senators Humphrey and Morse added the practical comment to this section of the Commission's Report that "only a few States, notably the more wealthy, have been able to initiate housing programs on an independent basis." The United States Housing Act of 1937 made a modest beginning to the provision of loans and contributions to local public-housing agencies. Acts of 1949 and 1954 gave the federal government a greater part in the major problem of slum clearance. An almost biennial Housing Act has become a feature of party politics on the national level, with the responsibility for slum conditions throughout the whole country gaining recognition as a collective obligation.

Family Allowances and General Care

In order to overcome the stigma of poor relief or public charity, several categories have been created of persons entitled to grants of public funds because of their circumstances. Britain, again, has systematized this concept, providing a useful illustration of it in operation. The most notable example is that of family allowances for mothers, who receive a lump sum for expenses on the birth of each child and a continuing allowance thereafter for a period of about three months. Widows and orphans are also entitled to government benefits as of right. Workers injured in the course of their employment are guaranteed payments from the national Treasury. A peculiarly British feature is a grant toward funeral allowances, implementing literally the slogan of security from the cradle to the grave. The area of general assistance to indigents, formerly covered by poor relief, remains subject to the hated "means test," requiring proof of destitution by the recipient. In the United States, a more cautious approach has been made to public assistance for the economically deprived and unfortunate. General relief remains a State responsibility, varying according to the capacities and outlooks of the various States. Assistance from the federal government takes the form of grants for aid to dependent children, the blind, and totally disabled persons.

Costs and Consequences of Social Legislation

During the twentieth century, the burden imposed on the individual through taxation in industrialized states has become a major factor affecting social relationships and the degree of personal freedom that may be enjoyed. The two principal causes of rising state expenditures are national defense and social services. In the latter case, two contrasting viewpoints may be distinguished. A socialist theory regards higher taxation for improved social services as a means for the redistribution of the national income in a manner that will correct some of the inequities of laissez-faire capitalism. This point of view may be regarded as slightly old-fashioned in view of the increase in earning standards of the bulk of workers in terms of money income. Income-tax and sales-tax laws now make the average wage earner a principal contributor to government treasuries. A point is being reached in advanced industrial communities where the statistically average citizen pays in tax contributions in full for the protection afforded him by governmentally sponsored social services. The second attitude may be linked to the pragmatic concept of empirical collectivism. Technological advances have altered the circumstances of social living. Improvements that affect everybody—increased opportunities to move around and change jobs might be cited as an example—have to be paid for by the acceptance of wider areas of cooperative action. Social services are the latest field of joint endeavor imposed on the community by the necessities of its own organizational development.

The extent and character of a social-service program and its concomitant taxation is determined by factors that are essentially political. Partisan groups united in political parties seek to balance the estimated wants of a majority of the electorate against their proved disinclination to pay for them in personal taxes. This may not be considered a scientific method of planning social development, but it has the merit of being undogmatic, open to the lessons of experience, and, above all, consensual as an expression of representative democracy. In the American situation, the debate centers in the question of the stimulation of economic growth for public purposes in contrast to private satisfactions. A concrete example might be how much of the national resources should be expended in building and maintaining schools, as against, say, luxury apartment buildings and hotels. From the political point of view, the important fact is that government is now in a position to make effective decisions on such matters. If a majority of the electorate feels that the economy is being misdirected, they tend under present-day conditions to choose a government that will employ instruments that lie at hand to alter the economy to suit dictates of the popular will.

Another recent consequence of social-service legislation is the effect it is producing on mass decisions concerning war and peace. The major industrialized countries of the world, including the United States and Soviet Russia, have reached the point where the burden of armament costs imposes limitations on extensions of the social services. The ordinary wage earner is presented with the view of international tensions as a direct obstacle to his attainment of the "better life" through the use of his country's resources for cooperative advancement. What ultimate effects this may have upon power groups in control of policy making has yet to be determined. History, at least in modern times, indicates that great decisions concerning war and peace are seldom made by rulers without the conviction that they will obtain popular backing. Pursuit of the welfare state has perhaps shown the ordinary citizen in all countries the practical price he must pay for resort to arms.

In an earlier chapter it was suggested that politics deals with matters of serious concern. When the ramifications of social legislation as they affect individuals in their pockets and way of living are considered, it may be seen that the degree of seriousness is practical rather than theoretical. In consequence of the applicability of political decision-making in the sphere of social services to the everyday concerns of the individual, it may be predicted that the attitude of the bulk of the electorate toward political questions is likely to undergo increasing change. Distinction between practical affairs relating to economic and social standing and political matters is lessening. Struggles for power and office, mock battles of emotional oratory, constitute an insufficient "floor show" for the tax bill now being presented for payment. The individual voter is now participant in a business concern in which he invests an increasing part of his income and to which he looks for economic returns and services essential to his security. A long, hard look at the management of the concern monopolizing so much of his money would be very much in the tradition of the American character.

Notes

[1] In the Preamble to the Constitution, one of the objects for which the Constitution was established is declared to be "to promote the general Welfare." The Preamble, however, is not the source of any substantive power conferred on the government of the United States. Some express delegation of power must be found in the body of the Constitution (*Jacobson v. Massachusetts.* 197 U.S. 11 [1905]). What is known as the "general welfare" clause is contained in Article I, Section 8: "The Congress shall have Power to lay and collect Taxes, Duties, Imposts and Excises, to pay the Debts and provide for the common Defence and general Welfare of the United States. . . ."

[2] Coker, Francis W., *Recent Political Thought,* New York: Appleton, 1934. See also Shields, Currin V., "The American Tradition of Empirical Collectivism," *The American Political Science Review,* 1952, **46,** No. 1, 104-120.

[3] *Pierce v. Society of Sisters,* 268 U.S. 510 (1925).

[4] Parker, John, *Labour Marches On,* Baltimore: Penguin, 1947, p. 201.

[5] Hogg, Quintin, *The Case for Conservatism,* Baltimore: Penguin, 1947, p. 146.

Supplementary Readings

Dahl, Robert A., and Lindblom, Charles E., *Politics, Economics and Welfare,* New York: Harper, 1953.

Eckstein, Harry H., *The English Health Service: its Origins, Structure, and Achievements,* London: Oxford, 1959.

Finer, Herman, *Road to Reaction,* Boston: Little, Brown, 1945.

Fleisher, Wilfrid, *Sweden: The Welfare State,* New York: John Day, 1956.

Glueck, Sheldon (ed.), *The Welfare State and the National Welfare,* Cambridge: Addison-Wesley, 1952.

Hayek, Friedrich A., *The Road to Serfdom,* Chicago: University of Chicago Press, 1944.

Marsh, David C., *National Insurance and Assistance in Great Britain,* London: Pitman, 1951.

Mendelsohn, Ronald, *Social Security in the British Commonwealth, Great Britain, Canada, Australia, New Zealand,* London: Oxford, 1954.

Poole, Kenyon E., *Public Finance and Economic Welfare,* New York: Rinehart, 1956.

Robson, William A. (ed.), *Social Security,* London: G. Allen, third edition revised, 1948.

Chapter 16

Political Aspects of Agriculture and Labor

Politics and Landholding

The origins of most Western political systems may be traced to problems arising from land tenure. Solon launched Athens as a constitutional democracy through the bold use of law to rid the economy of an intolerable burden of mortgage debt. Roman politics in the days of the Republic may be best understood in terms of the social consequences of successive land grabs, first that of the Roman tribes against their Etruscan and Latin neighbors and then the economic subjugation of the small farmer by a landed aristocracy operating great estates (latifundia) with slave labor. Collapse of republican institutions may be said to have commenced with the two Gracchi revolts in 133 and 123 B.C. when demand for redistribution of the land evoked civil war and the trend to dictatorship manifested in the rule of Marius, Sulla, Pompeius, and finally Julius Caesar.

Feudalism, which afforded a few centuries of stable social life to Western peoples after the collapse of Roman imperialism in savage anarchy, may be described as at once a system of land tenure and a system of government. It would be premature to assume that the institution of government, even in technologically advanced lands, has divorced itself from its primitive function of distributor of the land. Of course, physical possession or use of land no longer serves as the main access to means of production in industrialized countries. Government control of land tenure has merged into a general, state-protected pattern of property rights in an exchange economy that blurs distinctions between control over instruments of production and enjoyment of consumer goods. However, a skeleton of the traditional relationship between government and landholding still remains in the most civilized nations, causing political institutions to assume special responsibilities in this area.

The greater part of the world, both in territory and population, has not yet divorced production from the soil. There, control over the land amounts to almost total power to determine the structure of society. An illustration may be drawn from a Report by a British Royal Commission concerned with the problem of bringing African tribal communities into the structure of a modern state.

East Africa is at present predominantly an agricultural region and the income produced by the agricultural industry seems certain to remain a major ingredient in the geographical incomes of the territories. Land policy must be directed towards the removal of those conditions which prevent the available land from being effectively utilized, and equally towards the creation of conditions which will facilitate the application of technical knowledge, labour and capital in proportions suitable over the long period to the generation of maximum income. . . . What may be called individual rights of land tenure must replace the tribal controls which now exist.

Here again we have a conflict between the basic features of the traditional tribal economy and the requirements of a modern and more productive system. Many Africans have already come to appreciate and understand the implications of this conflict. . . . But this process of change has not been adequate for the needs of the region as a whole. . . . We, therefore, think that it is imperative to introduce a new land law which will ensure that private interests in land are recognized, which will provide that they shall be determined by a process of adjudication and duly recorded, and which will enable them to be bought and sold. This new land law necessarily involves the abandonment of policies which maintain customary tenures. . . . But these decisions must be taken as matters of national policy and be made effective through the laws of the territories. . . . We consider that a decision to give effect to this policy is as important for East Africa as was the compilation of the Domesday Book for England in the eleventh century.[1]

The measured words of this Report cover proposals to make fundamental changes in African society through a government-sponsored revolution in land tenure. In brief, an existing framework of economic security for the individual based on communal land occupation is to be replaced by a leap into compulsory individualism in matters relating to personal or family livelihood. The naked power of the political state may hardly be stretched further. The existence of latent and always inherent functions of government capable of revolutionizing society by changing legal rules concerning the relation of individuals or groups to the land from which they derive almost their whole livelihood is a significant factor in present-day world politics. Communist China has embarked on what is probably the most daring social experiment of the century through establishment of communes, politically ordered and controlled bodies through which alone their people are granted access to the land. India, Indonesia, Malaya, and most of non-Communist Asia are struggling with government land policies that will outdo the Communist revolution in increased productivity and social contentment. It is probable that the fate of government—whether it achieves popular representative forms or assumes a totalitarian cloak—depends throughout the greater part of Asia and Africa on the success or failure of land policies.

Politics in industrialized countries plays an equivocal role in relation to land and its cultivation. An ancient principle that all land lies within the dominion of the state and is held in private tenure from the state as ultimate proprietor has become an abstract legal theory. At the same time, land is not always admitted into the prevailing market economy in the same manner as other forms of property. A political *mystique* that places cultivation of the land in a special niche of its own apart from other forms of production still haunts European politics. Quintin Hogg, a foremost exponent of British Conservatism, makes a curious distinction between profit-making and good husbandry as a political responsibility of government in dealing with land cultivation.

When you go to a typical British farm to-day you see the result not of a good or a bad farmer (though a bad farmer may ruin a good farm in a surprisingly short space of time). What you see is the concentrated result of some twelve generations of good husbandry, the devoted effort which for over four centuries Englishmen have lavished *on the land*. I emphasize the words *on the land* because, though all the farmers worked for profit and the labourers for hire, neither the farmers nor the labourers received the true reward of their effort. The real reward redounded to the benefit of England; not just the Englishmen of that time, but of the Englishmen of a future time. They returned to the land in the form of manure, good drains, sound fences, and deeply cultivated fields more than they took out of it by way of sustenance for man and beast. . . . That is good husbandry, and that is the fundamental attitude of the Conservative Party to farming, and to industry for that matter. The profit motive is accepted and is used as the normal driving force, but it is not to be permitted to dominate, for if it does we shall do violence to the heritage which we have received from of old.[2]

That this is not empty rhetoric is proved by the continuance of severe wartime restrictions on landed proprietors by successive Conservative regimes. Use of land for farming purposes in Britain is no longer the sole concern of the owner of the land. Farming committees organized under governmental authority pass upon the farming practices of their neighborhood. If standards of good husbandry are not being observed, the owner loses control over his land. Justification of this disregard of the claims of private ownership may only flow from conviction that it is an overriding function of government to promote good husbandry.

France also holds the land on which the food of its people is grown separate from other types of property. Thus an ordinance of December 27, 1958,[3] was passed to protect young farmers against certain practices of land monopoly which made it difficult for them to find available land to farm. The government instituted a system whereby no person or company could increase his holdings beyond a certain maximum acreage without first obtaining an official permit. Politics in postwar as in prewar Italy remain distorted by an unsolved agrarian crisis; land held in great latifundia or plantations in the southern regions reduces the peasantry to an ill-nourished life of partial serfdom. An American observer points out that "The regions of Calabria, Lucania, and Apulia are the Achilles heel of Italy and perhaps of Western Europe as a whole. Their problem is basically agrarian, and it is intricate because of local diversity."[4] The regime of Franco in Spain has its basis in the fact that aristocrats constituting approximately one five hundredth of the population own 51 per cent of the land; wealthy farmers another 35 per cent; 1,000,000 small farmers own 11 per cent; 1,250,000 one-acre peasants 2.2 per cent; and there are about 2,000,000 landless agricultural workers.[5] A basically agricultural society constituted along such lines presents almost insuperable obstacles to the establishment of popular representative government.

Revolutionary outbreaks in Caribbean and some Central American lands frequently center in attempts to solve problems concerning the distribution of land by political means. The Castro regime in Cuba, for example, risked both internal disorder and loss of external support through adoption of a radical policy of land redistribution. Fundamental issues were involved which no popularly based government could ignore. The island has soil and climatic conditions which would make possible diversified farming and an ample food supply for its inhabitants. Yet all the evidence indicates malnutrition and severe dietary deficiencies affecting more than one third of the population. Historical reasons which led to a one-crop economy must bear most of the blame.[6] Oversimplification of the solutions possible through political remedies for these and similar problems is a constant threat to the stability of government through a considerable part of the less economically privileged portion of the world. A proper use of modern technology to raise living standards may require cultivation of land in large holdings rather than in small family-size farms. Responsibility lies ultimately with the political state to judge the long-term interests of the community and to order the relations of individuals and groups to the land accordingly. These decisions are peculiarly difficult and painful for government to make, as they seem to lie outside normal self-operating mechanisms of a market economy.

Government and the Nation's Food Supply

An obvious function of the political order in any country is the maintenance of an adequate food supply for the nourishment of the people. Even the United States—probably the most fortunate area in the world in natural resources and the technological means to exploit them—has maintained governmental interest in this matter. Political measures in support of agriculture have a long and fascinating history in the development of the American social system. Opening up the western public domain for settlement by the Homestead Act of 1862 gave a particular character to the democratic tradition in North America. In the same year, the Department of Agriculture was created—perhaps the most outstanding service agency produced by the federal government. Personal relationships built up between county agents of this Department and farmers provided one of the most realistic contacts the rural community enjoyed with national government. Integration of food producers into the national economy was advanced by the work of these trusted advisers, who were at the same time national, State, and local officials. A long-continued policy of providing marketing aids, services, and credit facilities to farmers has gradually involved the federal government in responsibilities towards agricultural production of a vast complexity.

There are several themes interwoven into the pattern of federal action which should be distinguished from one another in order to obtain a clear view of the nature and limits of government responsibility. In the first place, government interference with operations of an international market economy through import tariffs imposed for the benefit of domestic industry had an adverse effect on costs of agricultural production, particularly as regards the significant portion that had to be sold in the open markets of the world. Efforts of government to redress the imbalance brought about through its actions took many forms, most of them unsatisfactory. An expert debenture plan, proposed and defeated as an amendment to the Smoot-Hawley Tariff Act of 1930, elucidates the guilt complex of a political order biased in favor of industrial expansion. Under this plan, exporters of farm products were to receive a bounty which in effect was to be subsidized out of customs receipts on imports of industrial products. Eventually, the series of Agricultural Adjustment Acts, with their concepts of "parity" prices and crop loans to producers at various levels of the parity figure, involved the national administration and Treasury in commitments concerning which it would be difficult to forecast the end.

However, government responsibility since the two world wars has taken on a sharper and in some ways more practical edge in relation to food production as an essential factor in the preservation of national security. During both wars, government used its powers to bring about increased agricultural production, disposing of surpluses to its partners in the war effort. Besides a clear obligation to the farmer to accept some responsibility for the consequences of its actions, government retains a direct interest in preserving agricultural potential at a high level so that it would be instantly ready for the emergencies of future war. Neither productive land nor the farmer can be mothballed for future use, as has been done with shipping, for example; basic defense necessities play a considerable part in determining the nature of government commitments under conditions of an uneasy peace.

2.

A third factor influencing government policies has been the rise of political pressure groups organized as a natural reaction to the assumption of state responsibility in an individualistic sphere of private endeavor. Farm blocs, though politically important, may not be said to be either a primary or continuing cause of political intervention in the agricultural economy. Until, however, government has clarified the nature of its responsibility in this field and obtained recognition of the need for its policies from substantial majority interests throughout the community, the gadfly action of farmers' organizations may be expected to play an important part in domestic politics.

3.

An historical phase in which the dominant industrial nations of the West were able to treat food production as part of an internal market economy is perhaps in the process of passing. Lord Boyd Orr, a former Director of the Food and Agricultural Organization of the United Nations, estimates that between 75 and 85 per cent of the world's population are hungry, in the sense that their diet is inadequate to maintain health and prevent suffering from nutritional diseases.[7] With two great military power blocs confronting each other basically over the question as to who is to possess dominant economic and cultural influence over the underdeveloped majority of the world's population, the role of food supplier has assumed new importance. Demand for many of the products of agriculture has moved from the field of a national market economy into a political realm involving problems of security and long-term international policy that may be determined only by the government of the state. The British concept of government responsibility for

4.

"good husbandry" on a national basis may be in the process of being replaced by political definitions of husbandry on a world level. Should the Communist-controlled bloc achieve such a definition in advance of the Western nations, they may win an advantage future generations would find it hard to overcome.

Labor Organization

In the perspective of history, the organization of workers for the purposes of collective bargaining constitutes a comparatively new force in society. The legal and political readjustments required of political states to accommodate this development have caused acute social tension. Before the first half of the nineteenth century, combinations of working men to bargain with their employers were technically illegal as combinations in restraint of trade in both the United States and Britain. A Massachusetts judgment in the case of *Commonwealth v. Hunt* (1842)[8] removed the stigma of unlawfulness from workers' combinations seeking lawful ends by lawful means. The habit of repressive government action may be said to have died hard during the earlier stages of the industrial revolution in Western countries. Organized labor won its way to social acceptance through a struggle against the established political order that has left still visible scars, particularly among European workers, in the form of revolutionary and antigovernmental movements in trade-union ranks.

An early reluctance to integrate labor unions into the political and social order as generously as their counterparts, business corporations, has resulted in their acquisition of great power within an incomplete framework of public accountability. A grudging tribute to the power of labor may be quoted from a speech by a British Conservative Member of Parliament on the occasion of the repeal of the Trades Dispute Act in 1946.

It is a far cry from the Tolpuddle martyrs to the Labour Government of 1946. We are in the presence of the most powerful corporation that has existed in this country since the Roman Catholic Church was disestablished at the time of the Reformation. Here is an organization that claims more adherents than many members of the U.N. have subjects. It has gigantic sums at its disposal. It has many of the organs ordinarily associated with government. It has a sort of parliament or congress of its own.

The Trade Union Congress in Britain to which Mr. Quintin Hogg was referring is now equaled in power and influence by such groupings as the American Federation of Labor–Congress of Industrial Organizations (AFL-CIO) in the United States or the General Confederation of Labor in France. Though the problem of political assimilation cannot be said to have been solved satisfactorily in any Western country, it has been approached in two contrasting manners.

In the first instance the labor movement has been embodied in a responsible political party with a consequent obligation to win approval for its policies and actions from a majority of the electorate. This approach has been favored in Britain, Australia, and New Zealand, among other countries. It constitutes an endeavor of labor to integrate itself by its own self-discipline into a generally accepted pattern of political and social power. Thus, the President of the New Zealand Labour Party conference in 1951 warned his colleagues in the following terms:

> It must never be forgotten that in a country like New Zealand, not as highly industrialized as many other lands, Labour cannot rely for its support on industrial labour alone. Political Labour can only attain power by attracting the support and votes of other sections as well. Anyone who thinks otherwise is blind to the facts of history and of recent experience in this country.[9]

Though the real strength of the Labour Party in Britain, both as regards campaign funds and votes, lies in the trade-union movement, the Trade Union Congress is not formally affiliated with the political party. However, the separate unions composing the Congress are members of the party, in general, and entitled to representation at the annual party conference on the basis of one delegate for every 5,000 votes.[10] The voting strength of the union is decided by the number of their members prepared to pay the political levy and by the willingness of the union leadership to pass on a proportion of these sums to the Labour Party. Relationships between the Trade Union Congress leadership and the leaders of the Labour Party in Parliament are not formalized. Both groupings may be viewed as simultaneously patrons and clients of each other. Parliamentary leaders are dependent on union organization for funds and solid voting support in the country. Union officials have to look to the party in Parliament to protect and advance their particular interests through legislation and control of administration. By and large, it is a situation replete with what would be considered in the United States unacceptable conflicts of interest—for example, Labour Members of the House of Commons speaking openly on the floor as representatives of their respective unions rather than of the general electorate. The value of this partial solution lies in the responsibility to the whole community that has been imposed on the trade-union movement as the price of political and social power.

An alternative approach to the problem is that followed in the United States, where the labor movement concentrates its power as an economic and social force, using politics merely as an instrument for the winning of particular demands. One virtue of this attitude is that it does not place the industrial worker, as worker, in a separate political category of his own. This is a realistic appraisal of realities in American social organization, where economic status does not necessarily create different classes or kinds of citizens. At the same time, it raises a difficult question concerning the place of private government in relation to public government in a modern, industrialized state. There can be little doubt that the power unions have acquired over their members—and membership is for all practical purposes compulsory throughout a great many fields of industry—amounts to private government. What, then, are the functions of political institutions toward these great aggregates of power standing outside limitations of representative authority? A warning given by the American Civil Liberties Union in 1943, sharpened in recent times by the findings of Congressional committees, may be quoted in this respect:

> It is evident that unless the abuses in trade unions which have aroused widespread hostility are corrected, the drive for legislative control may not only undo the great gains for labor's rights of recent years, but also impose unwarranted restrictions. Those abuses arise largely from lack of democratic practices in many unions—resulting in the exclusion of Negroes, women and others qualified by their skills, in

limitation of membership by high fees, in control by autocratic cliques, or in a few unions by racketeers—and in the failure by some unions to hold regular and fair elections and to account to the membership for union funds.[11]

Lacking direct responsibility to the electorate through the political-party system, American labor presents government on both the national and state levels with delicate problems relating to its control. Approximately 30 per cent of nonfarm employees are enrolled in unions in the United States, as compared to figures between 50 and 75 per cent in Britain and Sweden. Protection of the nonunion worker against enrollment contrary to his personal wish or judgment has become an issue of State politics on the American scene. So called "right to work" laws affect the results of both State and national elections. On the federal level, the Sherman Act of 1890, directed against trusts, was used against organized labor in the Pullman strike of 1894, and its use confirmed by the Supreme Court in the "Danbury Hatters" case in 1908. Congress subsequently passed the Clayton Act of 1914 which gave unions a measure of equivocal freedom from the provisions of antitrust legislation. The preamble of the 1932 Norris–La Guardia Act contains a significant declaration of the responsibility of the general government toward labor organization.

Whereas under prevailing economic conditions, developed with the aid of governmental authority for owners of property to organize in the corporate and other forms of ownership association, the individual unorganized worker is commonly helpless to exercise actual liberty of contract and to protect his freedom of labor, and thereby to obtain acceptable terms and conditions of employment, wherefore, though he should be free to decline to associate with his fellows, it is necessary that he have full freedom of association, self-organization, and designation of representatives of his own choosing, to negotiate the terms and conditions of his employment, and that he shall be free from the interference, restraint, or coercion of employers of labor, or their agents, in the designation of such representatives or in self-organization or in other concerted activities for the purpose of collective bargaining or other mutual aid or protection; therefore the following definitions of, and limitations upon, the jurisdiction and authority of the courts of the United States are hereby enacted.

Subsequent legislation such as the National Labor Relations Act of 1937 has greatly extended the sphere of federal intervention under provisions of interstate commerce. A price for government protection is being exacted through denial of the facilities of the National Labor Relations Board to Labor organizations that are not prepared to have their officials sign affidavits to the effect that they do not belong to the Communist Party. The Taft-Hartley Act of 1947 ushered in principles of government control that are likely to stir partisan debate for several years. In summary, it may be repeated that organized labor in the United States has accepted a lesser degree of direct political responsibility for its actions to the general electorate than is the case in other highly advanced industrial nations. Consequently, government has to provide a place for this great social force outside the representative controls of party politics but still within the bounds of an internal order dictated by the community organized as a political state.

Regulation of Labor Conditions and Practices

Free-enterprise societies are founded for the most part on a system of private bargaining between individuals. Theoretically, conditions of employment are settled by each party negotiating to obtain the best terms for itself. Outside interference, particularly when backed by political power, has to be justified by the presence of exceptional circumstances. It may be confidently stated that, as regards general labor contracts in industrialized states, exceptional circumstances allowing for a measure of governmental regulation have become the norm. Perhaps this is not as paradoxical as it sounds, as the social environment that makes any form of fair bargaining between individuals possible is under constant change. A binding agreement is always a product of the rules of the state as well as the meeting of individual minds. Sir Henry Maine's formula, "from status to contract," describes the development of an economic and social order through political implementation. Bargaining, then, is only practical at any particular time or place under conditions determined by society organized in its political form. Chief Justice Hughes expressed this concept with the moderation of common sense.

It is manifest . . . that there has been a growing appreciation of public needs and of the necessity of finding ground for a rational compromise between individual rights and public welfare. The settlement and consequent contraction of the public domain, the pressure of a constantly increasing density of population, the interrelation of the activities of our people and the complexity of our economic interests, have inevitably led to an increased use of the organization of society in order to protect the very bases of individual opportunity. Where, in earlier days, it was thought that only the concerns of individuals or of classes were involved, and that those of the State itself were touched only remotely, it has later been found that the fundamental interests of the State are directly affected; and that the question is no longer merely that of one party to a contract as against another, but of the use of reasonable means to safeguard the economic structure upon which the good of all depends.[12]

A practical instance that troubled legislatures and courts in the first three decades of the twentieth century was whether the principles and terms of the American Constitution permitted State or federal governments to legislate minimum wages and hours of work for certain fields of employment. A dissenting opinion by Mr. Justice Stone in a 1936 case became the basis of a majority judgment one year later in the decisive case of *West Coast Hotel Co. v. Parrish.*[13] In the words of Mr. Stone:

We have had opportunity to learn that a wage is not always the resultant of free bargaining between employers and employees; that it may be one forced upon employees by their economic necessities and upon employers by the most ruthless of their competitors. We have had opportunity to perceive more clearly that a wage insufficient to support the worker does not visit its consequences upon him alone; that it may affect profoundly the entire economic structure of society and, in any case, that it casts on every taxpayer, and on government itself, the burden of solving the problems of poverty, subsistence, health and morals of large numbers in the community. Because of their nature and extent these are public problems. A generation ago they were for the individual to solve; today they are the burden of the nation.[14]

The Fair Labor Standards Act of 1938 inaugurated a nation-wide policy of federal control over minimum wages that brought American government into line with a preceding movement in other industrialized countries, started by New Zealand as far back as 1894.

The Settlement of Labor Disputes

Strikes are weapons of social conflict that have posed problems for governments of industrialized states somewhat analogous to the private wars of earlier times. On the one side a clear threat is raised to the internal order of the community, and on the other stands a necessity of permitting groups within a free enterprise society to exercise their full strength against each other within the limits of a competitive system. In Communist states, strikes are unthinkable for this very reason: they postulate an economy that results from free competition between individuals and groups and not from the enforced application of dogmatic standards. However, competition, as is the case with other tools of human association, must take place within an ordered framework of general consent. Government in the last analysis is responsible for supervising the rules of a game which may be played only if there are rules and an umpire.

The Commonwealth of Australia, a young and impatient arrival in the industrial order, has sought to cut the Gordian knot of private and public interest in labor disputes through a system of compulsory arbitration. Courts of Arbitration and Conciliation on both federal and State levels possess at least theoretical authority to settle disputes. The balance between advantage and disadvantage that has been discovered in practice has not proved sufficient to persuade many other countries to accept the Australian solution. First, Courts of law are not invariably competent, either through the methods they use or the experience of their judges, to settle complex labor disputes along economic or social lines. Secondly, if a labor organization rejects the court's findings and strikes anyway, the strike becomes one against the state, involving government as an interested party. Thirdly, in a federal state, such as Australia, conflict is bound to arise between the jurisdiction of federal and State courts in matters touching on direct social control of the economy. Though making labor and employer organizations responsible to the people through the processes of law has been in some ways a great advance, it has carried with it the less desirable concomitant of bringing living standards for the community to the decision of a court of law. Judges, though wise in judgment, may be deficient in understanding the capacities of economic forces to produce the material goods needed to satisfy their rulings.

In general, throughout Europe and the United States, government feels called upon to intervene only in the case of strikes of a certain character or order. What are known as "political strikes" are considered an immediate responsibility of the political administration. Such strikes are directed against the community as a whole or the government itself rather than aimed at employer groups. With the growth of nation-wide cartels in particular industries and the nationalization of sections of the economy, European governments have been increasingly faced with the problems of political strikes. The general strike in Britain in 1925 was an example of an attempt by a coordinated labor movement to use the strike weapon to force the government of the day to take action in the interests of the coal miners. The Trades Disputes Act of 1927 outlawed strikes of this nature, and though the Act itself was repealed by a subsequent Labour Government, it is questionable whether any future action of this nature would be held lawful. In Europe proper, "the myth of the General Strike"[15] was advocated openly as a means of keeping workers in revolutionary ferment.

A major difficulty has been to distinguish between strikes directed against the state and labor disputes on such a large scale or in such vital areas that they distress or even imperil the total economy. The United States uses the neutral-sounding term national emergency to describe situations that imperil the national health or safety, whatever may be the intentions of the parties responsible. Under the Taft-Hartley Act, the President is given limited powers to intervene under such conditions. However, little more than a postponement for eighty days can be achieved by the exercise of existing authority. With the growing integration of the economy into a defense pattern of related industries, responsibilities of government for maintenance of industrial peace become entangled with security considerations. Thus, in France, national railway strikes are met by mobilization of the striking employees into the armed services.

Regulation of Employment Practices

The early horrors of the industrial revolution in Britain and elsewhere were largely due to extreme doctrines of laissez faire interpreted to bar government from policing working conditions in industry. When governments once more assumed responsibility for the over-all health, safety, and morals of their citizens, employment practices became a fertile field for regulation. Child labor provides a dramatic example, particularly in the United States, where the prohibition of abuses of this practice on a nation-wide scale was long barred by a narrow interpretation of the commerce clause of the Constitution. An important change in the concept of the regulatory powers of government over social conditions may be traced in this controversy. When Congress first attempted to bar goods produced by child labor from interstate commerce by a statute of 1916, a majority on the Supreme Court ruled against its constitutionality in the case of *Hammer v. Dagenhart*[16] on the grounds that "the goods shipped are of themselves harmless." Mr. Justice Holmes dissented: "But if there is any matter upon which civilized countries have agreed—far more unanimously than they have with regard to intoxicants and some other matters over which this country is now emotionally aroused—it is the evil of premature and excessive child labor." Throughout the next twenty years, the court clung to the position that the regulatory power over commerce granted the national government by the Constitution amounted to a control over material goods and did not encompass social conditions involved in their production and distribution. The latter, according to the court, were subject only to the police powers of the States, and no national standards could be constitutionally imposed. This point of view, by no means purely legalistic, reflected a long-held tradition that national government—the only effective government in terms of the whole economic and social pattern—should function to promote physical facilities for industry and trade but may not interfere with the social consequences of economic forces. It was not until 1941 that the modern doctrine of governmental responsibility for the cure of social evils arising from unchecked economic competition was officially proclaimed in the case of *United States v. Darby*.[17] Congress had passed the Fair Labor Standards Act three years previously, and the constitutionality of the Act under the prevailing doctrines of the court was under challenge. Mr. Justice Stone demolished long-standing legal bastions of laissez faire in two sentences:

> The motive and purpose of the present regulation is plainly to make effective the Congressional conception of public policy that interstate commerce should not be made the instrument of competition in the distribution of goods produced under substandard labor conditions, which competition is injurious to the commerce and to the states from and to which the commerce flows. The motive and purpose of a regulation of interstate commerce are matters for the legislative judgment upon which the Constitution places no restriction and over which the courts are given no control. . . .

Among civilized peoples today, there is now general acceptance of the principle that supervision over conditions of labor is a primary function of government. Thus, the 1946 Constitution of Japan, drafted under the supervision of the Supreme Commander of the Allied Forces in occupation at that time, declares in Article 27: "Standards for wages, hours, rest, and other working conditions shall be fixed by law. Children shall not be exploited." Compensation for injury and health protection are normally subject to government regulation in advanced industrial nations. A recently assumed responsibility of government to promote closer association between employers and employees in industry is making some headway in European countries. Article 46 of the Italian Constitution of 1947 reads: "With a view to the economic and social advancement of labor, and in harmony with the requirements of production, the Republic recognizes the right of workers to collaborate, in ways and within limits established by law, in the management of business enterprises." The 1959 administration of General de Gaulle declared a social policy aimed at encouraging the development of various systems of giving workers a share in the enterprises in which they were employed. Tax exemptions are provided for corporations entering into contracts with their workers along the lines of profit-sharing bonuses, provision of workers' stock in the company and other partnership agreements approved by the government and the respective trade unions.[18]

Communist Labor Regulation

No question arises concerning acceptance of responsibility by Communist states for the fullest control over labor conditions and organizations. The position of the workers' own organizations, however, is equivocal. Though the right to form trade unions is recognized as a constitutional right, the trade union itself, as is the case with all public organizations, must be integrated into the Communist Party. As such, it is primarily an organ of government and not of worker representation. Where everyone is employed directly or indirectly by the state, there is, of course, no right to strike or opportunity to press demands outside regular Party and administrative channels. However, a bland assurance of the comfort of the working population is contained in Article 119 of the 1936 Constitution.

> Citizens of the U.S.S.R. have the right to rest and leisure. The right to rest and leisure is ensured by the establishment of an eight-hour day for industrial, office, and professional workers, the reduction of the working day to seven or six hours for arduous trades and to four hours in shops where conditions of work are particularly arduous; by the institution of annual vacations with full pay for industrial, office, and professional workers, and by the provision of a wide network of sanitoria, holiday homes and clubs for the accommodation of the working people.

Of course, "rest and leisure" are relative terms: among free peoples personal choice and self-organization play a major part in determining how much may be enjoyed; under Communist rule this is a high matter of state to be decided by the Party leaders in control of the government apparatus.

Public and Private Institutions of Government

A notable feature of the present century has been a commingling of public and private power in the general organization and control of society. Modern technology and ease of communication has confronted the ordinary individual with three masters of his social destiny: Big Business, Big Labor, and Big Government. These are not antagonistic or even widely different forces. It may be more realistic to visualize them as separate aspects of a single organizing force responsible for the nature of the economic order. Several reasons militate against clear demarcation of spheres of power. In the first place, institutional organization is basically similar in these three major organs of social power, resulting in like types of behavior patterns. Once a real gulf lay between merchants, princes, and craftsmen; now they resemble interchangeable units in a single institutional pattern. Restriction of the use of the term *government* to practices of political institutions is an archaic tradition. Matters relating to the control of men in almost all phases of their activities are as much the preoccupation of economic institutions as they are of the political state. Methods of administration and even representation of constituents resemble one another closely in business, labor, and governmental organizations. Relationships among the power groups in these bodies are influenced by the interchangeability of their leadership and by realization of a joint responsibility to the community for the ordering of social situations.

A devolution of governmental power has occurred as a consequence of the complexities of present-day social organization. This devolution has not been limited to a process of decentralization of governmental machinery, but has extended in part to organs of private government. Examples may be taken from the licensing powers granted to private associations. The right to practice medicine, law, or accountancy, or even to lay bricks, is now largely determined by private associations operating under direct or indirect grants of governmental authority. Though the power of government over the economic order has greatly increased during the present century, a significant part of this increase may be attributed to the use of governmental authority by economic institutions themselves. Perhaps this steady interlocking of all forms of social power and the decentralization of political authority marks a growth in natural cooperative forces of societies that enjoy the benefits of technology, general education, and ease of communication. The element of command and physical force is giving way to the influence of the expert and skilled organizer. At the same time, business and labor groupings find that disregard of the general interest in pursuit of private or institutional ends entails serious risks. Public opinion has organized itself to keep pace with the centralization of political and economic power. The citizen who may be voter, stockholder, employer, or trade unionist at one and the same time has no hesitation in using his power in any one capacity to protect his interests in any field. Under representative systems, wielders of political and economic power find themselves serving the same master—and one who is not reluctant to employ the strength of each to discipline the other.

Consequently, the participation of government in economic processes is matched by the involvement of business and labor organizations in governmental functions. This has led to a spreading of responsibility for the safeguarding of the general interest of the community and an increase of self-organization for this purpose. It may be noted that the principle of representation is central to the operation and continuance of this system. Where dogma and authoritarian leadership intrude, a fusion of political and economic power results in tyranny—Communist or fascist-nationalist. In free lands, however, interlocking institutions for the protection of the social order operate to elevate individual values. The test of legitimacy in the exercise of political or economic power has been reduced to the practical question as to whether total rather than partial interests of living beings are being served.

Notes

[1] *East Africa Royal Commission Report (1953–1955)*, Command 9475, London: Her Majesty's Stationery Office, p. 394.

[2] Hogg, Quintin, *The Case for Conservatism,* Baltimore: Penguin, 1947, pp. 120 and 121.

[3] "Ordonnance No. 58-1342 (27 Décembre 1958)" *Journal Officiel Paris,* 28 Décembre 1958.

[4] Wiskemann, Elizabeth, "Poverty and Population in the South," *Foreign Affairs,* October, 1949, **28,** 84-91.

[5] Stowe, Leland, *While Time Remains,* New York: Knopf, 1946.

[6] For a crusading discussion of this topic see de Castro, Josué, *The Geography of Hunger,* Boston: Little, Brown, 1952.

[7] *Ibid.,* p. x.

[8] 4 Metcalf 111.

[9] Quoted from Overacker, Louise, "The New Zealand Labor Party," *The American Political Science Review,* 1955, **49,** No. 3, 708-732.

[10] *Cf.* Hennessy, Bernard, "Trade Unions and the British Labor Party," *The American Political Science Review,* 1955, **49,** No. 4, 1050-1066.

[11] American Civil Liberties Union, *Democracy in Trade Unions, A Survey with a Program of Action,* New York: The Union, 1943, p. 3. For an account of the concept of private government in relation to unions see McConnell, Grant, "The Spirit of Private Government," *The American Political Science Review,* 1958, **52,** No. 3, 754-770.

[12] *Home Building and Loan Association v. Blaisdell,* 290 U.S. 298 (1934).

[13] *West Coast Hotel Co. v. Parrish,* 300 U.S. 379 (1937).

[14] *Morehead v. Tipaldo,* 298 U.S. 587 (1936).

[15] Sorel, Georges, translated by Hulme, T. E., and Roth, J., *Reflections on Violence,* Chicago: Free Press, 1950.

[16] *Hammer v. Dagenhart,* 247 U.S. 251 (1918).

[17] *United States v. Darby,* 312 U.S. 100 (1941).

[18] "Ordonnance No. 59-126 (7 Janvier 1959)" *Journal Officiel Paris,* 9 Janvier 1959.

Supplementary Readings

Barbash, Jack, *Taft-Hartley Act in Action 1947–1956, and, Essentials of a New Labor Policy,* New York: League for Industrial Democracy, new revised edition, 1956.

Foenander, Orwell de Ruyter, *Better Employment Relations and Other Essays in Labour,* Sydney: Law Book, 1954.

Griswold, A. Whitney, *Farming and Democracy,* New Haven: Yale, 1952.

Gulick, Luther H., *American Forest Policy; A Study of Government Administration and Economic Control,* New York: Duell, Sloan and Pearce, 1951.

Hardin, Charles M., *The Politics of Agriculture; Soil Conservation and the Struggle for Power in Rural America,* Chicago: Free Press, 1952.

Heagney, Muriel, *Arbitration at the Cross Roads: Digest of Opinion on Legal Wage Fixation,* Melbourne: 1954.

Kile, Orville M., *The Farm Bureau through Three Decades,* Washington: The Author, National Press Building, 1948.

Lens, Sidney, *Labor Unions and Politics in Britain and France,* New York: 1950.

McCune, Wesley, *Who's Behind Our Farm Policy?* New York: Praeger, 1957.

McKinley, Charles, *Uncle Sam in the Pacific Northwest: Federal Management of Natural Resources in the Columbia River Valley,* Berkeley: University of California Press, 1952.

Meek, Charles K., *Land Law and Custom in the Colonies,* London: Oxford, 1949.

Miller, Glenn W., *American Labor and the Government,* New York: Prentice-Hall, 1948.

Perlman, Mark, *Labor Union Theories in America: Background and Development,* Evanston: Row, Peterson, 1958.

Petro, Sylvester, *The Labor Policy of the Free Society,* New York: Ronald, 1957.

THREE

INTERNATIONAL

RELATIONS

Chapter 17

Nature of an International Order

Defense and aggression constitute primary functions of the political state. Because the need by organized groups to deal with their neighbors in terms of force has proved ineradicable in human history, politics has been in part organization for war and war an instrument of politics from the beginning of recorded events. The nation–state has won to preeminence as an improved means of providing defense for its citizen body or of satisfying their aggressive impulses. Political government as a whole is rooted in mankind's long experience of war and conditioned in its development by the likelihood and fear of wars to come. Relationships between states, then, are of the essence of the governing process, and do not constitute something extraneous to its structure or forms. The indignant citizen who asks: "What's the use of having a government if it can't deal with these Russians (or Chinese or Germans)" is making a sound analysis, if perhaps in oversimplified terms.

A more optimistic point of view might regard the development of international relations as a search for an external order to complement the internal order achieved by the nation–state. War and oppression could then be considered as passing phases, imperfect techniques for the accomplishment of a more ordered association for mankind as a whole. There is certainly nothing inevitable about war. It is a practice men have indulged in over a long period for much the same reasons as they engaged in the comparable ritual of human sacrifice, under a strong pyschological conviction that it was essential to the creation of order. The practical realities that must be met are tolerable relationships between organized peoples. Methods by which this may be accomplished constitute a problem in government. As peaceful trade succeeded to piracy and raids because it proved a more efficient and profitable method of group contact, so it is possible to conceive the end of violence as the arbiter of international relationships.

However, the conditions under which this desirable change might occur are linked to practical questions related to the organization of government on the national, or perhaps universal, level. Controversial issues abound on this topic. Does the organization of the world into separate governmental entities along nation–state lines increase the likelihood of war? Granted that no other form of world organization is foreseeable in the immediate future, what aspects of nation–state government tend to incite to war, and are these factors inseparable from the nation or archaic survivals inimical to its development? Such questions may not be answered by sweeping generalizations, however emotionally satisfying. Their solution requires a realistic appraisal of existing international patterns and an attempt to clarify the true objectives of organized peoples from the semantic haze of emotion-charged traditions and prejudices. It may be likened to Benjamin Franklin's heroic experiment to demonstrate the nature of lightning by flying a kite into a thunderstorm. Though it may be shown that awesome phenomena that had been held from time immemorial to be outside human control are natural events within man's technical capacities to handle, the daring experimenter is more than likely to be killed in the process. History does not relate how Mr. Franklin grounded himself against the lightning bolt, whether through prior knowledge or happy chance.

The means of war having been developed to an intolerable level by human ingenuity, examination of the forms of government needed to avert catastrophe on this level has become a matter of pressing urgency. Inevitably, it will be a painful process, carried out in terms of expedient measures to avert overwhelming danger rather than in accordance with some totally conceived plan. Indications of the extent to which the world has already progressed towards adapting its governmental forms to humanity's survival may be discovered by examination of some of the operative concepts in present-day international relations.

World Affairs

The hopeful-sounding term *world affairs* may be used as a proper description of a complex of geophysical facts. It does not, however, coincide at present with any political reality. There is no world organization responsible for the major cares of mankind, and, accordingly, no authoritative determination as to what are the principal interests or needs of the world's peoples as a single unit. What exists in fact is the organization of the bulk of mankind into several score independent nation–states, each claiming sole responsibility for the security and welfare of its inhabitants. On the political level, then, world affairs are mere resultants of international relations created by the coexistence of national states. The tendency of world affairs may be towards cooperation between peoples or armed struggle, depending on the character and policies of the national governments involved. A theory of government, such as Hitler's concept of race superiority, may commit peoples and their neighbors to relationships based on war and oppression. Marxism as interpreted by Lenin propounded the doctrine that the world was divided into capitalist, imperialist countries and oppressed colonial proletariats. The only possible relationship between the imperialist nations was one of war to further their expansion at one another's expense. Their relationship with proletarian peoples was bound to take the form of imperialist oppression. Lenin did not examine the nature of possible relationships between the proletarian and colonial peoples released from capitalist tyranny. Stalin provided a pragmatic answer by bringing all within military range (with the troublesome exception of Yugoslavia) under the protective guidance of Soviet Russia as the Mother of the New Socialist Age. It should be realized, however, that this Marxist-Leninist misconception of the modern world has influenced hundreds of millions of people to a belief in the inevitability of war as a way of life until the millennium of a world revolution is achieved.

National Interests

International relations may be conceived as logically determined by the national interests of the various countries of the world as interpreted from time to time by their separate governments. This realist point of view has been objected to on the grounds that it robs world order of a moral base, reducing international affairs to the unchecked competition of national ambitions. However, any alternative must express needs or ideals stemming from nonnational or supranational bodies. Lacking organization in governmental form, such groupings cannot express their point of view authoritatively or effectively. It seems more practical to accept the governmental structure of the nation–state as a determinant voice in settling world affairs in terms of its own concerns and limitations. Such acceptance makes it all the more important to give a meaning to "national interest" that will distinguish it from irresponsible selfishness or greed. Professor Morgenthau, a leading defender of the concept of national interest, provides this moderate description of the term.

> While the interests which a nation may pursue in its relations with other nations are of infinite variety and magnitude, the resources which are available for the pursuit of such interests are necessarily limited in quantity and kind. No nation has the resources to promote all desirable objectives with equal vigor; all nations must therefore allocate their scarce resources as rationally as possible. The indispensable precondition of such rational allocation is a clear understanding of the distinction between the necessary and variable elements of the national interest. . . .
>
> Finally, the national interest of a nation which is conscious not only of its own interests but also of that of other nations must be defined in terms compatible with the latter. In a multinational world this is a requirement of political morality; in an age of total war it is also one of the conditions for survival.[1]

Despite the effective preponderance of national interests, concepts of international interest held by individuals and groups in impressive numbers throughout the world may not be lightly dismissed. On the economic level, trade and business interests may reflect international rather than national standards for a great many people. Religious and cultural loyalties cannot readily be preserved or advanced on a national basis. Historical attempts to associate particular religious creeds with national power ended disastrously for organized religion and the political state itself. There are clearly important interests held by the individual on an international or world level that cannot be represented adequately by the government of his nation–state. Where traditions of limited, representative government predominate, national interests are restricted within the bounds allotted to domestic government that give individual citizens a measure of freedom to pursue economic, religious, and cultural interests along international lines in terms of associations other than that of their political state. A relic of monarchical theory perhaps persists in the identification of national interests with the absolute will of a single governing institution. In practice, this is not the case in the United States or like countries; national government speaks in the international field, as in any other, only in the restricted terms of those matters over which it has received authority by popular consent. If the ruthless interpretation of national interest by any government of a representative democracy should imperil the economic, moral, or physical security of the inhabitants, remedies exist whereby the government may be changed or further limitations placed upon the sphere of its activities. Of course, where a majority of the people themselves are determined upon the pursuit of aggressive or dangerous interests at whatever cost, only superior force from outside national borders can challenge their recklessness. One of the advantages of multinational organization of the world is that any single nation that oversteps bounds of acceptable behavior is likely to arouse its neighbors to just such a challenge. In light of the rapid growth of interdependence among organized societies, it is conceivable that an increasing number of peoples will conclude that their national interests are international and corporate in a world sense, and accordingly will instruct their governments to this end.

Universal Government

This is one of the most misused concepts of our times. Conceived of as a supergovernment dominating national governments and centralizing political powers throughout the world into a single institutional framework, it is little more than a pipe dream with slight resemblance to any existing pattern. The United Nations has suffered particularly in the United States from identification with this illusion. As a later chapter will point out, no existing international organization, including the United Nations, may claim governmental status in this sense. International or universal bodies in present times do not replace or override powers or functions of national governments. Instead, they operate in areas of general interest where national governments have proved ineffective through the limitations of their own structures. Thus, the practical matter of sending a letter or package from one part of the world to another over several national frontiers is beyond the capacity of any single nation–state. We do not consider the Congress of the Universal Postal Union a form of world government, though since 1874 it has exercised definite legislative powers in this technical field. It is recognized that, as regards postal services, telegraphs, certain aspects of world health, international air transport, and many other concerns of a closely linked world, institutions separate from national governments are required to create the minimum order needed for conduct of the world's business. If a universal order in this limited sense is regarded as parallel to, rather than conflicting with, national orders, its institutions may be viewed in a proper perspective as quasi-governmental. Even when major political issues are involved, as in the organization of certain parts of the United Nations, it may be seen that such authority as the world body may claim is supplementary to the power of national governments and dependent on their acceptance individually or jointly of the decisions of the United Nations as being in accordance with their national interests.

International Law

A society of nations as well as a society of individuals requires the cohesive force of law for its continued existence. However, the law of nations, or *international law* as it is now called, is analogous to, rather than identical with, law governing individuals in particular states. In the first place, the parties subject to such law are political states, not individuals. Therefore, only those forms of law that are applicable to corporate bodies are relevant to international law. As it has been long established that corporations acting in their corporate capacity cannot commit crimes, the whole field of punitive jurisdiction is removed from international law, at least in theory. Secondly, domestic law is based on the assumption that all individuals within its scope (the technical term is jurisdiction) are subject to physical control by a superior body, the sovereign power of the organized state. This permits of a situation where a judgment of a court of law amounts to a command enforceable by practical means. In international society, no supreme or sovereign body is acknowledged by its constituent members, independent and theoretically equal nation–states. Judgments rendered by courts of international justice, then, are enforced by means other than the application of physical force. Because of these differences, it is sometimes claimed that international law is not "true" law and is a useless barrier against world anarchy. Misunderstanding of the pragmatic nature of law in action is perhaps responsible for such an assumption. If that part of present-day domestic law that deals with corporate bodies were rejected as imperfect law, our social and economic structure would collapse. Similarly, if physical force was regarded as an essential element in the enforcement of any legal judgment, the conduct of business, and indeed ordinary life, would be beset with unusual hazards.

International law provides an invaluable instrument for the settlement of economic and social difficulties that lie outside the exclusive spheres of national states. Communication, trade, finance, labor, agriculture, narcotic and white-slave traffic, have all been made subject to international regulation based on agreements among nations. Such rules are enforced as part of the law of the land by individual states. Very early in its history, the United States Supreme Court ruled that

> the United States had, by taking a place among the nations of the earth, become amenable to the laws of nations; and it was their interest, as well as their duty, to provide, that those laws should be respected and obeyed; in their national character and capacity, the United States were responsible to foreign nations for the conduct of each state, relative to the laws of nations, and the performance of treaties. . . .[2]

It is now clearly established in the United States that international law to which the national government has subscribed by treaty or otherwise is part of the law of the land enforceable under the supremacy clause of the Constitution.[3]

Historically, international law has been associated with the rules of war and peace. Though agreement among civilized peoples to rules concerning the conduct of war—effective conventions concerning the use of poison gas in the second German war are an example—may have alleviated some of mankind's destructive tendencies, they have fallen far short of the prevention of war. Neither may domestic law be said to have prevented violent crime, but merely to have added an element of punishment in a number of cases. Areas in which war was formerly the principal method of settling international differences are gradually being reduced through multinational agreements accepting rules to be interpreted by international organizations or the International Court of Justice now associated with the United Nations. For example, wars such as that of Jenkins' Ear between Britain and the United States, or even the Spanish-American War, are almost inconceivable under present-day conditions of international arbitration and law.

Sources of international law are (1) usages among civilized peoples, and (2) multilateral agreements among nation–states along positive lines. The former are determined in a manner similar to the formation of common law, by examination of the practices of states and the writings of authoritative commentators in the course of deciding particular cases before competent courts. The latter sources have become the more important as the scope of international agreements has extended from formal treaties between nations into general world conventions codifying international practices and various forms of resolutions of international conventions on particular topics. Some confusion still arises from an identification of international law with a theory of natural law mandatory on mankind as a whole. Hugo Grotius, in his work *De Iure Belli ac Paci* (Concerning the Law of War and Peace, 1625), drew on the sources of Roman law as a form of absolute authority which he identified as *natural law*. Though Grotius admitted more eclectic elements in the formation of the contents of the law of nations, which he first enunciated, many of his successors, particularly Samuel Pufendorf (1632–94) committed the origins of international law to a framework of natural law theory. Introduction of moralistic and theoretically absolute concepts has led to efforts to codify international law within a forced pattern that promises more than the facts warrant. Both the previous history and present condition of international law are comprehensible in terms of a more modest concept of developing usages and growing areas of positive agreement. More relevant criticism of its content may be quoted from the late Professor Eagleton:

> The international law of today is sadly inadequate for the needs of the current world. It was made in the days when the Western European powers controlled most of the globe, and the law thus made is not satisfactory to the many new states which have come out from under that control and who object to the vested rights acquired by older states under that law; they therefore prefer political action to legal action.[4]

Collective Security

With the increase in the destructive consequences of war which may no longer be confined within the borders of the warring nations, the fact of world concern in the development of warlike tensions anywhere has become apparent. Though collective means of insuring peace are now recognized as desirable and even necessary for the survival of most individual nations, their implementation in practice has been negated by difficulties, suspicions, and evasions of responsibility. The basic principle of collective security is that aggressive war waged against any one state is a crime against all other states. Accordingly, it should be prevented, or, if that is not possible, punished, through joint action on the part of the organized states of the world. Under Article 10 of the Covenant of the League of Nations, members undertook "to respect and preserve as against external aggression the territorial integrity and existing political independence of all Members of the League." Article 16 of the Covenant declared that any member state that went to war in defiance of the terms of the Covenant was guilty of an act of aggression against all other members. Failure on the part of the major powers to implement the provisions concerning collective security, particularly in the instance of Mussolini's invasion of Ethiopia, was a principal factor in leading to the dissolution of the League.

The Charter of the United Nations contains more explicit and perhaps more practicable measures for the furtherance of collective security. Under Article 39, a Security Council composed of permanent members from the major powers and elected representatives of the smaller nations is entrusted with determining acts of aggression or potential threats to world peace. Obligations of all the members to supply military and economic means to implement decisions of the Security Council are detailed in Articles 43–47 but have never been tested in practice, owing to the early paralysis of the Security Council through use of the veto. What was established in fact by the United Nations Charter was a concert of powers to be responsible for the peace of the world. As this concert disintegrated almost in the moment of victory because of the defection of the U.S.S.R. from the Western powers, collective security on a world basis has never obtained a fair trial.

A limited form of world collective security based on what has become known as "permissive enforcement"[5] was elaborated to meet the Korean War crisis. A 1950 Resolution of the General Assembly of the United Nations (the Uniting for Peace Resolution) held that when the Security Council was prevented from acting through use of the veto the General Assembly could assume the function of deciding whether a threat to peace had occurred and what measures should be recommended to deal with the situation. Such recommendations could not be held obligatory on all members under Charter provisions; hence the description of permissive enforcement. Soviet Russia and its allies consider the procedure contrary to a proper interpretation of the original Charter. It is questionable whether this form of permissive enforcement of collective security aided the United States in the Korean struggle in a substantial, material manner. The moral support provided and the rallying of world opinion against Communist China was of probable value in limiting the scope of military action.

Collective security on a regional basis is at present organized much more realistically than world collective security. The North

Atlantic Treaty Organization possesses a fighting force, military bases, common strategy and command, constituting an organized defense body believed equal if not superior to any forces that could be raised against it in the rest of the world. Circumstances in which it would go into action short of direct attack on one of its members are not wholly clear. However, in the circumstances of the modern world, it may be considered an operational defense organization for the collective security of the Western region.

NATO

Balance of Power and Bipolar Systems

International relations as resultants of the operations of governmental systems tend to adapt themselves to a dominant order. Thus, for the first 400 years of the Christian era the world empire of the Romans dictated the forms and methods through which the peoples of the Western regions maintained contact with one another. A succession of European conquerors from Charlemagne to Napoleon have sought to reestablish the orderly concept of the *Pax Romana.* Nationalism, however, has proved a stronger lure than the benefits of uniformity. Once the existence is acknowledged of separate states with ineradicable national interests, the problem of international order becomes one of maintaining a balance of interests satisfactory to a combination of superior power. A classic example of the balance-of-power system in operation is provided by the foreign policy of Britain from the defeat of Napoleon to the outbreak of World War I in 1914. The balance of power is based strictly on the maneuverings of governments acting as unrestricted agents of national power. It may be classed as a game of governments played to a large extent in terms of military power and prestige. As such, it was suited to periods when the organized community regarded relations with other peoples principally in terms of defending themselves against attack or of seizing some economic advantage by the adroit use of force. In such circumstances, a people bound by law and even morality in their domestic relations could regard complacently the conduct of their external relations in terms of the polished scoundrelism of nineteenth-century diplomacy. True relationships between the peoples of separate states involving continuity in economic or cultural integration could never prosper under this system, where a shift in the diplomatic game could require that citizens of neighboring countries interrupt their joint pursuits to cut one another's throats at the command of their political governments.

Interdependence of the world's peoples has now become a factor in the limitation of the power of state institutions to dictate the external relationships of their nation. As the individual citizen in industrialized countries has come to develop concrete interests on the international level, governments have had to widen their perspective from narrow limits of military power and advantage to broader concepts of stable intercommunication. Perhaps part of the confusion of the modern world may be due to the fact that political institutions are not particularly competent to insure or direct this type of relationship between peoples. A good part of the active and profitable interchange among national groupings is being carried on at present by nongovernmental bodies: economic corporations, scientific and cultural organizations. Governments rooted in their traditions of force and power are being reduced to the role of policemen guarding an international commerce they are incompetent to originate and ill-equipped to direct. Balance-of-power concepts, then, may be considered outmoded because power is no longer the main objective determining the relationships among peoples. Other factors, linked to cooperative economic advantage and cultural interchanges, influence powerful sections of national electorates. Though the military and the diplomats are still powerful, they have been downgraded in part at least from principals to agents in determining international relationships.

An admixture of popular concerns and governmental processes has led to a degree of bipolarization in the international order. A loose organization of blocs of nation–states dominates the present conduct of world affairs. The two most powerful blocs are ranged against each other in a power struggle covering the military, economic, and cultural fields. Less powerful blocs—the Asian-African bloc may be cited as an example—occupy fringe positions ranging from minor commitment to one side or the other to outright repudiation of the necessity for any power struggle. A major difference between this type of bipolar system and the old balance of power is that it extends beyond a narrow field of governmental policies to embrace issues that have immediate and concrete meaning to the bulk of individuals comprising the various state systems. It represents a true competition as to the future nature of an international order between opposing economic, cultural, and social systems. Governments act as agents of these wider systems, and their preoccupations with power and maneuver are subordinated to broader goals. Commitment of peoples rather than political states is at once the strength and danger of present-day bipolarization. The conflict is one for an ordered world in which masses of individuals holding diverse views on fundamental matters can find freedom to carry on their activities according to their own principles.

The Western world versus the Soviet system is, of course, no clear-cut description of the international scene; it may be identified, however, as a dominant motif affecting all other factors. A major question, which may determine human survival, is whether this rivalry must be settled by governmental action. Governments have developed force to an intolerable level as their chosen instrument of international action. Like the dinosaur, they have become prisoners of their protective devices. Arguments concerning cultural forms, or even as to which economic system works best, cannot be settled satisfactorily by intercontinental missiles with H-bombs in their nosecaps. The organizations created by industry, science, or religion are more competent to compete in this field as representatives of popular belief than are political institutions. A problem remains as to how government in both camps may best keep the field open for a competitive struggle by organizations that do not rely on physical force. Demands emanating from their constituent people provide incentive for governments to discover such solutions. It would be foolhardy for a Western writer to guess how Communist regimes might adapt themselves to those ends. In the family of free nations, however, resort to multinational organization as a substitute for hierarchical bipolarization appears to have promise. Multinationalism dilutes reliance on force by spreading control over striking power throughout many political systems with divergent views and approaches. Conversely, it encourages a wider base of economic and cultural cooperation for a world order acceptable to all members of its grouping. On the basis of realities of world rivalry, it seeks to isolate the opposing system by linking the uncommitted or wavering regions to the non-Communist side through bonds of practical advantage forged in terms of true equality.

Geopolitics

An alternative method of formulating the nature of an international order is to look beyond governments, their armies and their diplomats, to the true relationship existing between world areas in terms of their geographic location, natural resources, and organizing capacities of their inhabitants. This method has the advantage of introducing some objective elements of scientific appraisal into a topic saturated with subjective emotions. It may be no answer to a true patriot to show that his country is neither right nor wrong but merely inadequate to the tasks which it has set itself, but the information is of value to practical men. *Geopolitics* evaluates the relative advantage of a nation's position in the world in terms of size, contours, location, climatic and soil conditions, natural resources and industry, transportation and communication facilities, and, lastly, the organizational capacity of its people in terms of the political, economic, and social framework they have devised for their activities.

As a means of predictive knowledge, the geopolitical outlook possesses particular interest to the student of world affairs. An early pioneer in the subject, Admiral Mahan, in his book, *The Influence of Sea Power upon History 1660–1783,* published in 1890, correctly estimated the connection between command of the seas and America's future position in the world. The fact that he could not foresee air power or guided missiles merely underlines the tentative nature of any scientific prediction. The temptation to use the new method of analysis to generalize in wide terms on international development has reacted into the field of politics, sometimes with unfortunate results. Thus, while Mahan's views were a useful stimulant in his own land to the building of a two-ocean navy, other geopoliticians stirred up more questionable activity. At the beginning of the twentieth century, a Scots geographer, Sir Halford Mackinder, put forward his *heartland* theory, relating geographical factors to international events in terms of a pivot area composed of the land mass of eastern Europe and all of Asia north of the mid-Asian mountain belt. He predicted truly enough that the Russian steppes and Mongolia would become a great center of economic power. Mackinder's theory was elaborated by General Haushofer under Hitler's auspices to justify a Germanic mission to seize the heartland from the Slav and to elevate the policy of *Lebensraum* into a scientific necessity.

An American scholar, the late Professor Spykman, in his book *America's Strategy in World Politics* (1942), questioned Mackinder's heartland thesis and offered a counter thesis, that control of the surrounding oceanic and territorial *rimland* was of greater importance. This theory may be said to be reflected in military terms by the ring of overseas bases established by the United States and her allies. Though it may be some time before geopolitics can claim the status of an exact science, its contributions have been and will continue to be of considerable importance. Political emotionalism on the part of governments and peoples alike is curbed in a useful manner by clear statements concerning the natural bases of power. Again, nations are encouraged to develop their strongest factors, which in turn makes them more valuable members of a world community, through this form of objective analysis. Dangers lie, as the past has shown, in the distortion of this infant science to provide justification for ambitious political schemes advocated by unscrupulous leaders. As long as channels of free communication remain open, however, the criticisms of other scientists should constitute sufficient safeguard. A particularly hopeful aspect of the development of geopolitical standards is that it has provided individuals and nongovernmental bodies with a means of evaluating external policies of their government. By bringing the political instruments of foreign policy under control of an informed electorate, geopolitics may greatly advance the objective of a world order adapted to modern scientific technology and in accord with the practical wishes of the bulk of mankind.

completely nonsense.

Notes

[1] Morgenthau, Hans J., "Another 'Great Debate': The National Interest of the United States," *The American Political Science Review,* 1952, **46,** No. 4, 976-977.

[2] *Chisholm v. Georgia,* 2 Wall 419 (1793).

[3] *Cf. The Paquete Habana,* 175 U.S. 677.

[4] Eagleton, Clyde, "Legal Matters," *Annual Review of United Nations Affairs, 1955-1956,* Eagleton, Clyde and Swift, Richard N. (eds.), New York: New York University Press, 1957, p. 141.

[5] *Cf.* Haas, Ernst B., "Types of Collective Security: An Examination of Operational Concepts," *The American Political Science Review,* 1955, **49,** No. 1, 40-62.

Supplementary Readings

Claude, Inis L., Jr., *Swords into Plowshares; the Problems and Progress of International Organization,* New York: Random House, second edition, 1959.

Eagleton, Clyde, *International Government,* New York: Ronald, third edition, 1957.

Friedmann, Wolfgang G., *An Introduction to World Politics,* London: Macmillan, second edition, 1952.

Gyorgy, Andrew, *Geopolitics; the New German Science,* Berkeley: Universersity of California Press, 1944.

Hartmann, Frederick H., *The Relations of Nations,* New York: Macmillan, 1957.

Kalijarvi, Thorsten V., et al., *Modern World Politics,* New York: Crowell, third edition, 1953.

Kohn, Hans, *The Idea of Nationalism,* New York: Macmillan, 1944.

Levi, Werner, *Fundamentals of World Organization,* Minneapolis: University of Minnesota Press, 1950.

Mackinder, Sir Halford J., *Democratic Ideals and Reality,* New York: Holt, 1942.

Mangone, Gerard J., *A Short History of International Organization,* New York: McGraw-Hill, 1954.

Mills, Lennox A., and McLaughlin, Charles H., *World Politics in Transition,* New York: Holt, 1956.

Morgenthau, Hans J., *Politics Among Nations; The Struggle for Power and Peace,* New York: Knopf, second edition revised and enlarged, 1954.

Niebuhr, Reinhold, *The Structure of Nations and Empires,* New York: Scribner, 1959.

Palmer, Norman D., and Perkins, Howard C., *International Relations, The World Community in Transition,* Boston: Houghton Mifflin, second edition, 1957.

Spykman, Nicholas J. (ed. Nicholl, Helen R.), *The Geography of the Peace,* New York: Harcourt, Brace, 1944.

Toynbee, Arnold J., *The World and the West,* New York: Oxford, 1953.

Chapter 18

Organs and Methods of International Relations

An examination of the methods through which international affairs are influenced by organs of government is conditioned by the objectives attributed to government in this sphere. A tempting analogy is that of a contest, a struggle among states in which the sole purpose of each state is to win for itself advantages that advance its interests over its neighbor's. The history of European civilization gives substance to this point of view, particularly during the monarchical period when ruling dynasties and classes were able to echo Louis XIV's dictum *"l'état c'est moi."* With the democratization of political government, the right and power of leadership groups to commit whole peoples in a mysterious but deadly game understood only by the elect became more questionable. As domestic government transformed itself into a means of expressing the aggregate interests of individuals through representative institutions, so the conduct of foreign affairs shifted emphasis to a community rather than institutional basis. A hitherto suppressed question gained increasing significance: what does the ordinary citizen gain from a struggle between states? Because more-or-less effective control over the institutions of government is now generally in the hands of ordinary citizens, the answer to this question determines the organization of the instruments for the carrying out of external policies.

It may be ventured that the average individual in an industrialized community possesses interests—economic, religious, and cultural—that extend beyond the political organization of his nation–state. In brief, some type of world order is needed to supplement the national order if modern man is to grasp his full opportunities. As no controlling political institutions exist for the world as a whole, national governments become agents responsible to their citizens for the preservation of some such order. Acceptance of such responsibility alleviates the concept of a naked power struggle between states into a form of competition between governments as to the type of world order to be established by joint endeavor. Where government based on consent is regarded as an instrumentality of society, its external policies may no longer be based on its own institutional aggrandizement.

Representative government has endowed with a new and broader character the traditional means through which political states conduct their relations with one another. These means may be summarized as (1) diplomacy, (2) war, (3) economic arrangements, (4) scientific and cultural exchanges, (5) ideological campaigns. Popular control over the instrumentalities devoted to these ends has not been won easily, and may still be considered imperfect in many countries. However, throughout the industrialized sections of the world, individuals have come to regard governmental institutions as agents for the furtherance of their concrete interests in the field of international relations. In consequence, relations with its own internal citizenry are now a major factor in policy determinations by organs entrusted with the conduct of external affairs.

The Machinery of Diplomacy

Practical considerations require that there should be a single channel through which a political state may negotiate with other states. In former times, a sovereign, generally a living monarch, could be identified readily as the one person entitled to speak for the nation–state. Representative government has blurred the concept of sovereignty into a convenient legal fiction, and it has become necessary to make explicit constitutional arrangements concerning the focus of power over foreign policy. As the American Constitution was conceived at a time when this change was beginning to take effect, the solution it provided has been widely followed elsewhere. A few terse phrases in Article II determine who will speak for the United States in the world outside.

> He [the President] shall have Power, by and with the Advice and Consent of the Senate, to make Treaties, provided two thirds of the Senators present concur; and he shall nominate, and by and with the Advice and Consent of the Senate, shall appoint Ambassadors, other public Ministers and Consuls. . . . he shall receive Ambassadors and other public Ministers.

This grant of authority, along with the status of Commander in Chief of the armed forces, suffices to make the Presidential office the Constitutional agent for dealing with other nations. The formal check contained in the provision requiring Senatorial consent to treaties and appointments, and the perhaps more important check implied by the power of Congress to grant or withhold money, maintain the character of the President as agent of a representative system of government. Another provision, giving Congress the power to declare war, has lost its significance in the last century. Wars nowadays do not need to be declared; they may be otherwise arranged by whoever possesses the negotiating powers.

The President's office is part of a complex of representative institutions. Though he is the focal center for all negotiations with foreign states, his power to initiate and implement external policy may be accounted a relative authority. It is relative to the popular support his policies may win within and outside Congress. Probably, it is also relative to the degree of confidence his views inspire in the expert apparatus on which he must rely. Nevertheless, in the past and in the foreseeable future, control by the President has proved, and is likely to continue to prove, the factor of definitive importance to other national governments seeking relations with the United States. Internal checks do not alter the fact that the American nation speaks with a single voice, that of the President, in the comity of nations. It may be significant that the 1958 Constitution of the French Republic, though not strictly a presidential system, gives to the President of France analogous authority to that of the American President in the field of foreign affairs.

Parliamentary systems normally make the administration in its Cabinet form responsible for the conduct of foreign affairs. On the surface, the legislature, to whom the Cabinet is directly responsible for all its actions, may appear to have greater powers of intervention and decision than is the case under presidential systems. In practice, however, ministerial leadership of the legislature insures more undivided control over external affairs than is often possible under a doctrine of separation of powers. In Britain, for example, the formal theory of the constitution is that the Crown engages in all negotiations with outside nations through the exercise of the royal prerogative. There is no legal requirement that Parliament should ratify treaties or agreements before they become binding commitments. The more important conventions of the constitution, however, make the Government of the day answerable in parliamentary debate and question hour for both the formation and implementation of policy. An administration, possessing the confidence of the legislature, is granted through custom and practical considerations considerable freedom to negotiate without having to explain or defend each policy development.

Diplomatic negotiation is an art involving high degrees of professional skill. Knowledge of languages, of the history of foreign peoples, economic conditions throughout the world, the political and social structure of modern nations, are all required to establish a proper basis of communication between political states. Expert organization for diplomacy is an important element in national security. The diplomatic profession retains continuity with age-old traditions, and its great institutional centers, the Foreign Office in England, the Quai d'Orsay in France, and the American State Department, compete with one another in terms of professional competence. No major nation can afford to be outclassed by its rivals in the organization and employment of diplomatic skills. For these reasons, the character and attitude of ostensibly subordinate and service institutions are a major factor in the formation and implementation of foreign policy.

During the first century of their national existence, lived in comparatively secure isolation, the American people suspected and distrusted the profession of diplomacy. Their instinct probably was sound, in light of prevailing social conditions. Britain and the European nations that were the principal rivals of the young United States had crystallized their diplomatic machinery into a class instrument. The excuse of expertness gave reactionary social forces in these countries an opportunity to isolate the machinery of diplomacy from the rising tide of democracy. To play the European diplomatic game meant, through the greater part of the nineteenth century, enmeshment in a web of class assumptions and customs. American indifference to the pretensions of aristocratic diplomacy forwarded the cause of democracy outside its own borders. By the start of the twentieth century, however, diplomacy, like soldiering, had been thrown open to a wider competition of talent. Since that time the United States Department of State has had the task of creating a network of foreign and consular officers—there are now about 6,000 Department of State personnel serving abroad—and a planning and operative staff at home equal, if not superior, to any other organization for diplomatic purposes elsewhere in the world.

The problem of relating expertness to popular control has by no means been solved in the United States or in any democratic state. "Open" diplomacy excites an often ill-informed intervention from power groupings lacking in perspective and full responsibility for the future security and welfare of the country. The press and other organs of public communication are among the greatest offenders in this respect, handicapping the United States particularly in many of her negotiations with states where opinion expression is conducted under more responsible conditions or placed under direct governmental supervision. Legislative intervention in the organization and operation of a foreign-service structure may be even more costly to the national interest. In some ways, it is comparable to control of a hospital staff by political bosses. Advancement of partisan political advantage at the cost of professional standards may cause as grave injuries to national security as open subversion. The committee system of the American Congress permits individual legislators to interfere in the organization and operation of the Department of State in an irresponsible manner. At least, the responsibility is mainly to themselves and their immediate colleagues, as neither the President nor the general electorate finds it easy to hold them to account for the consequences of their intervention. As an example of Congressional influence on organizational structure there may be cited the fact that the United States is the only major country in the world that fails to pay the expenses of its principal ambassadors. A deliberate withholding of appropriate salaries and expense accounts is made by Congress in order to reserve these posts as rewards for wealthy benefactors to party funds or to representatives of important financial and industrial interests. The President of the United States has to conduct a foreign policy by the results of which the people of the United States live or die through an expert organization that Congress has pruned, raided, bullied into conformity with passions or prejudices of the moment, and infiltrated with its committee chairmen.

The position of Secretary of State or Foreign Minister is a critical one in relating the expert knowledge of the professional diplomats to the policy outlook of elected officeholders. The ideal Secretary should be a powerful and respected figure in the partisan world of politicians, while at the same time he has the knowledge and capacity to understand and supervise the work of his expert advisers. Responsibility for formulating or implementing major policy lines does not properly belong to this minister. In the United States, it is the obligation of the Secretary of State to carry out the President's foreign policy. Britain's Secretary of State for Foreign Affairs receives instructions on policy from the Cabinet, where the Prime Minister generally possesses a deciding vote. Soviet Russia has made it clear that her Foreign Minister is a mere agent of the Kremlin hierarchy and is not free to initiate policy. Though secretaries and ministers do not create policy, they determine to a large extent the quality of administration given to the implementation of any policy. They achieve this by linking in their own persons the political organization of party government to the expert machinery of diplomacy. Understanding and motivation needed to win support from legislatures and the electorate originate from the activities of foreign secretaries as political figures and spokesmen for the world of expert knowledge.

The organizational pattern of foreign services now follows with some notable gaps and lapses the functional relationships among states. It was not until the first quarter of the twentieth century that the United States and Britain broke down traditional barriers separating the diplomatic from the consular services, elevating economic relationships to almost equal standing with political negotiations. The Rogers Act of 1924 and a subsequent Act of 1949 created a single Foreign Service of the United States embracing both diplomatic and consular posts. Career officers normally obtain experience in both types of positions. Britain amalgamated diplomatic and consular posts into one Foreign Service in 1921. However, a tradition of the superiority of the diplomat on the political level over his colleague dealing with matters of trade has persisted until at least very recent times. This has had significant influence in overemphasizing political differences among peoples and underemphasizing common interests to be found in economic cooperation. The internal organization of a state department or foreign office may not be divorced from policy making on the highest level. An imperfect balance on the level of information obtained from foreign lands, or an occupational bias affecting matters held to be of primary importance, can distort the negotiating capacity of even the greatest power.

Among the unresolved questions in the structure of the American State Department is that of administrative responsibility for the vast foreign-aid programs. At issue is more than the "empire building" rivalries common among bureaucratic organizations. The character of America's relationship with a great part of the world depends upon whether economic aid is to be subordinated to political diplomacy or made a major instrument of a new and more cooperative type of foreign policy.

Control over intelligence reports constitutes another organizational problem affecting policy determinations on the highest level. It is obvious that foreign policies will be based in large part on information received concerning the actions and intentions of other governments. Collection and evaluation of this information thus exercises a controlling influence over subsequent steps in policy making. Traditionally, embassies and consulates have been the eyes and ears of their governments overseas, with somewhat dubious assistance from the military, who have been seldom troubled by scruples in their quest for interesting facts concerning potential enemies. The stresses of hot and cold wars on American nerves have created a certain hypersensitivity on the question of the sources and value of information from abroad. Secret information has come to be considered almost the only type worthy of attention. Painstaking collection and analysis of facts concerning open happenings in the economic, social, or political fields has been downgraded to routine preparation of background material. A new service, shrouded in satisfying secrecy, the Central Intelligence Agency, has been granted responsibility for collecting and evaluating information for the use of the highest policy-making officials. This comparatively untried experiment raises some questions concerning the relation of administrative services to the process of reaching final policy decisions. As the C.I.A. has no functions to perform in the implementation of policies, by what standards does it evaluate the multitudinous facts it collects? A foreign-service officer obtaining information in the course of his duties is trained to examine and evaluate in terms of practical situations he is dealing with, thus relating the information into an operative pattern. The C.I.A. man, however, if he ventures beyond neutral, academic standards in his evaluation, would seem to have little recourse but to follow an irresponsible bias emanating from an institutional hierarchy. This difficulty is not peculiar to the United States but is shared with most major countries where reliance on secret agents has become endemic. Though the world network of secret intelligence possesses a dramatic appeal, it may be accounted an antidemocratic force divorcing top political decision-makers not only from the experience and opinions of their administrative subordinates but also from fruitful contact with informed opinions in the general community. How may the public follow the foreign policies of a government whose actions are based for the most part on closely guarded information from unknown sources?

A hopeful development in the apparatus of international relations is the organization of cultural contacts. Acknowledgment of cultural interchange as an instrument of foreign policy introduces individual standards into what was hitherto an area dominated by institutional abstractions. Of course, traditional instrumentalities of diplomacy and war have sought to subordinate the new organs of cultural intercourse into propaganda auxiliaries. However, the necessity in this field of employing a wide range of nonofficial talent renders difficult the distortion of such programs by administrative hierarchies. In the United States, Congress, under the Information and Education Act of 1948,[1] authorized the State Department to engage in cultural activities abroad involving means of mass communication. A more restricted but perhaps more fruitful program was launched by the Fulbright Act of 1946.[2] Under the provisions of this Act, exchange of teachers and students between the United States and other countries was financed by the United States government. As the funds were drawn from proceeds of the sale of American war supplies abroad that could not conveniently be converted into United States currency, a burden on the taxpayer was not immediately apparent. Britain placed intercultural relationships on a governmental basis by the establishment in 1934 of the British Council, an organization responsible for the sponsoring of centers of British culture outside the national boundaries. Though funds for the Council are supplied by the government, it is controlled by a Directorate appointed by the administration from representative cultural authorities.

METHODS OF DIPLOMACY Diplomacy, as distinct from war—a distinction that has to be made in practice with considerable caution—may be said to center in the making of agreements with other states. Treaties constitute the principal form of international agreements. They may be compared to civil contracts in that their binding characteristics result from observance of legal standards. Acceptance of international law, in the sense of a binding obligation to observe treaties, is, then, the cornerstone of world relationships on a diplomatic level. History has shown it to be an uncertain support: a majority of the great Powers have violated their treaty obligations at some time or other in the struggle for power. Germany led the way to twentieth-century disregard for treaty observance through her cynical "scrap of paper" interpretation of a treaty obligation to respect Belgian neutrality in 1914. Soviet countries have followed this lead enthusiastically with additional reservations on the binding nature of treaties made between "capitalist, imperialist" nations and "Marxist, proletarian democracies." The assumption of an international order regulated by solemnly made and scrupulously observed treaties may no longer be considered valid—if it ever was. This does not imply that treaties are useless as a major foundation for international relationships, but merely that they are insufficient by and in themselves. A complex of power realities has to be constructed to supply an enforcement background for any particular treaty or class of treaties.

Diplomacy has to merge with war before an international order based on treaty observance can be insured. However, short of war, diplomatic methods may be used to construct systems of alliances or understandings between groups of nations that may make breaches of certain types of treaties dangerous to an offending state. If the alliance is a formal one among several countries, it will take the form of a *multilateral treaty*, that is, a single document subscribed to by a number of Powers. There are many other types and degrees of alliances, ranging from strong bilateral agreements to mere understandings of common action in case of certain limited eventualities. The field is one for expert professional negotiation, often based on secret information and objectives that may not be disclosed fully to the general public of the participating states.

An American objection to secret treaties or alliances based on diplomatic maneuvering was expressed by President Wilson. This objection went deeper than scruples of personal morality; it challenged basic relationships among states that were not founded on the true consent of their inhabitants. Under present-day conditions, it may be granted that no major country possesses the power to stand alone, militarily, economically, or culturally. Therefore, limited international understandings are imperative, though the form of such relationships may vary from traditional diplomatic alliances to new developments in the area of cooperative action. For some time to come, traditional diplomacy may be expected to retain a vital function both in the preservation of national interests and in the safeguarding of some semblance of an international order. Its methods necessitate that a considerable measure of freedom and authority be granted to the expert negotiator. At the same time, its limitations demand close supervision of the objectives of negotiation by the representative institutions of the national communities concerned.

The Use of War

It is tempting in the sixth decade of the twentieth century to treat of war as if its effect on an international order were a matter of historical moment rather than present concern. Certainly, it seems unlikely that the type of experience that war brought to those born in the first decade of this century will be repeated in the lives of their descendants. Technology has rendered obsolescent patterns of war that had persisted since the invention of gunpowder. There remains, however, a concept of military force capable of potential variations of form, which, up to the present, has never been absent from any final determination of relationships among organized communities. Though the methods and instrumentalities through which this force manifests itself remain fluid, its objective has been consistent throughout history. The purpose of military force in international affairs is to reduce the will to resist demands. Conquest, occupation, victories, blockades, bombardments, and other ingenious means have been devised to achieve this single aim of submission. Obviously, then, if the political institutions of an enemy state can be subdued by means other than attack by organized armies, such methods will be preferred, on grounds of efficiency and costs, if not morality.

An analogue to the macrocosm of military power in the present-day world may be drawn from the microcosm of expeditionary forces used to subdue primitive communities. At the beginning of the twentieth century, a military column of mounted or foot soldiers was required to engage in hand-to-hand combat to subdue fighting tribesmen and then occupy the territory until the ruling hierarchy had been forced into acceptable behavior patterns. Later in the century, air attacks destructive of villages or population concentrations often achieved the same ends without use of ground forces. Still later, widespread dread of air bombardment could be used to break the will of settlements through the mere passage of aircraft bearing threats. Similarly, though on a much wider scale, military force tends to assume the form of a destruction potential that, once in the hands of an opponent, is too terrible to resist. Thus, military effort is translated from the battlefield into the factories and scientific laboratories of the great Powers. The ability to employ military threats profitably becomes the monopoly of a very few nation-states. Even for them, the concept of profitable applications of the dreadful instruments at their disposal becomes exceedingly remote.

The principle of deterrence appears to have become dominant

in the use of military power in determining international relationships. Combined with a bipolar system of world power, the Big Deterrent may be controlled only by the leading nations, and even in their case in conjunction with so many other Powers as to render it an international rather than national instrumentality. If the United States as an unquestioned guardian of thermonuclear power is taken as an example, it may be observed that her warlike capacities now depend on a network of overseas bases in the territories of allied nations. Successful defense or attack without the assistance of large blocs of lesser countries is almost inconceivable nowadays for either the United States or the U.S.S.R.

Deterrent warfare, unlike previous wars, may be said to be waged continuously. Under the name of the Cold War, it commits the economies and political systems of the major Powers to relentless competition in a race for definitive superiority. To quote from the 1958 findings of the Committee on Economic Development:

> From 1930 to 1939, the United States spent, on the average, a little over 1 per cent of its gross national product on national security. From 1955 to 1957, when the extraordinary expenditures of the Korean War were over, these outlays averaged nearly 11 per cent of the gross national product. . . . As long as the Communist bloc is bent on aggressive expansion, we prefer to exert pressure on it and to present it with initiatives of our own. Our self-imposed restriction against military aggression does not bar us from taking the offensive in other ways. By accelerated research and rapid technological advance in our own weapons and those of our allies, we could, for example, repeatedly render the military equipment of our opponents obsolete, and greatly increase the strain upon the Communist economies. . . . The United States need not turn into a "garrison state," but it may have to divert to national security a larger proportion of its output than formerly and forego standards and practices that impair the nation's strength but are not at all indispensable parts of our way of life.[3]

For the foreseeable future, a competitive balance of military preparation rather than actualities of force is likely to determine the nature of the international order. A perhaps underemphasized factor is a degree of internationalization of armed forces arising from the interdependence of the national forces within each opposing bloc. With national governments no longer in unchallenged control of their military power, international purposes and objectives may yet be imposed on the employment of military force on a major scale anywhere in the world.

Economic Cooperation

From the individual point of view, the most promising development in international relationships since 1945 has been the growth in economic cooperation. Interdependence of national economies is a practical phenomenon affecting the material welfare of individuals everywhere. The political institutions of national governments have been slow to adapt themselves to the realities of this situation. Accordingly, the experimental and somewhat makeshift arrangements that have been entered into to meet urgent economic crises of the postwar years have opened up potential avenues for new forms of profitable relationships. As the United States remains, despite growing Soviet competition, the most influential center of economic strength in the modern world, her policies in this respect have determined a basic pattern.

TARIFFS One presumed national interest of the United States, dominant during the nineteenth and the early part of the twentieth centuries, was the theory of *protection.* Industrial development appeared tied to safeguarding national industries against a flood of imports from abroad through the imposition of high tariff duties. This separated America from cooperative action with free-trade countries, led by Britain, that were seeking to operate in terms of an integrated world economy. After the first German war, it was discovered that enormous war debts owed to the United States by her European allies could not be paid off because the European countries were unable to earn dollar exchange obtainable only through import of their goods into the American market. In 1934, largely through the efforts of Secretary Cordell Hull, the Reciprocal Trade Agreement Act was passed, allowing the President to negotiate tariff reductions on a bilateral basis in return for concessions from the other nation involved. This power in the hands of the President proved of great importance in forming desirable economic relationships with European and other lands after the second German war.

An international movement towards general tariff reductions was started in 1947 by the conclusion of the General Agreement on Tariffs and Trade (GATT). Under the authority of the Reciprocal Trade Agreement Act, the United States government was able to participate in this movement to the extent of negotiating many bilateral treaties with other countries that conformed to standards adopted by GATT. However, it cannot be claimed that tariff barriers have been relegated to a realm of international control in the United States or elsewhere. A conflict between presumed national interest and international order remains acute. During the summer of 1959, organized labor in the United States made proposals for new laws to bar "sweatshop" imports produced by foreign workers operating under substandard labor conditions.[4] Difficult choices have to be made on a popular level between immediate, sectional advantages and the long-term benefits of international economic cooperation.

FOREIGN AID An imaginative act of international statesmanship was carried out by President Truman and his Secretary of State, General Marshall, in the proposal and signing of the Foreign Assistance Act of 1948.[5] The Marshall plan accepted economic cooperation with the greater part of the Free World as an essential national interest of the United States in the present world situation. The costs to the American taxpayer were great, but results in terms of the reestablishment of a powerful self-sustaining Europe were highly advantageous to American security. Further, the whole world was given convincing proof that the United States was endeavoring to combat Communist imperialism by the creation of a true international order based on generous economic cooperation and not on military dominance. The full consequences of this daring departure in statesmanship on the preservation of Western civilization cannot be fully evaluated until greater historical perspective has been achieved. However, the principle that the United States should use its economic strength purposefully to pursue world policies that coincide with its national interests has altered both the balance and character of international diplomacy.

Marshall plan.

A valuable consequence of the American initiative in the field of economic aid was the impetus applied to efforts of the European nations themselves to integrate their economies. The Organization for European Economic Cooperation (OEEC) was formed at American insistence to engage in joint planning for the use of American aid in European recovery. In 1949, a Council of Europe was formed by ten states, including Britain, France, Belgium, and Sweden among others. The aim of the Council was to promote economic and social fields of joint responsibility without trespassing too deeply into difficult questions of political sovereignty. From the beginnings of this Council, several revolutionary developments in economic cooperation on a regional basis have resulted. The Schuman Community, inaugurated in 1951, binds six of the coal- and steel-producing European nations (France, the German Federal Republic, Italy, Belgium, Netherlands, Luxembourg) to regulate their production and marketing arrangements in coal and steel under the guidance of a High Authority. The same six nations agreed in 1957 to form a European Atomic Energy Community (Euratom) and in the same year a European Economic Community for the establishment of a common market. The activities of this inner group of European countries have stimulated peripheral lands such as Britain and the Scandinavian nations to enter into closer trading agreements to complement and balance the economic unification of the original six.[6]

American policies in economic diplomacy shifted with the successful conclusion of the Marshall plan in 1951 to narrower concepts of economic assistance for defense purposes under the Mutual Security Program. However, a major challenge to the free world became apparent in the attempts by the Soviet nations to attract the two thirds of the world's population living under conditions of primitive technology into their fold. This threat could not be met by diplomatic maneuvering or increased armaments. United Nations statistics show that about one out of every two persons live where there is not enough food and with a daily intake only 400 calories above starvation level and 750 calories below that of the more fortunate one third of mankind.[7] Impoverished peoples cannot be reached by arguments of power and prestige. A stark fact facing the modern world is the imbalance of consumption that deprives the bulk of humanity of the opportunity of benefiting from technological civilization. The former colonial empires of the European Powers were dealing with this situation in a leisurely and sometimes imperceptible manner when they were caught and to a large extent swept away in a world-wide surge of nationalism. Communism saw and still sees its major opportunity for world domination in this situation. The United States has had to improvise with new and untried instrumentalities in this critical field of world relations. Though on the surface it may appear primarily a social and economic problem, governments are involved on the survival level. Control of the productive resources and labor potential of underdeveloped lands, particularly if exercised in the exclusive manner of Communism, is equivalent to mastery over industrial civilization.

In the words of the Chairman of the Committee for Economic Development:

> Tying economic aid exclusively to military policy ignores the fact that the Communist threat in the underdeveloped world is not solely—not even primarily—military. Foreign aid is one way—probably the best way we have—of countering Communist subversion abroad. It enables us to meet the legitimate needs and desires of the underdeveloped countries for greater economic growth. . . . Once economic development is given full weight and independence in our foreign policy, the way is open for an imaginative approach to the problem. Once there is greater public understanding of the critical need for economic development, we can mount the kind of program designed to do in the underdeveloped world what the Marshall Plan did in Western Europe.[8]

The growing emphasis on economic arrangements in the creation of an international order affects the traditional claim of political governments to monopolize the conduct of relationships between organized peoples. Business corporations and financial institutions organized on an international basis are frequently more competent to carry out profitable interchanges among peoples than state administrations. When government does assume responsibility, it may find itself operating in fields that lie outside its functions in domestic matters. A slackening of national bonds in economic matters appears an inevitable development, with the authority of the political state being shared with nonofficial bodies in the establishment of profitable relationships among communities separated by national boundaries. The international order of the future may not be primarily a political order; its governmental structure may be equaled or surpassed by parallel economic or cultural organizations serving individuals on a nonnational basis.

Scientific and Cultural Relationships

Science may be said to have existed on an international basis since the time of the ancient Greeks. Historically, however, political government has hindered or at least ignored the international character of science or culture. The growing practical importance to the individual of a "free" science in a world-wide sense has forced a change in government attitudes. Political monopolies and repressions are best countered, in general, when the services the political state can render its individual citizens are equaled or surpassed by benefits from other types of organizations. Thus, science may claim to have won its way in present times to a measure of international freedom by convincing the bulk of the community that it had more to offer in concrete advantages than the prejudices of their politicians. An outstanding example of the triumph of international science was the International Geophysical Year commenced in 1957.[9] The Executive Director of the United States National Committee for the Year declared it to be "the single most significant peaceful activity of mankind since the Renaissance and the Copernican Revolution." In any case, it represented an unexpectedly vigorous advance of scientific cooperation over the suspicions of sixty-six governments with their institutional leanings towards secrecy and national monopolies. The apparatus that launched the IGY may be examined as a prototype of nongovernmental organizations in the field of international relations. The International Council of Scientific Unions (ICSU) is composed of thirteen unions representing different scientific fields, such as mathematics, biology, astronomy, etc., together with the National Academies of Science or equivalent bodies from forty-five nations. In many, if not all, countries, National Academies are subject to direct or indirect control by the political government. However, when their representatives sit with the acknowledged world leaders of scientific research, they achieve a considerable measure of independence from nationalist politics. The success of the IGY has given a stature to the International Council of Scientific Unions in the eyes of world opinion that may empower this body to become the focus of a limited type of nonpolitical world organization. If the development and freedom of science can be removed from the control of political institutions, an important part of the practical life of individuals will be rendered free of national boundaries.

Nonscientific forms of cultural interchange remain either at a minor level of importance for the nonspecialist or are firmly controlled by political governments. The field of opinion formation is not one that national states are prepared to abandon in the foreseeable future. Countries where the liberal tradition is strong restrain government officials from too flagrant interference with the flow of ideas, but such restraint seldom affects authoritarian regimes either of the right or left. Perhaps one of the reasons why national governments continue to exercise authority in this area is the indifference of the ordinary individual in most lands to intercultural exchanges. Language barriers, localized educational traditions, and many other factors tend to make the bulk of any community suspicious of cultural notions from abroad. This prevailing intellectual provincialism strengthens the hands of political institutions in sustaining "thought control" along nationalist lines.

International Organs of Propaganda and Subversion

An ancient trick in the struggle for power between governments is an attack on the loyalty of a people to its own political institutions. To achieve destruction of an enemy government through internal revolution is an economical method of gaining a power advantage. In order to play this game on the international level, it is necessary to advance some ideology superficially attractive to influential groupings everywhere, and not too obviously identified with the particular interests of the propagandizing nation–state. Religious divisions provided a useful school for politicians in this art during the period of the Reformation and Counter Reformation. The separation of a ruling hierarchy from a prevalent popular creed offered many opportunties for external intervention. Thus, when James II of England proclaimed his Catholicism in the face of the Protestant majority of his people, foreign powers supporting Protestantism were able to score an international triumph through the substitution of the Protestant champion William of Orange for the Stuart monarch. Religion has now, on the whole, ceased to be a significant means of effecting political subversion. However, the socioeconomic doctrine of Marxism has appeared on the world stage as a powerful successor to religious differences in turning men's loyalties against the political institutions of their own nation–states.

As the United States in the economic field is the protagonist of world relationships based on cooperation, so the Soviet Union may be held the champion of ideological conquest. Of course, other countries, including the United States, seek to promote their way of life among other peoples by means of cultural persuasion. Soviet Russia, however, goes beyond a competition of ideas into an organized attempt to infiltrate the political, economic, and cultural institutions of other states with groups that have been detached from their national loyalties and rendered obedient to instructions from the Soviet hierarchy. This practice may be accounted a hostile action responsible in large part for that condition of armed tension known as the Cold War. The instrument through which the Russian nation–state pursues its ends by these means is the international Communist Party. According to Marx, the Communist Party was a mere instrumentality of the proletariat and inseparable from the working classes. Lenin and Stalin, however, converted the Party into an instrumentality of the Russian state that could use any class or group of people anywhere to promote the interests of the state hierarchy. Under this latter philosophy, national Communist parties may be manipulated to adopt any economic or political line that might bring benefits to the U.S.S.R. in its struggle for world power.

Considerable difficulty has been encountered among free nations in meeting this Communist Party instrumentality of international aggression. Political parties normally are considered organs of domestic opinion in countries under representative government; as such, the only checks imposed on them emanate from the will of the electorate and ordinary provisions of law. A body that takes the form of a national political party though dedicated to imposing the will of a foreign Power endangers the whole system of representative government. Some states cut the Gordian knot by specifically outlawing the Communist Party within their borders, thus forcing its members to reveal their true intentions in the form of illegal, subversive activities. Other nations, of which the United States is one, find constitutional obstacles to any outright prohibition of a national Communist Party. At the same time, they restrict known Party members in a number of ways, denying them access to positions in government service or to key posts in economic or social life. In the case of *Dennis v. United States*[10] the Supreme Court, after an exhaustive six-month trial in a lower court, held proven "that the literature of the Party and the statements and activities of its leaders . . . advocate, and the general goal of the Party was, during the period in question, to achieve a successful overthrow of the existing order by force and violence."

Subversion, then, has become an active force in international relationships. One unexpected result has been to involve ordinary individuals more closely in the relationships among states. In attempting to appeal to communities over the heads of their established governments, the Soviet nations have provoked countermeasures from national governments in the education of their citizens concerning the true issues at stake. A personal and emotional flavor has been imparted to international affairs that had been absent from the Western world since the time of the religious wars.

Notes

[1] Public Law 402, 80th Congress, Second Session, of January 27, 1948. H.R. 3342, Washington: United States Government Printing Office, 1948, **62,** Part I, 6-14.

[2] World Peace Foundation, *Documents on American Foreign Relations, 1945–1946,* Princeton: Princeton University Press, pp. 758-760.

[3] The Committee for Economic Development, *The Problem of National Security,* New York: 1958, pp. 7, 10, 11.

[4] *The New York Times,* August 17, 1959.

[5] World Peace Foundation, *Documents on American Foreign Relations,*

1948, Princeton: Princeton University Press, pp. 195-220. For a brief account of the operation of the Act see Carleton, W. G., *The Revolution in American Foreign Policy,* New York: Random House, revised edition, 1957, pp. 52-64.

[6] For an account of the development of European unification see Zurcher, Arnold J., *The Struggle to Unite Europe 1940–1958,* New York: New York University Press, 1958.

[7] *Pooling Skills for Human Progress,* New York: United Nations Department for Public Information, 1955.

[8] Zellerbach, J. D., *Our Stake in Economic Development Abroad—an Address,* New York: Committee for Economic Development, 1956, p. 8.

[9] For an account of the International Geophysical Year see Sullivan, Walter, *The International Geophysical Year,* New York: Carnegie Endowment for International Peace, 1959. (International Conciliation No. 521, January 1959.)

[10] *Dennis v. United States,* 341 U.S. 494 (1951).

Supplementary Readings

Almond, Gabriel A., *The American People and Foreign Policy,* New York: Harcourt, Brace, 1950.

Ashton-Gwatkin, Frank, *The British Foreign Service,* Syracuse: Syracuse University Press, 1950.

Beloff, Max, *Foreign Policy and the Democratic Process,* Baltimore: Johns Hopkins Press, 1955.

Buck, Philip W., and Travis, Martin (eds.), *Control of Foreign Relations in Modern Nations,* New York: Norton, 1957.

Cook, Thomas, and Moos, Malcolm C., *Power Through Purpose,* Baltimore: Johns Hopkins Press, 1954.

Elliott, William Y., chairman, *The Political Economy of American Foreign Policy; Its Concepts, Strategy, and Limits; Report of a Study Group,* New York: Holt, 1955.

———, chairman, *United Nations Foreign Policy; Its Organization and Control; Report of a Study Group,* New York: Columbia, 1952.

Gross, Feliks, *Foreign Policy Analysis,* New York: Philosophical Library, 1954.

Halle, Louis J., *Civilization and Foreign Policy,* New York: Harper, 1955.

Kennan, George F., *Realities of American Foreign Policy,* Princeton: Princeton University Press, 1954.

Leonard, Leonard L. (ed.), *Elements of American Foreign Policy,* New York: McGraw-Hill, 1953.

Lippmann, Walter, *Isolation and Alliances; An American Speaks to the British,* Boston: Little, Brown, 1952.

London, Kurt, and Ives, Kent, *How Foreign Policy Is Made,* Princeton: Van Nostrand, 1949.

Morgenthau, Hans J., *In Defense of the National Interest,* New York: Knopf, 1951.

Nicolson, Sir Harold, *Diplomacy,* New York: Oxford, second edition, 1950.
Schuman, Frederick L., *The Commonwealth of Man: An Inquiry into Power Politics and World Government,* New York: Knopf, 1952.
Stuart, Graham H., *American Diplomatic and Consular Practice,* New York: Appleton, 1952.
Thayer, Charles W., *Diplomat,* New York: Harper, 1959.

Chapter 19

Universal and Regional Organizations

In a previous chapter, a distinction was drawn between universal or world government and international organization. This distinction is of importance in understanding the character and functions of the large number of nonnational bodies that have begun to play a significant part in world affairs during the twentieth century. *Universal government* implies subordination of national governments and the assumption of their traditional responsibilities. *International organization* is supplementary to the powers of independent and sovereign nation–states. It may be said to fill in the interstices in mankind's political, economic, and social necessities neglected through the limited range of the national state. A further growth in the interdependence of peoples and their economies may, at some time in the future, make these gaps in the organization of mankind of greater importance than the order imposed by the limited capabilities of nation–states. An obvious example is that of peace, which has never been achieved under a system of sovereign states. However, in the actualities of the present times the bulk of the world's peoples are not prepared to accept any form of universal organization as superior to the governments they have chosen for the purpose of conducting their particular affairs. A survey of international organization must still be based on the premise that it is supplementary to but not dominant over national governments. Accordingly, individual citizens of the various states look to their own governments as their agents in determining the scope and functions of international organization. Supranational bodies remain forms of intercourse between governments, not peoples.

Nature of the United Nations

The United Nations may be regarded as the confluent point of two streams of human achievement and aspirations. To avoid confusion over the capacities and objectives of this body, it is desirable to keep the consolidation of previous gains made in international cooperation separate from the projected hopes of advances in wider fields of peace, security, and world justice. In terms of its historic origins, the United Nations may be regarded as successor not only to its immediate predecessor, the League of Nations, but to the whole loose body of international arrangements for political, economic, and social cooperation. By arranging these together under a single deliberative and administrative body, an advance was made in world politics analogous to the combination in business of numbers of unrelated enterprises under the logically efficient management of a cartel or trust. However, the type of international enterprise, whether it was the Universal Postal Union or the idea of a Concert of Powers for the maintenance of peace, carried with it the limitations inherited from its historic development. In this sense, the United Nations brought nothing new into the field of world cooperation beyond a useful concept of efficient centralization for improved organization and practice.

At the same time, the United Nations was a true creation occurring at a moment in history when peoples demanded from their governments some new approach to the tragic cycle of war and uneasy peace. Of course, a long previous tradition of dreams and plans for universal peace influenced the shaping of this world body. Though it did not spring full grown onto the world scene, the United Nations provided an institutional structure for what had theretofore been loosely organized aspirations. Perhaps it would be more accurate to say that institutional means were provided for a possible implementation of hopes through future agreements and developments. Certainly, the novel features added to world organization by the United Nations did not constitute instrumentalities

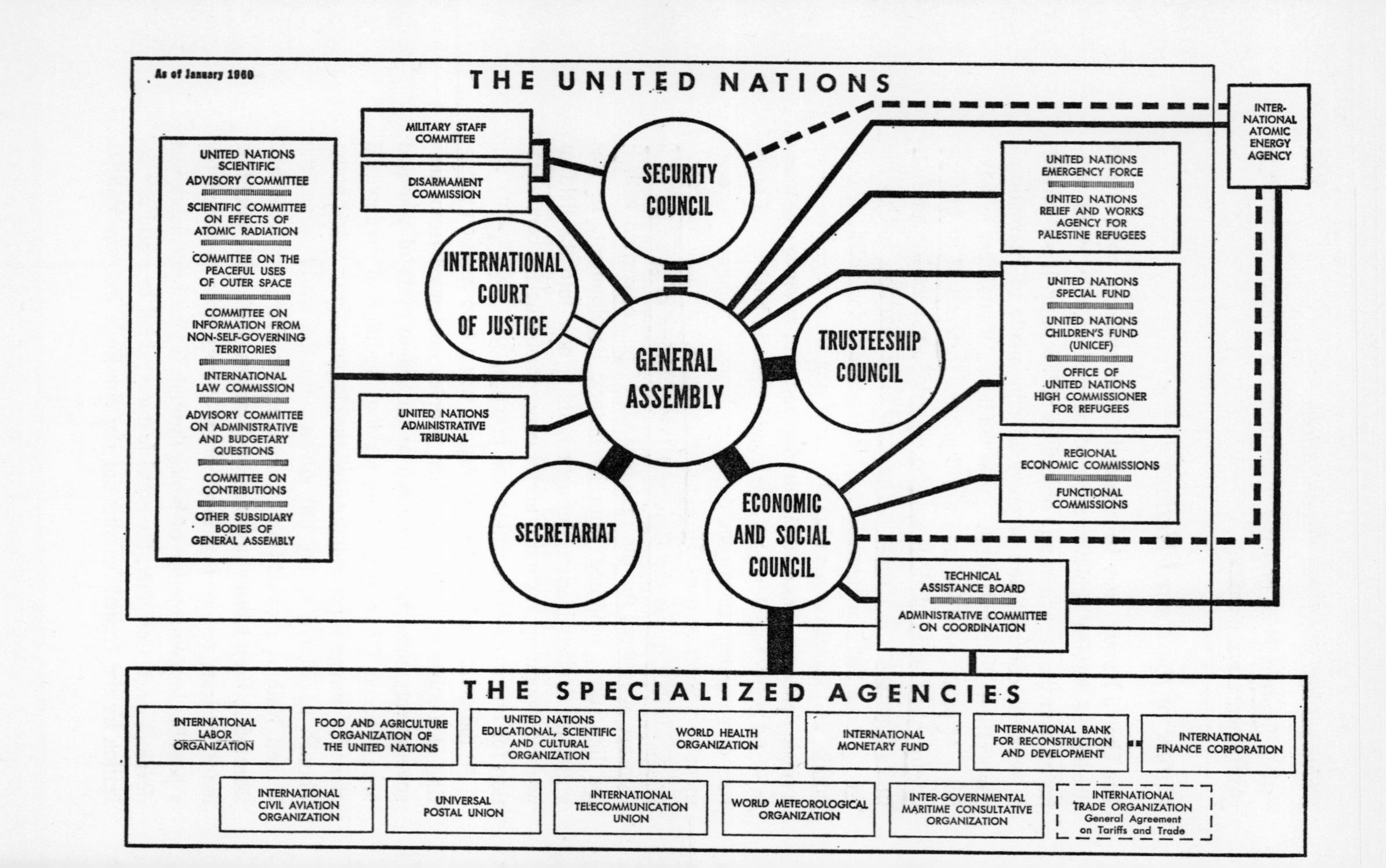
As of January 1960
THE UNITED NATIONS
MILITARY STAFF COMMITTEE
DISARMAMENT COMMISSION
SECURITY COUNCIL
INTERNATIONAL ATOMIC ENERGY AGENCY
UNITED NATIONS SCIENTIFIC ADVISORY COMMITTEE
SCIENTIFIC COMMITTEE ON EFFECTS OF ATOMIC RADIATION
COMMITTEE ON THE PEACEFUL USES OF OUTER SPACE
COMMITTEE ON INFORMATION FROM NON-SELF-GOVERNING TERRITORIES
INTERNATIONAL LAW COMMISSION
ADVISORY COMMITTEE ON ADMINISTRATIVE AND BUDGETARY QUESTIONS
COMMITTEE ON CONTRIBUTIONS
OTHER SUBSIDIARY BODIES OF GENERAL ASSEMBLY
INTERNATIONAL COURT OF JUSTICE
GENERAL ASSEMBLY
UNITED NATIONS ADMINISTRATIVE TRIBUNAL
TRUSTEESHIP COUNCIL
UNITED NATIONS EMERGENCY FORCE
UNITED NATIONS RELIEF AND WORKS AGENCY FOR PALESTINE REFUGEES
UNITED NATIONS SPECIAL FUND
UNITED NATIONS CHILDREN'S FUND (UNICEF)
OFFICE OF UNITED NATIONS HIGH COMMISSIONER FOR REFUGEES
REGIONAL ECONOMIC COMMISSIONS
FUNCTIONAL COMMISSIONS
SECRETARIAT
ECONOMIC AND SOCIAL COUNCIL
TECHNICAL ASSISTANCE BOARD
ADMINISTRATIVE COMMITTEE ON COORDINATION
THE SPECIALIZED AGENCIES
INTERNATIONAL LABOR ORGANIZATION
FOOD AND AGRICULTURE ORGANIZATION OF THE UNITED NATIONS
UNITED NATIONS EDUCATIONAL, SCIENTIFIC AND CULTURAL ORGANIZATION
WORLD HEALTH ORGANIZATION
INTERNATIONAL MONETARY FUND
INTERNATIONAL BANK FOR RECONSTRUCTION AND DEVELOPMENT
INTERNATIONAL FINANCE CORPORATION
INTERNATIONAL CIVIL AVIATION ORGANIZATION
UNIVERSAL POSTAL UNION
INTERNATIONAL TELECOMMUNICATION UNION
WORLD METEOROLOGICAL ORGANIZATION
INTER-GOVERNMENTAL MARITIME CONSULTATIVE ORGANIZATION
INTERNATIONAL TRADE ORGANIZATION
General Agreement on Tariffs and Trade

of power capable of insuring world peace under all foreseeable conditions.

Organization of the United Nations

Because of its origin in the general revulsion against war following the defeat of Germany and Japan in 1945, the organizational plan of the United Nations was conceived largely in terms of mechanism on an international scale to prevent aggression and to promote the peaceful settlement of disputes. Failures of its predecessor, the League of Nations, served as pointers for planning a more effective structure. However, the Charter of the United Nations sought to embody in an organizational framework several almost incompatible objectives. Chapter I, Article 1 of the Charter commences:

> The Purposes of the United Nations are: (1) To maintain international peace and security, and to that end: to take collective measures for the prevention and removal of threats to the peace, and for the suppression of acts of aggression or other breaches of the peace, and to bring about by peaceful means, and in conformity with the principles of justice and international law, adjustment or settlement of international disputes or situations which might lead to a breach of the peace.

Article 2 lays down certain Principles to be observed in the achievement of this and other Purposes. Among these principles are: "The Organization is based on the principle of the sovereign equality of all its Members," and again:

> Nothing contained in the present Charter shall authorize the United Nations to intervene in matters which are essentially within the domestic jurisdiction of any state or shall require the Members to submit such matters to settlement under the present Charter; but this principle shall not prejudice the application of enforcement measures under Chapter VII.

Concepts of "sovereign equality" and the right to do what they please within their own borders render nation-states too irresponsible to constitute disciplined members of an effective organization for collective security. Accordingly, the machinery devised by the United Nations to further peace was loose and experimental. It has developed along lines that approximate more closely to realities of the power balance between national groupings than the ideal postulates enunciated in the Charter.

Nevertheless, an institutional setting was given to a new force in world affairs that may be loosely described as "world opinion." This force is new in the sense that it is a product of the technical leap forward in communication that has taken place during the twentieth century. Its strength is at present indeterminate, but there are indications that it is based on a conviction held by large numbers of individuals everywhere that they possess certain basic interests in common. In effect, the citizen bodies of various nations have had their attention focused on problems of international relations and the methods employed by their respective governments in dealing with them. The total facts of the situation and the views of all other peoples have been established in dramatic manner. In consequence, national electorates have been able to instruct their own governments from a basis of information and understanding of their own involvement as individuals in a manner unknown in the past history of nation–states. World opinion, then, is in reality national opinion broadened to include the interests of individuals as participating entities in a world community. It serves to accentuate the character of national administrations as agents of their citizens in the operation of an international order of individual as well as institutional concern.

THE SECURITY COUNCIL Implementation of an international order based on peace was conceived by the framers of the United Nations Charter as necessitating acknowledgment of existing realities of power. Accordingly, the principal organ of the world body entrusted with responsibility for dynamic action was a Security Council composed of five permanent members and six non-permanent members. The permanent members were selected from what were presumed to be the major Powers: the United States, the Soviet Union, the United Kingdom, France, and the Republic (now the Nationalist Government) of China. Nonpermanent members, elected by the General Assembly, have a two-year tenure of office. Voting procedures weighted the balance of authority heavily in favor of the permanent members. Issues were divided into two categories: procedural and substantive. Though procedural matters may be decided by an affirmative vote of seven members, substantive issues require the vote of seven members *with all the permanent members concurring*. As the question of whether a matter is procedural or substantive is itself a substantive issue, this procedure provides each permanent member with a veto power over subjects to be considered or acted upon by the Security Council. The Soviet Union has cast over eighty vetoes in its determination to prevent any form of international action not dictated by its wishes.[1]

The principal responsibilities of the Security Council were intended to be furtherance of peaceful settlements of disputes between nations and the organization of collective security should all negotiations fail to stem aggression. Chapter VI of the Charter gives the Security Council authority to intervene at all stages in disputes between states to persuade the antagonists to accept a peaceful settlement. Should all such efforts fail, however, Chapter VII declares: "The Security Council shall determine the existence of any threat to the peace, breach of the peace, or act of aggression and shall make recommendations, or decide what measures shall be taken in accordance with Articles 41 and 42, to maintain or restore international peace and security." Economic sanctions and collective use of armed force are measures open to the Security Council under the provisions of these Articles.

Despite the East–West tensions inhibiting true collective action during the past ten years, the Security Council has employed the provisions of Chapter VI to encourage settlement in several dangerous disputes: the presence of Soviet troops in Iran; India's and Pakistan's conflicting claims to Kashmir; the Palestine question; Indonesian accusations against The Netherlands. A major test of the effectiveness of the United Nations as a bulwark against aggression occurred when North Korea invaded South Korea. Owing to the temporary absence of the U.S.S.R. from the Security Council, consideration was accorded as a breach of world peace. When Russia returned to the Council to veto action, the Fifth General Assembly passed the Uniting for Peace Resolution, establishing both a Collective Measures Committee and a Peace Observation Commission. This action in June, 1950, shifted responsibility for peace to a considerable extent from a paralyzed Security Council to a less inhibited Assembly. In the implementation of collective-security measures in the Korean dispute, sixteen nations sent military forces and over forty contributed material aid in some form.

THE GENERAL ASSEMBLY The principle of representation in world organization is embodied in the General Assembly of the United Nations. A method of election is provided for nations that did not sign the original Charter in 1945. The Security Council recommends and the General Assembly decides whether an applicant nation is a "peace-loving state" and able and willing to carry out the obligations of the Charter. That these are not empty phrases may be seen from the long-continued refusal of both the Council and the Assembly to consider the application for membership from Communist China until such time as her conduct removes the stigma of aggression placed on her during the Korean dispute. Other recently created states such as Malaya, Ghana, and Indonesia have been admitted readily as member states.

A representative body acquires significance according to the scope of the matters it is entitled to discuss. Of course, discussion must terminate in meaningful action; in national representative bodies this normally takes the form of legislation. International assemblies lack legislative authority but they pass Resolutions of varying binding force on their constituent members. It is a shallow and unsatisfactory view to judge the work of an international assembly by the power it possesses to achieve strict enforcement of its decisions. If an analogy is insisted upon with legislative bodies of sovereign states, then the analogy in historical propriety should be made with such bodies in their formative periods. England's Parliaments in the reign of Elizabeth I passed many apparently futile Resolutions against Monopolies, among other things. It can hardly be denied that such Resolutions were the start of a sequence that culminated in effective antitrust laws emanating from the Congress of the United States.

The deliberative powers of the General Assembly are wider than any hitherto possessed by an international organization, both as regards the original grant and the liberal interpretations placed on the Charter's authorizations. Articles 10 and 11 empower the Assembly to discuss and make recommendations concerning "any questions or any matters within the scope of the present Charter

. . ." and, again, "any questions relating to the maintenance of international peace and security brought before it. . . ." Perhaps the only effective check on the wide range of topics the Assembly feels free to debate is the provision in the Charter against intervening "in matters which are essentially within the domestic jurisdiction of any state." What constitutes domestic jurisdiction as distinct from matters of international concern has to be decided more by the conscience of the Assembly than by any clear-cut rules. Thus, the Assembly has claimed full right of discussion on the topic of race relations within South Africa, on the ground that government policies are provocative to other nations in India and Africa. Conversely, it is unlikely that the Assembly would consider itself entitled to debate school segregation in Arkansas or elsewhere in the United States.

The Assembly is organized around a system of Standing Committees for each of the major subject divisions on its agenda. These committees consist of the full membership of the parent body sitting under committee rules to permit free discussion and the drafting of resolutions to be submitted again to the membership in formal plenary sessions. This procedure, a common parliamentary form, encourages debate and a certain amount of flexible bargaining among delegates. The principle committees are:

First Committee (Political and Security Questions)
Second Committee (Economic and Financial Questions)
Third Committee (Social, Humanitarian, and Cultural Questions)
Fourth Committee (Trusteeship and Non-self-governing Territories)
Fifth Committee (Administrative and Budgetary Questions)
Sixth Committee (Legal Questions)

During the first fifteen years of its existence, the General Assembly has not established itself as a decision-making body of paramount importance in the settlement of world affairs. It may be questioned whether any representative gathering of comparable size and diversity could be expected to function as a direct governing body even if it controlled—which the United Nations does not—adequate machinery for the enforcement of its rulings. However, the effectiveness of the General Assembly lies in the fact that it has provided a new dimension to the field of negotiations between governments. Collective negotiation represents some advance toward a viable international order. In the absence of a reliable system of collective security, it may prove the bridge between the historic condition of warring independent states and a new world order based on cooperative action to achieve common interests. Of course, it may be believed—as powerful groupings in many countries do believe—that disputes among nations are too fundamental to be resolved by any means other than total submission on the part of one of the protagonists. In such a case, international order can result only through the establishment of a universal empire by the most powerful nation or combination of nations.

THE SECRETARIAT As a by-product of its growth, the United Nations has created the beginnings of a civil service for international administration.[2] Approximately 7,000 employees are paid directly out of United Nations funds, of whom more than half work in the headquarters offices and the remainder in the field scattered throughout the world. Besides these, there exist a less organized international bureaucracy attached to the specialized agencies (discussed later in this chapter) as technicians or administrators. The Secretary-General is the chief administrative officer of the United Nations. He is appointed by the General Assembly upon recommendation of the Security Council. Besides bearing responsibility for providing administrative services to the United Nations as a whole, the Secretary-General is accorded a political role of his own. Under Article 99, "The Secretary-General may bring to the attention of the Security Council any matter which in his opinion may threaten the maintenance of international peace and security." The first and second holders of this office, Trygve Lie and Dag Hammarskjold, have proved themselves skilled diplomats to whom the great and small powers have entrusted several important and delicate missions.

The administrative pattern emerging in United Nations affairs provides practical building blocks for the establishment of international services in political as well as economic and social matters. That these services are permissive rather than compulsory remains an important element in their development under present world conditions. Areas of interest to governments and peoples are being demarcated as subject to control by methods and standards common to all. Many problems remain to be solved before a fully efficient international administrative service can take its place among ranking political institutions in the world. For example, the General Assembly has required that the Secretary-General appoint at least four nationals of each of the eighty-three member states to his administrative staff. An integrated service employing trained men in suitable positions is difficult to contrive under such conditions. Nevertheless, the administrative capacities of the United Nations Secretariat surpass the abilities of its political organs to assume responsibility in wider fields.

ECONOMIC AND SOCIAL COUNCIL (ECOSOC) Economic matters provide the most fruitful area for international cooperation, because the increasingly integrated nature of a world economy clashes with the diversity of political government. Under the Charter, the Economic and Social Council is empowered to "make or initiate studies and reports with respect to international economic, social, cultural, educational, health, and related matters and may make recommendations with respect to any such matters to the General Assembly, to the Members of the United Nations, and to the specialized agencies concerned" (Article 62). Composed of eighteen members elected for three-year terms by the General Assembly, the Council is not an independent organ ranking alongside the Security Council but is directly responsible for its actions to the Assembly. In fact, the Assembly through its Second Committee has tended to by-pass ECOSOC in dealing directly with many important economic transactions.[3]

As a coordinating body, ECOSOC has supervised the planning and operation of Technical and Financial Assistance programs to underdeveloped countries. In 1954, ECOSOC established the Commission on International Commodity Trade (CICT), a body designed to prepare "measures aiming at the maintenance of a just and equitable relationship between the prices of primary commodities and the prices of manufactured goods in international trade."[4] Stabilization of commodity prices constitutes one of the major problems separating the interests of technically developed cultures from the mass of mankind engaged in primary production. Though neither ECOSOC nor the General Assembly has been able to achieve an agreed solution, this thorny problem has at least been brought to the debating stage on a world level. Three international commodity agreements, covering sugar, tin, and wheat respectively, have been made under the auspices of the United Nations. Though the United States is opposed to commodity agreements in principle as harmful to free enterprise, it has taken an active part in the Wheat Agreement of 1956.

I.D.

Another major resultant of the operation of ECOSOC has been the creation of regional economic commissions to handle world economic problems on a regional basis. There are now four such bodies: the Economic Commissions for Europe (ECE), for Asia and the Far East (ECAFE), for Latin American (ECLA), and for Africa (ECA). These regional commissions are of particular value to underdeveloped nations that need to pool planning skills and resources in order to progress along technological lines. ECOSOC also serves as a coordinating body between the politically organized and slanted General Assembly and the separately organized specialized agencies that represent a previous tradition of international cooperation along nonpolitical lines.

TRUSTEESHIP COUNCIL Though perhaps one of the least powerful among the major organs of the United Nations, the Trusteeship Council represents a daring assumption of international responsibility. Article 75 of the Charter declares that "The United Nations shall establish under its authority an international trusteeship system for the administration and supervision of such territories as may be placed thereunder by subsequent individual agreements." In relation to its Trust territories, then, the United Nations is a sovereign body with direct responsibilities to the inhabitants of these areas. The Trusteeship Council does not, however, engage in direct administration in the name of the United Nations. For each Trust territory, a Trusteeship Agreement is entered into with an Administering Power, generally the former colonial sovereign or its conqueror in war. This arrangement represented a considerable advance over the *mandate* system introduced by the League of Nations for the international supervision of colonial possessions surrendered at the close of the first German war. The Permament Mandates Commission was little more than an advisory body with slight powers of intervention in the affairs of a mandated territory. The Trusteeship Council has been provided with effective control mechanisms: it is empowered to send Visiting Missions to the

Trust territories and to hear petitions from individuals or groups from within these areas. The most important Trust territory is Tanganyika in East Africa, with a population of approximately 8,500,000. The next in significance, if not in size, is Ruanda-Urundi in the Belgium Congo. An original hope that the Trust system would be adopted for almost all colonial possessions has faded beyond recall. However, though Trust territories represent a bare foothold for international supervision in the colonial world, they have been used to some extent as pilot plants to influence administration in the larger colonial areas of which they are an integral part. The international tail has aimed at wagging the colonial dog.

poor imagery

A major obstacle to vigorous action on the part of the Trusteeship Council lies in its composition: the Charter requires that it shall be equally divided between representatives of nations administering Trust territories and noncolonial Powers. Another limiting factor is the inability of the Trusteeship Council to accept direct administrative responsibility itself should the Administering Authority on the ground fail to carry out its instructions. As Administering Authorities are sovereign nations carrying out the task with their own resources in money and man power, they are subject to persuasion but not command. Despite these handicaps, the record of the Trusteeship Council in influencing the direction of colonial affairs, both within Trust territories and in the larger colonial field outside, has been impressive. The focusing of world attention through United Nations instrumentalities on the equivocal colonial relationship has resulted in substantial changes. Pressures engendered by the General Assembly, to whom the Trusteeship Council is responsible, have placed the Council in a difficult position during recent years. As the Assembly now contains a large number of nations recently freed from colonial tutelage, it is constantly pressing the case for independence for Trust territories. Administering Authorities are reluctant to commit themselves to definite time schedules, which would have repercussions on neighboring colonial possessions. Their privileged position on the Trusteeship Council permits them to use this body as a brake on rash Assembly action.

Under Chapter XI of the Charter, United Nations members administering non-self-governing territories that have not been transformed into Trust territories pledge themselves to "accept as a sacred trust the obligation to promote to the utmost . . . the well-being of the inhabitants of these territories." As a check on the fulfillment of this pledge, the colonial Powers are required to transmit regularly to the Secretary-General information relating to economic, social, and educational conditions in the territories for which they are responsible. Though interpretation of this requirement (Chapter XI [e]) is a subject of controversy between the colonial Powers and the Assembly, it has been employed to advance the conception that colonial administration is now an international rather than purely national matter. The border line between United Nations Trust territories and national colonies is being steadily eroded in terms of world standards. A Committee on Information created by the General Assembly reviews the annual returns and makes them the basis of admonitory Resolutions addressed to the colonial Powers. In general, the Assembly is extending its claim to act as supervisory authority over both the Trusteeship Council and the separate colonial nations.

THE SPECIALIZED AGENCIES It has been previously observed that the United Nations was constructed on a base of operating intergovernmental agreements and agencies. In so far as these were nonpolitical, their autonomous character was respected, though the Charter requested that they be brought into relationship with the United Nations through agreements entered into with the Economic and Social Council (Articles 57 and 63). A distinction may be drawn between agencies intended to operate on a permanent basis and special agencies created by the General Assembly to fulfill a specific and limited function. Generally speaking, the specialized agencies are concerned with that aspect of international organization devoted to the improvement of social conditions. They operate in areas where politics and power tactics are insufficient to deal with the realities of human needs and deprivations. Each of these agencies possesses its own organization, linked with, but not subordinated to, the other organs of the United Nations.

A brief notation of the specialized agencies may delineate their character, though it cannot describe their operational significance.

Know this page

The Universal Postal Union (UPU) established in 1874, served and still serves as the basis of world communication through postal services.

The International Labor Organization (ILO), created at the same time as, but independently of, the League of Nations, is the watchdog of labor standards throughout the world. It has sponsored many international conventions, on forced labor and other topics.

The Food and Agriculture Organization (FAO), a United Nations creation to deal in scientific and technical terms with world problems concerning nutrition and agricultural production.

World Health Organization (WHO), established in 1946 as a center of world research and operational activities in raising health standards.

United Nations Educational, Scientific and Cultural Organization (UNESCO), a spirited and controversial body established in 1946 to encourage collaboration in science, culture, and education for the furtherance of peace.

United Nations Children's Fund (UNICEF), originally established as a temporary agency to provide food and supplies to children in war-devastated Europe. The Agency was made permanent in 1953 with the task of looking after the interests of children and mothers in underdeveloped areas.

United Nations Relief and Works Agency for Palestine Refugees (UNRWA). This may be classified as a temporary agency resulting from the intervention of the United Nations in the Palestine question. It is charged with a measure of responsibility for the welfare of approximately 1,000,000 Arab refugees. The United States contributes nearly 70 per cent of a budget averaging less than $40 million.

The International Monetary Fund (IMF), established in 1945 primarily as an instrument to promote exchange stability.

The International Bank for Reconstruction and Development (IBRD), established in 1945 as an agency to promote capital loans for economic development.

The International Finance Corporation (IFC). This agency was created in 1956 to further economic development, particularly in underdeveloped areas, through coordination of the flow of private capital.

Technical Assistance Board (TAB), a coordinating body that now directs the Expanded Technical Assistance Program (ETAB), operated mainly through the Specialized Agencies and the United Nations Technical Assistance Administration.

The International Civil Aviation Organization (ICAO), an operating body for the enforcement of a 1947 Convention on the subject of international civil aviation.

The International Telecommunications Union (ITU), established in 1865 with the beginnings of telegraphy, this body services world telecommunication.

The World Meteorological Organization, a data-gathering and research organization established in 1878.

The International Atomic Energy Agency (IAEA), established in 1957 as the body responsible for international activities concerned with the peaceful uses of atomic energy.

Operation of the United Nations

In some ways it is unfortunate that the United Nations dropped its original designation as the United Nations Organization. Its present title suggests the existence of a coherent governing body—an unwarranted assumption in view of the realities of the situation. "A coordinating body for multifarious international and intergovernmental activities of widely varying degrees of importance" might be a more accurate description. Imposing governmental form on the structure of the United Nations might be likened to an attempt to sculpture a bowl of alphabet soup. Political government always rests on the existence of a governing body with decision-making powers. This factor, in the case of the United Nations, is supplied neither by the Security Council (under existing or foreseeable conditions), the General Assembly, nor the Secretariat. Nevertheless, to describe the United Nations as a mere debating society is equally misleading. The function of this world body is to extend the area of peaceful cooperation among both governments and peoples. Discussion is only one of the means employed in the fulfillment of this responsibility. Perhaps the most fruitful method has been the establishment of nonpolitical administrative machinery to further common international interests accepted as matters of mutual concern by agreement among the member states. The limitation of political government to "domestic concerns," and the slow substitution of functional, administrative institutions for the clash of sovereignties in the ordering of economic and social affairs that extend beyond the borders of any one nation, constitutes the principal justification for the continued existence of the United Nations.

Regional Arrangements

Nationalism, though it has swept through the modern world with the drive of a universal religion, satisfies only a portion of human needs. It cannot feed a people or provide the basic security needed to advance material welfare to the extent that technological discoveries have made possible. Consequently, a countermovement of economic and social integration across state boundaries may be detected, normally below the level of political organization, but increasingly breaking through traditional concepts of state sovereignty. The political state as the supreme bond of social unity is being challenged by the actualities of human progress. In any Western country, the individual citizen has acquired interests, economic and cultural, that require for their satisfaction the operation of institutional networks of a supranational nature. Governmental structures are under pressure to adapt themselves to this development. Because these needs are practical and immediate, they cannot await universal solutions but tend to resolve themselves on a regional level—one step removed from the independent nation–state.

European history since 1945 illustrates the growing conflict between traditional concepts of the independent nation–state and the drive toward economic union. Professor Zurcher concludes his study on *The Struggle to Unite Europe: 1940–1958* in the following terms:

In Europe, at least, the finger of time may well write finis to the isolated state system that comes down from the eighteenth century. It has become increasingly clear to the leadership of Western Europe that such a system cannot provide the degree of integration that will ensure the social and material values that contemporary political organization is expected to achieve and foster. Indeed it has become apparent that the national states themselves cannot survive or the cultural values of national groups be safeguarded unless some broader form of political integration than that provided by nationalism eventually emerges. The decade since the end of World War II has underscored this conclusion and brought conviction to more than one outstanding European statesman and moral leader. The ancient framework of the national state system may and doubtless will persist indefinitely without much overt change, but its internal decay, brought about by its failure to secure the moral and material aspirations of the rank and file, will become increasingly apparent as time moves on. What will supplant that system, moreover, is clear. The European Movement has supplied or will supply the alternative in Europe. The future of political organization in Western Europe lies with the concept of regional and continental integration fostered by the movement.[5]

Besides the Council for Europe, the Schuman Community for Coal and Steel, and other economic bodies described in Chapter 18, the European movement has envisaged formation of a political community that would approach true federation in the American sense. An important preliminary step toward this objective, the establishment of a European Defense Community, was arrested by a hostile vote in the French National Assembly in 1954. A weaker form of military cooperation, known as the Western European Union, was accepted in 1955, but it lacked a federal character. The impulse towards closer political association is stalled, at least for the time being, principally through the uncertainty of the French people as to their true future. Endangered by an internal military threat to democratic institutions, and torn between its role as exponent of European culture and its heritage as an imperial African Power, France stands at a crossroads hesitating between choices that may determine the future of Europe as well as her own.

INTERNATIONAL COMMISSIONS A minor form of regional cooperation is exemplified by agreements entered into by major Powers for joint action in areas where they possess scattered dependencies. The Caribbean Commission was established in 1946 by Britain, France, and The Netherlands, and officially joined by the United States in 1948. The purpose of this body is to coordinate economic and social planning in the regions for which the constituent Powers bear responsibility. A small permanent staff was formed and conferences are held at intervals.

In 1947 a similar body with stronger emphasis on technical and scientific research was formed in the South Pacific area. Its constituent members are Britain, France, The Netherlands, Australia, New Zealand, and the United States.

ORGANIZATION OF AMERICAN STATES The relationship of the United States to the Latin American Republics has varied between indifference and intervention. True regional cooperation has been hindered by inescapable differences in cultural outlook, economic conditions, and military power. With Canada remaining aloof, it is questionable whether even a true geographical area is involved. However, since the enunciation of the Monroe Doctrine in 1823, the United States has accepted limited responsibility for the security of this area. Unilateral responsibility became increasingly difficult in face of Latin American resentment, and the establishment of a multinational organization to safeguard regional security became an objective of United States foreign policy. The Bogotá Conference of 1948 gave definitive form to the Organization of American States. Inter-American Conferences, held every five years and attended by all the constituent nations, serve as the supreme representative organ of the Organization. A permanent body, the Council of the Organization, acts to some degree as an executive organ and a provisional instrument of consultation. The Council, with headquarters in Washington, is composed of one representative from each member state (normally the country's Ambassador to the United States). However, a more potent instrument is provided in the Meeting of Consultation of Ministers of Foreign Affairs. This body may be summoned to deal with any pressing situation at the request of any member, confirmed by a majority of the Council of the Organization. In terms of the diplomatic machinery involved, the Organization of American States may be accounted a successful experiment in regional cooperation.

On the more fundamental level of economic and social cooperation, success is not so apparent. The Organization provides for three organs of the Council: the Inter-American Economic and Social Council, the Inter-American Council of Jurists, and the

Inter-American Cultural Council, together with a General Secretariat of the Organization, in which is embodied the former Pan American Union. These bodies have not as yet progressed above the level of technical committees. At the root of the problem lies the overwhelming economic preponderance of the United States. Any action for the furtherance of the economic development of the area would almost certainly have to be financed from and by the United States. With all member states possessing a single and equal vote, the United States is naturally reluctant to commit her funds to plans over which she could exercise little control.

The British Commonwealth

Though the unique structure of the British Commonwealth does not constitute a regional pattern—its component members are the United Kingdom, Canada, Australia, New Zealand, South Africa, India, Pakistan, Ceylon, Ghana, and, awaiting membership in 1960, Nigeria—it represents an approach to intergovernmental cooperation differing from the contractual obligations of the United Nations. A New Zealand Prime Minister once described the Commonwealth ties as "independence with something added." The additional factor includes exchange of views, information, and even administrative machinery below the policy-making level, in a manner that permits individual citizens of each Commonwealth country to share certain governmental organizations in common. Thus, Commonwealth lands with comparable social-security arrangements, the United Kingdom, Australia, and New Zealand, have reciprocal agreements permitting citizens who migrate from one country to another to carry with them portions of their social-security protection.

An assumption of basic friendliness and common interests, founded in part on institutional development along historically similar lines, permits an interlocking of governmental machinery at all levels. Accordingly, close liaison is maintained in matters of defense, education, and scientific research through exchange of facilities. Perhaps the most conspicuous area of cooperation is in the economic field. About half the external trade of Commonwealth countries (representing one third the total of world trade) is conducted among members or within the colonial empire for which they are responsible. A system of *imperial preference* provides for tariff concessions within the Commonwealth group. A more important bond is the *sterling area,* to which all Commonwealth lands with the exception of Canada belong. The association is not compulsory but arises through a pattern of trade, making the use of sterling as an international currency desirable. Its consequences include the maintenance of central reserves in London and close intergovernmental discussions on non-sterling expenditures. A Commonwealth Economic Conference in 1952 described the character and degree of economic cooperation in the following terms:

> The Conference agreed that Commonwealth countries would work together to achieve certain broad objectives. They have no intention of seeking the creation of a discriminatory economic bloc; rather their objective is, by strengthening themselves, to benefit the world economy generally. Accordingly, the following principles were agreed upon as governing the approach to the whole range of subjects under discussion:
>
> (a) Internal economic policies designed to curb inflation and rises in the cost of living should be steadily followed.
>
> (b) Sound economic development should be encouraged with the object of increasing productive strength and competitive power, providing employment and raising standards of life.
>
> (c) A multilateral trade and payments system should be extended over the widest possible area.
>
> The application of these principles will require individual action by Commonwealth Governments, cooperation among them and international action with other trading nations and existing international organizations. . . .
>
> The Conference therefore agreed to seek the cooperation of other countries in a plan to create the conditions for expanding world production and trade. The aim is to secure international agreement on the adoption of policies, by creditor and debtor countries, which will restore balance in the world economy on the lines of "Trade not Aid" and will, by progressive stages and within reasonable time, create an effective multilateral trade and payments system covering the widest possible area. . . .

One of the most effective consequences of Commonwealth cooperation has been the Colombo Plan for Cooperative Economic Development in South and South-East Asia. Under this Plan, originating at a Commonwealth Foreign Ministers Conference in 1950, financial and technical assistance is given for the development of Commonwealth and other countries in South and Southeast Asia. The United States associated itself as a donor nation, and practically all non-Communist lands in the area are now members in the Plan. Besides facilitating a pooling of governmental credit for development purposes, the Plan includes a Technical Cooperation Scheme under which experts and instructors are sent to the member countries in the Colombo Plan area and equipment required for technical research is supplied.

The organizational structure of the Commonwealth serves to facilitate communication and voluntary cooperation among independent states. As there is no central governing body, it is in no sense a federation nor does it impose on its members rigid obligations of the kind embodied in the Charter of the United Nations. As a voluntaristic institution, it is capable of operating with a minimum of legally conceived organization. A vague sense of entity is supplied by the designation of the reigning British monarch, the Queen, as Head of the Commonwealth. Basically, this is a courtesy title carrying with it no executive functions.

The principal organs of the Commonwealth are informal conferences, of which the Commonwealth Prime Ministers Conference, held every few years, is the most important. Other conferences held since 1945 include Finance Ministers, Defense Ministers, Supply Ministers, Foreign Ministers, Economic Conferences, and one on Nationality and Citizenship. These conferences are informal in the sense that they do not result in resolutions binding on the governments represented; they are primarily consultative gatherings. On the administrative level, the United Kingdom Commonwealth Relations Office serves as a channel for mutual consultation and exchange of information. Each Commonwealth nation is represented in the capital of other members of the Commonwealth by a High Commissioner of ambassadorial rank. A particularly effective administrative device is exchange of views on the departmental level without the intervention of political bodies. A traveler in the

Australian deserts or through the Arctic wastes of Canada is more than likely to encounter the rolled umbrella and bowler hat of the ubiquitous British Treasury official. Beneath the governmental level extends a network of semiofficial and unofficial consultative bodies mentioned in Chapter 2.

As a model of international cooperation, the British Commonwealth would be difficult to imitate. Its origins are rooted in historical events that brought many diverse peoples and lands under common institutional patterns. One lesson, however, is conveyed by its continued existence: Peoples and cultures may enjoy independence without closing the doors on practical cooperation with other organized nation–states. Given mutual trust, institutional machinery evolves almost of its own accord to handle areas of common interest.

Notes

[1] For a brief review of the development of United Nations action see Eichelberger, Clark, "Ten Years of the United Nations," *Annual Review of United Nations Affairs, 1955–1956,* Eagleton, Clyde, and Swift, Richard N. (eds.), New York: New York University Press, 1957, pp. 184-207.

[2] For an account of the Secretariat in action see Chamberlin, Waldo, "Administrative Matters," *Annual Review of United Nations Affairs 1955–1956,* Eagleton, Clyde, and Swift, Richard N. (eds.), *op. cit.,* pp. 159-183.

[3] *Cf.* Trager, Frank N., "Economic Affairs," *Annual Review of United Nations Affairs 1955–1956,* Eagleton, Clyde, and Swift, Richard N. (eds.), *op. cit.,* pp. 35-68.

[4] ECOSOC Resolution 512 A (XVII) April 30, 1954.

[5] Zurcher, Arnold J., *The Struggle to Unite Europe: 1940–1958,* New York: New York University Press, 1958, pp. 208 and 209.

Supplementary Readings

Chamberlin, Waldo, *A Chronology of United Nations Affairs,* New York: Oceana, 1959.

Deutsch, Karl W., *Political Community at the International Level: Problems of Definition and Measurement,* New York: Random House, 1954.

Duggan, Laurence, *The Americas: The Search for Hemisphere Security,* New York: Holt, 1949.

Feller, Abraham H., *United Nations and World Community,* Boston: Little, Brown, 1952.

Goodrich, Leland M., and Simons, Anne P., *The United Nations and the Maintenance of International Peace and Security,* Washington: Brookings, 1955.

Harvey, H. J., *Consultation and Co-operation in the Commonwealth,* New York: Oxford, 1952.

Jennings, Sir Ivor, *The British Commonwealth of Nations,* London: Hutchinson, 1948.

Mangone, Gerard, *A Short History of International Organization,* New York: McGraw-Hill, 1954.

Masters, Ruth D., et al., *Handbook of International Organizations in the Americas,* Washington: Carnegie Endowment for International Peace, Columbia University Press, 1945.

Underhill, Frank H., *The British Commonwealth: An Experiment in Co-operation among Nations,* Durham: Duke University Press, 1956.

Vandenbosch, Amry, and Hogan, Willard N., *The United Nations; Background, Organization, Functions, Activities,* New York: McGraw-Hill, 1952.

Zurcher, Arnold J., *The Struggle to Unite Europe 1940–1958,* New York: New York University Press, 1958.

Chapter 20

Relations with Underdeveloped Peoples

Throughout history, peoples have encountered one another on the cultural level of similarity or of difference. Institutional development of international relations, as discussed in preceding chapters, has occurred principally through contacts among communities in like stages of technological growth and social organization. Where dissimilar cultures have clashed, imperialism has constituted the principal alternative to war.

Imperialism may be distinguished from international relations because it denies to one of the parties the integrity of nationhood. The motivation behind imperialism is the expansion of a well-organized state at the expense of other peoples. There are two aspects of such expansion: one, the concept of assimilation, illustrated in modern times by the French *mission civilisatrice;* the other, the fact of exploitation of the physical and labor resources of a materially backward region in terms of the economic pattern of the imperial Power. In practice, assimilation and exploitation are linked together; the emphasis is determined by the form of self-justification adopted by the expanding culture. Thus, the British colonial empire has been, and still is, an enterprise using British law and order to establish advantageous economic relations with less advanced peoples. Though the final objective is political independence for the colonies, such freedom is posited on the creation of economic and social similarities that will bind the former colonies into a trading complex with their imperial benefactor.[1]

By the seventeenth century, a cleavage in terms of material

power had appeared between peoples dwelling in countries with a temperate climate and the rest of the world's inhabitants in tropical and subtropical lands. Asia, Africa, Central and South America, Caribbean and Pacific islands, became accessible to European intruders, possessed of aggressive strength out of all proportion to their numbers—and, one might add, their moral responsibility. In these early days, an obligation to spread the Christian religion provided uncertain justification for a practical pursuit of slaves, gold, ivory, and spices. Toward the end of the eighteenth century, an export trade in slaves from West Africa was conducted at the rate of about 100,000 a year. Though the ivory and spice trades were not, in their origins, harmful, they paved the way for later penetrations of more serious nature. The quest for gold created a Spanish empire in America based on brutality and degradation. Transportation played a primary role in the expansion of European culture. Ships, particularly the full-rigged sailing vessel, gave Western man an advantage in mobility. This superiority over the Arab dhow and other rivals was employed, in the first place, by nonpolitical groupings—merchant adventurers, slave traders, buccaneers—to impose their will on the trade routes of the world. At least the initial harm done to other peoples by Western expansion arose through the absence of governmental control over the wide-roving freebooters. Responsibility on the part of the political state for imperial expansion came later with the advent of mechanical industry and the development of bulk transport. Acceptance of political responsibility was entered into reluctantly and only when the misbehavior of individuals or trading groups had offended Western standards of morality or imperiled trade relations with other cultural groups. Thus, the British East India Company, having established itself in a trading station in 1641, was permitted to become political ruler of a vast continent. Though the British government established progressive control over this majestic trading corporation both at home and in India, it was not until 1858 that the Company was formally dissolved and the British Crown became the official ruler of India with Victoria's assumption of the title Empress of India.

Control over contacts of private groupings with peoples of dissimilar culture, then, became a governmental matter more by default or necessity than through conscious intention. Throughout the nineteenth century, the economic dog ran well ahead of its political master in establishing European influence among Asian and African peoples. A pattern of colonialism gradually integrated the forceful methods of the Western trader and settler in tropical lands into the legal and political structures of Western civilization. The forerunners of the industrial revolution—Britain, France, The Netherlands—carried the main burden of empire building. They acted, however, to some extent as agents for a unified industrial culture founded on the maintenance of world trading routes and the exploitation of physical resources everywhere, principally to advance living standards for Western peoples. In consequence, a dominant technological culture has appeared in the world dependent for its continuance on a delicate balance of relations between materially advanced peoples occupying a minor portion of the earth's surface and the bulk of mankind dwelling among partially developed resources. This industrial civilization is neither politically nor socially united—Communism and capitalism oppose each other at every turn; therefore, the path of its future survival and development is involved in bitter internal struggle.

The Present Situation

Involvement of government, primarily an instrument of the nation-state, in the settling of relations between peoples presents novel and difficult problems. Before government can act effectively, its actions must be related to its basic functions, in this case, the maintenance of the military and economic security of its own people. Realization that internal security has become dependent on equitable relations with underdeveloped peoples is an essential prerequisite to policy formation on the part of popularly controlled governments. In this connection, a statement by President Eisenhower on the eve of his departure to consult with European heads of government in the summer of 1959 may be quoted.

> The trip has several purposes. . . . To suggest to each of the several Heads of Government that we, together, explore ways and means in which our Governments may equitably and effectively cooperate in helping solve one of the most pressing problems of our time, that of

assisting to advance the cultural, health and living standards of the almost two billion people in the world who are citizens of the newly developing or underdeveloped countries. [The President's formal statement ended at this point, but he was reported as continuing extempore.] With respect to this last purpose, I want to say that this today, if not merely one of the most pressing problems, could easily be the most. Two billion people are going to find some way of expressing their convictions that they do not have to live in conditions that are completely unsatisfactory by any minimum standard that we set up for humans; and unless the civilized world, not just ourselves, but the civilized world is willing and ready to share in the burdens of making it possible for these people to achieve progress in this area, this world is going to have tough going.[2]

President Eisenhower's concern reflects the gravity of the problem raised for national governments by a world situation over which they as individual states can exercise little control. Great economic movements—a population explosion occurring in regions least able to feed extra mouths or employ additional hands, advances in physical communication destructive of old patterns of consumption and production—threaten the political and social world balance on which Western civilization hitherto rested. The immediate danger, of course, arises from Communist efforts to displace Western nations from their established positions in underdeveloped countries. Though the immediate consequences of Communist successes in this field might be disastrous to the economic and political structures of the West, Russia herself as an advanced technological culture cannot escape the deeper implications of the present division of the world between the haves and the have-nots. Political institutions lie at the heart of the problem; with the aid of modern technology they have provided means for the organization of the discontent induced by conscious poverty. Politics may now hit back at seemingly impersonal economic laws. Responsibility for deprivation and misery can no longer, as in the historical past, be confined to local economic factors, but has been raised to the level of world organization, involving prosperous peoples and the use to which they put their resources. For the sake of illustration, immigration laws may be cited as one of the methods used to protect comparative economic abundance from being overrun by hungry hordes from outside. Until modern transportation by land, air, and sea was developed to its present extent, there was slight opportunity for impoverished peoples to better their conditions by migrating to more highly developed areas. Now, it is at least physically possible that tides of distressed people could pour into the industrial centers of Europe and North America, producing social chaos and a collapse of living standards. Australia, set within easy access of the teeming millions of India, Japan, and China, preserves its particular character through rigid application of a "white Australia" immigration policy. Political power and not economic law enforces immigration restrictions, and to that extent enjoyment by Western peoples of their comparative advantages is based on their political strength as against the rest of the world.

It is no longer practicable to separate economic control from the political base on which it rests. Thus the economic structure of Indonesia was established by the Dutch over a period of centuries in a manner that channeled substantial profits to the Dutch entrepreneur. Rebellion and independence literally dispossessed the Dutch, placing both direction of the economy and its profits in the hands of indigenous politicians. Another example is the seizure of the Suez Canal by the government of Egypt. It is apparent that successful political organization can be used not only to protect the internal standards of prosperous lands, but also to seize the established investments abroad of Western capital and to deny access to resources vital to the development of industrial civilization. Economic blackmail remains a legitimate and increasingly effective weapon of national governments. With politics threatening to dissolve the world economic order in anarchy, national governments, singly or in conjunction, must seek to impose political solutions on problems that arise through disparities in national or regional wealth.

The nature of a political solution to the conflict between technologically developed and underdeveloped peoples may be divided conveniently into three parts. First, there is the traditional colonial answer, which, though now fading from the world scene, has left behind it a heritage that must be taken into account in practical planning. Secondly, there is the basically American concept of economic assistance, shorn of political ties but conditioned on observance of Western capitalist standards; contemporary with this is a rival Communist offer of technical aid at the cost of ideological assimilation. Thirdly, there is the beginning—at present a weak beginning—of cooperative international action through the United Nations or regional bodies such as the European Common Market or the Organization of American States.

The Colonial Heritage

Colonialism, in the present-day use of the term, describes the political control of an underdeveloped people whose economic and social affairs are directed by a dominant Power. Areas subject to colonialism are rapidly shrinking both in size and importance. New Guinea in the Indian Ocean and portions of Central and Eastern Africa remain the stronghold of the colonial pattern.[3] In the final communiqué of the Asian-African Conference at Bandung in 1955, the following denunciation of colonialism was proclaimed by the twenty-four attending nations.

> The Conference is agreed:
>
> (a) in declaring that colonialism in all its manifestations is an evil which should speedily be brought to an end;
>
> (b) in affirming that the subjection of peoples to alien subjugation, domination, and exploitation constitutes a denial of fundamental human rights, is contrary to the Charter of the United Nations, and is an impediment to the promotion of world peace and cooperation;
>
> (c) in declaring its support of the cause of freedom and independence for all such people, and
>
> (d) in calling upon the powers concerned to grant freedom and independence to such peoples.[4]

This position probably represents a majority view in the United Nations at the present time. It does not, however, provide immediate, practical solutions to the problem of bringing primitive tribal societies into profitable contact with technological civilization. Whether or not the European empires of the past injured more than they benefited the peoples they controlled is a question for history to decide. In any case, a pattern of contact was established which must run its course, irreversible through moral fiat. Tutelage of such primitive peoples as inhabit New Guinea through political rule by their advanced neighbors appears inevitable. The undeveloped physical resources of these areas cannot be left neglected under conditions of modern communication. In the absence of government responsibility, the inhabitants would be cruelly victimized by private adventurers armed with the weapons of modern technology. However, the true problem of modern colonialism centers in these areas, principally in Africa, where a minority of European stock has established itself as permanent residents and looks to the home government to help it perpetuate its dominance over the indigenous majority. Algeria in North Africa and the Federation of the Rhodesias and Nyasaland in southern Africa constitute the outstanding examples of settler colonies. In some ways they may be regarded as vestigial exceptions to a general liquidation of the colonial system.

Since 1945, the British colonial empire has resolved itself rapidly in favor of the political independence of its component parts. Starting with the grant of independence to India and Pakistan in 1947, Burma, Ceylon, Ghana, Malaya, Singapore, and Nigeria were freed from political control. A clear intention to accord similar freedom to other regions as soon as the inhabitants proved themselves capable of stable self-government was expressed by the metropolitan government. White settler colonies in Africa, with their demands for the establishment of guarantees for the continuance of white supremacy before losing the protection of the mother country, constitute the remaining unsolved problem in the liquidation of the colonial empire.

France, under the inspiration of de Gaulle, transformed her empire by the establishment of the French Community. Now, in the great regions of West and Equatorial Africa formerly under French rule, political control lies unequivocally in the hands of the indigenous peoples. In North Africa, Tunis and Morocco regained their independence, and only Algeria remains as a bastion of colonial rule. There, the presence of a million Europeans engenders a harsh conflict of loyalties. Portugal, in her unabated control over the African provinces of Mozambique and Angola, remains the most stubborn exponent of the colonial principle among European nations. By assimilating her African regions as provinces of European Portugal (though denying Portuguese citizenship to the bulk of the inhabitants), Portugal has evaded supervision of her colonial rule by international agencies such as the United Nations. The Portuguese state itself, however, through its denial of representative forms of government, constitutes a weak anomaly in the Western system of powers. Its future development will probably rest on events and policies beyond its internal power to control. Soviet Russia has continued the colonial expansion in central Asia inaugurated by its tsarist predecessor. Revolutionary Communism has proved more ruthless than the imperial regime in the subjugation of the Central Asian peoples. Absolute assimilation to Communist economic and social policies at any cost to freedom was the policy conceived and enforced by Stalin. Communist China apparently is pursuing the same policy in relation to Tibet and other bordering regions.

Though European colonialism is now in varying stages of dissolution, the pattern it has established remains the basis of relations between technologically advanced cultures and underdeveloped peoples. Political dominance during the nineteenth and early part of the twentieth centuries created discontinuities in traditional indigenous cultures, forcing them to accept values that had been evolved in the Western process of industrialization. There appears to be no turning back from this accelerating movement toward similarity in material standards of living. However, the resources of the lands in which two thirds of the world's peoples dwell are unequal, in their present stage of exploitation, to the task of supporting mass standards of well-being equivalent to those enjoyed in the West. Consequently, the advancement of the greater part of mankind must be carried out on credit, with the only possible creditors being the industrially established nations. Old-fashioned colonialism was one method of ensuring that an underdeveloped area would be credit-worthy—it was somewhat similar to putting a bailiff on the premises. Though such harsh means are no longer tolerable, the great outflow of capital from Europe into colonial lands was a major factor in the transformation of the modern world. Thus, in 1957–58, Britain contributed over a billion dollars in public funds to its colonial territories, and France and Belgium made equivalent grants. Private capital also sheltered itself under the colonial umbrella, confident that many of its risks would be underwritten by political power. The need for long-term investment capital and high-priced technical skill has not lessened with the abandonment of colonial rule. However, the conditions under which such needs may be satisfied by Western nations have changed radically, with a consequent recasting of economic relations.

Another consequence of the colonial pattern was the establishment of a belief or delusion in the reality of "white supremacy." This has been harmful to the manners and morals of Western peoples in general and disastrous to the outlook of the awakening nations of Asia and Africa. Time will probably heal wounds inflicted in cultural pride and dignity, but an interim period of suspicion and even dislike appears an inescapable part of the colonial heritage. World Communism, which has effectively avoided racist prejudices, finds this its most useful weapon in separating Western nations from their former clients among underdeveloped peoples. However, neither Soviet Russia nor Communist China has succeeded in establishing a credible pattern of tolerance in ideological matters outside racial characteristics.

Though colonialism was guilty of aggravating barriers of race and culture, it served to strengthen institutional ties of lasting moment between Western civilization and the rest of the world. Principles of representative government have become known to Asiatic and African peoples through direct experience under colonial rule. Educational systems and modern organizations of industry and commerce have been transplanted into the social systems of peoples who might not have been able to sustain them through their own cultural development for many generations. Common languages have been introduced, enabling tribal groups to gain national solidarity and communicate with the industrially organized portions of the world. The discoveries of medical science and the moral discipline of the Christian religion have been propagated among primitive peoples. In general, colonial rule supplemented the technical leap forward in physical communications which has compelled the world's peoples into closer contact with one another. The forced growth of nationalism as a political reaction to colonial subjection is itself a consequence of the rapid

Westernization of the inhabited regions of the globe. With a few outstanding exceptions, colonialism is no longer an issue dividing the world's peoples. However, the central problem of devising equitable methods of contact between industrialized and underdeveloped regions remains unsolved by the demise of colonialism. Freedom that carries with it the penalty of hunger in the midst of apparent plenty will not long satisfy more than half the world's population.

Economic and Technical Assistance

Though the principle of economic and technical assistance to underdeveloped countries has now received world-wide acceptance, the United States is entitled to rank as its principal protagonist. For a brief period in its history, the United States appeared to have fallen into a European pattern of overseas expansion. The doctrine of Manifest Destiny beckoned towards colonial adventures in the Pacific and the Caribbean. In 1898, Hawaii was annexed and the Philippine Islands, Puerto Rico, and Cuba were prizes of victory in the Spanish-American War. However, circumstances and the American character combined to throttle colonial ambitions. There was no pressing economic need, as in the case of Britain and France, to sustain the burden of overseas rule, and the libertarian American spirit found the practice of oppressive government irksome. From the start, improvement of material economic and social conditions in Pacific and Caribbean lands challenged American enterprise, particularly in terms of sanitation, road building, and educational facilities.

When the Philippines were freed from Japanese occupation, their independence was proclaimed on July 4, 1946. In the same year, Congress passed the Philippine Rehabilitation Act, granting $620,000,000 for repair of war damage. The record in Puerto Rico is even more impressive. After four hundred years of Spanish colonialism, Puerto Rico was a land of poverty-ridden stagnation. In 1952, Puerto Rico, transformed into the land with the highest per capita income in the Caribbean and the second highest in Central America, was granted the status of Commonwealth within the American Union, a constitutional position that accorded the island full self-government except in matters of external affairs, defense, and some questions of foreign trade and general taxation. From the human point of view, this has meant that a life expectancy of forty-six years has been altered to one of sixty-eight years within a few decades. This achievement has been accomplished through the opportunities offered to a hard-working and well-disciplined community by generous grants of economic and technical assistance from continental America. Cooperation on all levels in the establishment of private industry as well as technical aid from departments of the United States government has turned Puerto Rico into a show place of what an underdeveloped country can accomplish in the rapid improvement of living standards.

American experience in providing economic and technical assistance to impoverished lands was translated into a doctrine of world-wide application by President Truman in his inaugural address in January 1949:

> We must embark on a bold new program for making the benefits of our scientific advances and industrial progress available for the improvement and growth of underdeveloped areas. . . . We should make available to peace-loving peoples the benefits of our store of technical knowledge in order to help them realize their aspirations for a better life. And, in cooperation with other nations, we should foster capital investment in areas needing development. Our aim should be to help the free peoples of the world, through their own efforts, to produce more food, more clothing, more materials for housing, and more mechanical power to lighten their burdens.

This solemn acceptance of American responsibility for bridging the gap between the privileged and underprivileged peoples of the world has never been retracted, though methods employed have varied from the idealistic Point Four Program to the narrower limits of Mutual Security projects. Foreign aid, even when linked to long-term security considerations, must gain acceptance on the taxpayers and consumers level as a reasonable burden on the national income. Despite hesitations and misgivings, inevitable to a government under popular control, the United States has proved itself willing during the last decade to contribute generously to underdeveloped peoples without demanding any corresponding right of political control. In the years 1956–58, public capital extended to underdeveloped areas outside Europe amounted to approximately $8.5 billion. Of this total sum, the United States supplied $5.2 billion, the International Bank for Reconstruction and Development $925 million, and Britain and France the bulk of the remainder.[5] The flow of private capital to underdeveloped areas during the same period amounted to $5.9 billion, of which the United States supplied $3.4 billion. As a permanent pattern of relations with underdeveloped areas, the unilateral form of assistance proffered by the United States has certain obvious defects. Because the recipients undertake no obligations directly related to the interests of the United States, it is hard to justify to the American taxpayer the heavy costs to the public Treasury. Consequently, a tendency arises to confine grants to uses related to mutual defense. Such activities contribute little to the economic growth of underdeveloped areas and lay the United States open to the charge of practicing a form of military colonialism.

Technical assistance, or the loan of technical skills to promote development, is on the surface a less costly and more desirable form of mutual aid. In India and elsewhere, American agricultural and other experts have performed valiant feats benefiting indigenous culture and winning valuable good will for the American cause. Again, in a world dominated by nationalistic politics, exchange of technical skills is fraught with practical difficulties. Either the expert finds himself subordinated to local political considerations which may misuse his talents, or, if he exerts an independence needed for the proper fulfillment of his task, he is suspected of acting as agent for the powerful nation which contributed his services. It is clear to American eyes that Soviet technicians in underdeveloped lands are primarily concerned with advancing the interests of Communism. Consequently, similar suspicions concerning capitalist motivations on the part of American experts may be anticipated among uncommitted peoples.

The International Approach

A situation under which one third of the world's population controls approximately 85 per cent of the world's income, leaving 15 per cent to satisfy the needs of the remaining two thirds, is of obvious concern to international bodies. Economic disparities of this fundamental nature must be taken into account in the establishment of a world order by political means. Some of the methods through which the United Nations has attempted to assume responsibility for this problem have been described in previous chapters. The International Bank for Reconstruction and Development, the International Finance Corporation, and the Expanded Technical Assistance Program provide a working framework which might support the more ambitious concept of a Special United Nations Fund for Economic Development. However, the shifting of the onus for economic development from the shoulders of a few industrialized nations to a world organization is a great deal more than a question of the setting up of appropriate machinery. The resources for development, in capital and technical skills, must still be drawn from prosperous and technologically advanced communities. As these constitute a small minority in the family of nations, it is difficult for them to pool their resources under the leadership of an organization in which the have-not nations possess a voting majority. Governments founded on representative principles lack effective power to commit their taxpayers' funds in such a fashion. Though the United Nations may lead in elucidating problems and pioneering methods in relation to the economic development of impoverished countries, the prospect of its becoming the effective center of action in this respect appears utopian.

Projects for cooperative international action on a regional, rather than a world-wide, basis are, perhaps, of greater promise. Thus, the Colombo Plan, previously described, has had a limited success in enlisting assistance from major industrial nations toward the improvement of economic conditions in South and Southeast Asia. The Plan has permitted the client nations to control their own development projects and the contributing Powers to determine the direction and extent of their aid. A less clearly organized method of cooperative capitalization is indicated for underdeveloped territories under the aegis of members of the European Common Market. France and Belgium have made it known that their partners in the Common Market, West Germany in particular, will be given opportunities to share on equal terms in joint developmental enterprises in overseas areas attached to them by political ties. Though this represents a considerable advance on national exploitation of colonial areas, control over development appears too heavily weighted in favor of the industrialized purveyors of capital and technical skills. Nationalist sentiment in newly liberated regions may prompt the fear that economic colonialism is replacing political colonialism. The Organization of American States constitutes another potential instrumentality for cooperative economic development. However, the United States would have to provide a major share of the resources to be employed in stimulating such development. To reconcile this obligation with the voting equality of all states in the Organization offers insuperable difficulties to effective planning.

The Clash of Ideologies

For many centuries, the establishment of equitable relations between a civilization based on technology and the bulk of mankind practicing an agrarian economy has been hindered by the national rivalries of the industrialized Powers. Lenin seized on this factor to describe imperialism as the final stage of monopoly capitalism, condemning the capitalist world to destruction by internecine warfare and less advanced peoples to ruthless exploitation. These prophecies have been disproved by events: nationalistic imperialism by Western nations no longer constitutes a threat to peace, nor have underdeveloped nations become the helpless victims of capitalist exploitation. However, the Communist thesis has been maintained and developed as an instrument of Soviet aggrandizement. Technological progress for two thirds of the world's inhabitants, according to the Communist creed, is conditioned on renunciation of Western economic patterns and acceptance of a Marxist ideology. This division of purpose between major sections of industrial civilization aggravates the difficulties of bringing the material benefits of technological culture to the majority of mankind.

Underdeveloped peoples are now presented with mutually contradictory paths to advancement, enticing them to play off one system against the other for immediate gains. Continuity of planning or effective pooling of capital and technical skills to lessen the gap between national standards of living is hampered severely. The objective of promoting continuous material advancement through efficient use of local resources becomes subordinated to the question of the adoption of one social and economic system in preference to its rival. A form of ideological imperialism threatens to fill the vacuum left by the withering away of national imperialism. External aid, conditioned on the sacrifice of essential freedoms of social choice, revives the ancient dilemma of materially weak peoples in face of highly organized economic and military power.

Perhaps more important is the cleavage wrought in an essentially unitary industrial culture by divergent views concerning its relations with the agrarian portion of mankind. The Communist heresy (properly so called because it is a recent divagation from historical, economic, and social patterns) has arrested any direct, cooperative attack on the major problem of mankind—the raising of living standards throughout the world. In place of the main problem, a question of methodology is raised as a barrier to action. By demanding acceptance of Communist ideology as the price of material progress, the Soviet nations have thrown the practical problems of economic development into an arena of conflict between freedom and cultural tyranny. Accordingly, the primary effort of Western civilization is diverted from the spread of economic goods to a defense of its own traditions and freedom.

This defense takes two forms, both harmful to the prosperity of the bulk of mankind. First, a large proportion of the surplus wealth that might be employed by Western nations in the development of backward economic regions is diverted into a competition in armaments with Soviet Powers. Secondly, relations between Western nations and underdeveloped areas are confused by the need to advocate Western standards and patterns as against aggressive Communist infiltration. The continuity of indigenous culture is distorted in its natural development by pressure to accept Western molds that may safeguard it against the lures of Communist ideology.

Ideological lines between Western and Communist nations have hardened to such an extent that peaceful conversion from one camp to another is no longer seriously entertained, except in the case of a few border states. The alternative of forceful conversion under conditions of atomic warfare bears a terrifying cost. Accordingly, the lines of conflict, economic, ideological and even military, of the world's great Powers are tending to center in the underdeveloped regions. Decisive resources and overwhelming man power are at stake. Though this may hasten the integration of the world's economy, it carries with it the menace of a new imperialism based on the ruthless application of a dogmatic ideology. Political institutions on the level of national governments remain the principal instrumentalities through which this situation must be met. The improvement of government, and above all the spread and intensification of systems of representation from the domestic to the international level, constitutes the best hope for the survival of mankind.

Notes

[1] *Cf.* Adam, Thomas R., *Modern Colonialism: Institutions and Policies,* Studies in Political Science, New York: Random House, 1955, pp. 6-9.

[2] *The New York Times,* August 26, 1959.

[3] *Cf.* Adam, Thomas R., *Government and Politics in Africa, South of the Sahara,* New York: Random House, 1959.

[4] Kahin, G. M., *The Asian-African Conference,* Ithaca: Cornell University Press, 1956, p. 81.

[5] These and following figures from *The New York Times,* September 6, 1959.

Supplementary Readings

Adam, Thomas R., *Government and Politics in Africa South of the Sahara,* New York: Random House, 1959.

———, *Modern Colonialism: Institutions and Policies,* New York: Random House, 1955.

Bingham, Jonathan B., *Shirt-Sleeve Diplomacy: Point 4 in Action,* New York: John Day, 1954.

Burns, Sir Alan, *In Defense of Colonies: British Colonial Territories in International Affairs,* London: Macmillan, 1957.

Frankel, Sally Herbert, *The Concept of Colonization,* London: Oxford, 1949.

Furnivall, J. S., *Colonial Policy and Practice; A Comparative Study of Burma and Netherlands India,* New York: New York University Press, 1956.

Hancock, Sir William K., *Wealth of Colonies,* New York: Cambridge, 1950.

Hobson, John A., *Imperialism,* London: Macmillan, 1933.

Kolarz, Walter, *Russia and Her Colonies,* New York: Praeger, 1953.
MacInnes, C. M. (ed.), *Colonial Administration* (Colston Papers), London: Parthenon Press, 1950.
Myrdal, Gunnar, *Rich Lands and Poor,* New York: Harper, 1958.
Pratt, Julius William, *America's Colonial Experiment,* Englewood Cliffs: Prentice-Hall, 1950.
Staley, Eugene, *The Future of Underdeveloped Countries,* New York: Harper, 1954.
Strausz-Hupé, Robert, and Hazard, Harry W., *The Idea of Colonialism,* New York: Praeger, 1956.
Walker, Eric A., *Colonies,* New York: Cambridge, 1944.
Winslow, E. M., *The Pattern of Imperialism,* New York: Columbia, 1948.

Bibliography

Adam, Thomas R., *Government and Politics in Africa South of the Sahara,* New York: Random House, 1959.

Adam, Thomas R., *Modern Colonialism: Institutions and Policies,* New York: Random House, 1955.

Afros, John L., "Labor Participation in the Office of Price Administration," *The American Political Science Review,* 1946, **40,** No. 3.

Albig, William, *Modern Public Opinion,* New York: McGraw-Hill, 1956.

Alderfer, Harold F., *American Local Government and Administration,* New York: Macmillan, 1956.

Almond, Gabriel A., *The American People and Foreign Policy,* New York: Harcourt, Brace, 1950.

Ambassade de France, Service de Presse et d'Information. Speeches and Press Conferences, No. 119, October, 1958.

American Civil Liberties Union, *Democracy in Trade Unions; A Survey with a Program of Action,* New York: The Union, 1943.

American Political Science Association, *Toward a More Responsible Two-Party System,* New York: Rinehart, 1950.

Amery, L. S., *Thoughts on the Constitution,* New York: Oxford, second edition, 1953.

Anderson, William, and Weidner, Edward W., *State and Local Government in the United States,* New York: Holt, 1951.

Arendt, Hannah, *The Origins of Totalitarianism,* New York: Harcourt, Brace, 1954.

Aristotle, *The Politics of Aristotle,* tr. and ed. Barker, Ernest, New York: Oxford, 1948.

Ashenhust, Paul H., *Police and the People,* Springfield: Charles C Thomas, 1957.

Ashton-Gwatkin, Frank, *The British Foreign Service,* Syracuse: Syracuse University Press, 1950.

Bagehot, Walter, *The English Constitution,* New York: Appleton, 1914.

Bailey, Sydney D. (ed.), *Parliamentary Government in the Commonwealth,* London: Hansard Society, 1951.

Bailey, Sydney D. (ed.), *Parliamentary Government in Southern Asia,* New York: American Institute of Pacific Relations, 1953.

Bailey, Sydney D. (ed.), *Political Parties and the Party System in Britain,* New York: Praeger, 1952.

Baker, Newton D., "On Executive Influence in Military Legislation," *The American Political Science Review,* 1956, **50,** No. 3.

Barbash, Jack, *Taft-Hartley Act in Action 1947–1956, and, Essentials of a New Labor Policy,* New York: League for Industrial Democracy, new revised edition, 1956.

Barker, Ernest, *Reflections on Government,* New York: Oxford, 1958.

Barnard, Chester Irving, *The Functions of the Executive,* Cambridge: Harvard, 1938.

Barron, Richard, *Parties and Politics in Modern France,* Washington: Public Affairs Press, 1958.

Beard, Charles A., *An Economic Interpretation of the Constitution of the United States,* New York: Macmillan, 1935.

Becker, Carl L., *Freedom and Responsibility in the American Way of Life,* New York: Knopf, 1945.

Becker, Carl L., *Modern Democracy,* New Haven: Yale, 1941.

Beer, Samuel H., and others, *Patterns of Government: The Major Political Systems of Europe,* New York: Random House, 1958.

Beer, Samuel H., "Pressure Groups and Parties in Britain," *The American Political Science Review,* 1956, **50,** No. 1.

Beer, Samuel H., *Treasury Control: The Coordination of Financial and Economic Policy in Great Britain,* New York: Oxford, 1956.

Beloff, Max, "The 'Federal Solution' in its Application to Europe, Asia and Africa," *Political Studies,* 1953, **1,** No. 2.

Beloff, Max, *Foreign Policy and the Democratic Process,* Baltimore: Johns Hopkins Press, 1955.

Benda, Julien, translated by Aldington, Richard, *Treason of the Intellectuals,* New York: Morrow, 1928.

Benson, George C. S., *The New Centralization,* New York: Rinehart, 1941.

Berle, Adolf A., Jr., *The 20th Century Capitalist Revolution,* New York: Harcourt, Brace, 1954.

Berman, Harold J., *Justice in Russia,* Cambridge: Harvard, 1950.

Bingham, Jonathan B., *Shirt-Sleeve Diplomacy: Point 4 in Action,* New York: John Day, 1954.

Birch, A. H., *Federalism, Finance, and Social Legislation in Canada, Australia, and the United States,* New York: Oxford, 1955.

Blaisdell, Donald G., *American Democracy under Pressure,* New York: Ronald, 1957.

Board of Governors of the Federal Reserve System, *The Federal Reserve System: Its Purposes and Functions,* Washington: United States Government Printing Office, first edition, 1939.

Bosanquet, Bernard, *The Philosophical Theory of the State,* London: Macmillan, fourth edition, 1951.

Bowie, Robert R., and Friedrich, Carl J., *Studies in Federalism,* Boston: Little, Brown, 1954.

Brady, Alexander, *Democracy in the Dominions,* Toronto: University of Toronto Press, second edition, 1952.

Brogan, D. W., *Politics in America,* New York: Harper, 1955.

Brown, George W. (ed.), *Canada,* Berkeley: University of California Press, 1950.

Brown, W. Jethro, *The Austinian Theory of Law,* London: John Murray, 1906.

Bryce, James, *Modern Democracies,* New York: Macmillan, 1921.

Buck, Philip W., and Travis, Martin (eds.), *Control of Foreign Relations in Modern Nations,* New York: Norton, 1957.

Burkhead, Jesse, *Government Budgeting,* New York: Wiley, 1956.

Burns, Sir Alan, *In Defense of Colonies: British Colonial Territories in International Affairs,* London: Macmillan, 1957.

Burns, James M., and Peltason, Jack W. (eds.), *Functions and Policies of American Government,* Englewood Cliffs: Prentice-Hall, 1958.

Bush, Vannevar, *Modern Arms and Free Men,* New York: Simon and Schuster, 1949.

Campion, Sir Gilbert, et al., *British Government since 1918,* London: G. Allen, 1951.

Cardozo, Benjamin N., *The Nature of the Judicial Process,* New Haven: Yale, 1921.

Carleton, W. G., *The Revolution in American Foreign Policy,* New York: Random House, revised edition, 1957.

Carlyle, Thomas, *Sartor Resartus; the Life and Opinions of Herr Teufelsdröckh,* New York: Doubleday, 1937.

Carr, Robert K., *Federal Protection of Civil Rights,* Ithaca: Cornell University Press, 1947.

Carter, Byrum E., *The Office of Prime Minister,* Princeton: Princeton University Press, 1956.

Cassirer, Ernst, *The Myth of the State.* New York: Doubleday, 1955.

Catlin, George E. G., *Science and Method of Politics,* New York: Knopf, 1927.

Chaffee, Zechariah, Jr., *Three Human Rights in the Constitution,* Lawrence: University of Kansas Press, 1957.

Chamberlin, Waldo, *A Chronology of United Nations Affairs,* New York: Oceana, 1959.

Chandler, Albert R. (ed.), *The Clash of Political Ideals,* New York: Appleton, revised edition, 1949.

Chapman, Brian, *The Prefects and Provincial France,* London: Macmillan, 1953.

Chisholm v. Georgia, 2 Wall 419 (1793).

Clark, Jane P., *The Rise of a New Federalism,* New York: Columbia, 1938.

Claude, Inis L., Jr., *Swords into Plowshares,* New York: Random House, second edition, 1959.

Cohen, Morris R., *Law and the Social Order,* New York: Harcourt, Brace, 1933.

Coker, Francis W., *Recent Political Thought,* New York: Appleton, 1934.

Cole, G. D. H., *Guild Socialism Restated,* London: L. Parsons, 1920.

Cole, G. D. H., *Social Theory,* New York: Frederick A. Stokes Company, 1920.

Cole, Taylor, and others, *European Political Systems,* New York: Knopf, 1953.

The Commission on Intergovernmental Relations, *A Report to the President for Transmittal to Congress,* Washington: United States Government Printing Office, June, 1955.

Commonwealth of Australia Constitution Act 1900.

Constitution of the Republic of France, promulgated October 4, 1958.

Constitution of the German Democratic Republic, promulgated October 7, 1949.

Constitution of the Italian Republic, 1947.

Constitution of the Swiss Confederation.

Constitution of the Union of Soviet Socialist Republics, 1936.

Constitution of the United States.

Cook, Samuel D., "Hacker's Liberal Democracy and Social Control: A Critique," *The American Political Science Review,* 1957, **51,** No. 4.

Cook, Thomas, and Moos, Malcolm C., *Power Through Purpose,* Baltimore: Johns Hopkins Press, 1954.

Corry, J. A., *Elements of Democratic Government,* New York: Oxford, 1947.

Corwin, Edward S., *The Higher Law Background of American Constitutional Law,* Great Seal Books, Ithaca: Cornell University Press, 1955.

Corwin, Edward S., and Koenig, Louis W., *The Presidency Today,* New York: New York University Press, 1956.

Cummings v. Missouri, 4 Wall 277, 18 L. Ed. 356 (1867).

Curtis, Charles P., Jr., *Lions under the Throne,* Boston: Houghton Mifflin, 1947.

Cushman, Robert, *Civil Liberties in the United States,* Ithaca: Cornell University Press, 1956.

Dahl, Robert A., and Lindblom, Charles E., *Politics, Economics and Welfare,* New York: Harper, 1953.

Dawson, R. M., *The Government of Canada,* Toronto: University of Toronto Press, 1947.

de Castro, Josué, *The Geography of Hunger,* Boston: Little, Brown, 1952.

de Grazia, Alfred, Jr., *Public and Republic: Political Representation in America,* New York: Knopf, 1951.

Dennis v. United States, 341 U. S. 494 (1951).

de Toqueville, Alexis, *Democracy in America,* Vintage Books, New York: Knopf, 1954.

Deutsch, Karl W., *Political Community at the International Level: Problems of Definition and Measurement,* New York: Random House, 1954.

Dimock, Marshall E., "The Administrative Staff College: Executive Development in Government and Industry," *The American Political Science Review,* 1956, **50,** No. 1.

Dimock, Marshall E., *Business and Government,* New York: Holt, third edition, 1957.

Dimock, Marshall E., *The Executive in Action,* New York: Harper, 1945.

Dimock, Marshall E., and others, *Public Administration,* New York: Rinehart, revised edition, 1958.

Djilas, Milovan, *The New Class,* New York: Praeger, 1957.

Duggan, Laurence, *The Americas: The Search for Hemisphere Security,* New York: Holt, 1949.

Dumbauld, Edward, *The Bill of Rights and What It Means Today,* Norman: University of Oklahoma Press, 1957.

Duncan v. Jones, 1936.

Duverger, Maurice, translated by North, Barbara and Robert, *Political Parties: Their Organization and Activity in the Modern State,* New York: Wiley, 1954.

Eagleton, Clyde, and Swift, Richard N. (eds.), *Annual Review of United Nations Affairs, 1955–1956,* New York: New York University Press, 1957.

Eagleton, Clyde, *International Government,* New York: Ronald, third edition, 1957.

East Africa Royal Commission Report (1953–1955), Command 9475, London: Her Majesty's Stationery Office.

Easton, David, *The Political System,* New York: Knopf, 1953.

Easton, David, "Walter Bagehot and Liberal Realism," *The American Political Science Review,* 1949, **43,** No. 1.

Ebenstein, William, *Today's Isms: Communism, Fascism, Capitalism, Socialism,* Englewood Cliffs: Prentice-Hall, 1954.

Eckstein, Harry H., *The English Health Service,* London: Oxford, 1959.

ECOSOC Resolution 512A (XVII) April 30, 1954.

Einaudi, Mario, "The Constitution of the Italian Republic," *The American Political Science Review,* 1948, **42,** No. 3.

Egbert, Donald D., and Persons, Stow (eds.), *Socialism and American Life,* Princeton: Princeton University Press, 1952.

Ekirch, Arthur A., *The Civilian and the Military,* New York: Oxford, 1956.

Elliott, William Y., chairman, *United States Foreign Policy; Its Organization and Control,* Report of a Study Group, New York: Columbia, 1952.

Elliott, William Y., chairman, *The Political Economy of American Foreign Policy; Its Concepts, Strategy, and Limits,* Report of a Study Group, New York: Holt, 1955.

Evans v. Gore, 253 U. S. 245 (1920).

Everson v. Board of Education, 330 U. S. 1 (1947).

Fainsod, Merle, and Gordon, Lincoln, *Government and the American Economy,* New York: Norton, revised edition, 1948.

The Federalist, Modern Library, New York: Random House, 1937.

Feller, Abraham H., *United Nations and World Community,* Boston: Little, Brown, 1952.

Finer, Herman, *The British Civil Service,* London: G. Allen, 1927.

Finer, Herman, *English Local Government,* London: Methuen, fourth edition revised, 1950.

Finer, Herman, *Road to Reaction,* Boston: Little, Brown, 1945.

Finer, Herman, *Theory and Practice of Modern Government,* New York: Holt, revised edition, 1949.

Finer, Samuel Edward, *A Primer of Public Administration,* London: Muller, 1950.

Fleisher, Wilfrid, *Sweden: The Welfare State,* New York: John Day, 1956.

Foenander, Orwell de Ruyter, *Better Employment Relations and Other Essays in Labour,* Sydney: Law Book, 1954.

Ford, Henry J., *Representative Government,* New York: Holt, 1924.

Frank, Jerome, *Law and the Modern Mind,* New York: Coward-McCann, 1930.

Frankel, Sally Herbert, *The Concept of Colonization,* London: Oxford, 1949.

Freeman, J. Leiper, *The Political Process,* New York: Random House, 1955.

Balance Sheet of the de Gaulle Administration, June 3, 1958–February 5, 1959. *French Affairs,* No. 84, New York: Embassy of France, Information Service, May, 1959.

Friedmann, Wolfgang G., *An Introduction to World Politics,* London: Macmillan, second edition, 1952.

Friedrich, Carl J., *Constitutional Government and Democracy,* Boston: Ginn and Co., revised edition, 1950.

Friedrich, Carl J., *Constitutional Reason of State, the Survival of the Constitutional Order,* Providence: Brown University Press, 1957.

Friedrich, Carl J. and Brzezinski, Z. K., *Totalitarian Dictatorship and Autocracy,* Cambridge: Harvard, 1956.

Frischknecht, Reed L., "The Democratization of Administration: the Farmer Committee System," *The American Political Science Review,* 1953, **47,** No. 3.

Furnivall, J. S., *Colonial Policy and Practice; A Comparative Study of Burma and Netherlands India,* New York: New York University Press, 1956.

Galbraith, J. Kenneth, *American Capitalism: The Concept of Countervailing Power,* Boston: Houghton Mifflin, 1952.

Galloway, George B., *Congress and Parliament; Their Organization and Operation in the U.S. and U.K.,* Washington: National Planning Association, 1955.

Galloway, George B., *The Legislative Process in Congress,* New York: Crowell, 1953.

Gettell, Raymond G., *Political Science,* Boston: Ginn and Co., revised edition, 1949.

Gibbons v. Ogden, 9 Wheat 1, 6 L. Ed. 23 (1824).

Gierke, Otto Friedrich von, translated by Maitland, Frederic William, *Political Theories of the Middle Ages,* Boston: Beacon Press, 1958.

Gladden, Edgar N., *The Essentials of Public Administration,* New York: De Graff, 1953.

Gledhill, Alan, *The Republic of India; the Development of Its Laws and Constitution,* London: Stevens, 1952.

Glueck, Sheldon (ed.), *The Welfare State and the National Welfare,* Cambridge: Addison-Wesley, 1952.

Goodrich, Leland M., and Simons, Anne P., *The United Nations and the Maintenance of International Peace and Security,* Washington: Brookings, 1955.

Gordon, Strathearn, *The British Parliament,* New York: Praeger, 1953.

Greaves, Harold R. G., *The Civil Service in the Changing State,* London: Harrap, 1947.

Green, T. H., *Lectures on the Principles of Political Obligation,* London: Longmans, second edition, 1942.

Greenwood, Gordon, *The Future of Australian Federalism,* Melbourne: Melbourne University Press, 1946.

Griffith, Ernest S., *Congress, Its Contemporary Role,* New York: New York University Press, 1951.

Griswold, A. Whitney, *Farming and Democracy,* New Haven: Yale, 1952.

Gross, Feliks, *Foreign Policy Analysis,* New York: Philosophical Library, 1954.

Groves, Harold M., *Financing Government,* New York: Holt, fourth edition, 1954.

Gulick, Luther H., *American Forest Policy,* New York: Duell, Sloan and Pearce, 1951.

Gyorgy, Andrew, *Geopolitics,* Berkeley: University of California Press, 1944.

Haas, Ernst B., "Types of Collective Security: An Examination of Operational Concepts," *The American Political Science Review,* 1955, **49,** No. 1.

Hacker, Andrew, "Liberal Democracy and Social Control," *The American Political Science Review,* 1957, **51,** No. 4.

Haines, Charles Grove, *The Revival of Natural Law Concepts,* Cambridge: Harvard, 1930.

Halévy, Elie, translated by Morris, Mary, *The Growth of Philosophic Radicalism,* Boston: Beacon Press, 1955.

Halle, Louis J., *Civilization and Foreign Policy,* New York: Harper, 1955.

Hammer v. Dagenhart, 247 U.S. 251 (1918).

Hanbury, Harold G., *English Courts of Law,* London: Oxford, second edition, 1953.

Hancock, Sir William K., *Wealth of Colonies,* New York: Cambridge, 1950.

Hand, Learned, (ed. Dilliard, Irving), *The Spirit of Liberty; Papers and Addresses,* Vintage Books, New York: Knopf, 1959.

Hardin, Charles M., *The Politics of Agriculture,* Chicago: Free Press, 1952.

Hartmann, Frederick H., *The Relations of Nations,* New York: Macmillan, 1957.

Hartz, Louis, *The Liberal Tradition in America,* New York: Harcourt, Brace, 1955.

Harvey, H. J., *Consultation and Co-operation in the Commonwealth,* New York: Oxford, 1952.

Hawke v. Smith, 253 U.S. 221 (1920).

Hayek, Friedrich A., *The Road to Serfdom,* Chicago: University of Chicago Press, 1944.

Hazard, J. N., *The Soviet System of Government,* Chicago: University of Chicago Press, 1957.

Heagney, Muriel, *Arbitration at the Cross Roads: Digest of Opinion on Legal Wage Fixation,* Melbourne, 1954.

Hennessy, Bernard, "Trade Unions and the British Labor Party," *The American Political Science Review,* 1955, **49,** No. 4.

Hermens, F. A., *The Representative Republic,* Notre Dame: University of Notre Dame Press, 1958.

Herring, Pendleton, *Presidential Leadership,* New York: Rinehart, 1940.

Hilsman, Roger, *Strategic Intelligence and National Decisions,* Chicago: Free Press, 1956.

Hinden, Rita (ed.), *Local Government and the Colonies,* London: Macmillan, 1950.

Hobbs, Edward H., *Behind the President,* Washington: Public Affairs Press, 1954.

Hobhouse, L. T., *Liberalism,* New York: Holt, 1911.

Hobson, John A., *Imperialism,* London: Macmillan, 1933.

Hocking, William Ernest, *Man and the State,* New Haven: Yale, 1926.

Hoffman, Ross J. S., and Levack, Paul (eds.), *Burke's Politics,* New York: Knopf, 1949.

Hoffmann, Stanley H., and Wahl, Nicholas, "The French Constitution of 1958," *The American Political Science Review,* 1959, **53,** No. 2.

Hogg, Quintin, *The Case for Conservatism,* Baltimore: Penguin, 1947.

Holcomb, Richard L., *The Police and the Public,* Springfield: Charles C Thomas, 1957.

Holcombe, Arthur N., *Human Rights in the Modern World,* New York: New York University Press, 1948.

Home Building and Loan Association v. Blaisdell, 290 U.S. 298 (1934).

Hook, Sidney, *Marx and the Marxists,* Princeton: Van Nostrand, 1955.

Humphrey's Executor [*Rathbun*] *v. United States,* 295 U.S. 602 (1935).

Hunt, R. N. Carew, *Marxism, Past and Present,* New York: Macmillan, 1955.

Hunt, R. N. Carew, *The Theory and Practice of Communism,* New York: Macmillan, 1950.

Huntington, S. P. *The Soldier and the State; The Theory and Politics of Civil-Military Relations,* Cambridge: Harvard, 1957.

Hurtado v. California, 110 U.S. 516 (1884).

Huzar, Elias, *The Purse and the Sword; Control of the Army by Congress Through Military Appropriations, 1933–1950,* Ithaca: Cornell University Press, 1950.

Hyneman, Charles S., *Bureaucracy in a Democracy,* New York: Harper, 1950.

Ilbert, Sir Courtenay, *Parliament,* New York: Holt, 1911.

Iojrych, A., "The Role of the Executive in the Modern State—U.S.S.R.," *International Social Science Bulletin,* 1958, **10,** No. 2.

Jackson, Robert H., *The Supreme Court in the American System of Government,* New York: Cambridge, 1955.

Jacobson v. Massachusetts, 197 U.S. 11 (1905).

Jenks, Edward (ed.), *The Book of English Law,* London: John Murray, 1928.

Jennings, Sir Ivor, *The British Commonwealth of Nations,* London: Hutchinson, 1948.

Jennings, Sir Ivor, *Cabinet Government,* London: Cambridge, second edition, 1951.

Jennings, Sir Ivor, *Modern Theories of Law,* London: Oxford, 1933.

Jennings, Sir Ivor, *Parliament,* London: Cambridge, second edition, 1951.

Johnson, Eldon L., "The Accountability of the British Nationalized Industries," *The American Political Science Review,* 1954, **48,** No. 2.

Jones, Stanley W., *Public Administration in Malaya,* London: Royal Institute of International Affairs, 1953.

Kahin, G. M., *The Asian-African Conference,* Ithaca: Cornell University Press, 1956.

Kalijarvi, Thorsten V., et al., *Modern World Politics,* New York: Crowell, third edition, 1953.

Kaufmann, William W. (ed.), *Military Policy and National Security,* Princeton: Princeton University Press, 1956.

Kelsen, Hans, *The Communist Theory of Law,* New York: Praeger, 1955.

Kennan, George F., *Realities of American Foreign Policy,* Princeton: Princeton University Press, 1954.

Kern, Fritz, translated by Chrimes, S. B., *Kingship and Law in the Middle Ages,* Oxford: Blackwell, 1939.

Key, Valdimer O., Jr., *Politics, Parties and Pressure Groups,* New York: Crowell, third edition, 1952.

Kile, Orville M., *The Farm Bureau through Three Decades,* Washington: The Author, National Press Building, 1948.

Kirk, Russell, *The Conservative Mind; From Burke to Santayana,* Chicago: Regnery, 1953.

Klain, Maurice, "A New Look at the Constituencies," *The American Political Science Review,* 1955, **49,** No. 4.

Koenig, Louis, *The Invisible Presidency,* New York: Rinehart, 1960.

Kohn, Hans, *The Idea of Nationalism,* New York: Macmillan, 1944.

Kohn-Bramstedt, Ernst, *Dictatorship and Political Police; the Technique of Control by Fear,* London: Routledge, 1945.

Kolarz, Walter, *Russia and Her Colonies,* New York: Praeger, 1953.

Konvitz, Milton R., *Fundamental Liberties of a Free People: Religion, Speech, Press, Assembly,* Ithaca: Cornell University Press, 1958.

Koontz, H., and Gable, R., *Public Control of Economic Enterprise,* New York: McGraw-Hill, 1956.

Kropotkin, P. A., *The Conquest of Bread,* New York: Vanguard, 1926.

Laroque, Pierre, "The Role of the Executive in the Modern State—France," *International Social Science Bulletin,* 1958, **10,** No. 2.

Larsen, J. A., *Representative Government in Greek and Roman History,* Berkeley: University of California Press, 1955.

Laski, Harold J., *The State in Theory and Practice,* New York: Viking, 1935.

Laslett, Peter, *Philosophy, Politics and Society,* New York: Macmillan, 1956.

Laswell, Harold D., *National Security and Individual Freedom,* New York: McGraw-Hill, 1950.

Lasswell, Harold D., *Politics: Who Gets What, When, How,* New York: Meridian Books, 1958.

Lasswell, Harold D., *Power and Personality,* Boston: Chapman and Grimes, 1949.

Lasswell, Harold D., and Kaplan, Abraham, *Power and Society,* New Haven: Yale, 1950.

Lauterpracht, Hersh, *An International Bill of the Rights of Man,* New York: Columbia, 1945.

Leiserson, Avery, *Parties and Politics: An Institutional and Behavioral Approach,* New York: Knopf, 1958.

Lens, Sidney, *Labor Unions and Politics in Britain and France,* New York: 1950.

Leonard, Leonard L., *Elements of American Foreign Policy,* New York: McGraw-Hill, 1953.

Lerner, Max, *America as a Civilization,* New York: Simon and Schuster, 1957.

Levi, Werner, *Fundamentals of World Organization,* Minneapolis: University of Minnesota Press, 1950.

Lewis, Ewart, *Medieval Political Ideas,* New York: Knopf, 1954, Vol. I.

Lidderdale, D. W. S., *The Parliament of France,* London: Hansard Society, 1951.

Lindsay, A. D., *The Modern Democratic State,* New York: Oxford, 1947.

Lippmann, Walter, *Isolation and Alliances: An American Speaks to the British,* Boston: Little, Brown, 1952.

Lipson, Leslie, *The Politics of Equality,* Chicago: University of Chicago Press, 1948.

Livingston, W. S., *Federalism and Constitutional Change,* New York: Oxford, 1956.

Locke, John, (ed. Cook, Thomas I.), *Two Treatises of Government,* New York: Hafner, 1947.

Loewenstein, Karl, *Political Power and the Governmental Process,* Chicago: University of Chicago Press, 1957.

London, Kurt, and Ives, Kent, *How Foreign Policy Is Made,* Princeton: Van Nostrand, 1949.

McCloskey, Robert G. (ed.), *Essays in Constitutional Law,* New York: Knopf, 1957.

McConnell, Grant, "The Spirit of Private Government," *The American Political Science Review,* 1958, **52,** No. 3.

McCune, Wesley, *Who's Behind Our Farm Policy?* New York: Praeger, 1957.

McGrain v. Daugherty, 273 U.S. 135 (1927).

Machinery of Government Committee, Haldane Report. Command 9230 of 1918, London: His Majesty's Stationery Office, 1918.

McIlwain, Charles Howard, *Constitutionalism, Ancient and Modern,* Great Seal Books, Ithaca: Cornell University Press, revised edition, 1958.

MacInnes, C. M. (ed.), *Colonial Administration* (Colston Papers), London: Parthenon Press, 1950.

MacIver, R. M., *The Web of Government,* New York: Macmillan, 1947.

McKenzie, Robert T., *British Political Parties,* New York: St. Martins, 1955.

MacKenzie, W. J. M., "The Structure of Central Administration," Institute of Public Administration, *British Government since 1918,* London: G. Allen, 1951.

MacKinder, Sir Halford J., *Democratic Ideals and Reality,* New York: Holt, 1942.

McKinley, Charles, *Uncle Sam in the Pacific Northwest: Federal Management of Natural Resources in the Columbia River Valley,* Berkeley: University of California Press. 1952.

Macridis, Roy C., *The Study of Comparative Government,* New York: Random House, 1955.

Maine, Sir Henry, *Ancient Law,* Everyman's Library, London: Dutton, 1917.

Maine, Sir Henry, *Popular Government,* London: John Murray, new edition, 1890.

Mangone, Gerard J., *A Short History of International Organization,* New York: McGraw-Hill, 1954.

Maritain, Jacques, *Man and the State,* Chicago: University of Chicago Press, 1951.

Marriott, J. A. R., *The Mechanism of the Modern State,* London: Oxford, 1927.

Marriott, J. A. R., *Second Chambers,* London: Oxford, new edition revised, 1927.

Marsh, David C., *National Insurance and Assistance in Great Britain,* London: Pitman, 1951.

Masters, Ruth D., et al., *Handbook of International Organizations in the Americas,* Washington: Carnegie Endowment for International Peace, Columbia, 1945.

Mayo, Henry B., *Democracy and Marxism,* New York: Oxford, 1955.

Meek, Charles K., *Land Law and Custom in the Colonies,* London: Oxford, 1949.

Mendelsohn, Ronald, *Social Security in the British Commonwealth,* London: Oxford, 1954.

Merriam, Charles E., *Systematic Politics,* Chicago: University of Chicago Press, 1945.

Meyer v. Nebraska, 262 U.S. 390 (1923).

Meyers, Marvin, *The Jacksonian Persuasion: Politics and Belief,* Stanford: Stanford University Press, 1957.

Meynaud, J., et al., "The Role of the Executive in the Modern State," *International Social Science Bulletin,* 1958, **10,** No. 2.

Michels, Robert, translated by de Grazia, Alfred, *First Lectures in Political Sociology,* Minneapolis: University of Minnesota Press, 1949.

Michels, Robert, *Political Parties,* 1949.

Mill, John Stuart, *On Liberty.*

Mill, John Stuart, *Considerations on Representative Government.*

Miller, Glenn W., *American Labor and the Government,* New York: Prentice-Hall, 1948.

Mills, Lennox A., and McLaughlin, Charles H., *World Politics in Transition,* New York: Holt, 1956.

Milne, R. S., "Britain's Economic Planning Machinery," *The American Political Science Review,* 1952, **46,** No. 2.

Minersville School District v. Gobitis, 310 U.S. 586 (1940).

Moodie, A. E., *Geography Behind Politics,* New York: Rinehart, 1948.

Morehead v. Tipaldo, 298 U.S. 587 (1936).

Morgenthau, Hans J., "Another 'Great Debate': The National Interest of the United States," *The American Political Science Review,* 1952, **46,** No. 4.

Morgenthau, Hans J., *In Defense of the National Interest,* New York: Knopf, 1951.

Morgenthau, Hans J., *Politics Among Nations: The Struggle for Power and Peace,* New York: Knopf, second edition revised and enlarged, 1954.

Morley, John, Viscount, *On Compromise,* The Thinkers Library, London: Watts, 1956.

Mott, Rodney L., *Home Rule for America's Cities,* Chicago: American Municipal Association, 1949.

Myers v. United States, 272 U.S. 52 (1926).

Myrdal, Gunnar, *Rich Lands and Poor,* New York: Harper, 1958.

National Security Act of 1947.

Nebbia v. New York, 291 U.S. 502 (1934).

Neumann, Sigmund (ed.), *Modern Political Parties, Approaches to Comparative Policies,* Chicago: University of Chicago Press, 1955.

New State Co. v. Liebmann, 285 U.S. 263 (1932).

Nicolson, Sir Harold, *Diplomacy,* New York: Oxford, second edition, 1950.

Niebuhr, Reinhold, *The Structure of Nations and Empires,* New York: Scribner, 1959.

Overacker, Louise, *The Australian Party System,* New Haven: Yale, 1952.

Overacker, Louise, "The New Zealand Labor Party," *The American Political Science Review,* 1955, **49,** No. 3.

Palmer, Norman D., and Perkins, Howard C., *International Relations,* Boston: Houghton Mifflin, second edition, 1957.

The Paquete Habana, 175 U.S. 677.

Parker, John, *Labour Marches On,* Baltimore: Penguin, 1947.

Perlman, Mark, *Labor Union Theories in America: Background and Development,* Evanston: Row, Peterson, 1958.

Petro, Sylvester, *The Labor Policy of the Free Society,* New York: Ronald, 1957.

Pfeffer, Leo, *Church, State and Freedom,* Boston: Beacon Press, 1953.

Pierce v. Society of Sisters, 268 U.S. 510 (1925).

Plamenatz, John, *Mill's Utilitarianism; reprinted with a Study of the English Utilitarians,* Oxford: Blackwell, 1949.

Poole, Kenyon E., *Public Finance and Economic Welfare,* New York: Rinehart, 1956.

Pound, Roscoe, *Justice According to Law,* New Haven: Yale, 1951.

Pratt, Julius William, *America's Colonial Experiment,* New York: Prentice-Hall, 1950.

President's Committee on Civil Rights, *To Secure These Rights,* New York: Simon and Schuster, 1947.

Presthus, R. Vance, "British Town and Country Planning: Local Participation," *The American Political Science Review,* 1951, **45,** No. 3.

Pritchett, C. H., *The American Constitution,* New York: McGraw-Hill, 1959.

Public Law 304, 79th Congress, Second Session, February 20, 1946, S. 380 Employment Act of 1946, Washington: United States Government Printing Office, 1946.

Public Law 402, 80th Congress, Second Session, January 27, 1948, H.R. 3342, Washington: United States Government Printing Office, 1948, **62,** Part I.

Ranney, Austin, *The Doctrine of Responsible Party Government,* Urbana: University of Illinois Press, 1954.

Read, Sir Herbert, *Anarchy and Order: Essays in Politics,* London: Faber, 1954.

Rich, Bennett M., and Burch, Philip H., Jr., "The Changing Role of the National Guard," *The American Political Science Review,* 1956, **50,** No. 3.

Reith, Charles, *British Police and the Democratic Ideal,* London: Oxford, 1943.

Reith, Charles, *Police Principles and the Problem of War,* London: Oxford, 1940.

Roberts, Owen J., *The Court and the Constitution,* Cambridge: Harvard, 1951.

Robson, William A., *The British System of Government,* New York: Longmans, third edition, 1948.

Robson, William A., *Civilization and the Growth of Law,* New York: Macmillan, 1935.

Robson, William A. (ed.), *The Civil Service in Britain and France,* New York: Macmillan, 1956.

Robson, William A. (ed.), *Great Cities of the World; Their Government, Politics and Planning,* New York: Macmillan, 1955.

Robson, William A., *Introduction to French Local Government,* London: 1953.

Robson, William A. (ed.), *Problems of Nationalized Industry,* New York: Oxford, 1952.

Robson, William A. (ed.), *Social Security,* London: G. Allen, third edition revised, 1948.

Roche, John P., and Stedman, Murray S., *The Dynamics of Democratic Government,* New York: McGraw-Hill, 1954.

Rosenblum, Victor G., *Law as a Political Instrument,* New York: Random House, 1955.

Ross, J. F. S., *Elections and Electors,* London: Eyre and Son, 1955.

Rossiter, Clinton, *The American Presidency,* New York: Harcourt, Brace, 1956.

Sabine, George H., *Marxism,* Ithaca: Cornell University Press, 1958.

Sait, Edward McC., *Political Institutions: A Preface,* New York: Appleton, 1938.

Sapin, Burton M., and Snyder, Richard C., *The Role of the Military in American Foreign Policy,* Short Studies in Political Science, New York: Random House, 1954.

Sawer, G., et al., *Federalism in Australia,* Melbourne: F. W. Cheshire, 1949.

Schlatter, Richard, *Private Property,* New Brunswick: Rutgers University Press, 1951.

Schriftgiesser, Karl, *Lobbyists,* Boston: Little, Brown, 1951.

Schuman, Frederick, *The Commonwealth of Man,* New York: Knopf, 1952.

Schumpeter, Joseph A., *Capitalism, Socialism and Democracy,* New York: Harper, second edition, 1947.

Shields, Curren V., "The American Tradition of Empirical Collectivism," *The American Political Science Review,* 1952, **46,** No. 1.

Shubik, Martin, *Readings in Game Theory and Political Behavior,* Short Studies in Political Science, New York: Random House, 1954.

Smith, Edward C., and Zurcher, Arnold J. (eds.), *New Dictionary of American Politics,* New York: Barnes and Noble, 1955.

Smith, Louis, *American Democracy and Military Power,* Chicago: University of Chicago Press, 1951.

Smith v. Allwright, 321 U.S. 649 (1944).

Sorel, Georges, translated by Hulme, T. E., and Roth, J., *Reflections on Violence,* Chicago: Free Press, 1950.

Spahr, Margaret (ed.), *Readings in Recent Political Philosophy,* New York: Macmillan, 1935.

Spiro, Herbert J., *Government by Constitution,* New York: Random House, 1959.

Spykman, Nicholas J. (ed. Nicholl, Helen R.), *The Geography of the Peace,* New York: Harcourt, Brace, 1944.

Staley, Eugene, *The Future of Underdeveloped Countries,* New York: Harper, 1954.

Stanley, Timothy W., *American Defense and National Security,* Washington: Public Affairs Press, 1956.

Stein, Harold (ed.), *Public Administration and Policy Development: A Case Book,* New York: Harcourt, Brace, 1952.

Steiner, G. A., *Government's Role in Economic Life,* New York: McGraw-Hill, 1953.

Stowe, Leland, *While Time Remains,* New York: Knopf, 1946.

Straetz, Ralph A., *PR Politics in Cincinnati,* New York: New York University Press, 1958.

Strausz-Hupé, Robert, and Hazard, Harry W., *The Idea of Colonialism,* New York: Praeger, 1956.

Stuart, Graham H., *American Diplomatic and Consular Practice,* New York: Appleton, 1952.

Sullivan, Walter, *The International Geophysical Year,* New York: Carnegie Endowment for International Peace, 1959.

Swisher, Carl B., *American Constitutional Development,* Boston: Houghton Mifflin, second edition, 1954.

Tawney, R. H., *Equality,* New York: Harcourt, Brace, 1931.

Terminiello v. Chicago, 337 U.S. 1 (1948).

Thayer, Charles W., *Diplomat,* New York: Harper, 1959.

Thomson, David, *Democracy in France: The Third and Fourth Republic,* New York: Oxford, 1954.

Toynbee, Arnold J., *The World and the West,* New York: Oxford, 1953.

Truman, David B., *The Governmental Process: Political Interests and Public Opinion,* New York: Knopf, 1951.

Underhill, Frank H., *The British Commonwealth: An Experiment in Co-operation among Nations,* Durham: Duke University Press, 1956.

United States v. Darby, 312 U.S. 100 (1941).

Vandenbosch, Amry, and Hogan, Willard N., *The United Nations; Background, Organizations, Functions, Activities,* New York: McGraw-Hill, 1952.

Viereck, Peter, *Conservatism: From John Adams to Churchill,* Princeton: Van Nostrand, 1956.
Vinogradoff, Sir Paul, *Common-Sense in Law,* New York: Holt, 1914.
Waldo, Dwight, *The Study of Public Administration,* New York: Random House, 1955.
Walker, Eric A., *Colonies,* New York: Cambridge, 1944.
Walker, Harvey, *The Legislative Process,* New York: Ronald, 1948.
Watkins, Frederick M., *The Political Tradition of the West: A Study in the Development of Modern Liberalism,* Cambridge: Harvard, 1948.
Weldon, Thomas D., *States and Morals,* New York: McGraw-Hill, 1947.
Weldon, Thomas D., *The Vocabulary of Politics,* Baltimore: Penguin, 1952.
West Coast Hotel Co. v. Parrish, 300 U.S. 379 (1937).
Wheare, Kenneth C., *Federal Government,* New York: Oxford, third edition, 1953.
Wheare, Kenneth C., *Modern Constitutions,* New York: Oxford, 1951.
Wheeler-Bennett, John W., *The Nemesis of Power,* London: Macmillan, 1953.
White, Leonard D., *The Administrative State,* New York: 1948.
White, Leonard D., *Introduction to the Study of Public Administration,* New York: Macmillan, fourth edition, 1955.
White, R. J. (ed.), *The Conservative Tradition,* London: Nicholas Kaye, 1950.
Whitney v. California, 274 U.S. 357 (1927).
Winslow, E. M., *The Pattern of Imperialism,* New York: Columbia, 1948.
Wirszubiski, Chaim, *'Libertas' as a Political Idea at Rome during the Late Republic and Early Principate,* London: Cambridge, 1951.
Wise v. Dunning, 1902.
Wiskemann, Elizabeth, "Poverty and Population in the South," *Foreign Affairs,* October, 1949, **28**.
Wolf v. Colorado, 338 U.S. 25 (1948).
World Peace Foundation, *Documents on American Foreign Relations, 1948,* Princeton: Princeton University Press.
Wormuth, Francis D., *The Origins of Modern Constitutionalism,* New York: Harper, 1949.
Woytinsky, W. S. and E. S., *World Population and Production: Trends and Outlook,* New York: Twentieth Century Fund, 1953.
Wright, Quincy, *A Study of War,* Chicago: University of Chicago Press, 1942.
Young, Roland, *The American Congress,* New York: Harper, 1958.
Zeller, Belle, and Bone, Hugh A., "The Repeal of P.R. in New York City —Ten Years in Retrospect," *The American Political Science Review,* 1948, **42,** No. 6.
Zellerbach, J. D., *Our Stake in Economic Development Abroad—an Address,* New York: Committee for Economic Development, 1956.
Zurcher, Arnold J. (ed.), *Constitutions and Constitutional Trends since World War II,* New York: New York University Press, 1951.
Zurcher, Arnold J., "The Presidency, Congress, and Separation of Powers: A Reappraisal," *Western Political Quarterly,* 1950, **3**.
Zurcher, Arnold J., *The Struggle to Unite Europe, 1940–1958,* New York: New York University Press, 1958.

Index

Administration, Theory of, 6
AFL-CIO, 347
Africa, 21, 33, 340-341
Afrikaner Party, 241
Afros, John L., 185
Agencies, administrative, types of, 194-198; classification of, 193-194
Aggression, 363
Agricultural Conservation Programs, 183
Agriculture, and government, 343-346
Agriculture, Department of, 183-184, 344
Algeria, 431
Ambassadors, 384-385
Amendments (to United States Constitution), 38-43; First, 142, 279; Second, 174; Fifth, 138; Fourteenth, 91, 138, 142, 286; Eighteenth, 40; Twenty-first, 40; (to State constitutions), 100
American Civil Liberties Union, 348-349
Anarchism, 244-246
Angola, 431
Appeal, 144
Appropriations Committee, 111
Aristocracy, 286
Aristotle, 3-4, 20, 21, 23, 36, 275
Arkansas, 167
Army, 167-169, 175-176; civilian control over, 169-173; and compulsory service, 173-175
Army Organization Act, 175
Assemblies, legislative (*See* Legislatures)
Assemblies, representative, functions of, 110-117
Athens, 99
Atomic Energy Commission, 126, 182
Augustine of Hippo, Saint, 7
Australia, 13, 27, 30, 168, 255, 328, 347, 352, 420, 429; constitution of, 42; suffrage in, 91-92
Authority, 8; in constitutions, 36-38; political, 52-53
Autocracy, 21; Soviet, 76
Autonomy, regional, 251-252
Auxiliary service agency, 193

Bagehot, Walter, 237
Baker, Newton D., 172
Bakunin, M., 245
Balance of power, 373-376
Baldwin, Stanley, 73
Ball, John, 234
Bandaranaike, S. W. R. D., 212
Bandung Conference, 430
Barker, Sir Ernest, 12, 14, 308
Becker, Carl, 25
Belgium, 28, 68, 394
Bentham, Jeremy, 235
Berle, A. A., 313
Beveridge Report of 1942, 324, 326
Bias, in courts, 150
Bicameralism, 108-110
Bill of Rights, 40, 48-49, 132
Black, Hugo, 279
Bolshevik Party, 206
"Bossism," 214-215
"Brain trust," 58
Brandeis, Louis D., 276, 310-311

Britain, 28, 97, 98, 111-112, 199, 210, 212-213, 215, 221, 230-231, 239, 266, 280, 341-342, 346-347, 349, 394, 431; bicameralism in, 109-110; civil service in, 184-188, 191; constitution of, 37, 40-41, 44-45, 60; court system of, 145, 148; education in, 330-331; judicial system of, 136, 139; legislative body of, 124-125; ministerial office in, 68-73; national planning in, 260, 297, 299; nationalization of industry in, 197-198, 308; Parliament of, 113-115; police forces in, 157, 159, 163-164; referendum in, 101; regional governments of, 254-255; schools of, 288-289. (*See also* Commonwealth of Nations)
British Broadcasting Company, 197-198
British Commonwealth, 420-423
British East India Company, 426
British Transport Commission, 197, 309
Bureaucracy, 77, 78, 190-193; administrative agencies of, 193-198; French, 188-189; and government, 179-181; Soviet, 190
Bureau of the Budget, 62
Burke, Edmund, 16-17, 85, 86, 206, 211
Burma, 21, 212, 431
Business, 21; government regulation of, 310-312, 314-316

Cabinet (United States), 62
Cabinet form of government, 67-75
Calhoun, John C., 233
California, 101, 103, 222
Cameroons, 100
Canada, 13, 27, 28, 30, 255, 308, 419, 421
Candidates, 206-207
Cardozo, Benjamin N., 133
Caribbean Commission, 418-419
Carlyle, Thomas, 43-44, 84
Cartels, 314
Castro, Fidel, 343
Central Asia, 432
Central Intelligence Agency, 63, 387
Ceylon, 212, 421, 431
Chase, Salmon Portland, 12
Chicago, 259
Child labor, 354
China (Communist), 14, 17, 432, 433; constitution of, 37; land distribution in, 341
Church, established, 232
Churchill, Winston, 44-45, 98
Cicero, 54
Cincinnati, 263
City manager, 266-267
Civil law, 141-142
Civil rights, 233, 237; and equality of opportunity, 284-287; freedom of belief, 278-282; freedom of speech, 276-278; personal privacy, 282-284; as standard of order, 273-276, 292-293
Civil Service, 178, 179, 222-223; British, 184-188, 191; local, 265-267; United Nations, 410; United States, 181-184, 188
Class system, and socialism, 238-239; and welfare state, 319, 323
Clayton Act, 143
Code Napoléon, 137
Coker, Francis W., 320
Cold War, 345-346, 391. (*See also* Ideology)
Cole, G. D. H., 89
Coleridge, Samuel T., 54-55
Collective bargaining, 291-292
Collective leadership, 21
Colombo Plan, 422, 437
Colonialism, 425-427, 430-434
Commission on International Commodity Trade, 411
Commissions, international, 418-419; regulatory, 195, 196
Commissions on the Organization of the Executive Branch, 182, 187-188, 191, 196
Common law, 14, 115-116
Common Market, 437-438
Commonwealth Economic Conference, 421
Commonwealth of Nations, 31-32, 420-423
Commonwealth Parliamentary Association, 32
Commonwealth v. Hunt, 346
Commonwealths, 31-33
Communication, 203
Communism, 242-244, 356, 439, 440
Communist Manifesto, 22, 88
Communist Party; cell of, 215; international, 398-399; Russian, 22,

76, 88, 118, 206; and Soviet management, 190
Congress, United States, 120, 122-123, 126. (*See also* House of Representatives, Senate)
Conservatism, 228-234
Constitution, United States, 8, 16, 24, 37, 38-40, 45-46, 48-49, 56, 57, 382; on judiciary, 135, 144-145; separation of powers in, 28-29. (*See also* Amendments)
Constitutionalism, 36, 233
Constitutions, 49-50; amendments to, 38-43; definition of, 36; and government structures, 43-47; importance of, 16-17; and law, 30-31; political authority in, 36-38; State, 66-67
Constitutions of Clarendon (1164), 40
Contract theory, 47
Coolidge, Calvin, 168
Cornwall, 255
Corporations, 18, 82, 151-153; and government control, 313-314; public, 197
Corsica, 168
Council of Economic Advisers, 63-65, 298
Counties, 258-259
Courts, 133-137; organization of, 144-147, 148-150
Credit, government control of, 301-307
Criminal law, 142
Cuba, 343, 434
Cultural divisions, 256
Cultural exchange, 387-388, 397

Debate, in legislatures, 122
Decentralization, 257
Decision-making, 6
Declaration of Independence, 50
Defense, mutual, 435, 436
Defense, Secretary of, 62, 171
de Gaulle, Charles, 168
Democracy, 24, 26, 99
Democratic Party, 205, 209
Demos, 25
Dennis v. United States, 399
de Tocqueville, Alexis, 83, 250
Devolution, 249
Dicey, A. V., 200
Dictator, 20-21
Dictatorship of the proletariat, 22
Dimock, Marshall, 181
Diplomacy, 381-388; methods of, 388-389
Direct primary, 102, 103
Discrimination, 286-287
Discussion, in representative government, 23-24
Disraeli, Benjamin, 41-42, 230, 231
District Attorney, 148-149
Dominance, 6
Dominican Republic, 164
Douglas, William O., 277
Dreyfus Affair, 287
Due process of law, 137-180

Eagleton, Clyde, 371
Economic and Social Council, 411-412
Economic assistance, 386, 429-430
Economic cooperation, 392-397
Economic development, assistance for, 437-438
Economic growth, 336
Economic order, 356-358; control of resources in, 307-310; corporations in, 313-314; and government, 295-297, 312-313
Economic programs, 238-239, 240
Economic Report of the President, 64
Eden, Sir Anthony, 72
Education, 258, 321; opportunity for, 287-290; State responsibility for, 328-332
Egypt, 21, 429
Eisenhower, Dwight D., 427-428
Election, systems of, 90-103
Election expenses, 221-222
Electoral college, 92
Elites, 237
Elizabeth II, Queen, 72
"Empire-mindedness," 11
Employment practices, government regulation of, 354-356
England, 23, 89, 156, 165, 179. (*See also* Britain)
Equity, 143-144
Estates of the Realm, 23, 89
Euripides, 15
Europe, regional arrangements in, 417-418
European Atomic Energy Community, 394
European Defense Community, 418
Executive, concept of, 56-58

Executive powers, 28; and legislatures, 125-127

Factions, 204
Fair Labor Standards Act, 351-352, 355
Family allowances, 335-336
Farm blocs, 345
Fascism, 240-241
Faubus, Orville, 167
Federal Bureau of Investigation, 126, 161, 162, 163, 182
Federal Republic of Germany, 30
Federal Reserve System, 304-307
Federal Trade Commission, 66
Federalism, 28, 251-252
Feudalism, 339
Field, Stephen Johnson, 132
Food, in Cold War, 345-346
Food and Agriculture Organization, 415
Force, 363; and law, 131
Foreign aid, 393-396
Foreign policy, 381-382; military role in, 171-172
Foreign relations, United States, 59-60. (*See also* International Relations)
Foreign Service, United States, 386
France, 68, 75, 89, 146, 165, 168-169, 232, 280, 282, 324, 353, 355, 382, 394, 418; bicameralism of, 109, 199; bureaucracy in, 188-189; centralized government of, 253-254; constitution of, 37-38, 42-43, 46, 49; economy of, 303-304; judiciary of, 136-137; voting in, 92-93
Frank, Jerome, 133
Frankfurter, Felix, 275, 281
Frankpledge system, 156
Free association, 290-292
Freedom, 8, 275; of thought and speech, 276-282. (*See also* Civil rights)
French Community, 27, 28, 431; and constitution, 30, 32-33
Frischknecht, Reed L., 183-184
Fulbright Act, 388
Full Employment Act of 1946, 298, 316
Functional representation, 89-90
Funeral allowances, 335

Galbraith, J. K., 314
Garrison, William L., 235
General Assembly, United Nations, 408-410
"General welfare," 320
Geography, and state, 12-13
Geopolitics, 376-377
Germany, East, *see* Federal Republic of Germany
Germany, West, 27, 30, 68, 74, 95, 97; constitution of, 38
Ghana, 49, 74, 87, 187, 283, 408, 421, 431
Gibbons v. Ogden, 195
Gordon, George, 157
Government, 7, 19, 20; and agriculture, 339-346; and bureaucracy, 179-181; and control of economic resources, 307-310; democratic, 25-26; and economic order, 295-297, 312-313, 356-358; economic planning by, 297-301; federal, 27-28; institutions of, 18; by interest groups, 22-23; and labor, 348-355; law officers of, 147-150; limited, 19; local, 260-268; objectives of, 273-274, 275; regional, 250-258; regulation by, of business and industry, 310-311; representative, 23-24; responsible, 54, 113-114; types of, 20-33; universal, 367-368, 402. (*See also* Force)
Government boards, 196-198
Granger movement, 235
Grants-in-aid, 259-260
Green, T. H., 15, 132
Grotius, Hugo, 370-371
Group organization, 6
Grovey v. Townsend, 208
Guild Socialism, 89

Habeas Corpus, Writ of, 283
Hacker, Andrew, 236
Haeckel, Ernst Heinrich, 20
Haldane Report, 191, 194
Halifax, Marquess of, 61, 131
Hammarskjold, Dag, 410
Hammer v. Dagenhart, 354
Hand, Learned, 133, 135
Hardin, Charles M., 184
Hare system of proportional representation, 97
Harlan, John Marshall, 275-276
Haushofer, Karl, 377
Hawaii, 434
Health services, 332-334

Heartland theory, 377
Hitler, Adolf, 165, 218, 240, 241, 377
Hobbes, Thomas, 8
Hogg, Quintin, 341-342, 346-347
Holland, 68
Holmes, Oliver W., 29-30, 354
Hooker, Archbishop Richard, 3, 8
Hoover, Herbert, 40
Hoover Commissions, 182, 187-188, 191
House of Commons, 69, 110, 196
House of Lords, 109, 110
House of Representatives, 37, 45, 55-56, 111, 210
Housing, 334-335
Housing Act of 1954, Title III, 257-258
Hughes, Charles E., 291, 350-351
Humphrey, Hubert, 334
Humphrey's Executor [*Rathbun*] *v. United States,* 66

Iceland, 13
Ideology, 211, 397-399; clash of, in under-developed areas, 438-440
Immigration laws, 428-429
Imperialism, 425, 438, 439
India, 27, 31, 74, 87, 187, 283, 341, 421, 431
Individual, representation of, 80-85, 105
Indonesia, 21, 140, 170, 212, 341, 408, 429
Industry, 354; government regulation of, 310-312
Initiative, 99-101
Injunction, 143-144
Intelligence reports, 386-387
Intercessio, 53
Interest groups, 204-205, 216-217; government by, 22-23; in local government, 263
International Atomic Energy Agency, 416
International Bank for Reconstruction and Development, 415
International Civil Aviation Organization, 416
International Council of Scientific Unions, 396, 397
International Court of Justice, 370
International Finance Corporation, 415-416
International Geophysical Year, 396
International Labor Organization, 415
International law, 368-371, 388
International Monetary Fund, 415
International organizations, 402-403
International relations, 363-365, 380-381; balance of power in, 373-376; collective security in, 371-373
International Telecommunications Union, 416
Interstate Commerce Commission, 66
Ireland, 254
Italy, 28, 68, 74, 89, 165, 253, 324, 342, 355, 394; church and state in, 280; Constitution of, 36, 42; Fascism in, 240-241

Johnson, Eldon L., 309
Joint Chiefs of Staff, 62, 171, 176
Judges, 145-146
Judicial powers, 28
Judicial review, 29, 138-140
Judiciary, 217
Justice, 8, 9, 61
Justice, Department of, 147-148
Justinian, 130, 140
Jackson, Robert H., 278
Japan, 355; constitution of, 36, 42, 48, 49
Jefferson, Thomas, 50, 132, 174-175

Kautsky, Karl, 239
Korean War, 372, 407-408
Kropotkin, P. A., 245
Khrushchev, Nikita, 21, 166, 300

Labor; child, 354; Communist regulation of, 356; conditions and practices in, 350-355; organization of, 346
Labor unions, 291-292; organization of, 346-350
Labour Party, British, 94, 212-213, 347-348
Landholding, and politics, 339-343
Laroque, Pierre, 189
Law, administrative, 139-140, 200-201; blue, 142; civil and criminal, 141-143; common, 140; and Constitution, 30-31; definitions of, 130-131; due process of, 137-140; and enforcement, 160; international, 368-371, 388; officers of, 147-150; public and private, 6, 141; and

state, 14-15; and trusts and corporations, 151-153
Lawmaking, by representative bodies, 115-117
League of Nations, 371, 403
Legislature, 127-129; cabinet leadership of, 120-121; committee system of, 119-120; discussion in, 117-118; and executive powers, 125-127; investigative powers of, 123-125; leadership within, 118-119; party discipline in, 122-123; and police power, 160
Legislation, social, 323, 335-337
Legislative powers, 28
Lenin, V. I., 88, 165-166, 242, 243, 365, 398, 438
Levellers, 234-235
Liberalism, 236-238
Liberty, *see* Civil rights
Lie, Trygve, 410
Lilburne, John, 234
Line agency, 193
Lippmann, Walter, 6
List system of proportional representation, 96, 98
Lobbies, 221, 222-223; munitions, 173
Local government, 260-265, 267; civil service in, 265-266
Locke, John, 47, 150
Lord Chancellor, 136
Louisiana, 162
Luxembourg, 394

MacArthur, Douglas, 60
Mackenzie, W. J. M., 191-192
Mackinder, Sir Halford, 377
Macmillan, Harold, 72
McReynolds, James Clark, 288, 329
Madison, James, 24-25, 109, 151-152, 204
Magna Carta, 40
Mahan, A. T., 376
Maitland, F. W., 152-153
Majority rule, 24
Malaya, 13, 341, 408, 431
Mandate system, 412
Mann Act, 162
Mao Tse-tung, 88
Marbury v. Madison, 29
Marius, 54
Market system, 295-296
Marshall, John, 29, 195
Marshall Plan, 393, 394
Marsilius of Padua, 260-261
Marx, Karl, 9, 21-22, 26, 88, 245, 307-308, 365, 398
Marxism, 365, 398
Mass media, 224
Massachusetts, 167
Matthews, Stanley, 138
Merit systems, 181-182
Metternich, Prince, 232
Military elites, 232
Military power, 167-169; civilian control over, 169-173; and compulsory service, 173-175
Mill, John Stuart, 82-83, 90
Minimum wages, 351-352
Ministerial orders, 68-69
Minister, office of, 67-73
Ministers, Council of, Soviet, 76, 77
Missouri Valley Authority, 252
Monarchy, 20, 68, 69
Money, government control of, 301-307
Monroe Doctrine, 419
Montesquieu, C. L., 112
Morgenthau, Hans, 366
Morley, John, 26-27
Morocco, 431
Morse, Wayne, 320, 334
Mozambique, 431
Multimember constituencies, 97-99
Municipal government, 261
"Munitions lobbies," 173
Mussolini, Benito, 89, 165, 240
Mutual Security Program, 394
Myers v. United States, 65

Nasser, Gamal Abdel, 21
National Coal Board, 197
National Guard, 163, 175
National Health Service, Britain, 333-334
National Labor Relations Act, 350
National Security Council, 62-63, 170-171
National Socialism, 241
Nationalism, 13, 239, 250, 417
Nation–state, 13-14, 38
Nations, interests of, 366-367
Near East, 21
Nebbia v. New York, 310
Nebraska, 110, 288
Nehru, Jawaharlal, 74
Netherlands, The, 28, 394
New Deal, 315, 321

New Guinea, 430, 431
New York City, 97, 259
New Zealand, 347, 352, 420
Nicaragua, 164
Nigeria, 13, 14, 27, 92, 251, 421, 431
Nkrumah, Kwame, 74
Norris-La Guardia Act, 143-144, 349
North Atlantic Treaty Organization, 373
Nyasaland, 431

Office, 77-78; definition of, 53; prerequisites for, 54-55; recruitment for, 84-85; sense of, 217
Office of Price Administration, 184
Old-age pensions, 325-326
Oligarchy, 22
Opportunity, equality of, 284-287
Organization of American States, 419
Orr, Lord Boyd, 345

Pakistan, 14, 17, 21, 140, 421, 431
Palestine, 415
Pan American Union, 420
Parity prices, for crops, 344
Parliament Act of 1911, 40
Parliaments, 58, 67-73, 89
Party, political function of, 203-211; organization of, 214-217; and public opinion, 219-220; and representation, 85-87; responsibility of, 217-219; single, 87; structure of, 211-213
Party politics, 63
Patria potestas, 18
Patriotism, 14
Pax Romana, 15, 373
Peace, public opinion and, 337
Peel, Sir Robert, 157, 230
"People," as political authority, 36, 38
"People's Courts," 135-136, 137, 147
Philippine Islands, 434
Philosophy, 227-228
Philosophy, political, 6, 8
Planning, economic, by government, 297-301; national, 260
Platforms, of political parties, 210
Plato, 7, 9
Plebiscites, 100
Plutocracy, 22
Point Four Program, 435
Police forces, authoritarian, 164-167; establishment of, 157-158; organization of, 161-167; principles of, 158-161; secret, 166
Policy, and political party, 209
Polis, 3-4
"Political animal," 5
Political association, 7, 9
Political science, 4, 11
Politics, and landholding, 339-343; practice of, 4-5; study of, 3-4; theory of, 4, 5-6. (*See also* Party, political)
Populist movement, 235
Port of New York Authority, 252
Portugal, 21, 89, 232, 431-432
Potestas, 53
Pound, Roscoe, 131
Power, 5, 9; balance of, 373-376; countervailing, 314; limitation of, 25-26; military, 167-173
Powers, separation of, 28-29
Prerogative power of Crown, 68
President, United States, 55, 111, 170; agencies presided over by, 62-65; appointing and removal power of, 65-67; election of, 92; and foreign policy, 382; functions of, 58-61; power of, 56-57, 113
Presidium, of Supreme Soviet, 31
Pressure groups, 220-223, 345
Primary election, 102, 103, 208
Prime Minister, 71-73, 119, 187
Privacy, assurance of, 282-284
Progressive Party, 235
Prohibition Party, 205
Proletariat, 22
Propaganda, 397-399
Property, private, 116, 150-151, 233
Proportional representation, 263-264
Proudhon, Pierre Joseph, 245
Prussia, 180
Public administration, 178-179, 198-199
Public administration, law and procedures arising from, 200-201. (*See also* Bureaucracy, Civil Service)
Public law, 6
Public opinion, 223-224; and political parties, 219-220
Public Health Service, 182
Public service, *see* Civil Service
Puerto Rico, Commonwealth of, 32, 434-435

Pufendorf, Samuel, 371
Puritans, 234

Quebec, 255
"Question Hour," 114-115

Radicalism, 234-236
Read, Sir Herbert, 246
Reason, and government, 7
Reciprocal Trade Agreement Act, 392, 393
Referendum, 99-101
Reform Act, of 1832, 40, 41
Regional government, 250-258
Reith, Charles, 159-160
Religion, 227-228, 398; established, 256; freedom of, 278-282, 290-291
Reorganization Act of 1939, 62
Representation, bicameralism in, 108-110; proportional, 80, 94-97. (*See also* Representative government)
Representative government, 23-24, 80, 87-88; by functional groups, 89-90; political party in, 85-87; role of individual in, 80-85
Republic, definition of, 53
Republican Party, 209
Rhodesias, Federation of the, 431
Rights, 15, 132-133, 141; and administrative law, 200-201
Roberts, Owen Josephus, 310
Rome, 15, 23, 373; government of, 53-54
Roosevelt, Franklin D., 58, 135, 321
Royal Commissions of Enquiry, 125
Rousseau, Jean Jacques, 23, 235
Ruanda-Urundi, 413
"Rule of law," 49
Rules Committee, House of Representatives, 119
Rural Electrification Administration, 315

St. Lawrence Seaway Development Corporation, 197, 308
Salazar, Antonio de Oliveira, 89
Sallust, 23
Sankey Report, 125
Sapin, Burton, 171
Schuman Community, 394
Science, in international relations, 396-397
Scotland, 140, 145, 148, 197, 249, 254-255
Scottish Grand Committee, 255
Scottish Office, 255
Secretariat, United Nations, 410-411
Security, 8; collective, 371-373; of person and home, 282-284; social, 325-328
Security Council, United Nations, 372, 406-408
Self-rule, local, 258-260
Senate, United States, 37, 46, 55-56, 63, 109, 119
Seniority rule, of United States Congress, 120
Separation of powers, 112-113
Sherman Anti-Trust Act, 313, 349
Sicily, 165
Singapore, 431
Slave trade, 426
Smith v. Allwright, 208
Smithies, Arthur, 316
Snyder, Richard, 171
Social contract, 47
"Social justice," 296
Social legislation, 335-337
Social security, types of, 325-328
Social Security Act, 322, 326, 327
Social services, *see* Welfare
Socialism, 238-240
Sorel, Georges, 89
South Africa, 421
South Africa, Union of, 104-105, 241
Sovereignty, 18-20
Soviet Union, 14, 17, 22, 27, 112, 169, 215, 398-399, 428, 432, 433; bicameralism of, 109; bureaucracy in, 190; cabinet government in, 75-77; constitution of, 30-31, 37, 43, 48; court system of, 146-147; economic planning in, 299-301; in international affairs, 374-375, 385, 394-395; judiciary of, 137; labor conditions in, 356; property rights in, 151; representative government in, 87-88. (*See also* Communist Party, Russian)
Spain, 21, 28, 232, 342-343
Speech, free, 277-278
Spykman, Nicholas, 377
Staff agency, 193
Stalin, Joseph V., 165-166, 398
State, 3, 9, 84; and individual, 47; modern, characteristics of, 11-20;

withering away of, 26, 245
State, Secretary of, 62, 385
State Department, 182, 384, 386, 387
State police, 162, 163, 167-168
States, 334; autonomy of, 251-253, 256-258; constitutions of, 66-67; and Social Security administration, 327-328
Statute of Westminster, 1931, 40
Statutory instruments, 68-69
Stein, Harold, 180
Stone, Harlan F., 351, 355
Strikes, 352-353
Subversion, 397-399
Suffrage, universal, 80, 90-92
Supreme Court, United States, 124, 133-134, 135, 144
Supreme Soviets, 118
Sweden, 239, 349, 394
Switzerland, 13, 27, 30, 90, 99, 109, 251; constitution of, 42
Syndicalism, 89, 245

Tacitus, 117
Taft, William H., 65
Taft-Hartley Act, 350, 353
Tanganyika, 413
Tariffs, 344, 392-393
Taxation, 110-112; for social services, 335-336
Technical assistance, 434-436
Technical Assistance Board, 416
Technology, and government, 26
Tennessee Valley Authority, 182, 197, 252
Terminiello v. Chicago, 277
Thailand, 21
Tibet, 432
Town Meeting, 99
Trade Union Congress, 346-348
Tradition, 7, 15, 232
Treasury, Secretary of, 62
Treaties, 388, 389
Truman, Harry S., 60, 67, 393, 435
Trusteeship Council, United Nations, 412-414
Trusts, 81, 151-153
Tunis, 431
Tyranny, 20, 165-166, 167, 243, 273

Underdeveloped peoples, present relations with, 427-430
Unemployment Compensation, 326-328
Unicameralism, 110
Union of South Africa, 104-105, 241
Unions, *see* Labor unions
United Arab Republic, 28, 140, 241
United Nations, 99-100, 368, 370, 372, 403-417; agencies of, 414-416; and economic assistance, 437-438; organization of, 405-414
United Nations Children's Fund, 415
United Nations Educational, Scientific, and Cultural Organization, 415
United Nations Relief and Works Agency for Palestine Refugees, 415
United States of America, 13, 19, 97, 98, 398; autonomy of states in, 251-253, 256-258; bureaucracy in, 199; civil service, 181-184, 188; conservatism in, 232-234; economic and technical assistance of, 386, 434-436; federal system of, 27-28; public office in, 55-56; radicalism in, 235-236; suffrage in, 90-91. (*See also* Congress, Constitution)
United States Housing Act, 334-335
United States v. Darby, 355
Universal government, 367-368, 402
Universal Postal Union, 368, 415

Van Devanter, Willis, 28, 124
Veterans Administration, 182
Veto power, in Security Council, 407
Vice-President, 63
Violence, 155
Voluntarism, 155-156, 183, 248
Voter, responsibility of, 104-106
Voting, compulsory, 91-92; direct or indirect, 92-93; preferential, 94-97; systems of, 80. (*See also* Elections)

Wales, 255
War, 363-364, 365, 370, 389-392; deterrent, 391; and public opinion, 337
Ways and Means Committee, 111
Weimar Republic, 95
Welfare, 335; American concepts of, 320-323; British and European attitudes toward, 323-325, 327
Welfare state, 319
West Coast Hotel Co. v. Parrish, 351
Wheare, Kenneth C., 27

"White supremacy," 433
Wilkes, John, 157
Wilson, Charles E., 173
Wilson, Woodrow, 59
World affairs, 365
World Health Organization, 415
World Meteorological Organization, 416

Zurcher, Arnold J., 417

Political Science is a source of undue grief to a improportionate numbers of other-wise well qualified students. It looses its flavor gradually until the student's taste-buds can sense nothing but a sort of blandness of indifference.